The Israeli Left

The Israeli Left

History, Problems, Documents

Peretz Merhav

SAN DIEGO • NEW YORK
A. S. BARNES & COMPANY, INC.
IN LONDON:
THE TANTIVY PRESS

The Israeli Left copyright © 1980 by A.S. Barnes and Co., Inc.

All rights reserved under International and Pan American Copyright Conventions. No part of this book may be reproduced in any manner whatsoever without written permission from the publisher, except in the case of brief quotations embodied in reviews and articles.

First Edition
Manufactured in the United States of America

For information write to:
A.S. Barnes & Company, Inc.
P.O. Box 3051
La Jolla, California 92038

The Tantivy Press
Magdalen House
136-148 Tooley Street
London, SE1 2TT, England

Library of Congress: Cataloging in Publication Data
Merhav, Peretz.
  The Israeli left.

  Bibliography: p.
  Includes indexes.
  1. Political parties—Israel. 2. Israel—Politics and government. 3. Labor Zionism—Palestine.
4. Right and left (Political science) I. Title.
JQ1825.P37M47   329.9'5694   77-84578
ISBN 0-498-02184-X

1 2 3 4 5 6 7 8 9 84 83 82 81 80

Contents

1	The Jewish Labor Movement in the Diaspora	13
2	Labor Zionism	20
3	Trends and Parties During the Second Aliya	31
4	Ahdut Haavoda and Hapoel Hatsair	36
5	From Ahdut Haavoda to the Formation of Mapai	46
6	Left Poale Zion	57
7	The Communist Party (from M.P.S. to Maki and Rakah)	70
8	Hashomer Hatsair	81
9	The Hashomer Hatsair Workers' Party	92
10	From Mapai split to the Formation of Mapam	102
11	Mapam—Experiment in Unity	112
12	The Difference Renewed	117
13	The Prague Trial—Split in Mapam	130
14	The Struggle for Peace and the Sinai War	139
15	Fighting Against Signs of Confusion	145
16	The Israeli Road to Socialism	152
17	The Kibbutz Movement	167
18	Reformism and Anti-Reformism in Israel	180
19	The "Ben Gurion—Lavon Affair"	200
20	L'Ahdut Haavoda and Mapam	213
21	Debating the "Alignment"	222
22	Split in Mapai	235
23	The Elections of 1965	242
24	The June 1967 War and Afterwards	250
25	The Struggle for a United Workers' Front	265
26	The Earthquake of '73 and Its Aftermath	285
27	The Economic Background (1966-1976)	294
28	Workers' Hegemony at Stake	313
Postscript		332

Appendixes		
I	State and Constitution	335
II	Population	337
III	Political Parties in the 9th Knesset	339
IV	Results of Knesset Elections 1949-1977	242
V	National Congress of the Histadrut	243
VI	Trade Unions, Workers' Parties and Youth Movements	348
VII	National Congresses of the Workers' Parties	354
VIII	Evolution of Workers' Parties in Diagram Form	357
IX	Chronological Table of Events	358
References		370
Index		379

Foreword

This book, an expanded version of a series of lectures given at the Hashomer Hatsair Seminar in Giv'at Haviva, is an attempt to survey and to analyze the historic roots and stages in the ideological development of the Israeli Labor Movement and of its various trends and parties. I hope that it will help the reader understand better the differences and the conflicts in view that divide these parties today.

The reader would do well to keep in mind the particular historical situation in which the parties and problems discussed in this book have appeared. The socialist workers' movements in the older capitalist countries form the highest stage in the development of the working class. In these countries the labor movement can look upon the existence of the working class as axiomatic: the capitalist economic system exists, the working class exists, and the great but single task is to organize the workers and to educate them toward class consciousness, occupationally and politically, for a radical change in the ownership of the wealth existing in the state. In Palestine, on the other hand, industry and modern agriculture were nonexistent and there were no Jewish workers and farmers at all. First of all a modern economy had to be built, a task which the Jewish bourgeoisie was neither interested in nor capable of carrying out. It was also necessary at first to transform the new immigrants from the ranks of the Jewish intelligentsia and petit bourgeoisie in the Diaspora into a class of people participating in physical labor in the basic branches of the economy (and primarily in agriculture), and into people whose socialist ideology would no longer be abstract ideas but concepts rooted in the reality of their lives as workers.

It is, therefore, impossible to understand the history of the labor movement in Israel (or to a great extent even the differences dividing it today), if we do not keep in mind that from its very beginning it was an organic part of the national renaissance movement of the Jewish people—Zionism. It was the idea of the Return to Zion and of rebuilding the ancient homeland that motivated young Jews in the Diaspora to leave their studies, careers and homes in the cities of Europe, to immigrate to Palestine and become workers and farmers. In so doing they believed they were serving as the vanguard for the masses of Jews who would come after, and laying the firm foundations for a reformed and healthy economic and social structure on which the socialist Palestine of the future would be built.

This special situation gave the Jewish labor movement in Palestine a dual historic role: (1) to build the country, settle its wastelands, establish an economy and create a working class rooted in the soil; (2) to organize the workers and educate them for socialism, to conduct class struggle both in trade unions and politics. *How to integrate these historic tasks in developing and changing circumstances*—this is the question that from the very earliest days up to the present has been the crux of the dispute within the ranks of the Israeli labor movement, and this subject is given a great deal of space in this book.

A second source of controversy within the Israeli labor movement has centered around the *road to labor unity*. Should the majority trend seek to impose unity on the minorities? Would this be practical and useful? And on the other hand, how can the left minority, voluntarily and on its own initiative, become part of a broader and unified party framework without giving up its own specific values and ideas? If the pioneering left-socialist wing of the labor movement is not able to join a broader party framework, how can it make its own contribution toward shaping the working class and in influencing its progress and creative efforts? These problems occupy labor movements, and their radical wings, everywhere. Amongst us, however, the problem of unity takes on a special character of its own, on the one hand—because of the far-reaching cooperation in action prevailing between all the Socialist-Zionist parties in the spheres of immigration, absorption, settlement and defense; and on the other— because of the fact of the existence of the General Federation of Labor (Histadrut) as the common supraparty framework for all the working class public and parties, making it possible to carry out the common imperatives and tasks in practice, despite the party and political divisions. I have devoted a great deal of space to describing and analyzing the differences of opinion and the experiments concerned with this problem of unity that has been part of the Israeli labor movement from its inception.

There is still a third point of controversy over the relationship between Jewish, Zionist and Israeli patriotism, on the one hand, and internationalism—with its moral, theoretical and political demands, on the other. Is the integration of Socialist-Zionism and international fraternity only a fine phrase, with the reality one of a fundamental conflict, and must Israeli socialists choose between patriotic loyalty and socialism? That is what the two poles of the Israeli labor movement—the communists and the reformists—have claimed, though of course with different conclusions, the first by betraying their own people's national movement, and the second by abandoning internationalism. Or a synthesis of the two is possible; perhaps they can be symbiotic to each other. This question became even more pressing when the relations toward security and foreign policy, between the need for self-defense and the striving for coexistence and peace had to be decided upon. This dilemma and the resulting differences in finding an answer have also been a permanent feature throughout all the stages in the history of the Israeli labor movement, and the reader will meet it again and again in the chapters of this book.

I hope that this book will help the reader to understand the problems of the Israeli labor movement in all its various parties and contribute in strengthening the ties between the Left in Israel and abroad.

The Israeli Left

1 • The Jewish Labor Movement in The Diaspora

The Fathers of Jewish Socialism

The Jewish labor movement was born within the socialist circles that began to form during the 1870s and 1880s in the Jewish centers of concentration in Czarist Russia, under the influence of the revolutionary fermentation among the Russian intellectuals. The first and best-known of these was the "Vilna Circle" (1872), which produced the fathers of Jewish socialism, Aharon Zundelevicz, Aharon Shmuel Liberman and others. Liberman differed from his colleagues by consistently and undeviatingly propagandizing in the Hebrew language. He published a proclamation in Hebrew and founded the "Hebrew Socialist Society" in 1876. In 1877, he established the first Hebrew socialist paper, *Ha-emet (The Truth);* after *Ha-emet* closed, his follower, Morris Winchevsky, published the *Asefat Hahamim (Council of Scholars)*, also in Hebrew. Liberman was driven by the police from one country to another, was arrested and tried, and, after finding his way to the United States, committed suicide in 1880. Like all socialist intellectuals of his generation in Russia, Liberman was influenced by populism (narodism); in the course of his exile and wanderings in Central and Western Europe, however, he gained a knowledge of Marxism and became the first Hebrew Marxist.

In its second stage, when Jewish socialism sought to break out of the narrow circle of intellectuals, youth and educated workers who knew Hebrew, and to appeal to the masses—"the people"—the balance swung in the direction of Yiddish, spoken by most people. In 1880 a "Group of Jewish Socialists" was organized in Geneva and set up the *Jewish Free Press* in order "to bring to the Jews in Russia and Galicia, in their spoken languages (Jargon) the ideas of socialism as these have been developed in theory and practice in Western Europe and America . . ."

During the 1880s and 1890s the centers of mass Jewish concentration (southern and western Russia, Poland, Lithuania and Galicia) were in the course of a capitalist development, which also led to far-reaching changes in the occupational structure of the Jewish masses. The proportion occupied in crafts increased greatly and a Jewish proletariat came into being. Acts of oppression on the part of the Czarist authorities also increased and led to mass emigration, mainly to England and the United States. This was the ground in which the Jewish socialist movement took root.

The former Russian-Jewish socialist immigrants began to develop ramified educational and organizational activities in the United States, in close contact with the local socialist movement. Under the leadership of Morris Winchevsky and Abe Cahan, a United Jewish Trade Union was set up in New York in 1888; the Arbeiter Ring (Workers' Circle)—mutual aid association—was formed in 1892; in that same year, the Jewish socialist monthly *Die Zunkunft* (*The Future*) appeared, and in 1897, the daily *Forvartz* (*Forward*). In Czarist Russia, where Jewish socialist activity—like socialist activity in general—was conducted in small clandestine groups, owning to conditions at the time, these groups took on a broader form with the establishment of the General League of Jewish Workers in Lithuania, Russia and Poland (popularly known as the Bund), in 1897 in Vilna.

The Bund

The Bund's founders had not intended to organize a new political party in the accepted sense, with a precise ideological program and detailed constitution, and with a clear division of functions between political party and trade union. What they wanted was an "inclusive association" that would embrace all the Jewish workers within the borders of Czarist Russia, without overstressing ideological demands or imposing organizational obligations that might deter the masses from joining. At its Founding Congress, it was decided that "the Bund embraces all the militant Jewish proletariat and opens its doors to every worker joining the struggle of the proletariat for a better life. Everyone looking for struggle, or seeing its need, will join the Bund; he will be an equal member with full rights. . . ." In keeping with this, socialism was not mentioned specifically in the Bund's full name; its founders preferred to hide behind the more "general" banner.[1]

At the outset, the Bund did not have any special views on the national question in general or on the "Jewish question" in particular. However, from the very beginning, differences of opinion on the subject appeared between its two components—the intellectuals and the workers. The

1. As we shall see later, the Bund's "original" approach to the problem of party organization, the basis of membership and the role of theory and program in the party, had significant influence on the Palestinian labor movement in its early years; this influence was especially pronounced in the approaches and views of "Ahdut Haavoda."

founders of the Bund coming from the intelligentsia considered themselves to be *Russian socialists* who had been given the task of conducting socialist agitation and organization in the "Jewish section" of the all-Russian proletariat. They accepted the Jewishness of those workers and the fact that they spoke Yiddish as "facts which had to be taken into consideration," and nothing more. That is, they considered the existence of a special and separate Jewish labor movement as only an intermediate and transitory stage, with their perspective being assimilation into the Russian (or Polish, etc.) people, to become part of its culture and proletariat.

In contrast with this view, the forecasts of assimilation and the desires for Russification were foreign to the *popular proletarian elements* within the Bund, who were subject to the direct pressures and influences of the special conditions in which the Jewish workers lived and struggled: dual discrimination and dual oppression—both as workers and as Jews. The popular elements within the Bund considered themselves at one and the same time to be both part of the all-Russian proletariat and members of the Jewish community in Russia, that is, members of an oppressed national minority.

At the beginning, the Bund tried to find an "original solution" for these diverging views on the question of assimilation, one characteristic of its general approach of avoiding theoretical and programmatic problems. In order to form a bridge between the various conflicts, formulas and wings, the Bund attempted to avoid dealing with this "delicate issue" and adopted a position of "neutrality"; it was all the same, no matter whether Jewish national existence in Russia was maintained or whether the forecast was assimilation. Even when, in the course of time, the Bund was compelled to formulate a real national program of its own, this remained without any historical perspective or any final aim.

The Bund's National Program

Under the pressure of reality and popular sentiment, however, the Bund was compelled to abandon the ideas of assimilation and Russification and, on the contrary, began more and more to reflect the national strivings of the Jewish workers. At the same time, however, conditions had not yet ripened in those years (the beginning of the present century) to the point of compelling it to adopt the territorial-Zionist solution of the Jewish problem. This solution was alien to the thinking and the customary concepts of the all-Russian labor movement in its various forms (including the Bund itself). It also was far beyond the immediate "personal" experience of the Jewish proletariat. Before the latter could come to such a revolutionary and far-reaching solution, it had to exhaust all the possibilities of finding "closer" and "more practical" answers, such as the struggle for the satisfaction of its national demands where it lived, emigration overseas, etc. This stage in the development of the national consciousness of the Jewish proletariat and of its allied intellectuals was also reflected in the Bund's "National Program." Its essential was the search for a nonterritorial national solution, while rejecting both assimilation and Zionism. Gradually, in the course of debate and internal struggle, the Bund adopted the demand for "National and cultural autonomy"[2] (adopted finally at the 6th Congress in 1903). This meant that the Jews, dispersed among other peoples, were bound as individuals to the national collective by the possibilities of cultivating a common national language, culture and education.[3]

The internal contradictions in its national program and the theoretical unclarity customary within the Bund left the way open for many of the leaders and cadres to leave the Jewish labor movement for activity and careers in the "general" labor movement (Russian and American). They also made it easier for important segments of the Bund, after the October Revolution and the establishment of the Communist International, to join the Jewish Section of the Soviet Communist Party (the *Yevsektzia*). We should recall that up till World War II and particularly in its early years, the Soviet regime maintained the Jewish culture (schools, papers, books, theaters, etc.) under the guidance of a special Jewish department of the Communist Party and a Commissariat for Jewish Affairs (as part of the Commissariat for National Affairs). A large segment of the Bund leaders believed that this satisfied not only the primary demand for civil equality of rights, but also the Bund's program of "cultural national autonomy."[4]

---

2. "National-cultural personal autonomy" (that is, as individuals and not as territorial bodies) was also the program of the Austro-Marxists, proposed for the solution of the struggle between the different national components of the Austro-Hungarian monarchy.

3. Labor Zionism, too, did not reject the demand for cultural national autonomy for the Jewish minorities in the Diaspora countries; on the contrary, this has been one of its chief demands from the Soviet government for Soviet Russian Jewry. Labor Zionism, however, rejected the idea of personal cultural national autonomy as a *solution* that could guarantee continued national existence, and looks on this autonomy only as a supplement for the right to emigrate to Israel—that is, for a Jewish territorial basis in Israel. (See quotations on the Bund at the end of this chapter.)

4. In its 12th Congress, Moscow, April 1920, the Bund voted by a majority to amend its program, to change its name to the "Communist Bund" and to cooperate with the Soviet regime. Finally, in March 1921, the Communist Bund amalgamated with the Yevsektzia and many of the former Bund leaders soon attained key positions in the Yevsektzia and the Commissariat for Jewish Affairs. At the beginning of the 1920s, there were splits in the Bund's sister movements in other countries and considerable minorities left to join the Communist parties. A. Merezhin, one of the Bund leaders in Russia, became a Yevsektzia leader and its secretary.

Contradictions, Failures and Achievements

One of the striking contradictions in the Bund's ideology was its denial of the worldwide character of the Jewish labor movement and its limitations of Jewish nationalism to the borders of Czarist Russia alone. The illogic of that conception was emphasized by the organization of counterparts of the Bund in Jewish areas of concentration in other countries. The flood of emigration pulled along many of the Bund members and even cadres and leaders, and they replanted their ideas and organizations overseas. In the United States, their influence was felt in the Jewish trade unions and in the Arbeiter-Ring mutual aid society, though these had come into being even before the formal establishment of the Bund in Russia. In 1912, the Jewish Socialist Society was established in the United States, largely under the influence of the Bundist immigrants. On a limited scale, there was a Jewish trade union and socialist movement also in England, and even in France. In the large Jewish concentration of Galicia (the part of Poland that had belonged to the Austro-Hungarian monarchy before World War I) a Jewish Social-Democratic Party, largely parallel to the Russian Bund, was established in 1905 (after previous failures). After the liquidation of the Bund in Soviet Russia, most of its activities were centered in Poland where it formed the dominant force within the Jewish labor movement. It was very active in establishing and guiding Jewish trade unions and cooperatives, in promoting cultural institutions and schools in the Yiddish language, and the like. The destruction of the Jewish centers in Poland and the other countries of eastern Europe removed the basis for the existence of a Jewish labor movement in the Diaspora, and the labor movement in the State of Israel remains almost its only heir. Though the remnants of the Bund (found mainly in the United States and France, but also in many other countries, and even in Israel) have generally not changed their fundamental opposition to Zionism, many of them have been compelled to accept the facts of the existence of the State of Israel and the strength of its labor movement, and for some this acceptance has reached the point of sympathy and even active support.

The theoretician of the Jewish proletariat in the Diaspora and the greatest leader and thinker of Labor Zionism, Ber Borochov, devoted a special chapter in his programmatic work, *Our Platform*, to a study of the Bund. His criticism is summed up in the thesis that "the tendency to grasp the Jewish question culturally, the way it is stressed by the Bundists, is undoubtedly reactionary, and shows all the signs of its petit-bourgeois origin." Borochov did not, however, ignore the achievements of the Bund which he considered to have been a necessary and important stage of development in the history of the Jewish labor movement.

The Bund has very much to its credit in its activity for the Jewish proletariat, and the Bund's name is inscribed in letters of gold in the history of the Jewish labor movement; future generations of the Jewish proletariat will erect it a splendid monument in Palestine. It cultivated the Jewish workers' consciousness of themselves as a class, educated them to organized struggle for their interests, developed their spirit of discipline and cultivated their democratic concepts . . .

(B. Borochov, *Writings* I, p. 226; Sifriat Poalim and Kibbutz Meuhad Publishers, 1955.)

SOURCES

. . . The Congress recognizes that a state like Russia, composed of many different nationalities, must in the future become a federation of nations with full national autonomy for each nation, regardless of the territory occupied by it . . . The Congress recognizes that the concept of "nation" can also apply to the Jewish people.

However, since the Congress finds that it is too early under present conditions to demand national autonomy for the Jews, it considers it sufficient to struggle to remove the special anti-Jewish laws; to stress the fact of the oppression of the Jewish nation and to protest against it while avoiding any inflation of national sentiment that could blur the class consciousness of the Jewish proletariat and lead it to chauvinism . . .

(From the Resolutions of the Fourth Congress of the Bund, 1901; S. Eisenstadt, *Chapters in the History of the Jewish Labor Movement,* II. pp. 14-15; Sifriat Poalim, Merhavia, 1954.)

. . . The Congress views Zionism as the reaction of the bourgeois classes to antisemitism and to the abnormal juridical position of the Jewish people. The Congress considers—the final aim of political Zionism, the attainment of a land for the Jewish people, as something that is not of great importance and does not bring an end to the "Jewish question" if only a small part of the Jewish people can be settled in that land. To the extent that Zionism thinks of settling in that land the whole of the Jewish people or a large part of it—the Congress considers it an illusion and an utopia. The Congress believes that Zionist propaganda intensifies national sentiments among the people and is liable to disturb the development of class consciousness . . .

. . . In agreement with the general position of the 4th Congress of the Bund in its Resolutions on this question, the 6th Congress formulates its Program on the Jewish question in the following clauses: (1.) Full civil and political equality of rights for the Jews; (2.) The possibility guaranteed by law for the Jewish population to use its mother tongue in its relations with courts of law, state institutions and the autonomous local and regional government administration; (3.) Cultural national autonomy: transfer of all the functions connected with the questions of culture (popular education, etc.) from the state administration and the autonomous local and regional governmental apparatus to the nation, in the form of special institutions, both local and central, elected by all the members on the basis of general, equal, direct and secret ballot.

NOTE: Cultural national autonomy does not affect the right of the central legislative authority to fix certain obligatory rules on questions common to all the nations inhabiting Russia, such as obligatory education, the secular character of education, etc., and the right to supervise the maintenance of these rules (From the Resolutions of the 6th Congress of the Bund, 1905; in Appendix to Ber Borochov, *Writings*, I, p. 365; Sifriat Poalim and Kibbutz Meuhad Publishers, 1955.)

2 · Labor Zionism

Poale Zion and Zeire Zion

The Palestinian labor movement drew its inspiration from two sources: the Zionist wing of the Jewish labor movement in the Diaspora and the pioneering and socialist wing of the Zionist movement.

A part of the Jewish socialist intelligentsia was disatisfied by the ambivalent "National Program" of the Bund. They wanted to free the Jewish labor movement from the straitjacket in which it found itself because of extraterritorial dispersion, the abnormal economic and social structure of the Jewish masses, and the fact that Jewish workers were concentrated mainly in secondary branches of production and small shops; they wanted to concentrate the Jewish people in the territory of Palestine. A great contribution toward preparing the ground for this change among Jewish labor-oriented intellectuals was made by Chaim Zhitlowsky, one of the outstanding personalities of the populist wing of Russian socialism. He tried to break down the cosmopolitan prejudices against Jewish nationalism that were prevalent among Russian socialists, at the same time attacking the Jewish socialist intellectuals for their assimilationist aims. In a series of striking articles in the general socialist and Bundist press ("A Jew to Jews," 1892; "Socialism and the Jewish Question," 1899; "Zionism or Socialism," 1899), he showed how vital it was for socialism and the revolutionary struggle to cultivate nationalism and national culture. He demanded that the Jewish minority be granted national and cultural autonomy and called on the Jewish socialist intelligentsia to return to their people and to cultivate its popular national culture.

Parallel to this ferment within the ranks of those intellectuals who were attached to the Jewish labor movement in its main centers, there were also ideological shifts within the ranks of the Zionist movement. Socialist ideas began increasingly to gain way in western and central Europe and even to penetrate into the ranks of the Zionist movement, whose leadership clung to the ideas of bourgeois liberalism. Only two years after Theodor Herzl's[1] "Jewish State," Nahman Syrkin published his book, *The Jewish Question and the Socialist Jewish State* (1898), in which he developed, under more realistic conditions, the idea of socialist Zionism that Moses Hess had forecast in his *Rome and Jerusalem* in 1862. Syrkin's main work was to convince the progressive Zionist public that the combination of Zionism

---

1. The founder of modern Zionism; called the first Zionist Congress (1897) and was the first President of the World Zionist Organization.

and socialism was possible and even vital for the full realization of Zionism. From the Second Congress (1898) onward Syrkin began to gather around him a growing and increasingly influential group of socialist delegates.

The societies that supported this combination of Zionism and socialism, both those within the Jewish labor movement and those in the ranks of the Zionist movement (including Zionist workers' societies that had not yet defined themselves explicitly as socialists), generally called themselves "Poale Zion" (The Workers of Zion). In the first stage, from 1899 to 1904, this was not more than a general term that did not imply any specific organizational affiliations on a world or even on a countrywide level, nor even the existence of any precise and unified program on how Zionism and socialism were to be combined. In this latter sphere, there were very great differences. There were those who rejected the class struggle and the struggle for socialism until after immigration to Palestine and were against participating in the revolutionary underground in the countries in which they were living. Others favored participating in trade union struggle but opposed political activity in the Diaspora. There were still others who put the stress on "immediate activity" (*Gegenwartsarbeit*), that is, on general political activity and on internal cultural and educational activity in the Diaspora, leaving the matter of Palestine as some kind of "ultimate goal" or apocalyptic vision. Some groups stressed their Zionism and the longings for social and national renaissance in the ancient homeland, while others saw the essential task in concentrating Jewish migration in some autonomous territory, if at all possible in Palestine, but without considering this as an unconditional prerequisite for the fulfillment of socialist Zionism. The Poale Zionist groups were also divided over the question of language: Hebrew or Yiddish. There were Marxists and supporters of populist socialism. Societies like these sprang up to some extent in central Europe, France, and England, but mainly in Russia (including Poland and Lithuania), Galicia, and the United States.

However, in addition to this dividing line between General Zionism and Workers' Zionism, another and no less fundamental fissure was also growing and deepening between diplomatic, *declarative* Zionism—the Zionism of meetings, debates and discussions of ultimate aims—and *practical* Zionism that put the emphasis on carrying out theory in practice. Among the circles of Zionist youth, students and younger intellectuals (especially in Eastern Europe), there were many who reacted to the impotence of the official Zionist movement by organizing groups of "Zeire Zion" (Youth of Zion) or groups with other names, like "Hatechiya" (The Renaissance) akin in spirit, and which favored democratizing the Zionist movement, beginning constructive activity in Palestine immediately, deepening Hebrew cultural activity and Zionist education, and, first of all, preparing to realize Zionism practically by immigrating and laying the foundations for a Jewish, Hebrew-speaking, democratic and progressive working society. In its social aims, the Zeire Zion of the first years of the present century was influenced by Russian populism (Narodism) in its early, national and democratic stage, by Tolstoy's ideas of morality, simplicity and the return to nature, and by the slogans of "going to the people" and of the pioneering role of the intellectuals.

Zeire Zion stood aloof from Poale Zionism mainly because it considered it a part of the Jewish labor movement in which (in all its branches, including the Zionist) it found such faults as "Diaspora mentality," unrootedness, verbosity, a "poverty of action," and the like. These differences continued even in later stages, when Russian populism had become "Populist *socialism*," and afterwards, when, under the influence of World War I and the February revolution, most of the Russian Zeire Zion identified themselves as "Zionist Socialists" (Z.S.) and some even adopted a Marxist viewpoint. Now it was no longer, of course, a difference with "Socialist Zionism" itself, as in the past, but with Poale Zion's *proletarian* Zionism—that is, the view of the Jewish proletariat in the Diaspora as the chief, if not the only, bearers of socialist Zionism. Zeire Zion (Z.S. and other groups close to them) wanted to establish the socialist Zionist movement on a much wider popular base. They also claimed that Poale Zion was one-sidedly stressing the objective economic aspect of the process of Zionist fulfillment, and differed with the Poale Zion view of Zionist realization as mainly a long-range historic prognosis, while they, the Z.S., emphasized subjective activity for immediate socialist Zionist realization, with all the personal obligations that involved.

When the second countryside Congress of the Russian Zeire Zion met in Petrograd in May 1917, most of the members considered themselves *personally* to be socialists of one shade or another. A minority defined themselves as "laborists," rejecting the socialist label either in principle or because of the argument that there was no room for a socialist party in the reality of Jewish life in the Diaspora and that it should be deferred until after immigration to Palestine and social and economic reformation there. In the terminology of those days, they were called "Socialists of the future."

The Congress did not take a decision on defining the Zeire Zion as a Zionist Socialist party: instead they declared themselves "The Popular Zionist Zeire-Zion Faction" in the General Zionist Organization. The Third Congress (in Kharkov, May 1920) finally adopted the name "Zionist Socialist Party" (generally called the "Z.S.") as an independent political organization. After some time, the laborist minority left, first to re-

---

2. These differences of approach remained in force even when the political differences disappeared, up till the final union of the Zeire Zion (Z.S.) and Poale Zion (Right) in 1925.

establish the Popular Zionist Zeire-Zion Faction, and finally, in 1923, to reorganize as The Zionist Labor Party Zeire Zion-Hitachdut.

Almost at the same time, there was a similar development in Poland, where the socialist-Zionist majority defined itself as "The Eastern Alliance of Zeire Zion," while the laborist minority became The Popular Zionist Hapoel Hatsair Faction.

On a world scale, the laborist Zeire Zion organized itself by countries, with Hapoel Hatsair as its center in Palestine, as the "World Union of Hapoel Hatsair and Zeire Zion," generally referred to as Hitachdut (Prague, 1920). The Socialist Zeire Zion (headed by the Russian "Z.S." and the Polish "Eastern Alliance") formed the Alliance of Socialist-Zionist Workers-Zeire Zion (1921).[3]

Only a few can be listed of the outstanding leaders of these two wings of Zeire Zion after World War I. For the Z.S.: Yisrael Merom (Mereminsky)—(Russia, Poland); Yitzhak Barali (Russia, Lithuania); Chaim Greenberg (Russia, United States); and Yisrael Bar-Yehuda (Idelson)—(Russia, Palestine). For the Laborist Zeire Zion (Hitachdut): Eliezer Kaplan (Russia, Palestine); Avraham Levinson (Russia, Poland); and Chaim Arlosorov (Germany, Palestine).

Trends and Conflicts within Poale Zion

The failure of the diplomatic efforts of the Zionist organization to obtain a charter for Palestine from the Turkish Sultan and the stagnation in practical Palestine activity brought on the *territorialist crisis in the Zionist movement* (the "Uganda Crisis").[4] This crisis also was evident in the young Poale Zion movement. Some of the Poale Zion Societies were drawn into the territorialist[5] stream and formed the Socialist-Zionist Workers Party

---

3. Since both this world alliance and the Poale Zion (Right) were affiliated with the Ahdut Haavoda Party in Palestine, their Palestinian counterpart exerted a great deal of pressure on them to unite, but this happened only in 1925, in Vienna, when the two alliances formed the "Alliance of Jewish Socialist Workers–Poale Zion united with Z.S." On its formation, this alliance was also joined by the Dror Socialist-Zionist Federation—also a wing of the Zeire Zion that had been active first in the Ukraine and afterward in Poland. The popular name of the parties united in this world alliance was Poale Zion–Z.S. After the union of Hapoel Hatsair and Ahdut Haavoda in Palestine in 1930, efforts went on to unite all the new Mapai's Diaspora parties. As a result of these efforts, the Union of the Jewish Socialist Workers Alliance Poale Zion (united with Z.S.) and the Hitachdut World Labor Party, shortened to the "World Union," was established. Incidentally, differences between the two parties were so great in Poland that union took longer (in Eastern Galicia it was formed only in 1933), while not until 1947 was it achieved for all of Poland.
4. A plan to settle Jews in Uganda (actually present-day Kenya), based on an offer made to the Zionist organization by the British Minister for the Colonies in 1903. The proposal aroused a heated debate within the Zionist movement.
5. A political movement within the Jewish people whose aim was to obtain an appropriate territory for concentrated Jewish settlement outside of Palestine, on the basis of political, or at least cultural, autonomy.

(known by the initials of its Russian name—S.S.). After the Uganda Plan was rejected by the 7th Zionist Congress in 1905, the territorialist S.S. Party, which had been established in December 1904, seceded from the Zionist movement and cut its ties with the other sections of Poale Zion. Among its outstanding personalities, we can mention Nahman Syrkin, Yaakov Lestchinsky, Zev Latsky (Bertoldi) and Moshe Litvakov (Chaim Zhitlowsky also belonged to it at one period).

The Poale Zion ranks also included at the start a literary group that was known in Russian as Vozrozhdenia (The Renaissance). The members of this group, too, like the territorialist S.S., refused to accept the distant fulfillment of the Zionist goal and, for the time being, looked for fields of activity and transition solutions. They believed in the possibilities of a national cultural renaissance even in the Diaspora (even if it was not an "eternal" one) but, in contrast to the Bund, rejected assimilation and "national neutrality." They also rejected limiting the demand for national cultural autonomy to the borders of Russia alone. They formulated their demand for every Jewish minority everywhere and stressed the worldwide character of the Jewish people and its problems. Also in contrast to the Bund, they expanded the demand for national cultural autonomy to include *political autonomy* as well, in the shape of a Jewish parliament (*sjem* in Russian) like all the other democratic national parliaments of the nations to be liberated by the revolution, and wanted to turn the Russian and Austro-Hungarian "jails of nations" into states with a federative national structure (hence their common name, "Sjemists"). According to this concept, the Jewish national parliaments in the various countries would serve not only as a framework for the achievement of cultural autonomy, but also as a juridical and governmental authority for the advancement of the realization of Zionist territorial concentration.

It is clear that this concept, arbitrarily divorcing the problems of national cultural renaissance from social and economic reality and its processes, and putting its faith in organizational and juridical solutions, could not comply with the Marxist analysis of the Jewish problem and its solution. The Sjemists actually were inclined toward populist socialism and maintained close ties with the Russian Social-Revolutionaries. After their final departure from Poale Zion, the Sjemists organized themselves as the Socialist Jewish Workers Party (known by its Russian initials as S.E.R.P.). It was founded in Kiev in 1906, and its leaders included Mark Ratner, Moshe Silberfarb and, at one period, Chaim Zhitlowsky. In 1917 the S.S. and the S.E.R.P. united to found a party known as the "United."[6]

6. Like the Bund, many members of the United tended to consider the Soviet government's cultivation of Yiddish culture and language in its early years as the fulfillment of their traditional demands for Jewish autonomy in the Diaspora. They combined with the Communist Bund—as the Komverband (Communist Union)—and together joined the Yevsektsia. M. Litvakov, one of the former Territorialist and United leaders, was one of the Yevsektsia's central personalities and the editor of its newspaper, *Emes (Truth)*.

After the departure of the Territorialists in 1904 and the Sjemists in 1905, the Russian Poale Zionists, headed by Ber Borochov, re-formed themselves on a straightforward Marxist and Palestinian basis. They established the Poale Zion Jewish Social-Democratic Party and formulated its program (in Poltava in March 1906), which was accompanied by a detailed theoretical exposition—"Our Platform"— written by Borochov. In England and the United States, Poale Zion parties had already been established in 1904. These parties also went through a period of ideological searching and organizational schisms which, along general lines, paralleled the development of the Russian Poale Zion. In 1907, in The Hague, the World Union of Poale Zion was formed.

Even after the organization and reformation of the Palestine-oriented Poale Zion by countries and as a worldwide party, it was still not a single camp. In Czarist Russia, the Poale Zion had been nourished by the revolutionary underground, of which it had been a part, and this led to its orthodox Marxist ideology and its consistent spirit of class struggle. On the other hand, the Poale Zion in the United States of America and Western Europe had been influenced by the compromising spirit that prevailed in the socialist movement in those countries. A middle-ground position between the Russian and Western trends was taken by the Galician movement, whose leader, Shlomo Kaplansky, belonged, together with Borochov and Syrkin, among the central thinkers and leaders of the socialist Zionist movement prior to World War I (1905-1918).

In Europe, the attempts to reunite the Poale Zion with the Territorialists and the Sjemists came to naught, owing largely to Borochov's determination to maintain the expressly Palestinian and Marxist character of the movement. The differences were not so strong or outstanding in the United States. In 1909 the American Poale Zion changed its program and reformulated it in a non-Marxist direction, as a practical and constructive program of action, and abandoning the principle of class struggle. After this decision, most of the Territorialists, headed by Nahman Syrkin and Baruch Zukerman, and the Sjemists, headed by Chaim Zhitlowsky, joined the party. Encouraged by these reinforcements, the Poale Zion in 1910 established its own mutual aid society, The Jewish National Workers Alliance (*Verband*) which became a very active economic, cultural and educational center for the Zionist wing of the Jewish labor movement in America.

The Marxist Basis of Labor Zionism

Before Borochov could begin to investigate the national question of the Jewish people, he had to turn his attention to the national question in general, and come to some theoretical clarity on that subject. For that reason, even before his *Our Platform,* he wrote his study on *Class Struggle and the National Question* (1905) and was one of the first Marxist theoreticians to deal with this subject fundamentally. In attempting to explain the dual division of mankind—"horizontally" by class interests and "vertically" by national differences—Borochov generalized the various signs of these national differences as "conditions of production." By this he meant the conditions for the relative differences and separatism, conditions which are not the same as the "relations of production," "forces of production," or "means of production," but which serve all these as a geographic, ethnic and historic frame. It is this frame that by dialectical interplay shapes the character of the (relative) specificity of any one society compared to the others; of any one national, social-economic-political formation compared to the rest, and, in this fashion, also is the cause of the "uneven development of capitalism" that Marxist theoreticians have indicated. The generalization of all these various conditions under which production is carried out, termed "conditions of production," as a concept parallel to and complementing the "relations of production," is Borochov's important theoretical contribution to Marxist doctrine on the national question. This formula, which Borochov established because of the extraterritorial situation of the Jewish people, by applying Jewish history in the Diaspora, is especially important for the dialectical analysis of the trends and processes of development of the Jewish anomaly and for the determination of the historic way *out* of this anomaly. The objective background for class struggle and social revolution is seen by Marxism as the conflict between new and developing forces of production and old and limiting relations of production; in the same way Borochov showed that national conflict (true conflict and not the kind in which nationalism serves as a disguise for reactionary class interests) occurs when the developing forces of production come into conflict with limiting conditions of production, and that "the national problem should, therefore, be defined as a conflict between the developing forces of production and the situation of the conditions of production." We find that Borochov's definition of the contradiction between developing forces of production and abnormal conditions of production (e.g., an oppressed national minority, a colony under the rule of exploitative imperialism, an extraterritorial people, etc.) gives us theoretically firm ground and a common denominator for the struggle for national liberation of peoples deprived of national independence and the national liberation movement of the Jewish people deprived of a territory and of a normal economic and social structure. It is because of this that one of the special signs of Jewish nationality is the fact that the social struggles, as well as the reactions and conduct of the various classes of most of the people within the state as well as of the members of the Jewish minority are determined not only along class lines but along both class and national lines in combination.

An important part of Borochov's national theory is his brilliant and penetrating analysis of the interests and attitudes of the various classes toward the conditions of production shared by the nation as a whole; and in the event that these conditions are disturbed, toward rectifying them. In the course of this analysis, Borochov uncovered the "relativity" of nationalism and the class and particularist economic limits to the nationalism of each of the different classes. He showed that only the nationalism of the working class was "real," progressive, and even revolutionary, since it was the working class that was interested most of all in normalizing the conditions of production, in halting the intervention of foreign forces of oppression that narrowed the proletariat's strategic base, and preventing the full development of the contradictions and the social class struggle within the nation itself. Not only is the proletariat most interested in national liberation, in true nationalism and only that— that is, in nationalism not formulated in conflict with the class struggle and which does not aim to blur class consciousness or weaken the momentum of social struggle—it is also the class that is most capable of taking its position at the head of the national movement and of leading it consistently to complete victory in the form of full liberation, both social and national, of the masses.

Borochov made a Marxist analysis of the social class structure of the Jewish people and of the inability of the impoverished and displaced petit bourgeoisie, who are the large majority of the Jewish people, to become absorbed in other occupations because of intensifying national competition. He found that the Jewish proletariat was concentrated in nonprimary and nonbasic branches of production, especially in small, backward enterprises destined to vanish because of the trends of development in the capitalist economy, and that this factor also limited the Jewish proletariat's ability to struggle along with its prospects of victory ("the weakness of the strategic base"). He made a thorough and fundamental analysis of the growing process of mass Jewish migration which supposedly was to serve as a way out of the situation. Emigration did not achieve this aim, since those who entered countries with a developed capitalist economy were merely permitted, again and again, into the cracks in this economy, to become absorbed over and over again mainly in the nonprimary branches, generally in small enterprises. The problem thus remains without a solution even in the country of immigration.

In this way, Borochov reached his conclusion that the solution did not lie in national-cultural renaissance in the Diaspora and in the struggle for national-cultural autonomy, nor in the Jewish worker's participation in the socialist class struggle shoulder to shoulder with the native proletariat, nor in undirected migration. The solution lay in directing this migration together with the social reformation of the Jewish masses, in normalizing their social structure, in their penetration into the primary branches of production, in establishing their place among workers, craftsmen, middlemen, and the free professions. In a word, the solution is the far-reaching productivization of the Jewish masses. Such productivization is possible only in a country that does not have a developed capitalist economy and where the structure of the economy would permit this fundamental penetration and reformation. What is more, this reformation cannot be carried out just in any country, in some territory arbitrarily set aside for this purpose, but only in a place to which the masses are sufficiently attached by tradition and sentiment, by ties of historic continuity, so that the productivization in itself, involving difficulties and suffering, would be combined with a vision of national liberation and of return to the land of the fathers. To sum up, the need for migration will increase despite the diminishing potentialities in the former lands of absorption, and thus the trend toward territorial concentration in Palestine will become more dominant. This concentration will be both a solution of the Jewish national question and the establishment of a firm strategic base for the class struggle of the Jewish proletariat. This territorial process will be fulfilled mainly by a "stychic" (automatic) process because of objective economic necessity and the decisive factor in promoting concentration and construction in Palestine in the *class struggle of the Jewish worker.*

SOURCES

Zionism and Socialism

If the Jewish State is to turn from hope to fact, from vision to reality, it must keep the ideals of justice and social wisdom before its eyes. . . . Zionism must, necessarily, be wedded to socialism if it wants to be the ideal of Israel as a whole, of the Jewish working public, of the Jewish proletariat in all its forms, of the middle class, the intellectuals and Jewish ideologists. In socialist dress, Zionism can belong to the whole Jewish nation. By joining together with socialism, Zionism will grow and increase in strength until it becomes a tremendous national desire.
(From "The Jewish Question and the Socialist Jewish State," by Nahman Syrkin, 1898; Syrkin's *Writings,* I [Hebrew], p. 50; *Davar,* Tel Aviv, 1929.)

. . . Zionism is not possible without Socialist Zionism. That is what broadens the concept of Palestine and makes it possible to begin immediately in materializing the Jewish State. It brings Zionism and the material and spiritual interests of the masses of the people into agreement and transforms Zionism into a great ideal for which it will fight and live. It arouses the healthy, enlightened and ambitious elements in Judaism and makes them the pioneers leading the camp. We Socialist Zionists

now raise the flag of true freedom for the Jewish people; we rejuvenate Judaism by bringing to every one of its cells—the great idea of Socialism.
> (From "A Call to Jewish Youth," Nahman Syrkin, 1901, ibid. pp. 73-74.)

Zeire Zion

... Zeire Zion stand on the basis of the general national Zionist principles and declare that Social-Democratic theory and practice cannot be applied by the masses of Jewish workers in their conditions of life as a class of people without proletarian class possibilities. The application of Social-Democratic theory and practice contradicts the national interests of the Jewish people and by its nature is assimilationist. The doctrine of Poale Zion as a Social-Democratic party contradicts the interests of Zionism.
> (From the resolutions of the Zeire Zion Congress in Kishinev, 1906, in Eisenstadt, *History of the Jewish Labor Movement*, II Hebrew, p. 709.)

Z.S.

... The Eastern Alliance of Zeire Zion sees the radical solution of the national and social problems of the masses of the Jewish working people in building society on socialist foundations and at the same time in creating a laboring center in Palestine. In its struggle for the realization of the Socialist-Zionist ideals, the Alliance relies upon the masses of the Jewish working people and especially upon those groups that do not live on the exploitation of others' labor. The fulfillment of the Socialist-Zionist ideals is only possible by organizing a class movement of the masses of the Jewish working people in both the Diaspora and Palestine in economic, political and cultural fields of activity.
> (From the program of the "Eastern Alliance of Zeire Zion [Z.S.]," Warsaw, 1920. See H. Merhavia, *People and Homeland* [Hebrew], Jerusalem, 1939, p. 638.)

The Territorialists

... The Socialist-Zionists, relying on the interests and the ideal of the Jewish proletariat and the broad working masses, see in the limited Zionist program for Palestine, that cannot meet the minimum conditions needed to implement our ideas, and all the results implied by that (small settlements, etc.)—a fundamental and basic diminution of the Zionist program. . . .
> (From the declaration of N. Syrkin at the 7th Zionist Congress, 1905, in the name of the S.S., on their secession from the Congress. The 7th Zionist Congress, Congress Proceedings [German], Berlin, 1905, p. 135. Published by the Zionist Executive.)

The Sjemists

The Jewish Socialist Workers Party considers itself a part of the international socialist camp. It conducts its activity in accordance with the decisions of the International Socialist Congresses. The basic element characterizing the program of our Party is the demand to establish extraterritorial national parliaments (Sjems—from which the name by which we are called is taken) which must, in our view, lead to a juridical solution of the national problem. The jurisdiction of the Sjem should not be limited only to matters of culture and education; it must also embrace those political and economic problems that are closely related to the historic conditions of development of the nation concerned. Especially as far as the Jewish people is concerned, the Party raises the demand that the Jewish national Sjem be granted, among its other functions, the right to take the necessary measures to concentrate Jewish migration in some free and unoccupied territory. In this, the Party sees the solution not only of the problem of migration, but also of the Jewish national problem in general. . . .

(From the resolutions of the Founding Congress of the Socialist Jewish Workers Party, April 1906; in the Appendix to Borochov's *Writings*, I, p. 383.)

3 • Trends and Parties During the Second Aliya

The Second Aliya[1] was born amid the revolutionary happenings in Russia during 1905–1907. These events aroused social unrest and the desire for social and national liberation among the Jewish masses; at the same time, however, these same historic developments were reflected among the Jews, first of all, by a wave of pogroms conducted by the Russian reactionaries in order to divert the attention of the masses. Many Jews were impelled to think of emigrating to the Land of Israel (Palestine) where it would be possible to fulfill these longings for liberation, justice and progress, free of anti-Semitism and pogroms, and without the feeling that, instead of being allowed to participate actively in the social struggle, the Jews were destined, because of their special situation and status among the nations, to take part only as passive and suffering subjects.

Afterward, during Stolypin's reaction in Russia, disappointment and despair were prevalent within the revolutionary movement; these moods found fertile soil among the Jewish intelligentsia. Y. H. Brenner and A. N. Gnessin, each in his own way, described this depression in their Hebrew writings, as D. Bergelson did in Yiddish. The despair and alienation following the attempt to become part of the revolution, and after the failure of the revolution and the mounting reaction and persecutions, encouraged the stream of Aliya. The ideas behind this immigration were later to find expression in the ideology of the Israeli working class.

From this point of view, we can find parallels between the Bilu'im[2] at the beginning of the eighties and the Second Aliya. The latter, however, came at a much later stage in the development of national and social consciousness.

In addition to these external influences, there were also the effects of a deep crisis in the Zionist movement after the wave of enthusiasm and achievements among the Jewish public during the first years of its existence. The attempts to obtain a charter for Palestine by diplomatic negotiations with the Sultan and the various powers had failed. After having played its diplomatic card, the Zionist movement had come to a dead end. Many of the more impatient were attracted by the Uganda Plan as an immediate way out. The Uganda Plan was rejected by the Zionist public, but even after this rejection the Zionist movement still did not go beyond

1. Immigration wave: First Aliya—1882–1900; Second Aliya—1901–1918; Third Aliya—1919–1923; Fourth Aliya—1924–1927; Fifth Aliya—1929–1940.
2. Pioneers during the First Aliya.

barren debates and abstract slogans and phraseology that led to no real implementation.

Many members of Zionist youth circles—students and young intellectuals—reacted to the incapacity of the official Zionist organization by creating groups of Zeire Zion (Youth of Zion), which wanted to democratize the Zionist organization, speed up the beginnings of practical work in Palestine, deepen Hebrew cultural activity and Zionist education and, especially, achieve Zionist realization by immigrating to Palestine and laying the foundations for a Hebrew-speaking, democratic and progressive Jewish society. In their social views, these Zeire Zion members were influenced by Russian Narodism in its earlier, national democratic stage; only gradually were their views all the more crystallized under social-revolutionary influences.

The Uganda crisis also left its marks on the Poale Zion (Workers of Zion) movement which had, till 1905-1906, served as a general label for all these circles, groups, and political shadings that supported both socialism and Zionism. Part of the movement was carried into "territorialism," and when the Uganda Plan was rejected by the Seventh Zionist Congress, they formed the Jewish Social Democratic Workers Party. The Poale Zion at first also included the Vosrozdeny (Renaissance) literary group, whose members were called "Sjemists" (see Chapter 2). After the territorialists and Sjemists left, Poale Zion was organized as a Palestinian (Palestine-centered, in the phrase of the time) and Marxist movement.

Many of the cadres of the Poale Zion were unable to agree with either the paralysis of practical Zionist activity or the factional struggle within Poale Zion in the Diaspora, and arrived at the decision to go to Palestine (Eretz Israel) immediately in order to contribute their share toward the territorial concentration of the Jewish people, and in order to conduct a *real* class and national struggle.

These were, therefore, the two main sources of the Second Aliya: the Zeire Zion immigration—national-democratic, nonclass-oriented, kindred in spirit to both the Haskala movement[3] and Hibat Zion[4]; and the Poale Zion—proletarian-Marxist, supporting internationalism and class struggle, striving to find a foothold among the working class strata, and believing firmly in the Yiddish language and a secular and progressive Yiddish culture. They continued to defend the primacy of Yiddish in Palestine, as well.

At the beginning of the Second Aliya (Petah Tikva—1905) there was an attempt to unify the Jewish workers in Palestine into a single organization, at the initiative of the Poale Zion. This initiative was rejected by some of the workers, and at the close of that year, two separate organ-

---

3. Enlightenment.
4. "Love of Zion" (predecessors of the modern Zionist movement).

izations were established: Hapoel Hatsair (The Young Worker) and Poale Zion.

At first, Poale Zion suffered from a degree of strangeness to Palestinian reality and tended to view it in terms of the problems and terminology of the proletarian-Zionist labor movement abroad. Slowly, however, they began to overcome this weakness and showed signs of acclimatization. They decided in favor of the Hebrew language and to participate actively in the Zionist Congress. They raised suggestions for constructive activities, established Hashomer[5] and participated in Hahoresh.[6] They established the Eretz Israel Workers' Fund (Kapai) in the interests of all Jewish workers, not only of Poale Zion.

B. Borochov (see Chapter 2) praised the development of the Poale Zion in Palestine. His explanation of the differences between Poale Zion and Hapoel Hatsair did not raise any supposedly ideological conflict between constructive activities and class struggle. He considered *support or rejection of class struggle* to be the main dividing line between the two parties, but while acknowledging this conflict, he listed a number of Poale Zion's constructive activities—such as founding Hashomer and participating in Hahoresh.

Besides Hapoel Hatsair and Poale Zion, there was also a third nonparty trend headed by B. Katznelson, D. Remez, S. Yavnieli and Y. Tabenkin. These men had not come, as had the Hapoel Hatsair, from general Zionist intellectual circles, but rather from the Jewish socialist movement. Before coming to Palestine, B. Katznelson had belonged to the territorialists and the Sjemist Renaissance Group. Y. Tabenkin had been a member of Poale Zion.

On reaching Palestine, these "nonparty people" did not find their place in either of the rival groups. Their socialist background separated them from Hapoel Hatsair, but they also differed with the Poale Zion because of its slow spiritual acclimatization to Palestine and its exaggerated orthodoxy in preserving the terminology and ways of thinking common to the proletarian-Zionist movement abroad. The "nonpartyites" also denied the justification for two parties and invested most of their public efforts in establishing, strengthening and expanding the authority of the joint regional committees and agricultural organizations, working for the establishment of a countrywide organization of agricultural workers.

Summing up this period, it can be said that the Palestinian Poale Zion had a large share in implanting Marxism and the idea of class struggle among the Palestinian Jewish workers, in fostering ties between the Jewish worker and the international Jewish workers' movement, in laying the

---

5. Hashomer (The Guard) was an organization set up to take over the protection of the Jewish settlements.
6. Hahoresh was a contracting organization whose purpose was to perform agricultural operations and thereby introduce Jewish workers into agriculture.

foundations of urban trade unions and the beginnings of trade union and educational activity among the Oriental communities, etc., in addition to their activities in Hashomer and Hahoresh.

The nonpartyites played a considerable role in laying the first foundations of what was later to be the General Federation of Jewish workers (the Histadrut). They also helped stimulate the changes that were taking place within Poale Zion at that time. Despair and revulsion prevailed among the Palestinian Jewish workers at any attempt at precise theoretical formulations and definitions by the methods and analyses existing within the international labor movement and proletarian-Zionism. Hapoel Hatsair was the consistent and militant protagonist for this "heretical" attitude which became a *Weltanschauung*, a "program" and a principle. In practice, with certain reservations and contradictions, it was also the attitude of most of the nonparty people. In contrast to their views during the Second Aliya, Poale Zion was infected by these views toward the end of World War I; in the course of acclimatization and liberation from Diaspora dogmatism, they went so far as to reject Marxism and Borochovism and to abandon the principle of class struggle.

Even after the departure of the territorialists and Sjemists, the formulation of the Borochovist platform in Poltava in 1906 and the foundation of The World Union of Poale Zion at The Hague in 1907, the Poale Zion in the various countries was not a unified movement from the point of view of ideology, style, mentality or stress. In Czarist Russia its members absorbed the atmosphere of the revolutionary underground of which they were a part, and were naturally orthodox Marxists and militantly socialist. On the other hand, the Poale Zion in central and Western Europe, as well as in the United States, were influenced by the reformist moods of the general socialist movements in their countries. We might say that the Russian Poale Zion were *the Zionists among the Jewish Socialists* and they had to face the heavy competition of the anti-Zionist trends within Jewish Socialism. In the West, the Poale Zion were the *socialists of the general Zionist public.* Those same groups of youth and progressive intellectuals who had joined the Zeire Zion in Russia went mainly into the ranks of Poale Zion in the West. In this way, we find a situation in which the Poale Zion of the West were often closer in their views and mentality to the Russian Zeire Zion than to their Russian Poale Zion comrades.

The Palestinian Poale Zion were connected, in their early days, to the Russian party and the militant and orthodox Russian influence was to be felt in their theoretical programs (the "Ramle Platform," 1906). In the course of time, however, these influences grew weaker, Poale Zion immigration from Russia came only in small trickles and ceased completely during the war. During World War I, the ties with the American movement were strengthened partly because two of their outstanding leaders,

David Ben-Gurion and Yitzhak Ben-Zvi, spent their exile in the United States, and partly also because of American Jewish volunteers for the Jewish Legion[7] and the meeting between the American and Palestinian regiments (within the American regiment in particular, Poale Zion was strongly represented).

Toward the end of World War I, the movement for unification grew stronger, fed by the expectation of "great days to come," of mass immigration and the recognition of the need to absorb the new immigrants. The surprising ease with which Poale Zion and the nonpartyites met and merged in 1919 was undoubtedly a result of the new "American" course within the Poale Zion in Palestine. American-style Poale Zionism, without the Marxist backbone and without the central principle of class struggle, could actually have been accepted not only by the nonparty people, but by Hapoel Hatsair as well, but for the latter's conservatism and suspiciousness. Actually, they differed only in aspects of mentality, style and stresses which had more to do with the past and differences of origin than with present reality.[8]

7. Regiments of Jewish volunteers from the United States, the British Empire and Palestine, who participated in the British conquest of Palestine.
8. The outstanding Poale Zion personality in Palestine, Yitzhak Ben-Zvi, never translated his radical theory into practice. David Ben-Gurion was never a Marxist or a Borochovist. The "Red Russian" version of Poale Zionism was represented in Palestine mainly by Yaacov Zerubavel, the man who edited the party's paper *Ahdut (Unity)*; while the integration of theoretical radicalism and practical activism was urged mainly by the Poale Ziönist Hashomer headed by Yisrael Gileadi (d. 1918), who founded Hahoresh and was the initiator of kibbutz settlement in the Upper Galilee. Ben-Zvi was eventually to become Israel's second President. Ben-Gurion, of course, was Israel's first Prime Minister, serving in that capacity for many years. Zerubavel was one of the heads of the Left Poale Zion after the split in 1920. (See Chapter 6.)

4 • Ahdut Haavoda and Hapoel Hatsair

Ahdut Haavoda (Unity of Labor) was founded in 1919. When the nonpartyites and Poale Zion raised the slogan of unity, toward the end of World War I, they were thinking of complete unity that would also include Hapoel Hatsair. According to this plan, Ahdut Haavodah would not be a party but, at one and the same time, a "settlement, trade union and political organization." At the Agricultural Workers' Congress in Petah Tikva in 1919, a unity committee was elected to draw up a program. (It included Berl Katznelson, David Remez, Shmuel Yavnieli and Yitzhak Tabenkin for the nonpartyites; Yitzhak Ben-Zvi and David Ben-Gurion for Poale Zion; and left two places open for Hapoel Hatsair.) This committee did not suggest any theoretical or programmatic limitations to the proposed union; its aim was a broad framework that would be as general and as embracing as possible. Hapoel Hatsair, however, did not send its representatives to the committee and refused to join Ahdut Haavodah. This refusal may be explained by its being a minority at the Congress and its fear of being outnumbered in the new union.[1] It considered the lack of any programmatic definition as a ploy and a trap. It apparently did not distinguish Poale Zion's rightward trend and, on the contrary, thought it saw a leftward trend on the part of the nonpartyites. In imagination, it saw itself facing a concentrated and disguised Marxist majority.

Hapoel Hatsair's failure to join created a new situation. Right after the Agricultural Congress, Poale Zion and the nonpartyites called a founding convention of Ahdut Haavodah without Hapoel Hatsair, though they still hoped that the latter would reverse itself and come in shortly. When this did not happen, Ahdut Haavoda was compelled to drop the original plan for full political and trade union unity and to declare itself a *party*. Despite this, however, it did not give up its general and nonprogrammatic character. It was still looking for immediate union with Hapoel Hatsair and kept the "door open." The first result of Hapoel Hatsair's isolationism and Ahdut Haavoda's formation as a party was to exacerbate relations between the two groups and cause fierce partisan competition for the support of the new immigrants.

1. In the Petah Tikva Congress there were 27 nonpartyites, 19 Poale Zion, and 12 Hapoel Hatsair delegates.

The Third Aliya was beginning to flow into the country: the members of Hechalutz, Zeire Zion, Hashomer Hatsair, and others. The new immigrants did not understand the reasons for the party struggle and were not ready to accept it. They had come armed with high hopes and with world-embracing ideas, and were afraid that this party conflict would defeat all these hopes and plans. Yosef Trumpeldor[2] turned to both parties with an appeal to end their rivalry and to unify federatively within a general organization of Jewish workers, with the political parties continuing their individual existence:

> When I left the country at the beginning of the war, there were two workers' parties here—Hapoel Hatsair and Poale Zion. They fought over ideas, but it was still possible to find joint answers for mutual problems. There was a unified agricultural workers' organization, and a joint Sick Fund. Now, there is nothing in cooperation. Hapoel Hatsair has its Employment Bureau and Ahdut Haavodah, its own Employment Office. There are two Sick Funds and two agricultural workers' organizations. The war is also being waged between two trends among the railway workers.
> ... Jewry stands before very important events. The coming months or years will decide the fate of the Jewish people in the Land of Israel—to be or not to be. Persecuted by unparalleled pogroms, actually slaughtered, the Russian Jews stand on the country's threshold and plead to be allowed to enter. The joint efforts of all workers are needed. Every minute is precious, everyone coming into the country will be saved from certain death or the life of a Marrano. Every minute too late will be considered a crime on our part. Strive to leave the partisan circles. Come, all of you, to the common task with wide-open fraternal hearts.
> ... The parties will continue to exist. The workers will elect delegates to a joint council. The method of elections will be proportional. The council will be non-partisan and will establish a joint institution. Parallel to the council, nonpartisan trade unions will be established.

The new immigrants rallied around Trumpeldor's appeal and the rival parties were compelled to yield to the demand. Trumpeldor himself did not live to see the fruits of his efforts—he fell in the defense of Tel Hai.[3] Months later, in December 1920, in Haifa, the General Federation of Jewish Workers (Histadrut) was founded. Ahdut Haavoda definitely established itself as a political party within the Histadrut, though still

---

2. Yosef Trumpeldor, a member of Hashomer during the Second Aliya, was one of the first to conceive of the idea of the *kvutsa* (commune). In Russia during World War I and afterward, he was active first in organizing Jewish Legions to fight with the British to free Palestine from the Ottoman Empire, and later in establishing the Hechalutz (Pioneer) organization. Trumpeldor became the symbol of Jewish self-defense and Jewish heroism. In his Zionist views he was close to the Left wing of Zeire Zion (the later Z.S.) and his socialist views to the Russian Social Revolutionaries (S.R.).

3. In the spring of 1920, Arab bands, overwhelmingly superior in number, attacked Kibbutz Tel Hai (in the extreme north of Upper Galilee). Yosef Trumpeldor, in command of Tel Hai, fell with a number of other defenders.

without deviating from its "generalness" and nonprogrammatic character. Its chief aim was the achievement of complete unity—meaning unity with Hapoel Hatsair. Large sections of the Zeire Zion immigration from eastern Europe, which had gone through a process of political radicalization under the influence of the Russian Revolution, now joined Ahdut Haavoda, after having compelled it to establish the Histadrut. This opened new channels of growth for the young party; on the other hand, this trend was a deep disappointment for Hapoel Hatsair, which had been the traditional address for Zeire Zion immigrants, and the party was suddenly faced with the difficult problem of finding membership reserves.

The Second Aliya slogan for unity and the establishment of the Ahdut Haavoda at the beginning of the Third Aliya had been necessary and justified. With the objective of forming a working class that was becoming aware of its separate existence and mission, there was vital importance in establishing an independent and inclusive class framework. In keeping with the differing historical conditions of every nation, this framework can be trade union or political in character, or, in a different combination of conditions, a class framework in which the separation between trade union and political activities has not yet taken place. Because of the lack of clear definition, there may be mistakes in the principles of the unification program, but the act of unification itself, at that stage, is necessary in order to further the cause of the working class and its movement for liberation. The conflict between trends and ideological streams over the way to conduct the class struggle is one of the distinguishing marks of the *second stage* in the development of the labor movement; this conflict eventually finds its expression in political party differentiation.

At the time of the Second Aliya, it was still unclear what form the desired union of Palestinian workers would take; whether it would be a federative union of parties (the form it actually received at the end of 1920 with the formation of the Histadrut) or whether it would take the form of the full and unreserved political trade union and settlement unity in the shape of Ahdut Haavoda (as Berl Katznelson and Yitzhak Tabenkin desired). Until the coming of the Third Aliya and the pressure it applied, these *two* possibilities had existed potentially.

The situation changed fundamentally after the General Federation of Jewish Workers (Histadrut) became an existing force. The stages of inclusive political unity, *in addition to the united Histadrut,* meant something very different from the original demand for the achievement of labor unity (Ahdut Haavoda). This was especially true since the demand for inclusive unity was very theoretically unclear on the division of functions and relations between the political party and a settlement and trade union association. The demand for unity, as formulated by the nonpartyites of the Second Aliya and later by the Ahdut Haavodah in its inception, tended to diminish the importance of the political party in our specific circumstances.

The emphasis on the idea of unity was not on its immediate utility, limited to the specific circumstances and the proximate stage of development; it was made into an eternal and sacrosanct principle, good and correct in itself, absolutely, without stressing the fact that such unity was possible only on the basis of some agreed-upon program that would be truly obligatory and unifying. The avoidance of any definite and precise program was not only the result of the tactical consideration of leaving the door open for Hapoel Hatsair; this lack of definition was stressed by the former nonpartyites *as a principle,* and given theoretical backing as the correct path for a "class party open to all" in contrast to the "closed sects," and other such arguments.

> . . . We, members of Ahdut Haavoda, are workers and our socialism is the socialism of work expressed in popular terms and in style that is derived from our own lives and feelings, and we have no need to put ourselves into mechanical forms. . . . We have no need to decide on any ideology—neither Zionist nor Socialist—but only our existence as Jewish workers. That says everything. (Berl Katznelson, 1919.)

If we were to evaluate this phenomenon of Ahdut Haavoda today, we would first of all see the great and positive aspect of its very appearance, its dynamism in settlement and defenses, its great share in building the Histadrut and Hevrat Ovdim,[4] the Hechalutz organization and its educational activity among youth both abroad and in Palestine. Ahdut Haavoda, or more precisely, a part of it, also is credited with creating one of the main kibbutz unions, the Kibbutz Meuhad (United Kibbutz Federation).

On the other hand, there were also negative aspects, including, first, the glorification of the idea of unification "at any price and under all circumstances," while depreciating the value of world outlook, theory or program. A second negative aspect was, as its rivals defined it, Ahdut Haavoda's "lust for power," its desire to *force* unity on its opponents, and in general, its intolerant attitude toward minorities among the working public.

We could mention also the "gdudism" (*gdud ivri*—Jewish Legion formed to fight alongside the British Army in World War I)—that is, the hope of receiving the Jewish State from Great Britain as a prize for military services, which began with the plan of establishing Jewish Legions under British patronage and ended with the one-sided "British orientation" taken for a long time by the Histadrut and the Zionist movement.

---

4. "Workers' Society"; official name, General Cooperative Association of Labor in Israel; legal framework embracing all the Histadrut enterprises, cooperatives, moshavim, kibbutzim, etc. (See Chapter 16).

The Third Aliya came imbued with ideals and utopianism. Utopianism was one of the clear distinguishing marks of all the sections of that immigration. It was this utopian vision that gave the new immigrants wings and imbued them with the determination and extraordinary energy to change the face of things, the sure faith that the various ideals and plans would be fulfilled in the near future.

The danger of utopianism lay not so much in itself as in the awakening after the inevitable failure, and the concomitant reactions of disappointment and despair, directed not at the utopian aspect but at the idea itself. Under the conditions of the Third Aliya, this utopianism led to a tendency to abandon either Zionism or socialism and class struggle.

One of its early aspects was the theory of exclusive, pure "constructivism," which is not to be confused with the positive value of constructive activity in itself. Constructivism as an exclusive concept was the belief that an increasing number of constructive activities could in themselves guarantee the success of Zionism and socialism, without resorting to the "traditional" methods of the international labor movement class struggle or the revolutionary struggle for power. Nahman Syrkin was the theorectician of this doctrine. After he had repented of his "territorialist deviations" (see Chapter 2) and joined the Poale Zion in America, he became a regular contributor to the party's Palestinian paper, *Ahdut*. After World War I, he came to Palestine with a Poale Zion delegation, and in a number of speeches and articles developed his idea of building the country on a cooperative basis, with national capital and a workers' economy, and without private capital or capitalism.

> Zionism faces two possibilities; one is that capital, both large and small, will flow in, in confusion, for fear of bolshevism, and start businesses, speculation, land competition, and bring in cheap labor from Egypt and Syria. Zionism will become a mockery for the Jewish worker and the Jewish nation; Palestine will become a refuge for frightened capitalists. The doctrine will be falsified and our land will belong to foreigners. The second is that the Jewish nation will make a great national effort, national capital will come, and Zion will be built on a socialist cooperative basis. Jewish labor will prosper, the spirit of Judaism living in the Bible, in the Prophets, in the Midrash, in Hebrew philosophy and Hassidism, will find its historical answer. If Zionism is imbued with this spirit, there will be a Jewish National Fund with an annual income of tens of millions, a national loan of hundreds of millions. Zionism will be able to turn to the entire progressive world for aid.
> (Nahman Syrkin, "The London Meetings," 1919, *Ahdut Haavoda Notebooks,* Vol. II, Tel-Aviv, 1922, p. 23.)

Syrkin, who became the uncrowned theoretician of Ahdut Haavoda, had an unquestioned share in the development of socialist Zionism, and especially the credit of being among its founders. It was not long after

Herzl had published his *Jewish State* that Syrkin publicized the daring idea of a Socialist Jewish State and initiated the crystallization of a socialist trend within the general Zionist movement. His main center of activity and source of inspiration was in central and western Europe and later in the United States, far from the centers of the Jewish labor movement in Czarist Russia and its revolutionary spirit. After his return to the ranks of Poale Zion, he became the spokesman for the clearly non-Marxist trend of "pure constructivism" and opposition to class struggle in Palestine, in contrast to and in debate with Borochov. Like large sections of the Third Aliya, both in the Gdud Haavodah[5] and Ahdut Haavoda, Syrkin was inspired by the socialist construction in the Soviet Union and found in it support for his idea of building the country and for the illusion of "pure constructivism." Ignoring the detail that in Russia that socialist construction had been made possible by class struggle, revolution and the final conquest of political power, they tried to apply in Palestine an "organizational and governmental" method of building socialism, without class struggle and without any political struggle to change the regime.

In view of the enmity of the Soviet Union and the world communist movement to the Zionist idea and enterprise and the liquidationary onslaught of the Russian Jewish communists and the Palestinian Communist Party (P.K.P.), Ahdut Haavodah used this utopian theory of pure constructivism to develop an attitude that may be defined as the belief in the "absolute particularity" of our conditions and problems, an "original socialism" which still fed the desires for "absolute independence" and the fears of "self-denial and mimicry." The special extraterritorial chaacter of the Jewish people all over the world and the specific solution for the Jewish problem (Ingathering of Exiles in Palestine, productivization, etc.), they seemed to be saying that they also *require an absolute particularity in the Palestinian workers' ways of thinking, activity and socialist organization.*

The truth is that our socialism will have to be "original" in some aspects and "universal" in others. Our socialism will have to be Marxist revolutionary and based on class struggle, but at the same time completely adapted to our special conditions. The true "originality" of our socialism and Marxism lies in class struggle here being indivisibly joined to construction and settlement; while that other kind of "original socialism" (namely, nonrevolutionary socialism, without class struggle), which actually only means reformism, is poles apart from any originality or Israeli particularity; it would rather seem to be a most unoriginal and "cosmopolitan" *copy of the reformist movements in other countries.*

Any one-sided evaluation of Ahdut Haavoda would be a deviation from

---

5. "Yosef Trumpeldor Labor Battalion": a kibbutz federation, one of the most important (and typical) creations of the Third Aliya (see Chapter 16).

historical truth. At the beginnings of that movement, it is true, seeds were sown that eventually were to grow into reformism. On the other hand, Ahdut Haavoda should not be viewed as a final and immutable phenomenon. From 1919 to 1930 it saw many changes.

There was something particularly attractive about Hapoel Hatsair of Second Aliya days—with its outstanding leaders, its moral and idealistic tension, its efforts to improve man and society, to revive the Hebrew language, to educate youth abroad, etc. It will always own the credit for having founded the kibbutz movement and begun the settlement enterprise, for having turned the Diaspora intellectual into a farmer with roots in his own homeland—in a word, for having begun the creative activity of the Jewish working class in Palestine.

As far as the idea of socialism was concerned, Hapoel Hatsair in Palestine, like Zeire Zion abroad, shared a wide range of views and formulas, from fundamental reservations to fundamental support. Most of these reservations were naturally not concerned with the moral elements of the future nonclass socialist society, but rather with the idea of the irremediable conflict between the classes, with class struggle and international workers' solidarity, as these were reflected in the Socialist International. All—both opponents and supporters of socialism alike—were agreed, however, that at least during the present historical stage there was no room for a socialist movement or international workers' solidarity, neither in the Diaspora nor in Palestine at the very beginning of construction. Here there was room only for Zionism as a movement for national, cultural, social and moral revival. According to them, the working class in Palestine had one single mission—the consistent pioneering fulfillment, in theory and in practice, of the one and only national and social ideal: *Zionism*.

This general and nonsocialist ideology led Hapoel Hatsair, from the start, into a number of errors and failures (as for example, appealing to the employers' "national consciousness" in order to promote the "Conquest of Labor."[6] The positive aspects of Hapoel Hatsair, however, were all in its immediate activities, most of which were mandatory under the conditions of the Second Aliya; its negative aspects were to emerge in the future, when its ideological confusions had to serve a working class expanding and developing in changing situations and in a developing economy.

---

6. The name given the efforts of the Jewish pioneers to take up labor and guard duty in the Jewish plantations, despite their lack of experience and training and the low level of wages.

What Our Socialism Is, and What It Isn't

What It Isn't

a. We absolutely reject all political socialism. We do not think that transferring the means of production to the State, that is, putting them in the hands of a bureaucracy of officials and parliaments, will bring any solutions to the social questions.

b. We utterly reject all materialistic viewpoints in comprehending either history or the situation of the worker. Any solution based only on increasing wages without a fundamental change in the workers' relationship to their work will not last, since there is no limit to men's lust for money when it is encouraged;

c. We reject any socialism which sees its main task in politics, which thinks of helping the worker to change his life by politics alone, by demands directed toward others and not, at the same time, toward the worker himself.

In What Way Are We Socialists?

a. In seeing the basis of future society as the self-labor of all its members;

b. in seeing the transfer of the means of production to the workers themselves as a prerequisite to any solution of the social question;

c. in contrast to all forms of Marxism, our socialism strives for fulfillment from the bottom upwards, and not the contrary. There will be no true revolution in humanity that is not accomplished in its cells first of all—in the family, the group. Our socialism, therefore, does not put the emphasis on politics, though we recognize it as a means of second or third importance, but rather on self-fulfillment in independent groups satisfying their own needs;

d. Our socialism emphasizes the equality of work. We strive for creative labor, and it is not all the same to us whether the worker obtains his wage from working the soil or from producing luxuries. We are prepared to build an altar to creative labor, but not to work and the worker as such. Because of this, we have been opposed to almost all the phenomena of Europe's official and vociferous socialism, because it always demands from others, because it does not consider the quality of labor, and considers it only in a quantitative, external process; because it educates the worker badly by cultivating his lust, his envy, and his hatred instead of love; neither love of work place nor love of nation; because it denies God!

(Hugo Bergmann, *Our Socialism*, Min Hayesod, Vol. II, Tel-Aviv, 1964, pp. 72-73.)

There is, therefore, no contradiction in appreciating Hapoel Hatsair's achievements during the Second Aliya and the criticism leveled against its ideology by its contemporary rivals, Ber Borochov and the Palestinian Poale Zionists. If there is any contradiction, it lies in Hapoel Hatsair itself, in the fact that its actions and pioneering enthusiasm were much greater than its theoretical clarity and its reservations concerning socialism.

Hapoel Hatsair lost its attraction during the Third Aliya. It was no longer the expression or the organizational and spiritual creation of the new immigrants. What once were to be its future mistakes now became present ones. When it failed to join Ahdut Haavodah and after the Histadrut was formed, Hapoel Hatsair also hardened its own organizational and tactical side, turning from a dominant movement into an opposition party. It concerned itself with guaranteeing its reserves from abroad, secured its ties with the Zeire Zion World Union (Hitachdut) and laid the foundations for the Gordonia Youth Movement. In Palestine, it continued its settlement activity to establish *kvutzot* and *moshavei ovdim*,[7] and at the same time fought for influence and for its share in the leadership of the Histadrut. Since a considerable number of Hapoel Hatsair's own immigration now went to the city, it was all the more compelled to deal with the problems of the urban worker, and thereby lost its traditional character as an agricultural movement.

Its preoccupation with the problems of its urban members and active participation in the Histadrut compelled Hapoel Hatsair, unwillingly, to take part in the trade-union class struggle,[8] but its idealistic-utopian viewpoint influenced its handling of trade union activity and its approach to the class struggle forced on it by the new reality, and gave them what was clearly a reformist and compromising character. It is obvious that, by itself, Hapoel Hatsair would not have been able to guide the construction of a reformist party under the new conditions, but it was destined to make a tremendous and even decisive spiritual and moral contribution to the large urban *and* rural party, after joining it. That was what happened with the establishment of Mapai.

These changes within Hapoel Hatsair were also reflected in changes in its leadership, with the mantle passing from Aharon David Gordon[9] to

---

7. The *moshav-ovdim* is a cooperative agricultural settlement based on individual family farms.
8. In the Second Aliya period Hapoel Hatsair was opposed to dealing with the urban workers or to any connections between the Federalism of Agricultural Workers and urban trade unions, since Hapoel Hatsair considered only agricultural workers as "counting," according to their view of Zionist realization. This was one of the points in dispute between Hapoel Hatsair and Poale Zion at that time.
9. A. D. Gordon was the spiritual leader and philosopher of Hapoel Hatsair. He came to Palestine at a late age during the Second Aliya and became an agricultural laborer and then member of the first *kvutza* (commune) of Degania. His emphasis on the Jews' need to return to physical labor came to be called "the Religion of Labor." He was a strong opponent of class struggle and Marxism, but earned his place in the history of the Palestinian labor movement as the father of the vision of once more taking root as a nation in the homeland, in labor and Hebrew culture.

Chaim Arlozorov.[10] Hapoel Hatsair had been fundamentally opposed to socialism, to internationalism of any kind, and to class struggle. In this period of change, Arlozorov introduced a fine distinction by rejecting only "Marxism," while supporting a "popular socialism." He rejected revolutionary socialism but came out in favor of reformism; his sophisticated analysis of the Second International led him to support it as, in his view, only a kind of "Socialist League of Nations":

> ... A movement whose aim is to place the Jewish people as a creative and equal member in the Socialist League of Nations and which, at the same time, in its depths, is a national movement in the true and highest meaning of that concept ... A movement that does not desire to build its socialism on the interests of one class, but on renewing production and reviving labor in Israel; a movement whose means are not those of inciting class against class or class domination, but those of creating a cooperative way of thinking and cooperative views among the people. A movement whose aim it is to conquer Israel by the willpower of idealism, to bring the Exile toward a national and social future and to renovate Hebrew culture while recognizing the historic unity of the nation....
> (C. Arlozorov, *The Popular Socialism of the Jews*, 1918.)

Syrkin's Poale Zionism also frightened him no more than did Ahdut Haavodah's "class struggle" after it had retreated from Borochovism. There were differences of mentality and way of thinking (mainly in drawing from traditional Jewish culture, as against Western culture and enlightenment, the differences between a man-centered method and one occupied with changing society, government, and economic systems), which still separated A. D. Gordon and Nahman Syrkin, despite their objective proximity. Between Arlozorov, on the one hand, however, and Syrkin and Katznelson, on the other, there were very many points of contact, both ideological and practical.[11]

In addition to these elements, which helped bring Hapoel Hatsair closer to Ahdut Haavodah, there was another decisive factor—serious changes that were taking place in Ahdut Haavodah itself.[12]

---

10. Chaim Arlozorov was a leader of Hapoel Hatsair in Germany. After immigrating, he became one of the outstanding younger leaders, first of Hapoel Hatsair and then of Mapai. He was Prof. Weizmann's close collaborator in the Zionist Executive. He was assassinated in 1933, apparently by Jewish fanatics.
11. In this, Arlozorov was not alone: most of the active members of Hapoel Hatsair of the Third and Fourth Aliya supported union with Ahdut Haavodah.
12. Among the leading personalities of Hapoel Hatsair were A. D. Gordon, Yosef Vitkin, Yosef Aronovitz, Eliezer Yaffe, Eliezer Shohat, Yosef Sprinzak, Yosef Baratz, Yosef Bussel, Levi Eshkol (Israel's third Prime Minister), Chaim Arlozorov, Eliezer Kaplan, Yitzhak Lufban, Menahem Bader and Yitzhak Gelfat (the latter two are now in Mapam). Included among the Ahdut Haavoda leaders were Berl Katznelson, David Remez, Yitzhak Tabenkin, Shmuel Yavnieli, Eliyahu Golomb, Moshe Beilinson, Aharon Zisling, Yisrael Bar-Yehuda, Moshe Sharet (Israel's second Prime Minister), Yitzhak Ben-Zvi, David Ben-Gurion, Yisrael Shohat, Shlomo Kaplansky, David Bloch-Blumenfeld, and Golda Meir (Israel's fourth Prime Minister).

5 • **From Ahdut Haavoda to the Formation of Mapai**

After the formation of Ahdut Haavoda, the strongest element in the party was not the former members of Poale Zion, but rather the nonparty people of the Second Aliya. It was *their* views and emphases that shaped the party. If the latter had been formed with the intention of merging Poale Zion and the nonpartyites and nothing more, they might have been expected to formulate some compromise program in which the ideas, terminology and formulations common to Poale Zion would have made some impression. Ahdut Haavoda was planned, however, as a merger of Poale Zion, the nonpartyites, and Hapoel Hatsair. It was therefore clear from the very beginning that only the program of the nonpartyites—which avoided theoretical definitions, sweetening the "bitter pill of socialism" for Hapoel Hatsair by stressing the originality of "Hebrew socialism," and replacing the accepted socialist terminology with terms taken from the Prophets—could serve as the common denominator for the merging groups. This fact did not change even after Hapoel Hatsair refused to join Ahdut Haavoda on its formation, since its place was kept open. It seemed reasonable to expect that the nonpartyites, rather than the Poale Zionists, could represent this program best, since they identified themselves with it and would sooner or later be better able to convince the suspicious members of Hapoel Hatsair that when they joined Ahdut Haavoda they would find at the head people with views similar to their own. Also, the fact that the Poale Zion elements were only negligibly represented in the Third Aliya, toward whose integration the new party had been formed, inevitably strengthened the role of the former nonpartyites in Ahdut Haavoda as a whole and in its leadership. The leading personalities of Poale Zion of the Second Aliya were occupied in those days with cultivating Ahdut Haavoda's links with the Poale Zion movement abroad, and in representing it in the Socialist International, the Zionist Executive, in the Vaad Haleumi, the Tel Aviv Municipality, and in "Hashomer." Despite the vital importance of these missions and the respect these persons continued to enjoy, they took little or no part in the policy decisions or daily administration of the party and the Histadrut. The only one among them who did become an organic part of the Ahdut Haavoda leadership was David Ben-Gurion, who even in Second Aliya days had been closer in concepts and stresses to the nonpartyites than to his Marxist fellow party members. Now he joined Berl Katznelson in the process whereby, step by step, the two won the leadership and the sole, unquestioned authority over Ahdut Haavoda.

Poale Zion's greatest strength lay among the members of Hashomer (with headquarters in the Kibbutz Kfar Gileadi). True, these members' influence derived primarily from their actions, their daring and vision, and they did not occupy themselves much with theoretical doctrine; despite this, and in striking contrast to the nonpartyites and some of the other members of Poale Zion, they knew how to tie the two ends together and to synthesize pioneering activity with class consciousness and loyalty to Marxism and Borochovism. This was the "Poale Zion tradition" of Hashomer that was firmly maintained by Yisrael Gileadi and, after his untimely death, by Manya and Yisrael Shohat and their comrades. From the very beginning of the union, there had been some tension between the members of Hashomer and the former nonpartyites who now headed the new party. Their arguments over the program of the Hagana (founded in 1920, replacing Hashomer), the ownership of the weapons amassed by Hashomer, etc., also reflected, either openly or otherwise, the struggle over Ahdut Haavoda's program or concerning whether the leadership should continue as the monopoly of Berl Katznelson and Ben-Gurion or should be a collective leadership including the heads of the former Poale Zion.

When the "Joseph Trumpeldor Labor Battalion" (Gdud Avoda) was formed in August 1920 by immigrants from Hechalutz and other socialist-Zionist organizations in the U.S.S.R., its ranks were joined by members of Hashomer. This historic meeting of the veterans of the Second Aliya and the new immigrants, and the integration of these two elements, offered great hopes for pioneering socialist Zionism. However, things turned out otherwise. From the party standpoint, Gdud Haavoda was composed mainly of Ahdut Haavoda members who were nonaffiliated. Its original program, however, included the aim of "strengthening the Federation of Jewish Labor (Histadrut) and of *directing it toward the aims of the Gdud* (author's emphasis). It was not long before this last clause took on a distinct meaning. Sharing Ahdut Haavoda's utopian illusions of the "immediate" fulfillment of Zionism and socialism, the Gdud considered it its right and duty to disseminate its authority and values among the working class, and even presented a separate list in the elections to the Second Congress of the Histadrut in January 1923, with the platform of equalizing the standard of living of all the Histadrut members, of opposing bureaucracy, and of recognizing the kibbutz as the only form of labor settlement. These aims, as well as the Gdud's separate appearance in the elections, were considered by the Ahdut

Haavoda leadership as the dangerous signs of future competition. After coming to this conclusion, they did everything they could to humble the Gdud, and exploited disputes within the Gdud itself in order to intervene in its domestic affairs, either on the party level or through the Histadrut. One outstanding (though not the only) act of administrative intervention was the Histadrut Executive Committee's decision in favor of partitioning the collective farm of Tel Yosef—Ein Harod. In protest against this administrative intervention, dozens of leading members of Ahdut Haavoda (Gdud members and especially members of Hashomer) left the ranks of the party. That intervention ultimately proved to have even more far-reaching effects.

The growing bitterness and hostility toward Ahdut Haavoda and the Histadrut leadership left a valuable part of the labor public vulnerable to the crisis of the Fourth Aliya,[1] when the utopian hopes of immediate fulfillment of Zionism and socialism were shattered on the rocks of unemployment, closed immigration, a pause in settlement, and political siege. From 1924 to 1926, this crisis and the widening rift with Ahdut Haavoda and the Histadrut led to the growth of a leftist ideological trend, breaking the traditional ties between Zionism and socialism and between pioneering construction and class struggle. When the Histadrut authorities and about half the Gdud members demanded the expulsion from the Gdud of the members of the militantly anti-Zionist "Workers' Faction" (Palestinian Communist Party), this "leftist tendency" opposed it, leading to even further deterioration in relations within the Gdud, until the final split in December 1926. In August 1927, some dozen of these "left Gdud" members, headed by M. M. Elkind, went to the Soviet Union where they founded an agricultural commune, called Via Nova (New Path), of short duration.

A serious examination of this tragic affair leads us to the opinion that if it were not for this bitterness, hostility, and hatred they might have overcome the crisis just as the other section of the working class overcame it, more or less.

In any case, there is no reason to look at the liquidationary leftist ferment in which some of the best elements of the Third Aliya and the Gdud became involved as historically inevitable, without considering the revelations of lust for power, the cult of centralism and the intolerance which characterized Ahdut Haavoda.

The resignation of the veteran Poale Zion element in protest, concentrated in Hashomer, from Ahdut Haavoda led to important qualitative

---

1. Fourth Aliya (1924–1926), also called "Grabsky's Aliya" because of the Polish Minister of the Interior who enacted a series of economic decrees which severely affected the lower-middle-class Jewish masses and led to a large middle-class immigration to Palestine. The result was an outburst of land speculation and other inflationary activities that brought on economic crisis, unemployment, and emigration.

changes in the cadres and leadership of the party. When some other personalities also left the party and its institutions, the remaining Poale Zion leaders were pushed out of positions of decision in the party and the Histadrut. The way was cleared for Berl Katznelson and David Ben-Gurion to assume positions of sole leadership and unshakable authority in Ahdut Haavoda and, while transforming it from a utopian movement to a reformist party, to continue striving toward the goal of union with Hapoel Hatsair.[2]

Hapoel Hatsair's refusal to join Ahdut Haavoda compelled the latter to draw to the full programmatic and organizational conclusions from its new situation as a political party. It was obligated to draw up a program and an organizational constitution. In 1919 and 1920, the party had shown itself capable of filling the needs of the hour. Now, in the same way, with the accelerated development of the capitalist economy from the Fourth Aliya onward, it should have taken the lead in the workers' activities and struggles, not only in broadening settlement activity but also in class struggle. It should have looked, both theoretically and practically, for a new synthesis on a higher level. This would have been a faithful continuation on the path of Poale Zion of the Second Aliya, in new circumstances and in larger dimensions. Ahdut Haavoda, however, developed in a completely different direction. During its first years, it was totally involved in strengthening the Histadrut, in reinforcing its control over Histadrut bodies and the kibbutz movement, in tightening the links with the World Union of Poale Zion (right wing) and its control over its reserves in the youth organizations—Hechalutz, Hechalutz Hatsair, and Freiheit abroad, the General Federation of Working Youth (Hanoar Haoved) and the Jewish Socialist Youth (Bahrut Sotsialistit Ivrit) in the country.[3]

Though *the problem of unification* was not tabled, it was considered temporarily to be not actual. Here we find a classic example of a situation in which total unity was unrealistic and impractical and yet still continued to influence the party; it was the historic orientation toward this unification and not its practicality or impracticality that shaped the character of the party. The effect of this orientation toward total and unconditional unity was first of all to freeze the development of the party itself. Matters that had to be taken up were not discussed on their own merits,

2. In the course of time, some of the Hashomer veterans who had left Ahdut Haavoda drew closer to "Left Poale Zion," which at that time formed the chief leftist socialist-Zionist opposition to Ahdut Haavodah and later to Mapai. Later, some of these joined Mapam when that party was established.
3. For Hanoar Haoved, see Chapter 17, subhead on "Pioneering Youth Movements." As to Bahrut Sotsialistit Ivrit, it was established in the spring of 1926 as the organization of the younger generation of Ahdut Haavoda, and later of Mapai. During the mobilization for the Palmah and the British Army, and during the Mapai split in 1943-1944, it ceased activity.

but always with the corollary consideration of how any specific step might affect the possibilities of eventual unity; whether it would "burn bridges" or widen the gap between the party and the candidate for unification. Thus, the orientation toward unity with Hapoel Hatsair, from the very outset, did away with any possibility of socialist programmatic chrystallization within Ahdut Haavoda itself. The contrary was true: definite signs began to appear, in varying degrees, of a rightward trend by the party's leadership and cadres. The traditional synthesis of pioneering construction and class struggle was replaced by an unreserved constructivism alone, accompanied by reformist practice in Histadrut activities, in interparty relations and in the Zionist movement, in an inclination toward the right wing of the international workers' movement and especially in the British Labour Party. As we have seen, this "new course" was guided by David Ben-Gurion and Berl Katznelson.[4]

This trend of development caused profound disillusionment in many former Poale Zionists, among the veterans who had helped found Ahdut Haavoda and the new immigrants coming at the end of the Third and during the Fourth Aliya. When Marxist terminology and the traditional fundamentals of Poale Zion were not included in Ahdut Haavoda's founding program, they comforted themselves with the fact that the essential content of these terms and fundamentals, and especially the principle of class struggle, were *actually* accepted in the party and that these "axioms" had not been included in the party program only so as not to put difficulties in the way of the future unification with Hapoel Hatsair, and so as not to prevent the Russian-Zionist-Socialist ("Z.S.") and Hechalutz immigrants from joining the party. In the course of the years, however, these former Poale Zionists became increasingly doubtful that Ahdut Haavoda was really acting according to the principle of class struggle and that the "axioms" still remained intact.

During the split in the World Union of Poale Zion in 1920, the members of the minority in the Polish Poale Zion movement disagreed with the suggestion to join the Communist International and favored participation in the Zionist Congress and the path of pioneering construction in Palestine (and, therefore, won the title of "Right Poale Zion"). Despite this, at least during the early years after the split, they remained faithful to the Marxist-Borochovist terminology and tradition. It is not surprising, therefore, that after immigrating to Palestine, they found it a difficult and lengthy process to adapt themselves to Ahdut Haavoda, which was bent on deserting the principle of class struggle.

4. Berl Katznelson was the outstanding personality and thinker of the "nonparty" group during the Second Aliya, of Ahdut Haavoda and eventually of Mapai, until his death in 1944. One of the leading reformist non-Marxists, and the theoretician of "exclusive constructivism" in the Palestinian labor movement, he played an important role in shaping and building the Histadrut.

This was the background, in 1924, for the formation of the first opposition within the ranks of Ahdut Haavoda—in the form of the Avuka (Torch) Group. This group was composed mainly of former members of the Polish (right) Poale Zion, but it was also joined by Marxist elements among the socialist Zionist youth arriving from the Soviet Union. The Avuka Group enjoyed the patronage of the veteran Ahdut Haavoda leader, Shlomo Kaplansky[5] and whose aim was to conduct Marxist education within Ahdut Haavoda and to secure the loyalty to class struggle, in practice as well as in theory. One axis of debate between Avuka and the Ahdut Haavoda leadership was the suggested union between the Poale Zion and the Zionist-Socialist (Z.S.) World Union, something which Avuka feared because of its negative effects not only on the movement in Poland but also on Ahdut Haavoda's trends in Palestine.

However, after this suggested union between the two world organizations became a fact (at the unification congress in Vienna in August 1925), tension relaxed. In the meantime, as some of the former Poale Zionists had managed to overcome their "pangs of adaptation" and had integrated into the Ahdut Haavoda leadership and the Histadrut apparatus, Avuka ceased activity at the end of 1925.

As we look back now at this opposition group, its organic fault immediately springs to the eye. It did not succeed in uncovering the sources of Ahdut Haavoda's rightward trend and hesitated to question the principle of "total unification" and the declared orientation on unification with Hapoel Hatsair that prevented the party's own socialist solidification. It ignored the critical character of the reformist course which it wanted to arrest by conducting Marxist education in the ranks of the Party. What is more, Avuka was not able to oppose the reformist and solely constructive policies with a leftist socialist-Zionist alternative of its own, one based on synthesizing class struggle and pioneering constructivist action. It was not possible to base a movement or an opposition, for any length of time, merely on disillusionment, discomfort, nostalgia, and loyalty to terminology.

The economic and political crisis that struck Palestine in 1926 and 1927, following the Fourth Aliya, had a considerable (and perhaps decisive) role in shaping the Palestinian labor movement. The gates were barred to Jewish immigration and unemployment was rife and spreading. On the one hand, there was an artificial expansion of the capitalist and speculative sector, accompanied by the formation of petit-bourgeois and Diaspora patterns in the cities; on the other hand, a stoppage of national settlement; and all this with a background of darkening political horizons and dim hopes for Zionist progress. Worst of all, this depression and crisis fell

---

5. Outstanding veteran Poale Zion and Ahdut Haavoda leader, later head of the Haifa Technion (Institue of Technology).

on the working class after years of rising hopes for what was to be the imminent fulfillment of both Zionist and socialist aims, as if pioneering initiative supported by national capital were sufficient without having to go through an extended period of capitalist development. Suddenly, with no warning, the Jewish workers fell from the peaks of their utopian hopes and illusions to the wells of stagnation, crisis, and despair.

Now was the time for the effects of the lack of clarity and the absence of precise definition of the relationship between pioneering constructive initiative and class struggle, characteristic of Ahdut Haavoda, to make themselves felt. During the peaks of the Third Aliya's constructivism, the problem of class struggle did not divide Ahdut Haavoda, since it seemed to be only a secondary matter, overshadowed by the pioneering activity. From the practical viewpoint neither one position nor the other on class struggle was too important. Reality was one of pioneering construction. There wasn't any opposition to the traditional principle of class struggle, without the members of Ahdut Haavoda having to test this principle in actuality. Now, however, in the crisis, and with the shattered hopes of the "short-cut," class struggle gained in importance and the hour of trial was at hand.

In the early, prophetic days of the movement abroad, generalized definitions of socialist Zionism or both Zionism and socialism might have been sufficient. Then, during the Second and Third Aliya the accepted formula was a kind of coexistence of constructivism and class struggle. From the crisis of the Fourth Aliya and onward, however, *the idea of a supposed contradiction between the two concepts began to take form.* Generally, this was not an officially declared contradiction in principle, but rather a kind of practical choice or parting of the ways. The intellectual nebulousness of the Third Aliya which could unite all began to give way, during the Fourth Aliya, to a widening differentiation, with the choice now represented as supposedly *either* pioneering constructivism *or* socialist loyalty and class struggle. From then on, in keeping with this, and for many years, some of the partisans of class struggle began to look on constructivism as a hindrance and brake; during the days of crisis and stagnation, some of them went as far as to despair of socialist Zionism altogether. Others, hesitating to integrate class struggle and constructive pioneering activity, began to transfer their utopian illusions speedily into compromising reformist practice, explaining and embellishing their inactivity and unreadiness to wage a consistent struggle for workers' interests with the excuse of "concessions and sacrifices for the sake of pioneering and building the country."

At the same time, our description of the effects of the crisis of 1926–1927 on working-class consciousness and development in Palestine would not be complete without pointing out, as the doctrine of the supposed conflict between pioneering and class struggle, the instructive and fertile effects which these ideas had on *Hashomer Hatsair*, then in the decisive stage of its ideological, political and organizational solidification. It was this lesson that emphasized the need to define the precise place and role of every one of the fundamental elements of a socialist Zionist, pioneering and working-class ideology, and to analyze the mutual relationships between these elements in the various stages of Zionist fulfillment. *This was the synthesis of class struggle and construction.* We shall go into this, however, in the chapter on Hashomer Hatsair.

The close of 1926 saw a revival of oppositionary activity in the Tel Aviv branch of Ahdut Haavoda, mainly by the remnants of the Avukah Group. This time, the stress was on problems of trade union organization and activity. This opposition, however, was quite limited and never attained the dimensions of an organized group with an organ of its own, and there did not seem to be many possibilities of arresting Ahdut Haavoda's trend toward reformism. As a result, the group's leading spirit, Zvi Coltun (a former Secretary of the Tel Aviv branch) despaired not only of changing the party, but of pioneering constructivism and even socialist Zionism in general, and in 1928 he went over with some of his associates to the ranks of the Palestinian Communist Party. Most members of the group disavowed his choice, but what he did shocked them and caused a temporary cessation of their activity.[6]

At the start of the Fifth Aliya (1928–1929) the debate over unification was renewed in both parties. Hapoel Hatsair inclined more toward Arlozorov's point of view in favor of unification; he was supported by the urban section of the party and the members working in Histadrut institutions in cooperation with Ahdut Haavoda there. The centers of resistance remained mainly in the *kvutzot* and *moshavim* which had hardly been affected by the internal changes within Hapoel Hatsair itself and within Ahdut Haavoda. (Incidentally, something very similar happened in Ahdut Haavoda: the rural section—the Kibbutz Homeuchad—was less influenced by Berl Katznelson and David Ben-Gurion's new course and were therefore less enthusiastic over the prospects of approaching unification.) Within Ahdut Haavoda, Katznelson and Ben-Gurion were moving as swiftly as they could toward unification, not only because of the "principle" in itself, but also, and mainly, because of their ever-growing proximity to the positions of Hapoel Hatsair in its new reformist and practical form. The arguments of theory and principle that accompanied these efforts were

6. After leaving Ahdut Haavoda, Coltun's doubts about Zionism rapidly turned into anti-Zionism. From 1930 on, he worked as a nonparty sympathizer on the editorial board of the anti-Zionist *Ha-Or*. In 1932, he joined the Communist Party. He was arrested by the British authorities and expelled to the Soviet Union in 1936. A few months later, he was arrested and in 1938 was executed.

actually more of a cover for the real aims. The former Poale Zion leaders (with the exception of Ben-Gurion, of course) had their reservations about this general enthusiasm, not so much because of their opposition to the reformist programs, but because of two other reasons: First, they considered the mentality and inhibitions of the party in the "World Union" (and of the Polish party in particular). These parties faced the heavy pressure of the more revolutionary rival mass parties among the Jewish workers, and only with great difficulty yielded to Ahdut Haavoda's demand to unite with the "Z.S." World Union in 1925; unification with the Hapoel Hatsair affiliate—Hitachdut, considered almost "general Zionists"—could have damaged their position considerably.

Second, it was not easy for the Poale Zion leaders to completely give up in principle their traditional fundamental axioms, and especially the principle of class struggle. Their defense of these traditional positions was mainly a matter of terminology, however. It was a formalistic and conservative orthodoxy, without adapting the principles of Marxism and Borochovism to the new conditions.

> .... Unfortunately, I cannot take part in the festival with a whole heart. Not because I oppose the unification of Ahdut Haavoda and Hapoel Hatsair into one party. I, too, look on unification as a victory for Socialist-Zionism. I am opposed, however, to "unification at any cost," to "unification despite everything," "unification at any moment." The matter of class consciousness has not been emphasized sufficiently. . . . The concept of "class consciousness" is not an empty phrase, but a special characteristic holding the recognition of the ties with the Jewish labor movement throughout the world and with the international labor movement in this country and abroad. . . .
> (Y. Ben-Zvi, *Notebooks*, Vol. 19, V, 1929.)

In the hour of decision, however, they gave up their opposition and halfheartedly or wholeheartedly supported the nonprogrammatic unification with the party that didn't accept socialism or class struggle—Hapoel Hatsair.

Of the nonparty personalities of the Second Aliya, Yitzhak Tabenkin was in a special position. In contrast to the others, he was a Marxist and had not agreed with Katznelson and Ben-Gurion's new course. However, though he continued to be considered one of Ahdut Haavoda's ideologists, he belonged more to the "spiritual leadership" than to the inner decision-making circles; especially, he was deeply involved in building the Kibbutz Hameuchad, in contrast to the divided and disintegrating Gdud Haavoda. Tabenkin could not ignore the fact that the unification of Ahdut Haavoda, in its present rightward trend, with Hapoel Hatsair would only culminate in the triumph of the latter's anti-

Marxism within the new party. On the other hand, he was unable to liberate himself from the attractions of the concept of "all-embracing unity" as an absolute and correct value transcending circumstances and relation of forces. He most certainly saw what was coming, but in the last analysis, the "principle" won and he, too, supported the unification.[7]

The center of opposition to the merger was found in the circles of the Third and Fourth Aliya, coming from the Russian Hechalutz, the "Z.S.," "Dror," and Socialist-Zionist youth organizations in Russia. True, their socialism was not Marxist and showed strong social-revolutionary tendencies. They were suspicious of "dogmatic formulas" that were "too precise." In their declaration on joining Ahdut Haavoda (in 1920) the Z.S. had still made their joining the party conditional on a promise to work energetically for union with Hapoel Hatsair. The members of Dror, who had moved from Russia to Poland and thus were deeply active in Hechalutz and Hechalutz Hatsair, had only with difficulty accepted unification with Poale Zion (Right).

Now, it was among these "nondogmatic" socialists that there were many whose experiences in this country had led them to question their own nondogmatism. The same thing happened as far as the unification was concerned. In the course of the years, they had been absorbed in Ahdut Haavoda, had been among the founders and builders of Kibbutz Hameuchad, and had become involved in the developing Palestinian reality. Now, face to face with the life of a worker, they had overcome many of their theoretical ideas. They had not been Marxists and partisans of class struggle from the start, but they had come to these ideas under the influence of reality. This phenomenon may perhaps be explained by the fact that they had not gone through the initial crisis of the Poale Zion, expressed in the gap between theories formed and crystallized abroad and the new conditions in Palestine. This problem was overcome by Poale Zion either by *ignoring* the new situation or by *deserting the theory* and cultivating an attitude of skepticism toward the possibility of any theory to meet our situation or to help change it. Unlike the former Poale Zionists in Ahdut Haavoda who were fighting rearguard battles in the course of retreat, these others were crystallizing and developing their views. (A somewhat similar process might be found in another part of the Third and Fourth Aliya—Hashomer Hatsair.) In any case, it was reality that aroused and moved many of the former members of the Z.S., Dror, etc., leftward. They provided most of the opposition to the unification with Hapoel Hatsair and many of them voted against

---

7. In 1929, the merger agreement was initialed and a referendum was conducted among the members of both parties. In Ahdut Haavoda 81.6 percent voted in favor, 16.6 percent were opposed, and 1.8 percent abstained. In Hapoel Hatsair 85 percent were in favor, 10 percent against, and 5 percent abstained.

it. Later, we will find their ranks forming the center of leftist opposition in Mapai, leading to the split in 1944.[8]

In the end, the open and consistent opponents of unification were an insignificant minority; most of the former Poale Zionists abstained.

Yitzhak Ben-Zvi, who had expressed some doubts about details of the program, now welcomed the merger and called it the natural continuation of the movement's tradition.

Tabenkin spoke at the Ahdut Haavoda Congress about his questions and fears but in the end voted for the merger, and the reformist leadership obtained its wish. In January 1930 the merger was completed and the Eretz Israel Workers Party (Mapai) was formed.

> A. Mapai recognizes that the labor movement in Eretz Israel is united in its historic aim: devotion to the establishment of the Jewish people in the Land of Israel as a free working people, rooted in all the branches of the agricultural and industrial economy and autonomously developing its own Hebrew culture; membership in the working class of the world, in its struggle to do away with class enslavement and social discrimination of every kind, to transfer the natural resources and means of production to the ownership of the working public and to establish a society of labor, equality and freedom.
> B. Mapai considers itself to be responsible for pioneering realization in the Zionist movement and a loyal member of the Socialist labor movement throughout the world. The Party participates in the Zionist Organization and its institutions, in the Socialist International, in Knesset Israel and in the institutions of self-government—as the representative of the Jewish workers in Palestine for active and responsible pioneering activity in all the spheres of the nation's and worker's life in the country and in all the causes of the Zionist and Socialist movements.
> (From the Mapai Program.)

---

8. We do not, of course, mean to imply that all those from the Russian Hechalutz, Z.S. and Dror, or even most of them, went through this course of development, but only emphasize that elements from these groups took a prominent place among the opponents of unification and later among the leftists in Mapai.

6 • Left Poale Zion: The struggle over Borochov's legacy

In Chapter 2 we saw how the Poale Zion in the various countries had divided, even before World War I, into orthodox Marxists (Russia), those wavering in the middle, as in Austria-Hungary and Palestine, and the anti-Marxists, in the United States and elsewhere. This was due to the influence of the general labor movement as well as the relative strengths and status of the rival parties in the Jewish labor movement in those countries, the social makeup of the Poale Zion parties, and other factors. This division deepened during the war years and especially after the outbreak of the 1917 Revolution in Russia. In the electrified atmosphere of the postwar period, after the victory of the October Revolution and the rising tide of revolutionary communism in the European and world labor movement, the rupture was inevitable. At the Council of the World Union in Stockholm in 1919, and its Congress in Vienna in 1920, the movement finally split into two separate World Unions, one "left" and one "right."

The dispute that led to the split moved around two main axes: the question of joining the Communist International and the question of participating in the Zionist Congresses.[1]

The fact that the Eastern European Poale Zionists voted for the Third (Communist) International was natural and understandable under the circumstances; the same was true of the issue of severing ties with the General Zionist Organization with its bourgeois leadership officially supported by the British government (the Balfour Declaration, etc.), which

---

1. The split occurred after the above Congress, by a vote of 179 to 178, decided to affiliate with the Communist International. (Since this vote was the first, they never came to voting on the question of participating in the Zionist Congress.) In keeping with the decision, the "Left Union" began negotiations with the authorities of the Communist International in order to win its recognition for Jewish territorial concentration in Palestine and to guarantee the continued existence of the (left) World Union of Poale Zion and its right to conduct Poale Zion agitation among Jewish workers in their lands of concentration. When these aims were not attained, the negotiations were terminated finally in the summer of 1922. The outstanding personalities of the "Left Union" included N. Nir, Y. Zerubavel, Hashin Y. Vescher, Moshe Erem, N. Barrou, A. Revutsky, Z. Abramowitz, and others. Among the outstanding personalities of the "Rightist Union," there were, in addition to the Ahdut Haavoda leaders in Palestine, S. Kaplansky, S. Z. Shazer (Rubashov), now the President of Israel.

was the same government that was heading the anti-Soviet campaign and intervention. All the traditional arguments of the Russian Poale Zionists against participating in the Zionist Congress suddenly took on infinitely greater importance in these circumstances. As a matter of fact, it may be said that on this issue, too, the decision taken by the Russian Poale Zion and their supporters in other countries was a natural and understandable one.

> ... The Russian Poale Zionists were different from their comrades in the other countries in their special emphasis on the Marxist and class outlook ...
> [B. Borochov, "History of the Poale Zion Movement," *Writings,* III. p. 6, Tel Aviv, 1966].

It is clear that the participation or nonparticipation in the Zionist Congress was only a signpost. Most of those who favored participation (headed by the Americans and to some extent also Ahdut Haavoda) also favored exclusive constructivism as a surrogate for the traditional paths of constructivism and class struggle. Those who were against participation underrated the value of the constructive working class role, of activities in Hechalutz and among the youth, and the like, in addition to class struggle.

The Right wing, Poale Zion's reliance on Borochov and on the Poale Zion tradition in the country from the time of the Second Aliya onward was very questionable. On the other hand, it seems as if the left wing Poale Zion, on these two questions of anti-reformism and the Zionist Congress, were loyal to Borochov's general views and considered themselves his legitimate heirs.

In any case, some reservations are in order.

First of all, Borochov had indeed opposed participating in the Zionist Congress but had been very far from considering it a vital problem of principle, as did the Left Poale Zion. After all, while in America, Borochov had bought the Zionist *shekel*[1] out of party discipline, though in other cases of a disagreement in principle, he had not avoided breaking party discipline.

> ... "The question isn't whether to participate in the Zionist Congress. Even if the Congress is bourgeois, Poale Zion might find it necessary to go there for tactical reasons, in order to influence the bourgeois Zionists. This question concerning the Zionist Congress isn't more than a detail. The question that is much more important and fundamental is the general one: how are Poale Zion to relate to the Zionist Organization—as a bourgeois, or as a general Jewish one embracing all classes among the Jewish people? Proletarians can also participate in certain bourgeois organizations if that can benefit the

---

2. Token of membership in the World Zionist Organization, conferring the right to participate in the Zionist Congress.

working class. The big question is whether they consider that organization to be alien and bourgeois, or general and theirs, too.
(Ber Borochov, "Zionists and Poale Zionists," 1915, in *Selected Writings*, II, in Yiddish, by the Jewish National Workers Alliance [Farband], New York, 1928, p. 292.)

What is more, Borochov's opposition to participating in the Zionist Congress was due not a little to his evaluation of the Congress as merely a debating platform, without practical activity, an estimate that undoubtedly had some grounds in the reality of those years. However, the debates at the Congress began to take on practical meaning and even importance after the Balfour Declaration, when the labor parties in Palestine attempted to win over the Zionist bodies to large-scale settlement activity, and succeeded.

Second, Borochov was, indeed, an "anti-constructivist," but his mind was open to every constructive act carried out in Palestine, certainly not excluding the labor settlements, the cooperative movements and the kibbutz, etc. The Left Poale Zionists did not differentiate like Borochov, between "constructivism" as a slogan implying the denial of class struggle, and supporting constructive activities in themselves.

. . . They [the "Social-Democratic" Poale Zionists] honor the Jewish National Fund and willingly support it because of its great national aims and popular activities; but they know that despite this the Jewish National Fund remains a bourgeois institution and in no manner a socialist one. As their own they consider only those funds and institutions in the service of the working class. That fund is the "Palestine Workers' Fund" [KAPAI] which was created by workers and belongs wholly to workers
(Ber Borochov, ibid.)

. . . The "Social-Democratic" Poale Zionists stand firmly on their belief that no socialism and no liberation can be possible by any other way except the class struggle. . . .
They also recognize more or less peaceful methods of activity by the labor movement, that is, in parliamentary activity and cooperative organization.
But they insist firmly that these peaceful methods can at most only ease the class struggle and serve as auxiliaries to trade union struggle and direct political action. These peaceful methods, however, can under no circumstances be a substitute for the direct struggle and take its place.
It is only a dangerous utopia to think that Palestine in particular can be different from all the other countries and that in it, in particular, there can arise a kind of colonization that will be free of capitalist elements. . . .
(Ber Borochov, *The Socialism of the local Poale Zionists*, ibid, Chap. 2, pp. 285, 287.)

. . . They (the Social-Democratic Poale Zionists) . . . view the coopera-

tive movement as a good thing, but cooperation isn't the center of the world. They think that cooperative settlement construction is a good method but not the only one and in any case it isn't socialist.
(Ber Borochov, ibid., p. 292.)

Third, the "authentic" reliance on Borochov of 1906 does not exhaust the problem of "loyalty" to Borochovism. After all, Borochov, for all his genius, was not able in 1906, in Russia, to do more than draw the general lines of development, the historic perspective. However, he would have called himself a pure utopian if he had tried his strength, in the circumstances of the time and place in which he worked, in giving an exact and detailed description of the way the historic perspective would be fulfilled, with all its twists and turns, in the future circumstances of the far-off country. True, dialectical, living Borochovism should have obligated the Poale Zion of the '20s to complement what Borochov said in his time, on the basis of the concrete reality of territorial concentration in fulfillment and of construction in a period of mass immigration, just as Lenin did for Marxism. If we turn our attention to the direction in which Borochov was hinting in the years after "Our Platform" and especially during the war, we find that the general direction hinted at in his last articles is toward the integration of cooperative settlement construction and class struggle.

... On the verge of a new chapter in world and Jewish history, at a time when the Jewish people faces great dangers and new attractive possibilities, we stand before the question: how shall we overcome the organizational weakness in Zionism? How shall we develop the maximum of fertile activity out of those deep feelings of sympathy felt by the masses of the people for the vision of renaissance in our land?
And this is the answer: national unity against the unity of the opponents of Zion
(Ber Borochov, "The Unity of the Anti-Zionists," 1911, in *Writings*, II, p. 395. Published by Sifriat Poalim and Kibbutz Hameuchad, 1958.)

The work of practical settlement in the country, with the experience obtained, the unavoidable mistakes and the sacrifices made, is what created the political facts that gave us today's results. Even if the Jewish colonies are weak, the settlement methods faulty and the Zionist institutions still young, in any case these did more, taught the people itself and the whole world more than thousands of fine programs and diplomatic negotiations. One watchman who fell had a greater share in the realization of Zionism than all our proclamations
(Ber Borochov, "Facing Reality," in *Writings* II (Yiddish), 1917, p. 260.)

In the past we thought that Zionism was a *stychic* process and that our main work was in removing the hurdles piled in our way. With this in mind we thought to leave all the work of construction to the bourgeoisie. Afterwards it was revealed that we were mistaken. There are mechanical stychic processes and there are organic stychic processes. Our mistake was in our thinking that the mechanical process had begun when in reality only the organic one had begun.

(From "Palestine in our Program and our Tactics," 1917, in the anthology *Ber Borochov: From Class to Nation* (German), 1932, p. 101.)

The atmosphere of those days, which were days of division in the "World Union" and of struggle against anti-Zionist liquidationism, moved both wings of Poale Zion further away from the path in which their party had developed and taken form in Palestine during the Second Aliya. The right wing opportunistic deviation was balanced by one of a sectarian left-wing character, which looked with suspicion at everything the right wing did or supported, including its pioneering construction activity.

From this point of view, Shlomo Kaplansky may be considered to be a loyal heir of the prewar Poale Zion tradition, in that he integrated settlement creation with loyalty to the principle of class struggle, in theory and in practice.

The role of the working class in Zionism is both a creative and liberating one. It fills its liberating role in Palestine itself by fighting on the positions that it won by the good old methods of trade union and political struggle. It also fulfills this role in the Zionist movement by impelling it by its criticism, its organizational strength, its mass education on the class egoism of the bourgeoisie, to take the path of democratic and socialist settlement, in accordance with the interests of the masses. By this it provides that large masses of workers will be able to penetrate into the new economy and that Palestine will be (in Herzl's words) 'a great workplace for the Jewish people'. The working class fills its creative role by reinforcing, by its free initiative, the bases of cooperation in the Jewish community, in work, production and consumption. In contrast to the 'private initiative' that is the idol of the capitalists, it sets up the collective initiative of the Jewish workers, which is becoming more and more collectivistic in nature and in activity. We should not draw a dividing line between the two roles and methods of work of the Poale Zion movement. They influence each other, the success of both depends, of course, to a great extent on our organizational strength and, above all, on the course of the great and final decisive conflict between capital and labor in the whole world. . . .

(From "Problems of Socialist Zionism," 1920, in *Vision and Fulfillment* by Shlomo Kaplansky, Sifriat Poalim, 1950, p. 72.)

During the time of the split and shortly afterward, Kaplansky erred in his international orientation (as a faithful pupil of Austro-Marxism); but in the last decade of his life he corrected his mistaken position. He took his place at the head of the League for Friendship Ties with the U.S.S.R., left his party after the split in Mapai, going first to the Tnuah Ahdut Haavoda, and then with the Hashomer Hatsair Party until Mapam. Kaplansky thus drew the full conclusions, both international and Palestinian, of loyalty to Marxist Poale Zionism. His sensitive and faithful Zionist and socialist sense helped him see that the theoretical development of Borochovism in the conditions that had taken shape after the Third Aliya had found its completion in the group that was not one of the traditional wings of Poale Zionist Borochovism, *in the Marxist-pioneering force of Hashomer Hatsair.*

The Foundation of Left Poale Zion in Palestine

After World War I, when Ahdut Haavoda and the Histadrut were established, Left Poale Zion had not yet appeared as a real and important factor in the country's political life. Most of the veteran and authoritative leadership was engrossed in the struggle over the World Union and, after the split, in building the Leftist Union organizationally and ideologically, and in negotiations with the Comintern over the recognition of Zionism, so that the Leftist Union could become part of the communist movement; while doing all this they were waging a life-and-death struggle with liquidatory trends and elements. The latter was prepared first to decrease the demands in the negotiations with the Comintern and, in any case, not to present them as ultimatums; later on, when the negotiations failed, they were ready to divest themselves of any real Poale Zionist content, whether it be by capitulating and accepting the Yevsektsia's arguments openly, or by a system of "procrastination" which put off the fulfillment of territorial concentration in Palestine until after the final victory of the world revolution.

A small minority of the Poale Zion in Palestine did not join the Ahdut Haavoda, and continued to maintain its separate existence. They were motivated by two aims that operated in combination. The first was the desire to preserve the loyalty to the Poale Zion tradition, to the "World (and later, Left) Union," and to combine this with a positive attitude toward the October Revolution and the Third (Communist) International. The second aim, like the first a reaction to the rightist trend, tended to abandon the traditional Poale Zion path and to find a compromise between the principles of proletarian Zionism and the anti-Zionist principles of the Yevsektsia.[2] More precisely, the Poale Zion minority that did not join Ahdut Haavoda was divided into a left Poale Zion trend

3. Yevsektsia: the Jewish section of the Soviet Communist Party. "Yevseks" became a synonym for a Jewish antinational and anti-Zionist Communist.

(Revutsky) and a liquidationist-Yevsektsia wing (Meirson). Their party was first called the "Socialist Workers Party" (MPS) and afterwards, with the growing Poale Zion immigration, changed its name to the "Jewish Socialist Workers Party." Nonetheless, the liquidationist trend remained the stronger.

After the split in the world Poale Zion movement in 1920 and the formation of the Left Union, and during the negotiations with the Comintern in 1921–1922, the Left Union showed three distinct trends. The first was the disguisedly liquidationist trend already described. The second, at the center and enjoying the support of the majority of the leadership (Zerubabel, Nir, Erem and others) was loyal, in principle, to the Palestinian program and fought the liquidationist trend, while trying to maintain the unity of the Left Union by making concessions to the liquidationists and holding up the schism until the conclusion of the negotiations with the Comintern. The center actually neglected practical Palestinian activity, concentrating mainly on the negotiations with the Comintern. The third, militantly antiliquidationist trend demanded immediate practical Palestinian activity, accelerated Poalei Zion immigration and efforts to achieve a united front with the Labor Zionist parties.

> ... The construction of a Jewish socialist Palestine can only come about in agreement with the main principles of revolutionary class struggle, and its development will take on strength with the development and victory of the social revolution. ... Bourgeois Jewish settlement, conducted up to now on the basis of private property and exploitation, has gone completely bankrupt, both socially and nationally. The growth and success of the Jewish settlement in Palestine have proven that Palestine can only be built by the immigration and settlement of large masses of Jewish workers, supported by their own labor and organizing their activity according to the aims of constructive and creative socialism. ... Together with class struggle we must even today—in the period of capitalism's transition to socialism—take all the practical and social-economic measures both in the Diaspora and in Palestine for socialist settlement in Palestine and the future dictatorship of the Jewish proletariat over Jewish life in Palestine. ...
> (From the Resolution of the "Poale Zion left bloc" at the Fifth World Congress, Vienna, 1920.)

In Russia, these conflicting trends led to the existence of two separate Left Poale Zion parties: one, the Jewish Communist Party, Poale Zion; the second, the Jewish Socialist Democratic Party, Poale Zion. The more Palestinian-oriented and militantly antiliquidationist wing that had been organized as an "Organizing Committee" (in Berlin) was expelled from the ranks of the Left World Union in 1922. Within Palestine the

Left World Union recognized the Jewish Socialist Workers Party (MPS) and later, in its new form, the Jewish Communist Party by the name of the similar liquidationist group in Soviet Russia. This party left the matter of loyalty to the idea of Jewish territorial concentration in Palestine as a matter of free choice for the members of the party. The Jewish Communist Party (Poale Zion) actually conducted something like a double set of books. It presented itself as the "Jewish Section of the Palestinian Communist Party," although there was no non-Jewish section; that is—toward Moscow it appeared as a non-Zionist territorial organization, while at the same time it presented itself to the Jewish public and the Poale Zion immigrants as a "Left Poale Zion party." Some of the party's members were opposed even to this "Zionist compromise" and organized an openly anti-Zionist Communist Party of Palestine (after the schism at the Congress in 1922). Parallel with these two Communist parties, two separate factions appeared in the Histadrut and trade unions: the "Workers' Faction" for the PCP; the "Proletarian Faction" for the CPP.

Those members of the Organizing Committee who came to Palestine, Zev Abramowitz and Yitshak Yitshaki, joined the group headed by Avraham Revutsky, who had left the Jewish Communist Party to form an "Initiating Committee for the Social Democratic Poale Zion in Palestine," and together set up the "Agitation Group of the S.D. Poale Zion" or, as it was called in short, "Poale Zion S.D." Under this name they appeared in the elections for the Second Congress of the Histadrut in the winter of 1922–1923. In March 1924 they established the Poale Zion Palestine Workers' Party.

After the failure of the negotiations with the Comintern, the liquidationists were expelled from the ranks of the Left World Union. The Russian Jewish Communist Party (Poale Zion) merged with the Yevsektsia[3] and the two wings in Palestine; the PCP and the CPP also merged and formed the united Palestine Communist Party (PCP) as the openly anti-Zionist and anti-Poale Zion local branch of the Comintern, in 1923.

In 1923 the World Union sent a delegation to Palestine to set up a loyal branch to replace the Jewish Communist Party, which had until then been recognized as its official Palestinian affiliate. Meanwhile, the Union and the Organizing Committee had merged in the Diaspora in 1924; as a result, the two groups also united in Palestine and formed the Left Poale Zionist Party in the same year.

---

4. The pro-Palestine Left Poale Zion continued to exist as a legal party in the Soviet Union until 1928.

The World Union and the Palestinian Party

Even now the Left Poale Zionists did not succeed in becoming an important factor among the working public in the country, or an alternative to Ahdut Haavoda or later to Mapai. Those workers who were not easy about the growing reformism faced a difficult choice. On the one hand, reformism, but which was active in the pioneering and settlement areas, and on the other, the Left Poale Zionists who were loyal to class struggle and revolutionary socialism but completely divorced from real creative Zionist activity, without which the class struggle lost all its purpose and prospects. In this situation the workers inevitably voted for reformism. They listened gladly to the Poale Zionists, and appreciated their incisive criticisms and analyses, but did not consider them an alternative to the reformistic leadership in guiding the construction of the country and the labor movement.

Those leaders who had come together in the country still looked on the Palestinian party (in keeping with the old tradition of Poale Zion) as only one of the branches of the "World Union." The Palestinian party was small and not very successful and members found comfort in their world movement, which was a serious and important force among the Jewish labor public abroad. In addition, they did not consider themselves authorized to change any of the aims and values of the world movement in order to meet the needs of the Palestinian party. Considerable sections of the Palestinian party did revolt from time to time against this stress on the World Party, in order to find greater contact with the wider public and the Palestinian youth. As a result of this and all kinds of ideological and tactical conclusions deriving from this revolt, the Palestinian Left Poale Zionist party split and reunited a number of times.[4] However, even the "activists" who were more rooted in the country and had even overcome their Yiddishism, established ties with youth groups in the Marxist circles, maintained their contacts with the veteran Poale Zionists within the Gdud Haavoda and looked for contacts with the remnants of the "Left Opposition" of the Fourth Aliya, etc.—even they—never went beyond such searchings and still, at that time, had not come to a revision of their position on participation in the Zionist Congress, their attitudes to the National Funds, etc.

However, with all due respect for these reasons, we still must look for an objective and sociological answer to the question we have raised. That answer is that Poale Zion did not grow and did not change first and foremost *because of their tiny share in the immigration flowing into the country.* Only such an immigration could have expanded their ranks in order to alter the real quantitative and qualitative relations between the "World Union" and the Palestinian party, to make the Left Poale Zionists face the

---

5. The sequence of events: 1928: split; 1931: reunification; 1933: split; 1942: reunification.

problems of training in the Diaspora and integration in the country, and to intervene in an increasingly active way in the "stychic process."

The main reason for this lack of immigration was an objective one; the social stratum within the Jewish people in the Diaspora that formed the Left Poale Zionists' bulwark was the Jewish proletariat, and it was precisely this class which, in the period during the two world wars, was in no hurry to immigrate, holding on to the last to whatever positions it held. The Jewish workers were afraid of the special kind of migration called *aliya*, which involved drastic changes in an unknown country and the adoption of new occupations. The immigration of the Jewish proletariat could only be conceived, and actually came about, when the time came, as a *stychic* process. The Jewish proletariat was destined to move from the Diaspora in masses only when dire necessity compelled it to do so. This is the reason for the special emphasis that Borochov put on the stychic factor in territorial concentration; the subjective, active element does find a place in his doctrine but yields pride of place to the automatic processes. We must recall that Borochov was not a general Zionist who came to socialism and the Jewish proletariat as a way of achieving Zionism. On the contrary, he was a "general" (Russian) socialist who found his place in the Jewish labor movement and, as the theoretician of this movement, outlined the Jewish proletariat's path to the solution of its national problem by territorial concentration in Palestine and building a strategic base for its class struggle. The same holds true for the Left Poale Zionists in the Diaspora and in Palestine.

Nonetheless, we should not ignore the subjective element, the spiritual distress of members and thinkers who saw their party in Palestine at a dead end without any illusions to obscure the dimensions of their failure. This was the beginning of the flow out of the party, both in the Diaspora and in Palestine, either into Mapai or into Hashomer Hatsair's Socialist League. It was the combination of all these factors plus the beginnings of mass immigration of Jewish workers from eastern Europe during the second half of the '30s that explains the change in Poale Zion (Left) in 1937-1939: their decision to participate in the Zionist Congress, to support the national funds, and the like.

Though they did not succeed in serving as an alternative or providing a starting point for an antireformist concentration on a pioneering Zionist basis, they have a well-deserved place in the Palestinian labor movement for their loyalty to Marxism and Borochovism, which they supported proudly despite their isolation, their stubborn attempts to remove the barriers and decrease the tension between labor Zionism and the world revolutionary labor movement, their unswerving support of class struggle during all those years when it was being abandoned by the majority in the Palestinian labor movement, their loyalty to the legacy of the October revolution, their sympathy and support of the socialistic construction in the Soviet Union, their devotion to international solidarity with the Arab workers, etc.

When the stychic immigration from eastern Europe finally came, it brought veteran Poale Zionists whose training and experience is now enriching the ranks of the pioneering left parties in Israel.

Sources Against Participation in the World Zionist Congress

a) ... The Jewish people as a whole is interested in the territorial concentration of the Jewish masses but every class strives for its class interests. The work of construction in Palestine, its aims and methods, differ among the different classes. The Jewish bourgeoisie wants to transfer to Palestine the old forms of exploitation of the capitalist society; the Jewish proletariat is striving to establish Jewish cooperation in labor there.

b) The Zionist Congress, composed of a bourgeois majority, can under no circumstances carry out the socialist work of construction in Palestine, work that is in deep contradiction to the interests of the Jewish bourgeoisie.

c) The character of the Congress, the nature of volunteering, from the very outset removes any possibility of fulfilling any decisions that may be carried by some accidental majority according to the spirit of the demands of the working class. The Zionist Congress therefore cannot be exploited by the proletarian for its own interests. Participation could only create harmful illusions among part of the working class and weaken its activity in independent proletarian construction in Palestine.

For these reasons, the Fifth World Congress of the World Jewish Socialist Workers Union, Poale Zion, declares its opposition to participating in the Zionist Congress ...

> (From the Resolutions of the World Congress of the Left Poale Zionists, Vienna, 1920.)

For an Activistic Palestinism

... Our Palestinian task must always be real and decisive for us; we shall consider every step we take in the light of the great concern whether it will indeed hasten the tempo of achieving the territorial center, that is, of the revolution in our lives, or the contrary. That obligates us, with all the means at our disposal, to intensify and accelerate the immigration, to oppose and overcome the dispersion of the flow of emigration to other countries, to make a wider opening in the wall still separating Palestine and the Jewish migrant. We cannot only recognize the importance of the process. It isn't a matter only of replying from time to time to some phenomenon or other—when these phenomena are decided for us from outside. We must have a program of how more and more to hasten the process of realizing the territorial center, and this program will decide on our work in all the countries and in all the areas of the Jewish worker's life.

It is self-evident that all this requires one more thing from us: to root out of ourselves all Palestinian minimalism and to draw out of our hearts the psychological element of minimalism—the inner feeling that Palestine is really a kind of uncomfortable appendage to our revolutionary tasks, which must first receive its certification in the seven seas of the "really revolutionary" work.

The Jewish working class will fulfill its revolution—the conquest of power in Palestine—in class struggle at all times and in every place, but only its consciousness will grasp the full decisive implications of Palestinism for its struggle.

> (From an article by Z. Abramowitz, "Palestine in our Program," in the pamphlet, *The Problems of Poale Zionism,* Warsaw, 1934; Yiddish.)

... There is a demand by a large part of the movement for activism in the Palestinian-territorialist field of activity, a field that had actually been neglected and left to the reformists. We are moving away from the proletarianizing youth that is preparing itself for immigration to Palestine, and this movement is alienated from us. We reject it because it is petit bourgeois, while this movement is actually bringing many elements to Palestine who, by their transition to a life of labor, are forming the main part, the decisive majority of Palestinian proletariat, which does not understand us and which we do not understand, and the traditional influence of the reformism has put its stamp on it and is working in it.

> (From an article by Z. Abramowitz, "The War of Ideas in the Poale Zion Movement," published in *Halochem,* Tel Aviv, October 19, 1934.)

Rejoining the Zionist Congress

Twenty-four years ago, at the initiative of B. Borochov, the Russian Poale Zion party decided to leave the Zionist Congress. In the course of time, this position was accepted as a fundamental tactical line by the Marxist Poale Zionists throughout the world. At that time, the Zionist Organization was mainly an ideological and propagandistic movement. Its class differentiation was on its first beginnings and the specific aims of the various potential classes. Though they already reflected the different potential class interests, they still related more to programs and aims than to the real day-to-day interests of large masses. Under those conditions, the negative attitude towards participating in the Congress was necessary for the movement in order to protect it from being eroded by the flow of general Jewish ideologies and to make it possible for it to win and organize wide masses of the Jewish working class in an independent proletarian movement, standing firmly on the soil of class struggle and its aim, together with the territorial solution of the Jewish question in Palestine and also for uncompromising war for the social liberation of the Jewish masses the world over hand in hand with the international proletariat. The economic and political development of Palestine fully ratified the fundamental assumption of Borochovist Poale Zionism concerning the historical force of the tremendous lever of class struggle in achieving the Jewish territorial center in Palestine.

> (From the Resolutions of the Tenth World Congress of the Left Poale Zionists, Tel Aviv, December 1937.)

... In this completely different historic situation, when the importance of Palestine in the lives of the broadest Jewish masses has gone up immeasurably, when the struggle over what is done in Palestine and around it concerns the real interests of wide Jewish masses, when the Zionist Organization, thanks to the tremendous development and the importance of Palestine, as well as to its internationally recognized authority, has become a factor of social force exploited by the bourgeois politics of interests in order to restrain the struggle of the masses of workers in Palestine, the Poale Zion movement faces the task of waging the struggle for a clear class line in defending the interests of the workers—also within the Zionist Congress and its institution . . . In accordance with the demands of the real struggle for the interests of the workers and the masses of the Jewish people, in loyalty to the revolutionary class tasks in the process of fulfilling the ideal of the Jewish territorial center in Palestine—the World Congress accepts the imperative imposed by the greater and riper needs of the Jewish workers and laborers in Palestine and the world, and decides to participate in the coming Zionist Congress in order to continue on this forum as well the class struggle on the conscious Jewish proletariat.

(From the Resolutions of the Tenth Congress of the Left Poale Zionists.)

7 • The Communist Party (from M.P.S. to Maki and Rakah)

The Israeli Communist Party had its beginnings in the leftist minority in Poale Zion that refused to join Ahdut Haavoda in 1919 and wavered for a number of years between a Left Poale Zion trend and anti-Zionist liquidationism ("M.P.S. Poale Zion"—the Socialist Workers Party Poale Zion"). In 1922 the partisans of these conflicting trends finally separated, and in 1923 two parties were established: The Party of the Left Poale Zion and the Palestinian Communist Party (P.C.P.).

As the only anti-Zionist party in the Palestinian Jewish community (except for the religious ultra-orthodox Agudath Israel), the P.C.P. attracted mainly disillusioned elements who had deserted the Pioneering Zionist camp both because of personal difficulties and because of what they thought were the dim prospects of the continuation and victory of the Zionist enterprise. (These came from the ranks of the Gdud Haavoda,[1] from Ahdut Haavoda,[2] during the crisis after the Fourth Aliya, from the Hashomer Hatsair kibbutzim in the early thirties,[3] from Left Poale Zion at the time of the "Anti-Fa").[4] Because of its anti-Zionist posture and its identification with the anti-Zionist slogans and programs of the reactionary leadership in the Arab national movement, the P.C.P. lost all influence among the Jewish public and did not succeed in growing, even during periods of economic or political crisis. Despite its outspoken desire for and attempts at Arabization, it also did not succeed in striking any roots within the Arab public during the British Mandate.

After Hitler's rise to power and with the growing immigration from the fascist countries, the Communist Party succeeded in absorbing left-wing

---

1. In 1926 the Gdud Haavoda (Labor Battalion) split and the liquidationist leftist wing which formed the core of the Left Opposition in the Histadrut, organized itself as the Left Gdud Haavoda, which soon disintegrated, some of its members going to the P.C.P.
2. The group centering around Z. Colton.
3. After the economic and political setbacks of the Fifth Aliya (1931–1932), some of the Hashomer Hatsair kibbutzim stemming from that same immigration wave went through an ideological crisis that ultimately led to some tens of members' leaving the kibbutzim and joining the P.C.P.
4. Shortened name of the League to Fight Fascism and Anti-Semitism that was established in 1934 by Left Poale Zion and in which members of the P.C.P. and persons moving between the two groups also participated.

antifascist refugees who did not, however, share the anti-Zionist tradition of the veteran Palestinian Communists. The prolonged disturbances during 1936-1939, the intensifying dispute between the Jewish community and the imperialist British administration, with the "White Paper" (the ban on immigration, the "land law"), illegal immigration, etc., led in 1939/1940 to some fermentation within the ranks of the party (the Emet group against the Kol Ha'am group), with some attempts to tone down anti-Zionist (actually also anti-Jewish) activity, by some complicated distinctions between Zionism and the existing Jewish community; between Zionist aliya and the "right of Jewish immigration," and the like. This, it was thought by the Emet (Truth) group, would help the party establish roots in the Jewish community.

This fermentation attained considerable dimensions during the war and at its end. In 1943 the party disintegrated into a number of factions—Jewish and Arab (the Arab League for National Liberation). The reasons we have listed were augmented during the war by the intense antifascist activity among the Jewish community (army mobilization, war efforts, etc.) as well as by the process of fascistization and nazification within the Arab national movement (headed by the Mufti of Jerusalem). There was also mass trade union activity among industrial workers, a radicalizing process among the Jewish workers which was reflected in the rise of Hashomer Hatsair and worsening relationships between left and right within Mapai. There were also growing pro-Soviet sentiments, etc.

After the adoption of the U.N. Resolution of November 1947, the P.C.P. changed its name from "Palestinian" to "Eretz-Israelian" and came out for an Arab-Jewish state within the boundaries of the former British mandate and based on the existing numerical relations. The question of Jewish immigration was to be decided "democratically" by the majority of the population, something that could only imply one thing—the banning of immigration.

On the establishment of the State of Israel in 1948, the P.C.P. once more changed its name to "Israeli" and attempted to unite the various Communist organizations within one single territorial party. The union with the Arab League for National Liberation was achieved and a unification agreement was reached with the Hebrew Communist Party (which had gradually emerged from the former Emet faction), with the question of the solution for the Jewish question and territorial concentration in Palestine left open temporarily, pending a free debate within the party. This agreement was not kept, and only a few months later, immediately after the elections to the First Knesset in the winter of 1948-1949, the majority, led by Mikunis, Vilenska, Wilner and Toubi, ejected the

Hebrew Communists and returned to its openly anti-Zionist positions.[5] The party looked upon Borochovism and the Zionist Left as expressions of "bourgeois nationalism," denied the universal character of the Jewish people and the Jewish question, and sought to distinguish between the State of Israel and its labor movement, and their pioneering functions toward the Jewish people and the Diaspora ("Israelism" versus Zionism).

The Israeli Communist Party (Maki) propaganda evaded the question of Jewish immigration, declaring that it supported integrating the immigration. In actuality, not only did it not do anything in the Diaspora to spur immigration, but it also did not refrain from urging Jewish Communists in the Diaspora to fight within the Jewish public and within their own parties against Jewish immigration to Israel from the Popular Democracies. In the Israeli-Arab dispute it adopted a unilateral stance on the side of the Arab rulers. In short, it saw its role and duty in justifying every one of the steps and tactics of Soviet policy, including justifying the Prague trials,[6] the libels against the Jewish doctors in Moscow, the denial of the right of national and cultural autonomy and of immigration for the Jews of the Soviet Union.

It was, therefore, not surprising that this party lacked any roots or prospects within the Jewish population. Within the Arab population, Maki's status was relatively strong for many years, both because its spokesmen vigorously attacked the "Military Administration" and because of its nationalistic Arab and pro-Nasserist propaganda. Arab nationalists considered it to be the only legal party fighting their struggle. In the course of time, however, increasingly wider circles within the Arab minority became convinced that the solution for their problems or guarantees for their future would not come from any imminent salvation by Abdul Nasser, accompanied by dreams of "irredenta" or slogans of "secession from the State," but by the Arab minority's integration into the country's life and economy, the relaxation of tension and the establishment of Jewish-Arab peace in the Middle East, and an alliance with the progressive forces within the Jewish majority. On the other hand, some of the Arab nationalists have in recent years begun to deny Maki their support in light of the worsening relations between Nasser and Arab Communists in Syria and Iraq, with the Arab nationalists trying their hand from time to time at organizing a political organization of their own (e.g., El Ard).

Maki's fundamentally mistaken path was not limited by this list of theoretical assumptions and practical political positions concerning the universality of the Jewish problem and its Zionist solution, the questions of immigration and security, the way to solve the Arab-Israeli dispute,

---

5. The majority of the Hebrew Communist Party, headed by the M. K. Elieser Preminger, joined Mapam.
6. See Chapter 13.

pioneering and the kibbutz movement, etc. The underlying problem was that a socialist workers party's mission and prospects of victory depended on the degree of its active and consistent identification not only with justified partial immediate matters, but also with the fundamental problem faced by the masses of the people, and on its answer regarding these fundamental problems; in other words—on its ability to be the left and pioneering pole of the national liberation movement as a whole, and its ability to prove that it alone, and not the center or the right, was the consistent expression of the popular strivings. If we apply this assumption to the conditions of the Jewish people and Israel, we cannot conceive of the starting point of the leftist struggle being cosmopolitan, anti-Zionist or non-Zionist, neutral or evading the fundamental problems faced by the Jewish people and the Jewish community in Israel. The contrary is true; the starting point for a leftist struggle must be that the bourgeois right and reformism, because of their class and ideological inhibitions, are incapable of consistently and effectively solving the political, economic and military problems whose solutions are a condition for full realization of Zionism. In other words, the starting point for the struggle against the bourgeoisie and reformism must be that they *are not sufficiently Zionist or pioneering*. It is only when the left's struggle against its opponents is waged on this level and context that it has any objectively historical prospects of convincing the large part of the laboring strata of the people of the justice and feasibility of Israel's socialism.

During the 60s, in the "de-Stalinization" era within many Communist parties, with the new slogans of "different paths to socialism" and the growing stress on national autonomy in general and of the individual Communist parties in particular, Maki also tried to become part of the new process by "softening" its positions, its propagandistic style and appearances on the Knesset platform, by freeing itself from the chains of total rejection of everything created in the country, and of all the other parties. It gave its reserved support to Levi Eshkol's government and his polemics with Ben-Gurion and Rafi and even rejected the hostile attitudes and warlike declarations of the Arab countries toward Israel, as those made by Nasser or Algerian President Ben-Bella, as well as the provocatively anti-Israel statements made by the President of Eastern Germany, Walter Ulbricht, during his visit to the U.A.R.

These moderating attempts aroused a bitter struggle between conflicting trends within Maki's leadership and cadres. The first, flexible trend was represented by Shmuel Mikunis, Moshe Sneh[7] and Ester Vilenska; the second, conservative and inflexible, rejecting the new course, was represented by Meir Wilner and most of the party's Arab leaders and

---

7. Formerly one of the outstanding leaders of Mapam, Moshe Sneh joined in 1954 the Communist Party of Israel (see Chapter 13.)

cadres. During the second half of 1964 this dispute broke out into open conflict and came to a lead at the beginning of 1965, with the approaching 15th Party Congress.

In addition to the theses for the Congress, the Party's papers, the daily *Kol Ha'am (Voice of the People)* and monthly *Zu Haderekh (This Is the Way)* publicized the two conflicting positions. *Kol Ha'am* also opened its columns to a debate over the theses. When the Mikunis-Sneh-Vilenska group won a decisive majority in the elections to the Congress (205 to 151), the rival faction refused to yield and the result was an open break, with both groups preparing to hold separate Congresses on the same day, June 23. Only the pressure and mediation of the foreign Communist delegations prevented a final break at the last minute. The Congress was postponed two months and new elections were agreed upon. The postponement did not, however, solve anything; the new elections once more gave the Mikunis-Sneh-Wilenska faction a majority, though a smaller one than before (175 to 167) and since the minority still refused to accept this, a split was inevitable. Toufik Toubi and Emile Habibi declared themselves an independent faction in the Knesset, and two separate Congresses were held on August 4 and 6. The Wilner-Toubi faction, which was supported by all the party's Arab members, faced the danger of a growing trend to replace the so-far accepted joint Jewish-Arab party structure by a return to the days of the one-time nationalistic Arab League for National Liberation, with the aim of becoming something like a "Palestinian F.L.N."[8]

The Mikunis-Sneh-Vilenska faction, for its part, faced two hurdles that apparently prevented it from transforming the "softened position" into a real change: (a) the militant anti-Zionist tradition which had, in the course of the years, become a psychological complex braking and distorting the necessary ideological processes; (b) the hesitation to take steps that were correct in principle and even necessary if the party was to take root and progress, when such steps required the party to disagree with and criticize Soviet policy on the Israeli-Arab dispute and on Soviet responsibility to initiate or support Jewish-Arab negotiations, on the attitude toward Soviet Jewry, etc.

In the 1965 election campaign, the Mikunis-Sneh wing used the party name (Maki) while the Toubi-Wilner faction adopted the name "New Communist List" (Rakah). This latter wing also tended to label itself "the Jewish-Arab Maki." In the elections to the 10th Congress of the Histadrut in September 1965, Maki received 1.58 percent of the votes, with the New Communist List receiving only 1.29 percent. On the other hand,

8. Thirty-five percent of (united) Maki's 3,000 members were Arabs. In the Party Congress elections in 1965, the Mikunis-Sneh group won 58 percent of all the votes, the other 42 percent going to Wilner-Toubi (all the Arabs plus 7 percent of the Jewish members). The fact that Maki (Makunis-Sneh) remained nearly without any Arab cadres and members put it in a "delicate position" both in Israel and in the world communist movement.

the latter received 2.27 percent of the votes to the Knesset elections (in November 1965) and won three seats, while Maki only received 1.13 percent and one seat. (In the 5th Knesset the united party had had five representatives—three belonging to the Mikunis-Sneh faction and two to the Toubi-Wilner wing). These changed relationships are explained by the support the Toubi-Wilner faction won among the Arab electorate, especially after the nationalist slate presented by El-Ard had been banned and Cairo Radio called on the Arabs to vote for the New Communist List.[9]

So long as the Israeli Communists did not find the courage to overcome their "traditional" inhibitions and their recent "softening" did not go beyond details of style, stress, propaganda and tactics, there were no real prospects for a fundamental change in their status as a sectarian minority with the Israeli public.

Ever since the 1965 split and especially after the war in June 1967, Maki has been moving rapidly away from the traditional Communist ideological and political positions in this country, in all their variants, and these changes began to go beyond the realm of "moderation" alone. By supporting the Six Day War and defining it as a defensive war for physical and national survival, it was led to an open and irreparable break with the proclaimed policies of the U.S.S.R and most of the world Communist movement. As a result, it also began to emancipate itself from the fear of going "too far away" from the official Soviet and communist positions, a fear that in the past had forced Maki to do a lot of maneuvering and had been one of the important difficulties it had to face in becoming part of the Israeli reality and in taking shape as an *Israeli* Communist party.

The fact that world communism and Arabs on the one hand, and Jews on the other, identify Israel with "Zionism," with "anti-Zionism" becoming a synonym for "anti-Israelism" or even anti-Semitism, compelled Maki to abandon its traditional anti-Zionism, without, however, declaring itself positively to be a Socialist-Zionist party.[10] This "fine" distinction found its concrete expression, for example, in the fact that Maki did not oppose Jewish immigration to Israel and did not find anything wrong with it, but did not consider that one of its tasks was to encourage immigration or to educate toward it in the Diaspora. Nor did it change very materially in the matter of combining class struggle with the constructive pioneering upbuilding of the Jewish homeland: whereas it had opposed this combination, and constructive activity in general, in the past, it later supported

---

9. In the elections to the 11th Histadrut Congress in September 1969, Rakah received 2.27 percent, with Maki receiving only 1.79 percent. In the Knesset elections in October 1969, Rakah won three seats, Maki one; in December 1973 Rakah, four, Maki ("Moked"), one; in May 1977, Rakah, five, Moked ("Sheli") one.

10. In the end of 1972, Pinhas Tubin, Maki's main representative on the Histadrut headquarters and one of the closest collaborators of the late Moshe Sneh, left Maki and returned to Mapam, getting fed up with Maki's hesitation to declare itself unequivocally socialist-Zionist.

it when done by others, without—like Mapam—considering this combination of constructivism and class struggle to be one of its own basic vanguard roles in the context of the political, economic and cultural life of the Jewish people and the State of Israel.

Recent Developments

In the early seventies, new differences emerged within Maki, mainly on three issues: the extent of national solidarity; qualified or unqualified opposition to the government; the attitude to Mapam, on the one hand, and to the various leftist anti-establishment splinter groups, on the other. In spite of the criticism of the Labor-Mapam Alignment, and in particular of Mapam's adherence to this alignment, the majority within Maki saw as its potential allies, at least on long range, Mapam and part of the Israel Labor Party, accompanying this perspective by harsh criticism of the marginal anti-establishment groups. Whereas the minority held the view that "it is doubtful if Mapam is still an independent socialist factor," and they advocated the establishment of a Left Forum, consisting of Maki, the "Left Alliance" (the so-called Riftin Group), "Siah" (New Israeli Left), Uri Avneri's Haolam Haze, and others, as an "activist alternative to the passive waiting for new constellations in the labor movement, in regard to Mapam and the Israel Labor Party." In their polemics they went so far as to accuse the majority of "having demoted Maki into a satellite of Mapam and the Alignment." At the 17th Congress of Maki (April 1972), however, the disciples of the late Dr. Sneh resoundingly defeated the minority led by Ester Vilenska, which never succeeded in enlisting the votes of more than 20 to 21 percent of the delegates.

After the 17th Congress, relations between majority and minority within Maki deteriorated more and more. Toward the Histadrut and Knesset elections to be held in 1973, the Vilenska group decided to join, together with the majority of "Siah" New Leftists–Uri Avneri's Haolam Hazeh, forming the MERI (Israel Radical Camp) election list. The Central Committee of Maki reacted by expelling the Vilenska group from the party: the expelled members called themselves the "Israel Communist Opposition," and have been accused by Maki of a "splitting, neo-Rakahist tendency." In spite of its fundamental perspective of "Left Labor Unity," comprising Maki, Mapam and part of the Labor Party, Maki could not for the present see any way of maintaining its representation at the Histadrut and the Knesset, other than by forming a joint election list with the more moderate minority within the Siah New-Leftists (who called themselves the "Blue-Red Movement," defining their group as radical socialist-Zionist), under the name of Moked (focus), and in June 1975 Moked turned from a temporary election alliance into a united political party.[11] Toward the elections of May 1977, Moked joined ranks with one of the splinter groups emerging from the former "Black Panther Movement" (a radical community movement of oriental Jews; see Chapter 27), as well as with the group of Independent Socialists and the Haolam Hazeh group, constituting "Sheli" (Camp for Peace and Equality).

Although Rakah made no progress whatever in attracting Jews as party members or voters, it gradually strengthened its position within the Arab minority, in particular by exploiting the grave mistakes and blunders made in this sphere by the Israel Labor Party. In the elections of 1973 they increased their parliamentary representation from three to four, and in 1977 to five. A remarkable success for Rakah were the municipal elections in Nazareth, in December 1975, when their Democratic Front for Development of Nazareth (Rakah and left intellectuals and merchants) won the majority in the Town Council, and Rakah Knesset Member Toufik Zayad was elected Mayor of Nazareth. In March 1977, at the start of the national election campaign, Rakah established a Democratic Front for Peace and Equality, together with some nonpartisan Arab nationalists on the one hand, and some of the (Jewish) former "Black Panthers," as well as with some other Jewish leftist splinter groups, on the other. In the national election of May 1977, the Democratic Front received nearly half the votes cast by Arabs (49 percent), as against 37 percent they had got in December 1973. In the elections for the Histadrut the picture was as follows: In September 1973 Rakah received 29 percent of the Arab vote, and the Democratic Front, in June 1977, 35 percent. Following the landslide victory of Likud in May 1977, a change of heart occurred within the Arab electorate. In the elections for the Histadrut, in June 1977, Rakah's Democratic Front could muster only 26,000 voters as against 80,000 five weeks before (in the national election). The swing was back to the Labor-Mapam Alignment.

Sheli did even worse: In the elections for the Histadrut, in June 1977, they polled only 1.12 percent, as against 2.74 percent in 1973; and their 26,000 votes in the national election of May dwindled in June, in the elections for the Histadrut, to less than 10,000.[12]

SOURCES

> The working masses of the Arab people are the only ones conducting a really active struggle—despite their treacherous leadership—against Zionist "Aliya" and the adventures of "conquest." If the Jewish worker

11. After hesitations and a long silence, and when Maki finally decided to merge with the New Left "Blue-Red" group to establish "Moked," veteran Communist leader Shmuel Mikunis, Maki's former Secretary-General, joined the Vilenska opposition group (June 1975). However, when this group agreed, in February 1977, to join Rakah in its newly established "Democratic Front for Peace and Equality," he walked out and retired from politics.
12. See also Chapter 28.

does not want the struggle to move into chauvinist channels, he must fight together with the Arab worker against the renewed Zionist adventures. . . .
> (From "The New Adventure of Immigration and its Implications"—*Farois*, organ of the P.C.P., No. 46/47, January, 1933.)

The Party calls you to the path of life and freedom. Separate yourself from the conquering Zionist camp . . . Only the Arab national movement and its victory are the trustworthy solution for the problem of the Jewish minority . . . We call on the Jewish public to join the strike and to continue the struggle for the following demands: the abrogation of the Mandate and the Balfour Declaration, a popular democratic legislative council, the stoppage of immigration and the conquest of labor and land . . .
> (From Proclamation for May 1, 1936, by the Central Committee of the P.C.P., from Shlomo Rechev, "The Party of Betrayal and its Metamorphoses," Hebrew, published by Mapam, Tel Aviv, 1950.

The June War and the Development in the Middle East

Just as every war, so the war in the Middle East of June 1967, was the continuation of a policy by other means, i.e., military means. It was the continuation of the policy conducted by the imperialist powers, first and foremost the U.S.A., and of the Israeli rulers toward the anti-imperialist regimes in the Arab states.

The June war was not a just war waged in self-defense in the face of aggression, but an aggressive war, well-planned for a long time both from the military and the political aspects.

The main aim of the war was to overthrow the anti-imperialist regimes in Egypt and Syria, to put an end to the policy of friendship and cooperation of these countries with the U.S.S.R. and other socialist countries, and to abolish the progressive economic and social reforms inside these countries.

In the beginning the imperialist powers had tried with the help of internal reaction in these and other Arab states, to cause the overthrow of these regimes by other means: by organizing counter-revolutionary coups d'etat, by economic pressure, by political bribery based on anti-communism, by military threats, etc. Only after all these means had borne no fruit, came the direct military blow.

It is impossible to understand the character of the June war without viewing it against the general background of development in the international arena in general, and the Middle East in particular during that period. . . .
> (From: "Theses for the 16th Congress of the Communist Party of Israel"; Information Bulletin, *Rakah*, Tel Aviv, 1969.)

The Zionist movement is therefore not a national liberation movement, as it does not set itself the aim of liberating any people or country from foreign rule. It is not a national movement at all, but a reactionary political movement of the Jewish bourgeoisie. Just as there is no "Jewish

exterritorial world people," there is no national extraterritorial world movement. Nor is it an Israeli national movement. It works against the national liberation of the people of Israel from dependence on imperialism, it collaborates with the colonial powers against the anti-imperialist national liberation movements in the Middle East and in other regions. . . .
(Ibid.)

There never was, nor could there be, a socialist Zionism. At the same time one must see that there exist socialist aspirations among many working people who are under Zionist influence. But in ideological as well as political respect, also the "socialist-Zionist" organizations have sided in all decisive struggles, in all tests of the times, with imperialism, against socialism and the movements for national liberation (thus in Tzarist Russia and other countries, where the struggle for socialism was conducted, thus in their policy towards the countries of socialism in the international arena, thus in the Middle East wars in 1956 and 1967).

The Leninist premise that bourgeois ideology and proletarian ideology cannot co-exist has been verified in the case of the "socialist Zionists," too! . . .
(Ibid.)

Stalin's thesis that every national movement is a bourgeois movement even if the proletariat "apparently" participates in it, applied to Zionism, distorted the view of reality. It is correct that the decisive influence on the policy and leadership of the Zionist movement was in the hands of the Jewish plutocracy—first of France, Germany, Great Britain and finally of the U.S. But in the countries of Jewish distress, especially in eastern Europe before and after the holocaust, the Zionist movement had a popular and broad national character and included masses from the discriminated against, persecuted and despairing strata of society that regarded immigration to Eretz Israel as their only salvation. This distinction between the summit and the popular public mass base was lacking in the communist approach to Zionism.

It also lacked the discernment of the dialectical development of the relationship between the Jewish community in Eretz Israel and British colonialism, in other words, between the Zionist undertaking and the mandatory government. According to the agreement between the Zionist summit and the British government, the mandatory British administration was obligated to help establish the "Jewish national home." In reality, this help was accompanied by severe hinderances and setting the two peoples against each other, but due to objective circumstances and subjective motives the Jewish community succeeded in achieving the crystallization of a nation in the years of the British protectorate over Eretz Israel in spite of all such interference. And here one thing was transformed into its opposite; the Jewish community that was established under the protecton of the British Empire came into total conflict with British policy and became a serious factor in the struggle for national liberation (1945-1948). The Jewish people in Israel was one of the main factors in the struggle against colonialism after the Second World War; it caused the British government to leave all of Eretz Israel and thereby played a major role in the battle against imperialism in the Near East.

In the struggle of the communist movement with Zionism insufficient thought was usually given to differentiate in the Zionist movement between the bourgeois right and the worker-pioneer left in which even a socialist left crystallized that revealed an ideological affinity to Marxism-Leninism.

The communist battle against Zionism also suffered from ignoring the constructive and socialistic-humanistic roles it fulfilled. With all its faults—the Zionist Organization, and especially its worker-pioneer wing, laid the foundations of a Jewish society in Eretz Israel and the State of Israel.

It goes without saying that the campaign of hate waged at present in a number of socialist states and with the participation of a number of Communist parties ostensibly against Zionism but actually against the Jewish people and the State of Israel should be reproved and rebuked. The identification of Zionism with imperialism and the comparison of Zionism with racialism and Nazism are insults to every Jew as a Jew . . .

(From: Moshe Sneh: "Theses for the Sixteenth Congress of the Communist Party of Israel," Maki, Tel Aviv, October 1968.)

I would like to say that also with regard to the question who are our potential real allies in the campaigns for a change in the Israel Government's foreign and domestic policy—there are changes taking place that strengthen the assumption of a Left block with the participation of Maki and Mapam. We do not object to a cooperation, contacts, joint actions with any of the other parties, movements and groups. However, we have not to answer the question with whom we shall demonstrate together tomorrow in front of the government offices in Jerusalem, but the question with whom we shall carry out the change we seek. Let us not change the options. Cooperate, act jointly—yes, and I do hope that in the next days, too, we shall make a joint effort with members of Siah and the "Left Alliance" who are prepared to give a hand to get Israel to adopt a better policy; but the strategical option of Maki is the establishment of a left workers' block in the Israel labour movement that is to carry out a changeover in that deterioration taking place in Israel's society. . . .

(Raoul Teitelbaum, Chairman of the Central Committee: "Summarizing the 17th Congress of Maki," in "Israel at Peace," No. 6, Organ of the Communist Party of Israel-Maki, June 1972.)

8 • Hashomer Hatsair (The Young Guardian)

The first Hashomer Hatsair immigrants arrived with the Third Aliya. They took an active part in the movement for the formation of the Histadrut and in its actual establishment, appearing in the elections to the First Congress in a joint list, together with "Hechalutz" and "Z.S." groups, called "The New Immigrants."

Most of Hashomer Hatsair's thinking in those days was devoted to man's improvement, to cultivating a personality striving for liberation from the false morality of the bourgeois world and to build a kibbutz society (the Shomer community) in which there would be better personal relationships between man and society.

Hashomer Hatsair grew up during the great national and social awakening that followed World War I, the October revolution and the hopes of peace and progress that stirred hearts throughout the world after the war. The first of the pioneer national and socialist youth movements among the Jewish masses, Hashomer Hatsair grew out of those same tremendous shocks, and especially the troubles that overtook the masses of Jews in eastern Europe (Petlura's pogroms in the Ukraine, whose reverberations reached Poland and Galicia, the pogroms in Lvov, etc.). Among the spiritual sources that nourished the young organization, we can list the influences of Hashomer, of A. D. Gordon and Trumpeldor, on the one hand, and the romanticism of the revolutionary anti-Tsarist underground, on the other; the influences of the "Free Youth Movement" and "youth culture" which first sprang up and were cultivated in prewar Germany, and of the philosophies, the literature, the psychology and the new pedagogy that in those days were looking for new values in experience and ideas. Together with these, from the beginnings of the twenties, there were already signs of Marxist influence, with the study of Marxism winning an important place within the movement (especially in Poland). It would not be altogether true to say that at the beginning of the twenties, Hashomer Hatsair was still completely strange to Marxism; it would be more exact to say that Marxism had not yet become a general theoretical starting point and guide in choosing its path, as it is today.

Some of these characteristics might have seemed to bring Hashomer Hatsair close to Hapoel Hatsair. And, indeed, A. D. Gordon showed a great deal of interest in the Hasohmer Hatsair immigrants and tried to find out what they were like. However, Hashomer Hatsair's roots in progressive European culture, its search for a scientific basis for human and social behavior and the first signs of revolutionary Marxism that were already appearing, built a wall between Hashomer Hatsair and Haspoel Hatsair even in those first days. Hashomer Hatsair also learned very soon that deep changes had taken place in Hapoel Hatsair since the days of its glory in the Second Aliya. It was the image from the past that had attracted the Jewish youth movement in Europe; now they met Hapoel Hatsair when it was turning into a separatist political party that did not understand the Third Aliya.

The lack of any organized ties between the groups of Hashomer Hatsair immigrants themselves and between them and the educational youth movement in the Diaspora led to the "Shomrim" (Hashomer Hatsair members) dispersing throughout the country and to wasting the strength of the Hashomer Hatsair immigration. In addition, the pioneering tension of the movement abroad declined and it went through a crisis of dangerous individualism. At a Hashomer Hatsair meeting at Kibbutz Bet Alfa in 1924, the need was stressed for a framework that would unite the Hashomer Hatsair immigration and serve as a guiding and absorbing center for the movement abroad. There were some at that meeting who differed with this: they had managed meanwhile to make ties with other political or kibbutz groups (Ahdut Haavoda, Gdud Haavoda) and demanded the freedom of choice and integration for every Shomer on arriving in the country.

The chief direct result of that meeting was to send a delegation to the movement in the Diaspora; there was also some clarification of the view that Hashomer Hatsair had a special mission to fill. Three years later, this idea was to be given material form.

The question of the framework was connected with the process of ideological refinement within the Hashomer Hatsair immigration. After they were absorbed in labor they came up against the real conflicts between worker and employer. At work they met the wider working public, with all its political trends, and could no longer concentrate only on the internal problems of the kibbutz society; they were obliged to devote thought to the problems of society in general and of labor, the working class and the class struggle in particular. In the same way that Hasomer Hatsair had earlier tried to apply analysis and science to subjects like pedagogy, psychology, philosophy, etc., it now attempted to answer the problems of sociology and politics. When it attacked these problems scientifically it could only come to a socialist outlook and the Marxist conclusions: class struggle, international solidarity (with workers throughout the world and with the neighboring Arab laborers), support for the socialist construction in the U.S.S.R., etc. As alert youths seeking the roots of things and believing in complete realization, they were less apt to choose the compromising reformist version of socialism than the revolutionary one.

Hashomer Hatsair's pioneering and settlement Zionism was a direct result of its origins and its collective educational experiences. It adopted and formulated its socialism and the principle of class struggle in the course of taking root in the country, in work and in the working public. Thus, in the middle of the twenties, we see the features of Hashomer Hatsair's particular ideological character: the synthesis of pioneering Zionism and revolutionary socialism, construction and class struggle.

In 1926 Hashomer Hatsair, together with circles close to it among the kibbutzim coming from the pioneering movement in the Diaspora and with part of Gdud Haavoda, presented the "Kibbutz List" for the elections to the Third Congress of the Histadrut. In its program the List criticized, from a leftist stance, not only Hapoel Hatsair, but also Ahdut Haavoda, though it kept its criticism separate from all the other leftist groups that did not take a similar stand of active support for pioneering settlement. One of the foci of the election campaign to the Third Histadrut Congress, to be held in 1927, was the question of the "separation of functions." From different standpoints, the Communist "Fraction," the "Left Opposition"[1] and Left Poale Zion all demanded the separation of the trade union and settlement functions of the Histadrut, that is, the establishment of two separate organizations, arguing that the combination of functions interfered with the class and trade union struggle that should be the sole task of a working class organization like the Histadrut.

This demand from the ultra left found unexpected support at the other rightist pole of the labor movement, in some of the smallholders' settlements belonging to the orthodox wing of Hapoel Hatsair. In the latter's view, the Histadrut should have occupied itself only with settlement, immigration, absorption and training, and should not deal at all with trade unionism and class struggle.

On this question of principle the Kibbutz List, Ahdut Haavoda, and most of Hapoel Hatsair came out against the liquidationary demand for the "separation of functions," but this correct joint stand found its full theoretical basis—the synthesis of construction and class struggle—only in the Kibbutz List program. In contrast to this, both Ahdut Haavoda and Hapoel Hatsair opposed removing the functions of settlement, absorption and education from the Histadrut because they considered these functions to be the essentials, with the class and trade union functions supernumerary, and nothing more.

Thus, even then, we begin to find the "dual front" on which Hashomer Hatsair was destined to fight for many years: against the right wing in the

1. The "Left Opposition" was formed during the crisis following the Fourth Aliya. It expressed the disillusionment and leftist rebellion by a part of the kibbutz movement (leftist trend in Gdud Haavoda, some members of Bet Alfa and Hefziba) against the exclusive constructivism of the Histadrut leadership, by one-sided emphasis on trade union functions and international communist perspectives.

Palestinian labor movement in its various parties and later, after the merger, in Mapai, for deserting or blurring the class struggle; against ultra-leftist denials of the constructive pioneering functions of the Palestinian labor movement and the Histadrut; against any undermining of the synthesis between construction and class struggle, between pioneering Zionism and revolutionary socialism; an inseparable synthesis which it considered then, and still considers today, to be the essence of the originality and particularity of our labor movement, the "Israeli path to socialism." In the program of the Kibbutz List in 1926 we thus already find the fundamental assumptions that were to be formulated a year later, with the establishment of the Kibbutz Ha'artzi of Hashomer Hatsair.

In 1927 Hashomer Hatsair's own organization was finally formed. The Kibbutz Ha'artzi of Hashomer Hatsair was established, declaring itself, on the basis of its ideological assumptions, a separate ideological and political trend within the Histadrut, in addition to its kibbutz and educational functions. The members of Hashomer Hatsair coming from Russia, Latvia, and part of the Lithuanian movement refused to join the common organization since they had joined Ahdut Haavoda and did not share the "ideological assumptions." Soon after, we find them among the founders of the Kibbutz Hameuchad. Even Bet Alfa, the oldest of the Hashomer Hatsair kibbutzim, did not join the Kibbutz Artzi as a whole; some of its members were affiliated with Ahdut Haavoda, while another part were under the influence of the "Left Opposition."

Hashomer Hatsair never rejected the label of "socialist Zionism," accepting it as a fact. In the Kibbutz Artzi's "Ideological Assumptions" Hashomer Hatsair, however, did not use that term in defining its synthesis of Zionism and Socialism, reflecting by this the fear of blurring the limits between these two different fields. In these "Assumptions" Hashomer Hatsair listed the three separate elements that formed a unity: Zionism, socialism, and kibbutzism, and instead of the label of socialist Zionism, coined the terms "Pioneering Zionism" and "Revolutionary Socialism," that is, the synthesis of these elements that complement rather than contradict each other, though they are not identical. What is more, the quantitative and qualitative relations between them are not fixed; they are rather a process in which any one of the elements may become dominant at some specific stage and thereby determine the character of that stage and that period.

For that reason, the "Ideological Assumptions" bring in the idea of stages. In the first stage, the Zionist element is the dominant one, including the imperatives of national solidarity and the like, though class struggle has, of course, already started. The second stage was defined as the period of heightening class struggle, social differentiation and the struggle for a socialist workers' regime.

This theory of stages found many opponents from the outside and, in the course of time, many critics within. The outside critics, each from his own starting point, left or right, argued against the very idea of the process. For them it was either one or the other: either Zionism, construction, etc., or socialism and class struggle. These are values that are fixed, almost eternal, that are correct and actual to the same extent at all times. The criticisms from within were not aimed against the idea of the process itself, but at the specific definition of the two stages; the argument was that the separation was made too formalistic; what they were really afraid of was that the second stage would be put off till it was too late. Some schematism, however, is only natural in formulating a new idea when we are interested in stressing its difference from the accepted views. Still, by pointing to a process in which the elements are in constant flux without marking distinct stages, we would only be paving the way for endless debate and countless mistakes in subjective analyses and evaluations concerning the progress of the process and the nature of the period. One cannot talk of a "developing process" without a concrete analysis of the present period and the one to come (the concrete changes from one stage to the next) and without fixing the practical aims and imperatives characterizing each specific stage after it has been analyzed and defined.

In any case, the fears of the internal critics were not substantiated; the "theory of stages" did not cut up the process as a whole and did not prevent the subjective element from keeping in step with the course of the objective historical process. On the contrary, it helped Hashomer Hatsair keep to the path of revolutionary realism and keep it from being drawn into opportunistic or ultra-leftist deviations.

What is more, the "Ideological Assumptions" of Kibbutz Ha'artzi, and the idea of integrating class struggle and construction, and the "theory of stages" in particular, were a vital modification and valuable theoretical development of Borochovism. It freed itself from the "stychic process"[2] that completely ignored the active subjective factor and the role of the revolutionary and pioneering element in the struggle for national and social liberation. This provided a theoretical dialectical basis to the reciprocal relations between pioneering Zionism and revolutionary socialism, between construction and the national cooperation of all sections of the people in the Diaspora on the one hand, and the developing class struggle in Palestine, on the other.[3]

2. In this context, the "stychic process" in an unorganized, undirected force working within society. Borochov's theory of the "stychic process" was based on his mistaken assumption that Jewish migration would inevitably be impelled, by the pressure of objective conditions and circumstances alone, in the direction of Palestine, without any guidance, education or subjective preparation, and that Palestine would also be settled and built "of itself," without any need for primary initiative on the part of the Jewish workers.
3. Hashomer Hatsair's reservations concerning the "stychic process" as originally formulated by Borochov (or later by Left Poale Zion) was not an abandonment of Borochovism but an extension of it. Borochov himself testified to this in his last speech before his

"Kibbutzism" was also defined in these "Assumptions" as a separate fundamental. It cannot be a "substitute" for the class struggle going together with construction—that is the highroad to socialism; but it can help both in fulfilling Zionism and in class struggle and the strife for a socialist Palestine. The Assumptions very clearly rejected the approach accepted in parts of the kibbutz movement (especially in the Gdud) which ignored the capitalist nature of the regime surrounding the kibbutz in deciding on the path and framework of the kibbutz. In actuality, the construction of kibbutz cells in a capitalist environment cannot be based only on propaganda or on planning and organization; under the conditions of capitalism, it implies *swimming against the stream*, made possible mainly by education from childhood, by a broad kibbutz framework allowing the greatest possible democracy and personal satisfaction. This led to the concept of the "organic kibbutz" which enjoyed a considerable degree of economic and social autonomy based (in additional to the social and personal preparedness) on the dialectical analysis of the kibbutz' potentialities within the capitalist environment, and inevitably using this analysis to decide on the kibbutz vanguard role as a fighting ideological and political collective.

Incidentally, what has been said here of the methods of building the kibbutz also holds good, to a great extent, for the workers' economy and workers' cooperation in general: concerning these two, Hashomer Hatsair, in the program of the "Kibbutz List," had already warned against the delusion of omnipotent centralistic organization, from the top downward, and demanded that it be based as much as possible on specific, conscious and enterprising human subjects, from the bottom up.

The Fifth Aliya (1929-1940) greatly increased the ranks of Hashomer Hatsair. Its own kibbutzim were generally established in the moshavot (capitalist agricultural colonies) where they came face to face not only with the hostile plantation owners but with the reformist practices of Hapoel Hatsair, Ahdut Haavoda (later Mapai), as well.

Hashomer Hatsair's answer to the demand for inclusive unification was positive in principle, but insisted on the existence of certain programmatic conditions ("Minimum Program") and on wide autonomy on kibbutz education and theory. At the unification Congress (of Ahdut Haavoda and Hapoel Hatsair) in January 1930, a statement in this spirit, signed by representatives of all the trends within Hashomer Hatsair, was broadcast. The Kibbutz Artzi Conference at Kibbutz Mishmar Haemek in 1930

death (at the Russian Poale Zion Congress in Kiev, 1917): "In the past, we thought Zionism was a stychic process and our main work was to remove hurdles placed in our path. From this viewpoint, we wanted to leave the work of construction to the bourgeoisie. Afterwards it became evident that we had been mistaken. There are *mechanical* stychic processes, and *organic* stychic processes. Our mistake was to think that the *mechanical* process had already begun, while in reality only the *organic* process had begun."

saw the final formulation of the clauses of the minimum program on the basis of which Hashomer Hatsair was prepared to join one of the existing parties. Toward Mapai, the demands were for class struggle, scientific socialism, organization of the Arab workers and Hashomer Hatsair's right not to belong to the Second International. Toward Left Poale Zion, the demands were for participation in the Zionist Congress, support of the National Funds, pioneer training in the Diaspora and the Hebrew language.

Almost from the Kibbutz Ha'artzi's foundation (and even earlier, among the leaders of the youth movement in the Diaspora) Hashomer Hatsair had debated the evolution of Mapai—that is, whether the demands for programmatic unity with Mapai had any basis in reality or whether the die had already been cast and Mapai had already become just another social democratic party with which any union was ruled out. There were also some who wanted to soften the programmatic conditions for unification with Mapai on the assumption that it would be possible to influence it from within. Hashomer Hatsair's leadership was opposed both to rejecting unification in principle and to unification at any price, and united the movement as a whole around readiness for unity in principle and strict maintenance of the conditions of the minimum program.

    2. After evaluating the development of political reality in Palestine and the path of the working class in the country and its tasks in the present period, the Council sees the need for unifying the forces of the working class in a broad class party that will be the instrument of the political activity of the Jewish working class in Palestine. This party must be established on the broad basis of a "minimum" program that will leave room for the existence of specific and more crystallized ideological conceptions and in which Hashomer Hatsair would be guaranteed the minimal conditions enabling it to fight successfully to bring its ideological values and political positions to the working class as a whole. This political unification of workers' movement in Palestine is a necessary process, but it will not be achieved by ideological blurrings and concessions in principles.

    3. The Kibbutz Ha'artzi can belong to a party which by its nature and actions would be able to include the following principles in its constitution as a minimum program:

    a. Class struggle as the element on which the program will be based in contrast to the system of "peace in industry" and its direct result—compulsory arbitration.

    b. An active position on the Arab question, which must find its concrete expression in joint organization in city and countryside.

    c. Full democratization in the political, cultural, economic and trade union activities of the working public.

    d. Cultural, educational and propaganda activities on the basis of scientific socialism.

    e. Participation in the World Zionist Organization and the National Funds.

f. Pioneering (Chaluziut).

g. Recognition of the vanguard role of the working class in the colonization effort in the country.

h. Complete support of the kibbutz movement and active struggle for its defense and development.

i. Hebrew culture and language.

j. The party's appearance on the international scene in accordance with its character as defined in these principles.

k. Our right not to belong to the two Internationals, because of our disagreement with both.

4. The Council points out that in addition to the principle of collective membership, guarantees for the ideological autonomy of the Kibbutz Ha'artzi in free organized collective ideological struggle, and the right to make public propaganda as the possessors of a specific and crystallized ideology, our special roles in the kibbutz movement and the youth movement make full kibbutz and educational autonomy obligatory as necessary conditons for our affiliation in the party.

(From: "Resolutions of the Kibbutz Artzi Council at Mishmar-Ha'emek, 1930")

... We too want unity and are prepared for it immediately. We don't demand of the members of Hashomer Hatsair that as a condition for unity they put their essentials to the test, whether these be principles of faith or ideology or science which they accept as an obligatory viewpoint, and that they undertake to accept what we shall impose on them and to abandon what we won't like. We, who maintain our unity as a party on the basis of obligatory views, do not agree that as a condition for unity we undertake to give up the freedom of views which everyone among us has; we do not agree that as a condition for unity we undertake to accept an obligatory view that will be imposed on us, concerning our views on matters of faith, ideology or science.

Matters of fundamental views deserve to be examined seriously in themselves within the united movement, and not decided by negotiations between the parties as a condition for something, even for something as great and important as unity. We members of the Eretz-Israel Workers Party (Mapai) are ready to unite as we are with the members of Hashomer Hatsair as they are. The questions in dispute? The united movement will find the answers.

(From "In order to know," by Berl Katznelson, *Writings* IX, pp. 193-194; published by Mapai, Tel Aviv.)

We don't want to unite with Mapai as it is, since we understand that then we wouldn't be able to remain after the union what we are today. We indeed demand autonomy and programmatic unity, but we know that what is decisive is the same principle that B.K. also mentions. We know very well that Mapai isn't a party with a theoretical program, as the Enfurt Program, for example. We know that union with Mapai is in the basis of obligation in acton and not in the basis of an obligatory view. Precisely because of that, precisely because this union imposes discipline on using action and deeds, we demand such programmatic guarantees as will prevent any forced discipline—a discipline that we will not be able to maintain morally without rebelling or breaking. We cannot enter the party in order to subvert it and every day weaken it in its ability to act. We demand a progammatic minimum of such a kind as will make it possible for us to cooperate in creativity and struggle, despite the differences in matters of faith, science and views. We know that after the union we shall find ourselves a minority without party seniority in a party with its own traditions, that is standing at the helm and utilizing the apparatus of the Histadrut and of its varied bodies.

Union cannot come by breaking what already exists. Union is an extended process towards internal unity. Successful negotiations on unity will only be successful if they are conducted on the basis of equality and not by liquidating the creative and militant independence of Hashomer Hatsair.

(From "Things as They Are," by Meir Yaari, *Hashomer Hatsair* 44, Merhavia, Nov. 16, 1939)

There was a second debate—which closely paralleled the first and continued for a long time—on the question of the "framework," whether the Kibbutz Ha'artzi was organizationally adapted to guide political activity effectively. There were some who demanded the establishment of an independent Hashomer Hatsair party, or at least a decision on such a perspective. This party would, of course, also include workers outside the kibbutz. The opposition to this demand based itself on two groups of arguments. The first, kibbutz arguments: the increased devotion to political and organizational activity that would inevitably follow such a step would be beyond the capacity of the kibbutzim which were already immersed in their own difficulties. The second was political: the formation of a new party would be an act of despair and of abandonment of the idea of wider programmatic class unification; as long as there was even a hope of such unification even in the distant future, the path should not be closed. Another argument was also raised that at the time of the "first stage" there was no objective need for the existence of parties; this was the period of "realizing communities" alone. This argument, however, soon disappeared in the course of the debate.

Mapai's development verified the worst premonitions, and it soon emerged as a typical reformist party. Even the presence of a kibbutz and pioneering wing within it was not strong enough to redirect this development or change this reformistic character. On the other hand, and not unconnected with this development, some hundreds of non-kibbutz workers voted, for the first time, for the Hashomer Hatsair list to the Histadrut's Fourth Congress (winter 1932-1933) and some of them began to organize into "circles of Hashomer Hatsair sympathizers." The Kibbutz Ha'artzi Council in Hadera in 1935 voted to "encourage these forces and persons," but the demand to establish a new organization (or even to decide on forming an independent political party) still did not win a majority, though it already had many supporters. Only two years later (in the winter of 1936-1937) the "Socialist League in Palestine" was formed to unite workers outside the kibbutzim as an organized political ally of the Kibbutz Ha'artsi.

With all the importance of this step, it was only a temporary solution and it was natural to believe that it wouldn't be long before the demand was raised (as it indeed was) by both the League and members of Kibbutz Ha'artsi not to delay any longer in setting up a single political party and, first of all, for doing away with the organizational and political divisions between the Kibbutz Ha'artsi and the Socialist League.

The question of the "framework" became even more serious after the elections to the Fifth Congress of the Histadrut (in the winter of 1941-1942) when Hashomer Hatsair won great political victory by rallying more than 20 percent of all the voters to its program and became the largest opposition in the Histadrut, second in size only to Mapai. These voters now included thousands of non-kibbutz workers, far more than the members of Hashomer Hatsair itself.

The Kibbutz Ha'artsi Conference at Mishmar Haemek in 1942, however, did not yet decide on unity with the League, though the old arguments and especially the "prospects of unification" did not have much weight. The main consideration now was the possibility of changes within Mapai itself as a result of leftist ferment (the so-called Siah Bet). The final decision was a moderate one: to watch this development and at the same time to "prepare the ground in order to lay the foundation" for the establishment of an independent party at the right time. Meanwhile, the links with the League would be tightened by joint meetings of the two central committees working by democratic decisions; a daily newspaper would be established, etc.

Although in principle it supported broad class unity, Hashomer Hatsair was far from making unit itself a principle and an absolute imperative. On the contrary, it approached this with very serious reservations and looked upon it only as a possibility, though most of the members who had come with the Third Aliya viewed it as a *desirable possibility*. In theory, the possibility of another kind of development was always assumed. The key to the decision in favor of one of these directions was seen to be the future developments within Mapai, which at that time included the vast majority of the politically conscious working public. It was only when Mapai showed itself to be clearly and unequivocally a typical reformist party (even to the satisfaction of those members who had waited a long time for further proof) by ousting from its ranks the leftist-pioneering minority, that Hashomer Hatsair began to come out clearly for a "union of the left."

A partial (and transient) union of this kind was achieved in the joint list of candidates presented by Hashomer Hatsair and Left Poale Zion for the elections to the Sixth Congress of the Histadrut (the "Left Front,"

1944). This election combination did not last long. Hashomer Hatsair's calls for union were not answered by the other parts of the left (Hatnua L'Ahdut Haavoda[5] and Left Poale Zion). The large majority of the movement decided, therefore (at the Nahariya Conference in 1946) that there was no longer any point in delaying the formation of an independent party. In February 1946, in Haifa, the Kibbutz Ha'artsi Hashomer Hatsair united with the Socialist League and formed the Hashomer Hatsair Workers Party.

Summing up the Socialist League's ten years of existence, it was possible to say that its establishment had been a daring experiment for a kibbutz movement like Hashomer Hatsair. There had been doubts about the degree of trust it could win among the workers in the city and countryside because of its close but organizationally complex ties with the Kibbutz Ha'artsi. Some had also feared that it would draw its membership only from former kibbutz members and the Hashomer Hatsair educational youth movement. The various fears proved groundless; the League succeeded in expanding its membership and influence far beyond the ranks of those two groups. It absorbed cadres and members who had left other parties. What is more, during the period of radical fermentation among the industrial workers, the League's ramified trade union activities brought it trade union activists coming from a completely different movement background, and with them workers for whom this was the first taste of political activity and party membership. Above all, the League revealed unreserved loyalty to Hashomer Hatsair in every trial, in the face of heavy attacks from without and bitter battles over unification and the removal of divisions within. It provided "individual" non-kibbutz wokers with living and convincing testimony that Hashomer Hatsair had decided to break out of its exclusive rural kibbutz limits and that its attitude towards political and trade union activity in the cities and the colonies was a serious one, from which there would be no retreat or regret.

The establishment of the Hashomer Hatsair Workers' Party marked a new and higher stage in Hashomer Hatsair's political activity among the urban workers. The last divisions between members sharing a common political view though living in different social forms were removed and those workers who were close to Hashhomer Hatsair's political views lost the last of their fears and suspicions concerning the degree of equality between the non-kibbutz workers who were members of the League and the kibbutz members of Kibbutz Ha'artsi.

---

5. The one-time Mapai left wing which seceded from Mapam in 1944.

9 • The Hashomer Hatsair Workers' Party

The Hashomer Hatsair Workers' Party existed for two stormy years of intensified struggle against the British rule, of fateful debate over the country's political future and the kind of regime that would be established. The Party fought against chauvinistic political programs that put their faith in agreement with imperialistic countries; it fought for a Jewish-Arab agreement that would satisfy the just national ambitions of the Jewish people returning to their country, and of the Arab community living in it (the League for Jewish-Arab Rapprochement)[1] and to win allies among the Arab workers in Palestine and in the neighboring countries. It endeavored to lead the struggle against British rule linked under all conditions with pioneering activity in immigration and settlement, to draw an ideological and political line between the working class and the fascist-Revisionist camp.[2] It worked to cultivate a pioneering and socialist culture by means of the Sifriat Hapoalim (Workers' Book Guild) and the Center for Progressive Culture, with the poets Abraham Shlonsky and Lea Gold among its outstanding personalities), and to win the sympathy

1. The "League for Jewish-Arab Rapprochement and Cooperation" was founded in 1939. In 1942 Hashomer Hatsair and the Socialist League adhered collectively, on the basis of a bi-national program. Their main partner in the League was the "Ihud" (Union) Society, a group of intellectuals headed by Prof. Martin Buber, Dr. Judah L. Magnes, Dr. Ernst Simon, and others. (The Ihud was preceded by the "Brit Shalom"—Peace Alliance—which had been established in 1926). The League worked together with the Arab "Falastin Jedida" (New Palestine Society), headed by Fawzi al-Husseini, who was assassinated in 1946 by nationalist Arab terrorists.
2. The "Zionists-Revisionists" were an extreme right-wing party in the Zionist movement. It was founded in 1924 by Vladimir Jabotinsky and fought against the "too compromising" policies of the Zionist Executive (headed by Prof. Haim Weitzmann) toward the English and the Arabs. It also supported an exclusive "political Zionism" as contrasted with Weitzmann's "constructive Zionism," and put the stress on military education. In the social field it was opposed to Socialism and class struggle, and showed a great deal of sympathy for the Italian "corporative state."
"Betar," its youth organization, was established in 1926, and in 1934 the "National Labor Federation" was founded in contrast with the Socialist Zionist "General Federation of Labor" (Histadrut). In 1935 the Revisionists seceded from the ranks of the World Zionist Organization and founded the "New Zionist Organization." In 1937 they left the "Haganah" (self-defense force) and established the extremist and terroristic "Irgun Zvai Leumi" (National Military Organization), generally known as "Etzel" or as "Irgun." In 1940 an even more extremist wing split away from Etzel to form the "Fighters for Israel's Freedom" (Lehi). After the establishment of the State in 1948, Etzel reorganized as a political party—"Tnuat Herut" (Freedom Movement), headed by the former commander of Etzel—Menahem Begin.

of the socialist world for progressive Zionist aims and to cultivate friendship and solidarity with the socialist countries, to unite the forces of the militant worker and pioneer camp in the "Union of the Left" and ultimately in the United Workers Party, which was established by fusion with the Ahdut Haavoda-Poale Zion Party.

In its "Ideological Assumptions," drawn up in 1927, Hashomer Hatsair set itself the basis of class struggle and revolutionary socialism. This was the reason for its opposition to the Second International, to which first Ahdut Haavoda and later Mapai were affiliated, and for its support for the socialist construction in the Soviet Union, support that deepened in the course of a number of years into principled support for the October revolution and the revolutionary path that had led to its victory.

In the beginning, Hashomer Hatsair had considered itself close to the leftist forces in the Second International (Prof. Max Adler and, to a lesser extent, Otto Bauer, and others) but it had always had its reservations concerning their remaining within the predominantly reformist Second International. When these left factions left the Social Democratic parties in some of the countries at the beginning of the thirties, Hashomer Hatsair endeavored to establish informational ties with these independent groups and their "International Bureau." It very soon became apparent, however, that most of the parties belonging to this Bureau were moving further away from their original positions, which had more or less been similar to Hashomer Hatsair's view on the international labor movement. They abandoned the role of serving as a catalytic agent for the establishment of unity in action between the rival wings of the labor movement and of establishing an independent Marxist revolutionary force that would support the Soviet Union and the socialist construction in process there, while at the same time clearly rejecting the Comintern's tactics and openly criticizing the bureaucratic falsification of proletarian democracy in the Soviet Union itself. When it became clear to Hashomer Hatsair that these groups were being strongly influenced by ultra-left and sectarian attitudes of opposition to the antifascist Popular Front and of condemnation of the foreign policy of the Soviet Union which was endeavoring in those years to form a power alliance against Nazi Germany, it moved away from the Bureau and severed its ties with it.

The ideological confusion prevailing for a while in the ranks of the world labor movement after the victory of fascism in Germany and during the Depression and defeats for revolutionary socialism in Vienna and Spain (1934) also left its signs in Hashomer Hatsair. Especially among the younger cadres, there were those who began to criticize Soviet foreign policy supposedly from the left and found the same "opportunistic common denominator" for the Soviet Union's joining the League of Nations, the principle of "collective security," the Popular Front, up to, first, the attempt to form an anti-German coalition and, afterwards, the Ribbentrop-Molotov agreement.[3]

At the outbreak of World War II, in September 1939, Hashomer Hatsair called on the Jewish community in Palestine to mobilize totally for the war effort against Nazi Germany and fascist Italy.

Concerning the way the Jewish community was to participate in this effort, Hashomer Hatsair rejected the policy of the Mapai leadership (at the head of the Jewish Agency and the Vaad Leumi[4]) to send Hagana cadres abroad to serve within the British Army on the European fronts. It considered this policy a reincarnation of the one-time "gdudism," i.e., the belief that in return for serving with the British, we would receive some political compensation after victory. Hashomer Hatsair considered the central Jewish war role to be the preparation to defend the country against the danger of a German-Italian invasion and against the threats aimed at the Jewish community by the Arab nationalists who were encouraged by the presence of Axis armies in the Middle East. This brought on an increasingly tense debate between Hashomer Hatsair and Hakibbutz Hameuchad on the one hand, and the Mapai leadership on the other, over the Palmach[5] and whether priority should be given to mobilizing into its ranks and other similar formations, or into the British Army. To this was added another debate over the form and frame of service in the British Army: as nationally-anonymous service units, something which Mapai was willing to accept for "lack of choice," or only as armed fighters in recognized Jewish units. This debate was decided in the course of the war when the British were compelled to organize Jewish units of artillery, transport, etc., and in 1940 with the formation of the "Buffs" (armed units to guard military installations, prisoners, etc., in Palestine). In 1942, a num-

---

3. The debate within Hashomer Hatsair over the evaluation of the Ribbentrop-Molotov agreement (the non-aggression pact concluded in August 1939 between the U.S.S.R. and Germany) was not limited to these two trends alone. Also among the opponents of the agreement were those who had, up to then, essentially supported Soviet foreign policy between 1934 and 1939 of working to isolate Nazi Germany. Some criticized the Soviet Union for not participating in the war that broke out between Germany and the Western countries, while still others thought that this nonparticipation, for the time being, was a result of the Munich policies that still prevailed in the West, but they denied the Soviet Union's need to express its temporary nonparticipation in the struggle by signing a non-aggression pact ... In any case, *the movement as a whole* sharply criticized the glorification and sanctification of the agreement by the Communist parties, presenting a temporary tactic of Soviet foreign policy as a "theoretical innovation" and transforming it into the ideological compass for all the workers' parties everywhere.
4. Havaad Haleumi (National Council) was the executive of the autonomous organization of the Palestinian Jews (Knesset Israel) in the British mandate era.
5. The Palmach was the Hagana's countrywide combat unit, and its mobilized striking force between 1941–48 and the beginning of the Israel Defense Army (until 1949). The Palmach mobilized its forces mainly from the ranks of the pioneer youth movements, with its bases mostly in the kibbutzim of Hakibbutz Hameuchad and Hakibbutz Ha'artzi. Ideologically and politically it was mainly under the influence of Hatnua L'ahdut Haavoda and Hashomer Hatsair.

ber of Jewish infantry regiments were formed, and finally, in 1944, the Armed Jewish Brigade. The members of Hashomer Hatsair took their full share in the Palmach, in the artillery and transport units, the infantry, the women's army, the Brigade, etc., participating in the fighting in the Libyan Desert, and through Italy; in the occupation of Austria, Germany and Belgium, and up to the meeting with the refugees of the Holocaust, the organization of the "Briha"[6] and illegal immigration to Palestine.

When the tidings were brought of the mass annihilation of the European Jews in the camps in the Nazi-occupied countries, as well as of the heroic uprisings in the ghettos and the activities of the Jewish partisans in the forests, under the initiative and guidance of the pioneering movements (in 1943–1944),[7] the national institutions and the kibbutz movement looked for ways of re-establishing contact and of saving as many as they could. The first attempt was made by the parachutists, working within the framework of the British Army, who were dropped in Nazi-occupied territory in 1944. Most of them, however, were captured and imprisoned, and some were executed. Nine of the 32 parachute emissaries were members of Hashomer Hatsair kibbutzim.[8] A new chapter in establishing contact was opened, as mentioned, at the beginning of 1945, when the members of the Brigade met the refugees, and the remnants of the pioneering youth movements in particular.

In the discussion on the conclusions to be drawn from the war effort as far as the relations with the British Mandatory Power (the White Paper government) were concerned, Hashomer Hatsair was opposed to any idea of a "political armistice" and was among those who demanded the breaking of the White Paper decrees limiting the settlement areas and closing the gates of the country to Jewish immigration. It also rejected the armistice in the class and trade union struggle that, according to Mapai, was required by the war effort. When, in 1941, the Mandatory Government enacted a law banning strikes and lockouts and establishing a government authority for compulsory arbitration, and the Histadrut leadership was about to send its representatives to this body, Hashomer Hatsair took its place at the head of the opposition to this step and charged Mapai with using the excuse of the war effort in order to carry out ideas and programs it had favored for a long time, without any connection with the war effort.

As a movement that had overcome inhibitions derived from a narrow nationalism, as well as other ideological prejudices, Hashomer Hatsair

---

6. Organization formed in Europe to bring the refugees to embarkation centers on their way to Palestine.
7. The commander of the Warsaw Ghetto Revolt in 1943 was Mordehai Anilevitz—one of the leaders of the Hashomer Hatsair youth movement in Poland.
8. One of them, Haviva Raik, a member of a Hashomer Hatsair kibbutz, was dropped into Slovakia in 1944. She participated in the revolt against the Nazis and was executed.

inevitably had to carry its theoretical starting point—revolutionary socialism—to its radical conclusions concerning the question of Jewish-Arab relations as well. The principle of class and international solidarity naturally also implied joint organization of Jewish and Arab workers. This was reinforced in the course of time by the situation in the Jewish colonies (*moshavot*) where it became evident that the Achilles heel of trade union organization and the struggle to introduce Jews into work in the orange groves was the existence of cheap Arab labor. As in the days of the Second Aliya, the worker was compelled to choose between turning to the plantation owners' "national conscience" or forging as wide a front as possible for his class struggles. It became clear that it was actually necessary to solve this problem of cheap and unorganized labor. Hashomer Hatsair advocated the joint organization of Jewish and Arab workers by a system of stages (national sections, organizing the regularly employed Arabs in the Jewish colonies), but it set its aim at the construction of an international workers' organization, without which socialist aims could not be achieved.

After some years, as bloody conflict became sharper, more frequent and more extended, Hashomer Hatsair found that the common class interests of the workers of the two peoples were not sufficient for a joint Jewish-Arab labor movement. The Arab worker was subject to the pressure of the nationalist atmosphere and affected by nationalist slogans and suspicions concerning the Jews. Without his own answer to the tangle of international relations, the Arab worker was unable to swim against the stream successfully. Hashomer Hatsair thus felt itself obligated to find an answer to the question of the relations between the two peoples. Even from the beginning, it had opposed the slogan of a "Jewish majority in Palestine." Instead, it formulated the slogan of "concentrating the majority of the Jewish people in Palestine and its environs," with the stress not on the status of majority (eventually to be used for domination), but positively, on a solution of the Jewish problem—that is—the concentration of millions of Jews in the country) who might ultimately become a large majority). The distinguishing characteristic of this slogan was the principle of "great Zionism," as opposed to the political principle of national domination. In the course of the anti-Jewish riots, and especially after publication of the Peel Report (1937)[9] and the great public debate over partition, and afterwards during and after World War II, at the time of the debate over the Biltmore Program,[10] it elaborated

9. After the disturbances of 1936 a Royal Committee of Investigation headed by Lord Peel studied the situation in Palestine and ultimately recommended the establishment of two separate states—a Jewish state and an Arab state.
10. The "Biltmore Program," the official political program of the World Zionist Organization from 1942–1947, was adopted at a meeting of American Zionists in Hotel Biltmore in New York, 1942. After it was ratified by the Zionist Action Committee in Jerusalem, it was called "The Jerusalem Program." Its essence was "that Palestine be established as a Jewish Commonwealth integrated in the structure of the new democratic world."

a socialist program as an alternative to partition—the bi-national state.

In those years, Hashomer Hatsair was the only group trying to give a principled and realistic answer to the problem of Jewish-Arab relations without giving up the vision of great Zionism, but also without ignoring or evading the recognition of the national and political rights of the neighboring people. The formula used by Left Poale Zion: "The common homeland" was vague and mere phraseology, since it avoided the basic question of national equality. The formula of the "Movement for Labor Unity" (Hatnua Le'ahdut Haavoda) that had split away from Mapai was: "A Jewish Socialist state in all of Palestine." Whatever its Jewish "justification," it could not pretend to offer a solution for the Arab national question. It was actually based, therefore, on the assumption of a conflict of national interests between the two peoples. In addition to these one-sided formulas and suggested solutions, Hashomer Hatsair had to combat other also one-sided solutions such as those suggested by the "Ihud" (which contained considerable essential concessions concerning the freedom and continuity of immigration, freezing the dimensions of the Jewish community in the suggested bi-national state, and others.

In contrast to these, Hashomer Hatsair suggested establishing a bi-national state which would not bind the freedom of immigration or freeze the numerical proportions of the two peoples living in the same state at numerical equality, as the "Ihud" suggested. The bi-nationality of the state would be expressed in the equality of both peoples in government, administration, economy, society, culture, education, language, religion and the like, regardless of the status of numerical minority or majority. This would hold good both during the first period in which the Jews would still be a minority, and afterwards when they would become the majority.... The bi-national constitution would be based on an advance agreement on the essential and decisive fundamentals (including freedom of Jewish immigration and settlement ties with the neighboring Arab states, etc.) so that there would be no constitutional way of changing them arbitrarily by a majority of votes, but only by mutual agreement.

In actuality, the real choice was not at all between the establishment of a Jewish state (with or without the addition of "socialist") in the whole and undivided Palestine, and dividing either territory or control. Hashomer Hatsair saw that the real choice was between the danger *that the whole of Palestine would be declared an Arab state*, whatever the specific formula or title, and the possibility, no matter how weak, that the two peoples would come to an agreement and divide either the territory or the control between them. If that was so, Hashomer Hatsair preferred dividing control in a whole and undivided Palestine, with the possibilities of immigration and settlement, over dividing the territory and thus limiting the room for settlement and mass immigration.

Hashomer Hatsair also argued that in practice it was futile to ignore the

Arab factor and the objective bi-national situation, and that the real results of the slogan of a "Jewish Socialist state in whole and undivided Palestine" would be accepting the Peel Plan, or something like it. "Siah B" (later, Tnua L'ahdut Haavoda) actually recognized this danger, and since it considered the possibility of partition as the greater evil, it demanded that for the time being the concern over ultimate programs for a political agreement in the country be dropped and that the emphasis be put on creating additional facts in the fields of immigration, settlement and security so that, eventually, it would be possible to realize the establishment of a Jewish Socialist state in the whole of Palestine.

Ultimately, none of these plans were fulfilled, neither that of Hashomer Hatsair (a united bi-national state with freedom of immigration) nor that of the Tnua L'ahdut Haavoda (putting off the decision until the Jews became a majority), nor that of Mapai (the Biltmore Program), which expected that Great Britain would grant a state in a whole or divided Palestine, by agreement and cooperation. The State of Israel came into being as part of a pioneering and mass struggle for the rights of immigration and settlement against the Mandatory power. It came into being in a war of independence against England and its satellites' armies, with the moral, political and very concrete help of the socialist countries headed by the Soviet Union. When it became evident that the realistic alternative to the partition proposal suggested to the U.N. Assembly was the replacement of the Mandate by the establishment of Palestine as a democratic state with a permanent Arab majority, Hashomer Hatsair stood in the breach and exerted all its efforts for the decision of Jewish independence that won the unreserved support of the majority of nations, including the Soviet Union and the Peoples' Democracies.

Hashomer Hatsair started on its road in the Diaspora far from revolutionary Marxism and class consciousness; in a continuous and developing process it went a long way in revolutionary and class development. Its particular contribution to the Jewish labor movement in Palestine was to raise the idea of the integration of pioneering construction and class struggle, as it had been conceived by Poale Zion in the Second Aliya and the early Ahdut Haavoda, to a higher level by justifying and developing it theoretically and politically as an *integration of pioneering Zionism and revolutionary socialism.*

The secret of Hashomer Hatsair's development, growth and cohesion lies in its "ideological collectivity." This does not only mean integrating the ideological and political spheres with other areas of full kibbutz collectivism and rejecting the existence of partisan ideological and political divisions within the organic kibbutz and in the Kibbutz Ha'artsi as a whole. This essential, which has proved its importance in the history of the kibbutz movement from the days of the Gdud Haavoda and onwards, is complemented by another and no less essential aspect: the principle of a regimen of free and penetrating discussion in a constant and systematic effort to attain reciprocal ideological influences and joint unifying conclusions. Hashomer Hatsair remained faithful to this principle in building its political force as a party when it left the kibbutz limits to join in establishing the Socialist League, later the Hashomer Hatsair Workers' Party and, finally, the United Workers' Party (Mapam).[11]

SOURCES

What regime will replace the British Mandate?

The Conference declares that the new world order that will follow victory cannot be established on foundations of peace, justice and equality, unless the problem of Jewish homelessness is finally solved.

The Conference urges that the gates of Palestine be opened; that the Jewish Agency be vested with control of immigration into Palestine and with the necessary authority for upbuilding the country, including the development of its unoccupied and uncultivated lands; and that Palestine be established as a Jewish Commonwealth integrated in the structure of the new democratic world.

Then and only then will the age-old wrong to the Jewish people be righted.

(From the Declaration adopted by the Extraordinary Zionist Conference, May 11, 1942 (Biltmore Resolution.)

A struggle for the fulfillment of the vision of the Socialist Jewish state, a regime that will be founded on international fraternity, cooperation and equality between the Jewish people returning to its homeland and the masses of the Arab people living in the country.

(From "The Program of Ahdut Haavoda-Poale-Zion, to the 22nd Zionist Congress," in *Davar*, October 27, 1944.)

The "Ihud" Society is for the union of Jews and Arabs in a bi-national Palestine based on the equality of both peoples, and for the union of a bi-national Palestine with the neighboring countries. This must be a regional union under the supervision of the United Nations.

... For long-term immigration policy we suggest that in a bi-national

---

11. Even as part of the larger party, the Hashomer Hatsair kibbutz as such continues to cultivate ideological collectivism and its internal cohesion as a branch of the party, with the program of the party as a whole serving as the contents of this collectivity. There has been a modification in the status of Hakibbutz Ha'artsi as far as this ideological collectivism is concerned: After joining the wider party framework, Hakibbutz Ha'artsi no longer served as a separate forum for political and ideological classification. This funciton was handed over completely to the party and its authorized bodies. The role of the Kibbutz Ha'artsi had been limited, in the theoretical field, to helping to deepen the all-party collectivism within the kibbutzim.

Palestine the Jewish community should be allowed to grow by immigration to half of the country's population in number."
> (From the Memorandum by the "Ihud" Society to the Anglo-American Investigating Committee, May 7, 1946. Published in *Ba'ayot*, No. 18.)

There is a way to understanding and agreement between the two peoples, even though there are many hurdles on this path. Agreement is necessary for the development of the country and the liberation of the two peoples. The condition for agreement is the principle of no domination by one nation over the other and the establishment of a bi-national state on the basis of political parity and full cooperation between the two peoples in the fields of economics, society and culture. Immigration is a political problem and within the framework of an inclusive agreement it will not be difficult to solve this problem on the basis of the country's economic absorptive capacity. This agreement between the two peoples must receive international ratification by the United Nations Organization and it must guarantee the Arabs that independent bi-national Palestine will join an alliance with the neighboring Arab countries.
> (From an address by Fawzi al-Husseini, leader of "Falestin al-Jadida," at a public meeting in Haifa, July 22, 1946, published in Mishmar, July 26, 1946.

5. The League considers the fundamental principles of Jewish-Arab agreement to be:

    a) Recognition of the right of the Jews to return to their historic homeland and to build their independent national lives there, recognition of the right of the Arabs of Palestine to an independent national life and their ties with the other parts of the Arab nation;

    b) the non-domination of one nation over the other—no matter what the numerical relations between the two peoples in the country;

    c) a bi-national regime in Palestine;

    d) a positive attitude towards Palestine's participation, as an independent bi-national entity, in a federation with the neighboring countries, when the conditions for that are prepared and after guaranteeing the fundamental rights and vital interests of the Jewish people returning to its homeland and the fundamental rights and vital interests of the Arab people living in the country . . .
> (From the program of the "League for Jewish-Arab Rapprochement and Cooperation," June 23, 1942, in *Israel and the Arab World*, by Aharon Cohen, pp. 287–288, Sifriat Poalim, Merhavia, 1964.

2. The Convention stresses the pressing need to change the political path of the Zionist movement, as defined by the "Biltmore Program." We shall intensify our struggle for the victory of the alternative policy whose fundamentals are: the undisturbed progress of the Zionist enterprise, real international control, the maintenance of political equality within a bi-national regime of Jews and Arabs in Palestine.
> (From the Political Resolution of the Founding Convention of the Hashomer Hatsair Workers Party in Eretz Israel, Haifa, Feb. 22,

1946, in "From convention to Convention—1946-1948, Resolutions and Summations," p. 5, published by *Hashomer Hatsair* Party, Tel Aviv, 1948.)

. . . In view of the standstill aims of British policy towards the Zionist enterprise and with the international discussion of the problems of Zionism and Palestine, the Hashomer Hatsair Council once more stresses that the only path which preserves the international status of Zionism and the Jewish National Home, that is related to progressive world policy and opens new horizons for the Zionist enterprise, is a Zionist policy based on political equality between Jews and Arabs in an undivided Palestine, replacing the British Mandate with international control by the three great powers in the name of the United Nations, continuing the undisturbed progress of the Jewish National Home, the development of the land for the benefit of both of its peoples, and speeding its march towards independence as a bi-national state.
(From the Resolutions of the Council of the Hashomer Hatsair Party, 27–29/6/47, ibid, pp. 14-15.)

Hashomer Hatsair welcomes the decision of the United Nations annulling the treacherous policies of the British government, rejecting the chauvinistic aims of domination of Arab reaction and opening a new page in the struggle of the Jewish people and Eretz Israel for independence . . .

Hashomer Hatsair will give loyal support to the establishment and construction of a Jewish state in part of Palestine. It will invest the best of pioneering forces in mobilizing the capacity of the Jewish people, in encouraging, training, organizing and absorbing immigration, in continuing the settlement enterprise and in reinforcing our defensive strength.
(From a statement by the Central Committee of Hashomer Hatsair Party, Nov. 30, 1947, ibid., p. 43.)

10 • From Mapai Split to Formation of Mapam

The worst fears came true—the fears of those within Ahdut Haavoda who were against unification with Hapoel Hatsair, as well as of those who accepted it for the sake of principle, without any great enthusiasm or illusions. The Ahdut Haavoda leadership, headed by Berl Katznelson and David Ben-Gurion, very swiftly merged with the Hapoel Hatsair leadership into a plainly reformistic trend. Those former Ahdut Haavoda members who desired to preserve their loyalty to the tradition of its best days found themselves an insignificant minority and were pushed aside.

The first focus for opposition to Mapai's reformistic course in its early days was provided by a group gathered around a journal called *Socialist Notes*. This opposition, whose beginnings were found in the ranks of Ahdut Haavoda in 1929, was composed, on the one hand, of former members of Zionist Youth and socialist-Zionist organizations coming from the Soviet Union, with strong Marxist inclinations and, on the other, by former members of (Right) Poale Zion from Poland. These were joined by other elements: at an early stage—building worker union militants from Tel Aviv who wanted to preserve and deepen the class content of the Histadrut's trade union activities, and—at a later stage—former members of the leftist Socialist German Workers Party—the S.A.P. Eventually, after lengthy debates, the Mapai Central Committee published a statement to the effect that all those who identified themselves with the group, cooperated with it or supported it, would be expelled from the party (Hapoel Hatsair, Oct. 28, 1932). As a result, some of the group's members accepted the verdict and remained within the party, while the majority left to organize itself as the "Union of International Socialists in Palestine."

As its basis, this opposition, which was essentially an ideological discussion group, had two fundamental assumptions: 1) that the period of pioneering and constructivist socialism had exhausted itself since national capital had ceased serving as the chief factor in building the country; 2) that true socialism necessarily involved active internationalism in all spheres of life, starting from joint labor organization (Jews and Arabs) to the struggle for the democratization of the Mandatory regime (a "legislative council," even with an Arab majority, and the like).

Since the activist anti-reformist elements in the Mapai ranks saw how the reformist course was growing in strength, supposedly in order to fulfill the pioneering tasks that guided Palestinian socialism into "constructive socialism" (without class struggle), they began to put the blame for the reformist decline in Ahdut Haavoda and Mapai on their responding to those pioneering and constructive tasks and tended to minimize the importance of these tasks (without opposing them). Despite its honest socialist aims, this group failed just because it attached its anti-reformism to minimizing the importance of pioneering; instead of attacking "exclusive constructivism" they criticized constructivism in general; and instead of refuting the Mapai thesis of the alleged contradiction between constructivist pioneering and class struggle and opposing it with their own leftist-pioneering alternative, they actually adopted Mapai's theory of the contradiction, though they drew the opposite conclusions. They envisioned a kind of "normal" Palestinian Social-Democratic Party (neither "constructivist" nor communist), but just another one of the affiliates of the (Second) Socialist International.

In actuality, however, the historic prospects for a leftist Israeli socialism lie in the measure of its success in refuting the thesis of a contradiction between building the country and class struggle, and in convincing the working class public that reformism itself inevitably acts as a brake on construction, only the integration of class struggle within construction being able to bring it to consistent fulfillment. *The Israeli Left will either be a pioneering one or be bound to liquidationist degeneration or— in the best of cases—to sectarian and barren isolation.* Today, looking back, we can say something that perhaps could not be seen so clearly then, early in the thirties—that the prospects of an anti-reformist socialist opposition *in the city* depended on its joining together with a leftist trend *in the kibbutz movement* based on loyalty to both pioneering radicalism and socialist radicalism. At the beginning of the thirties, however, these two leftist trends in city and kibbutz went their separate ways. And so it happened that in spite of this opposition group's desirable anti-reformist aims and the fresh thinking that marked its early steps, its "non-constructivism" made it easier for Mapai's reformistic leadership to attack it and to isolate it, so that its influence was hardly felt during the radicalizing process that was to affect large sections of the Palestinian workers in the second half of the thirties and the forties.[1]

1. After some time (1933–1934) most of the members of the group organized themselves as the "Union of International Socialists in Palestine," which was mainly an ideological discussion group. During the campaign against the Ben-Gurion–Jabotinsky agreement, the organization was quite active; it also mobilized sympathy, support and volunteers during the Civil War in Spain. After that, it devoted all its energies to supporting the Soviet Union in the war against Germany. In this field, the "Union" cooperated with the P.C.P., despite their fundamental differences with communism, and this cooperation helped deepen the differences within the Union itself. Actually, what united the members

However, the expulsion of the *Socialist Notes* group from the ranks of Mapai did not end the opposition to the leadership's reformistic course; on the contrary, this opposition even increased and went on to a higher stage. Four years after the foundation of Mapai, the first open mass conflict broke out over the ratification of the Ben-Gurion–Jabotinsky agreement in 1934 (between the Histadrut and the anti-socialist National Labor Federation) that gave a minority of workers in any place of employment the right to prevent a strike and to turn the dispute over to arbitration. The disagreement within Mapai threatened to burst the party asunder and there was no choice but to leave the decision to the general Histadrut forum by a referendum. In the public campaign in preparation for the Histadrut referendum in the spring of 1935, a triple front was set up of Kibbutz Hameuchad, Hashomer Hatsair and Left Poale Zion, with considerable support among the urban branches of Mapai.[2]

This same front was established in the great debate within the Zionist public after the presentation of the partition plan by the Royal Commission of Investigation headed by Lord Peel (1937–1939).[3]

In the years preceding World War II this leftist opposition once more appeared within Mapai, headed by part of the former Ahdut Haavoda who felt that Mapai's policies were betraying the Ahdut Haavoda tradition. This opposition was headed by the majority in Kibbutz Hameuchad. Oppositionary unrest also increased in Mapai's urban branches and especially in Tel Aviv and particularly among the building workers whose task was carried out under difficult conditions and who were compelled to move from one British military camp to another, and who felt themselves discriminated against as compared with the easier situation of the dominant groups in the Party's urban branches.

Overriding bureaucracy, growing social inequality among the workers (and within the party branches), limping trade union policies which no

---

of the group from the very start was the desire to provide a Marxist analysis for the economic and political situation in Palestine and to fulfill the principles of internationalism in Palestine itself (Jews and Arabs), and on the world scene (solidarity with the Spanish Republic and the Soviet Union). In other fields, there were many differences of stress and disagreements, particularly in evaluating the Zionist enterprise; these differences deepened during the cooperation with the P.C.P. and eventually led to the end of the Union in 1943. Some of its members found their way, later on, to Mapam; others joined Maki; while still others remained outside all political organizations.

2. In the referendum, held in March 1935, the agreement was rejected by a majority of 16,474 over 11,522.

3. In both these campaigns, the triple leftist front was not isolated in its opposition; in both it was joined by allies from the right within Mapai, and in the question of "partition," even by people from the bourgeois sector. What is important, however, is that in both these campaigns these three public forces appeared in a single front.

longer fitted the new needs and dimensions, were among the chief causes for the unrest in Mapai's urban branches.[4]

The Mapai opposition (Siah Bet) was active in mobilizing popular sympathy for the Soviet Union, a sympathy that took on greater scope among the Palestinian workers during the Red Army's war against the Nazi invaders. The Siah took an active part in the establishment and activities of the Victory League to Aid the U.S.S.R. at War ("V League"). At that same time, the Mapai right wing, stimulated by Berl Katznelson's political address at the Histadrut's Fifth Congress, attempted to rush through the Congress a reactionary resolution hostile to the "Forces of Tomorrow" (the Red Army, etc.). Kibbutz Hameuchad leader Yitzhak Tabenkin entered the fray with a bitter debate with Katznelson. The knowledge that Siah Bet would not vote for the resolution finally compelled the Mapai leadership to accept a resolution that was acceptable to the whole Congress.

The description of Siah Bet and of its continuation as Hatnua L'Ahdut Haavoda would not be complete without mentioning its enormous credit in developing the Hagana and Palmach, in illegal immigration and in the struggle against the British imperialist regime. There was a very serious debate between Hashomer Hatsair and Hatnua L'Ahdut Haavoda on how to conduct the struggle[5] but the historic truth is that the two parties were loyal and active partners in that struggle, just as they were partners in the Palmach and illegal immigration. However, it is also an historic truth that members of Hatnua L'Ahdut Haavoda were particularly active in guiding the struggle and in building the Palmach, with Yitzhak Tabenkin at their head.

---

4. The Tel Aviv opposition within Mapai took on organized form for the first time when it won a majority in the elections to the Mapai Tel Aviv Council in September 1937. The right wing within Mapai attempted to upset these results of a democratic test; the Party's Central Committee attempted to intervene, and these actions accelerated the process of consolidation of the various opposition groups as a party faction and their linking up with the official party opposition headed by the leaders of the Kibbutz Hameuchad. The opposition was called "Siah Bet" (Faction "B"). When it left Mapai in 1944 it was called "The Movement for the Unity of Labor" (Hatnua L'Ahdut Haavoda.)

5. Hatnua L'Ahdut Haavoda favored the "continuous struggle," that is, a general and unreserved conflict with the British armed forces. Hashomer Hatsair, on the other hand, favored a "selective struggle," coming into direct conflict with the British armed forces in defense of the fundamental and declared aims of Zionism and the Palestinian Jewish community—immigration, settlement, self-defense. In practical terms, this meant providing defense when illegal immigrants were brought to the shore, when settlements were made in areas banned by the "White Paper," resisting arms searches and confiscations. Hashomer Hatsair saw the need to win the support of most of World Jewry as well as progressive world opinion (including in Great Britain itself) for the struggle so as to frustrate the hopes of the British administration of evading its international obligations to establish a Jewish National Home by breaking the Jewish community in a military trial. Hashomer Hatsair also feared the inevitable loss of any distinctions between the continuous struggle and the terrorist activities of Etzel and Lehi, which could free the British of any restraints in carrying out their plans.

SOURCES

. . . The Congress declares that the Zionist Movement will untiringly continue and even intensify the struggle against the policies which were expressed before World War II in MacDonald's White Paper, and after the war, by the declarations of Bevin, Atlee and Morrison. In this struggle, the Jewish Community (Yishuv) in the country will defend immigration, settlement and self-defense, without any sacrifices being too dear, in the spirit of the mass migrations to the shores of the land, the resistence in Emek Hefer, Biria and Haifa, and with the force of mass non-acceptance whose first elements were laid in the Yishuv's plan of resistance. In this struggle, however, the Yishuv will reject terrorist methods and will isolate the fascist groups distorting the content of the political struggle of Zionism and endangering the Yishuv's force of defense.

(From Hashomer Hatsair's resolutions for the 22nd Zionist Congress, December 1946; in "From convention to Convention, 1946–48, Resolutions and Summations," p. 21, published by Hashomer Hatsair Party, Tel Aviv, 1948.)

. . . The Zionist Movement, the Jewish People and the Jewish Community in the country will not yield to the policies of the British government to liquidate Zionism and will not accept the war against Jewish immigration, the bar on settlement, the robbery of land, the theft of defensive weapons, the denial of rights and the oppression of the Yishuv. . . . For a popular, daring and continuous struggle against the policies of liquidation. . . .

(From the Resolutions of the L'Ahdut Haavoda–Poale Zion faction at the 22nd Zionist Congress; M. Breslavsky, *The Palestine Labor Movement*, III, p. 390. Tel Aviv, 1959.)

. . . Unrestrained and ill-considered activism, which has even led to a kind of armistice with the terrorist groups, had objectively aided our enemies and helped them move the center of gravity from the fundamental problems of our struggle to the questions of a military contest in Palestine. It has apparently brought additional publicity to the Palestine question, but in so doing has narrowed the circle of our friends in England and the world over. By putting the question of the regime at the center of the political discussions, and not the question of immigration, this activism has also made its contribution towards renewing the idea of partition . . .

(From the resolutions of Council of the Hashomer Hatsair Party, Tel Aviv, Feb. 10, 1946, *From Convention to Convention, 1946–48, Resolutions and Summations*, p. 10.)

. . . The Council of the Hashomer Hatsair Party once more points out the danger of the catastrophe that may be caused by the terror. Fascist terror is running wild without a stop and sabotaging the Zionist struggle. The enemy at home is helping the enemies outside who want to throw the country into a blood-bath on the eve of the international discussion . . . "

(From the Resolution of the Council of Hashomer Hatsair Party, Tel Aviv, June 27–29, 1947, ibid., p. 14.)

... In my humble opinion, there could not be at that historic period any "conventional" way of fighting against the enemy—even in the later period when the conflict between us and the British administration became more intense. Anyone who thinks that the Jews in Palestine could have fought the British like the Viet Cong the Americans is only mistaken. Anyone making general schematic comparisons of ways of fighting is misleading. Why couldn't they fight the same way? Because there is a difference between the kind of fighting of the Viet Cong, for whom I have all sympathy, who actually rule the country and are the majority in the country, and the struggle of the Jewish community that was a minority in the country. All the Viet Congs are in Vietnam and they fought earlier against the French and now against the Americans. The difference between us and Vietnam is clear: We were a minority in this country as the vanguard of the Jewish people... Therefore, anyone who says that he was at that period anti-imperialist or anti-British does not say by that that the war against the British regime had to be conducted under conditions unappropriate to the situation of the Jewish people. The relationship between the Jewish people in the country and the Jewish people in the Diaspora had to have an influence on the intermediary stages of the political struggle and the nature of the military struggle.

... The line of direct war against the British, against the British administration, against the British officers and soldiers, was a mistaken one. That is what I thought then and what I think now. What line wasn't a mistaken one? There had to be formed a *specific line of Jewish struggle* ... I think that it was absolutely correct ... that we looked for an independent, specific, national path ... what we called at that time the selective struggle.

What did this line base itself on? It said that the conflict with the Mandatory regime had to be connected first of all to those areas that are decisive for the fulfillment of Zionism: settlement and immigration, for the reason, too, that this struggle could rally around it all of the Jewish community, which it wasn't so easy to unite. For the reason that it could help us find allies in England and in other countries, especially since we are talking of the time of an anti-Hitler coalition, a struggle against the British for our rights could have united the Jewish Diaspora. The question of finding allies is not an insignificant one.

Fundamentally that was a correct line, one that matched our specific situation.

(Yaakov Riftin in symposium in *Maariv*, April 10, 1966.)

In the elections to the Mapai council that was to decide on the party's candidates for the Histadrut Congress (December 1938), the kibbutz and urban oppositions united into "Siah Bet" and obtained about a third of the votes. After that it fought with more or less success for its proportionate representation in the party organs and the Histadrut. On the other hand, the right wing ("Siah Gimel"—Faction C) remained the main, if not the sole representatives in outside bodies such as the Jewish Agency, the municipalities, etc. The results of the elections to the Fifth Histadrut Congress in the winter of 1941–1942 gave the leftist parties about 25 percent of the votes, and the latter, together with the Siah Bet Mapai delegates (about one third of the Mapai delegates) controlled half of the Histadrut institutions. In general, Siah Bet avoided openly breaking party discipline in the Histadrut Congress and Council (at most, abstaining from voting); in the closed meetings of the Histadrut Executive Committee (Vaad Hapoel), however, they allowed themselves greater freedom, and in the Tel Aviv Workers Council (the central organ of the local Histadrut institutions) where the combination of Siah Bet, Hashomer Hatsair and Poale Zion (Left) had a majority, the situation led to violent conflicts within Mapai and spurred its leadership's decision to purge the party of the opposition.[6]

At the Mapai Congress in Kfar Vitkin in 1942, the majority voted for an organizational party statute that imposed a heavy discipline on the party's representatives, abrogated proportional representation and banned factions. The struggle over these statutes continued throughout 1943, and in the spring of 1944, the Mapai leadership announced elections to the Sixth Histadrut Congress, with the party's candidates obliged to accept the discipline of the Kfar Vitkin decisions and the decisions of the party's Central Committee. This step put Siah Bet outside the party and it reformed in May 1944 as Hatnua L'Ahdut Haavoda (The Movement for Labor Unity) and presented its own list of candidates for the Histadrut Congress.[7]

The left within Mapai had exhausted all the possibilities of "influencing from within" and of struggling over the character and image of the "all-

---

6. Today, looking back, we can see that it was the ties formed between the Tel Aviv Siah Bet and the Kibbutz Hameuchad that saved it from the fate of the *Socialist Notes*, and turned it into a political mass movement, even if the ties to the Kibbutz Hameuchad sometimes served to slow down the momentum of the urban faction and to delay its final departure from Mapai.

In their popular character and mass bases the Tel Aviv Siah Bet really had the advantage over the opposition that preceded it. It, however, continued to suffer from Ahdut Haavoda's traditional disdain for theory or precise programmatic formulations. Thus, healthy class instincts and revulsion against Mapai's administration machine were not sufficient to take the place of a clear and well-founded theoretical program. Though the important close links with the Kibbutz Hameuchad were a source of spiritual, moral and organizational inspiration and strength, for a considerable part of the Faction's leadership they were primarily elements in the factional struggle for control over the Tel Aviv branches of the Party and the Histadrut. Despite their declared identification with the pioneering-leftist ideas of the Kibbutz Hameuchad, they very often revealed narrow trade unionist tendencies, and actually had never liberated themselves from the traditional factional maneuvering even after they left Mapai. With all these weaknesses it is not surprising that the Tel Aviv Siah Bet leadership for the most part did not succeed in finding its place within the pioneering left and gradually dispersed into the ranks of L'Ahdut Haavoda-Poale Zion, Mapai, Rafi, Mapam and Maki.

7. The Kfar Vitkin Congress is not important in Mapai history only because the decisions were shortly to lead to the split in the party. After adopting the centralistic organizational statute, giving the ruling elements full control over all rival internal organizations, Mapai inevitably took on the character of a machine party, without any democratic party life and with ideological tension and values pushed aside.

embracing class party." In the final analysis, however, the party's indefinite and nonprogrammatic character gave the reformist leadership some very decisive advantages, with the party continuously going more to the right. The left had no choice but factional organization, and as the pressure increased, to go on to revolt and disobedience to the arbitrary decisions of the majority. The left was justified in acting in this way because it was part of a reformist party that was vainly claiming to be "the mass party," "inclusive" and "undefined."

The left, however, left Mapai *against its will*. Formally, it had left; in actuality, it had been expelled despite its loyalty to the idea of "inclusive unity" and the "all-embracing class party." It had the choice of either total submission or of revolting and leaving the united framework and finally chose survival.

> ... Membership in the party is based on loyalty to the principles of the party, freedom of thought and debate, discipline in action.
> The party directs the activity of its members and representatives in the Histadrut, in the Yishuv, in the Zionist movement and the international labor movement.
> In all matters that fall within the realm of party activity, by the decision of its authorized institutions, members of the party act only according to lines authorized by the party and within the frame of its discipline.
> The party bans the existence of factions within it; members are not allowed to form factions or to be members of them (a faction is a grouping of members in a permanent special framework of any kind outside the authorized pattern of the parties and the Histadrut in order to deal separately with any matter or matters falling into the realm of party authority). ...
> All members will have to register anew on a form prepared in keeping with the statute by the secretariat by authorization of the Central Committee. This form will also serve for new members.
> (From resolutions of the third session of the Fifth Mapai Congress, Kfar Vitkin, October 1942. In *Ahdut Haavoda* III, pp. 175–196, Tel Aviv, 1964.)

> In the Party Congress in Kfar Vitkin a dangerous attempt was made to cut the thread of continuity in building the Party of the Workers of Eretz-Israel as a broad class party and to turn it into a plainly centralistic party based on decisions from above, a constitution creating an artificial majority and preventing any real cooperation, influence or development for the various trends within it."
> (From a statement by Siah Bet, Tel Aviv, Nov. 7, 1942; *Davar*, Nov. 22, 1942.)

It is, therefore, not surprising that in the years following the split, two contrasting trends stood out in the Tnua L'Ahdut Haavoda: one, represented mainly by the kibbutz section of the Tnua (though not all of it, and not only it), which did not accept the split and saw the chief task to be to achieve the *total unification*, not only between the Tnua and Mapai, but also, at the same time, with Hashomer Hatsair and Poale Zion. They considered the struggle for the fulfillment of this idea to be the historic mission of their new party, drawing their inspiration from the struggle to achieve full and inclusive labor unity toward the end of World War I.

> ... To many, the vision of the political unity of the labor movement seems to be a false and illusory one. Despite this, there is not and will not be any other way out for the movement and it has no other cure. This unity will be achieved if it will be the task of a large public movement of the workers of Palestine, putting all its decisive weight on the scales. We call on the workers of Palestine to turn the election campaign for the Histadrut Congress into a great public movement—a movement for the labor unity of the workers of Palestine. We want to be the organized center of this movement. We consider this to be our chief task. This will be our banner for the elections; we will carry this banner to every worker or living unit, to every settlement, to every group of workers in city and village, to every place of work, to the adherents of the house of labor mobilized in the tasks of war and security, and to all the pioneering youth. We shall call on all the workers of Palestine to rally around this banner, to organize in groups of cadres every place where the workers of Palestine live and work.
> (From "Statement of Meeting of Hatnua L'Ahdut Haavoda," in *Information Bulletin of the Tnua L'Ahdut Haavoda*, May 1, 1944.)

In contrast to this, there was a second minority trend (especially in the cities and among the younger elements of the Kibbutz Hameuchad) that understood that despite all due respect for the tradition of Ahdut Haavoda, and the principle of unity, in its time, this tradition and principle, under the new circumstances, had to be translated faithfully and concretely into *unity of the left* (with Hashomer Hatsair and Left Poale Zion, and without Mapai).

The starting-point for the leftist struggle within Mapai had been its reliance on the past, its identification with the movement before it had turned rightward and abandoned the values and tradition of Ahdut Haavoda. This reliance on the past during a struggle for the future is a common phenomenon in history and can, in certain circumstances, supply the energy for revolutionary advance. In any case, this was a natural starting-point for a left that was fighting a deviationist leadership abandoning the accepted values of the movement. The coin, however, had its other side as well—the sanctification of the past and the stressed reference to Ahdut Haavoda in its time, led the Mapai left wing and the Tnua L'Ahdut Haavoda to cultivate a tendency to perpetuate ideas and formulas which had been valid and progressive in their time but were no longer valid or progressive in the changed situation. In that way, they cultivated a kind of "revolutionary conservatism," pointing its shaft, indeed, against the reactionary revisionism within Mapai but inevitably also showing its signs to a certain degree when there was an objective need really *to change* theory in keeping with the changes of time and historic evolution, in the light of Marxist doctrine.

The chain of political events between the two U.N. sessions in July and November of 1947, when real prospects of ending the British Mandate and achieving national independence appeared on the horizon, worked to dull the traditional differences between the Hashomer Hatsair Party and the Ahdut Haavoda—Poale Zion Party (the last two had united in April 1946). The things all parts shared by the pioneering left triumphed over the differences and this accelerated process culminated in the foundation of the United Workers Party (Mapam) in Tel Aviv in January 1948, by the merger of the Hashomer Hatsair Workers' Party and the L'Ahdut Haavoda–Poale Zion Party.

11 • Mapam—Experiment in Unity

The United Workers' Party (Mapam) was founded on the eve of the declaration of the State, when the process of rapprochement between the Hashomer Hatsair Workers' Party and the L'Ahdut Haavoda-Poale Zion Party culminated in the union of these two parties in January 1948. It seemed to the groups that were joining together that the new political circumstances had dulled the traditional differences of the past. The debate between the partisans of the bi-national solution for the Jewish-Arab question and the supporters of the "establishment of a Jewish State in the whole of Palestine" had ended with the partition and the establishment of two separate national states. Within the State of Israel, which came into being in part of Palestine, there was no longer any room for debate over bi-nationalism. It was clear to the former partisans of bi-nationalism that the State of Israel that had arisen by partition had to be a *Jewish* State, just as it was clear to the opponents of bi-nationalism, as well, that the Jewish State would have to grant the Arab community living within its borders full civil equality and recognize it as a national minority with all the rights and obligations deriving from that recognition.

As for the question of "inclusive unity" of the labor movement, the members of the former L'Ahdut Haavoda considered this their declared aim, looking upon the establishment of Mapam as the first stage in the fulfillment of the total unification. In practice, however, no one among them attached any real meaning to this perspective in the given circumstances.

As for socialist views, when it united with Poale Zion in 1946, the Tnua L'Ahdut Haavoda had recognized Marxism, and though no discussions were held or formulas adopted on questions like the positive attitude in principle to the October revolution or the attitude to the dictatorship of the proletariat (at the time of the formation of Mapam elaboration of the party program and constitution were put off to the second congress), the rejection of reformism and the positive and sympathetic attitude toward the Soviet Union, the Red Army and the Soviet Union's U.N. Representative Gromyko's statement in favor of the Jewish State were shared by all the uniting forces and overshadowed the differences of principle on matters held by some members of L'Ahdut Haavoda.

On the other hand, the united movements shared the same pioneering Zionist outlook, as well as the vision and presentiment of the dangers facing the future of the State of Israel—the danger to its security, to its democratic and secular character, to the preservation of its neutrality, to the status of the pioneering forces and the situation and standards of living of the working class presented by the reformistic course. With these dangers in view, the union of all the anti-reformist pioneering and revolutionary forces seemed a supreme Zionist and socialist imperative.

There is no doubt that despite the subsequent failure of this union, the very attempt to unite the left and establish a broad pioneering Zionist, anti-reformist socialist party which could campaign for the support of the working public as an alternative to Mapai, was justified and correct. It was important to confront Mapai with a mass party that was not composed mainly of the members of any one specific immigration wave, youth movement or way of life (like each of the parties that had united in 1948). By combining Hashomer Hatsair, Hatnua L'Ahdut Haavoda, and Left Poale Zion, the new united party was given a broad demographic and social base, including different sections of the working class, the members of different immigrations and youth movements. Such unity could emphasize the historic continuity as regards both the Jewish labor movement in the Diaspora and the Second and Third Aliya in Palestine itself. Thus, in the given historic circumstances and in light of the perspectives for the future, as they then appeared to almost everyone, the unification answered a vital need and there were real prospects for its ultimate success.

The first years of the united party not only proved the vital need for its establishment and political activity but also seemed to justify the hopes for the eventual complete success of the merger. It is true that even in this period—during the War of Liberation—some bitter debates broke out and the "parity" between the two parts in manning party institutions and dividing functions, decided upon at the start as a temporary measure, led to more than a few difficulties, friction, and even minor crises. Still, it can be said of that period that the process of mutual rapprochement went ahead ideologically and socially and was reflected in "mixed votes" (not according to former party affiliations) and in close personal relationships. Perhaps, if it had not been for the deterioration of the objective political circumstances which had helped in the birth of the union and which were a prime condition for its success (or perhaps if this deterioration had even occurred at a later stage) the process of integration might have gone to completion. Unfortunately, however, developments were completely different.

SOURCES:

". . . I do not ignore the differences separating us from the L'Ahdut Haavoda-Poale Zion Party on a series of matters, some of them very serious ones. I do not erase the past from memory, though in political life, forgetfulness, like memory, is sometimes a condition for progress.

In the many meetings we have held with the members of the L'Ahdut Haavoda—Poale Zion Party, we conducted some serious and even very painful discussions. The final result, however, was a positive one. It demands daring, in the faith that the common basis is a trustworthy guarantee for the future. . . .

. . . After all this I now come to the conclusion that the bases we have formulated together hold a guarantee for the militant socialist-Zionist character of our new party. Why should we not believe that the party will go on to deepen this content in the course of its development? We have met midway and we have the right to believe that from now on the process of unification, of ideological integration, will be accelerated and intensified until it becomes complete and indivisible.

We don't believe in political unity without the basis of common political and ideological conceptions—an obligatory, guiding and educating program. That, however, is not enough. Political unity formed by the merger of two different parties without attaining social integration, the creation of a new militant comradeship—isn't worth the name. If the united party does not strive from its very first day to create a new cultural and social character bringing together the best of the two parties, it won't be worth the cost. For, only unity of this kind can transfer the parties' ideological values to all its members and turn its political program into the foundation on which it will build its ideological collectivity. It is the ideological collectivity that turns the party into a united force paving its way surely through the harshest trials.

The work we have to do is not easy. Our social and cultural sources were not the same, the histories of the uniting movements were different ones. These histories do not belong to the past alone, they live in every single one of us, work within us and every day shape our reaction to the problems of life. The task is a great one and if we are capable of carrying it out, the union will succeed. We shall have to use all our wisdom and social ability in order to remove the divisions, true and false, between us; to transfer our relationships to our party to our new party, generously, without too many calculations; to give it the best of our ability and our devotion, and if we do that—we shall succeed.

(From address by Yaakov Hazan at Second Congress of the Hashomer Hatsair Party, Tel Aviv, on the eve of merger with the L'Ahdut Haavoda-Poale Zion Party; in *Unification Congress*, pp. 73–75, published by Mapam, Tel Aviv, 1948).

. . . We shall bring with us to Mapai a new partner for unification, stronger than each of us was alone. I wish for Mapai that it grow in its independence and loyalty to its beginnings; that it grow in its fraternity and comradeship towards us—and then the day of unity will come.

Finally, I would like to say something private and personal. As one of the six members who, together with Remez, Yavnieli, Berl Katznelson, Ben-Gurion and Ben-Zvi, signed on Ahdut Haavoda's first proclamation, I consider myself faithful to that mission in this union of the militant and revolutionary part of the Palestinian labor movement. As such, we shall also build that *Ahdut Haavoda* (Unity of Labor) whose mission it is to be the vanguard of the people and the vanguard of socialism. . . .

(From an address by Yitshak Tabenkin at Founding Congress of Mapam; ibid., p. 29.)

... This union didn't start with the recent negotiations. It is the culmination of an era and the beginning of an era. For long we have been demanding this union and fighting for it, within the Palestine Workers Party (Mapai), with Hashomer Hatsair and with the fears and conservatism within. On the ruins of the Warsaw ghetto this banner was raised again by our comrades, the ghetto fighters. On the day the World War ended we sat down to negotiate union. We had a difficult path. It is in the midst of bitter struggle that we are concluding. The unity of forces, the removal of unnecessary divisions nourished by the past and not needed by the future—are the command of the hour. We are all listening to the pulse of these days.

(From address by L. Levite at the Sixth Council of the L'Ahdut Haavoda–Poale Zion Party, Tel Aviv, Jan. 22, 1948, on the eve of union with the Hashomer Hatsair Party; ibid., pp. 78, 82.)

2. The Party is unified in seeing the historic role of the revolutionary class struggle and of the establishment of a workers' regime to liquidate capitalism and all forms of national and social enslavement, for the establishment of a classless socialist society and a world of international fraternity.

The Party considers itself an inseparable part of the revolutionary labor movement in the war to repel the forces of capitalist-imperialist reaction threatening the peace of the World, and to root out the revelations of fascism, racialism and anti-Semitism; to secure the political and social ascension of the masses of workers; to conquer the key positions in the economy and the state for the working class; to defend the new popular-democratic states and to forge a true alliance with freedom- and peace-loving nations.

The Party will cultivate ties with the revolutionary workers movement in the world and lend its hand to the militant trade union and political international unity of the working class, founded on the national independence of the worker within his people and a firm alliance between the workers of the world and the Soviet Union, the first workers' state, carrying on the great project of socialist construction of our generation and fulfilling the historic mission of the October revolution, the mission of the working class throughout the world.

The Party, combining the values of Jewish and human culture and drawing upon the sources of revolutionary doctrine and the heroic tradition of socialism, will base its activity on educating and teaching the world outlook and the methods of class struggle of Marxism. The Party will persevere in fashioning a Jewish labor culture and in constructing a pioneering and socialist way of life.

On the UN Decision

... In the new political conditions created by the U.N. Decision, the Party will participate with all its strength, despite its basic rejection of the partition solution, in building the Jewish State and defending it.

The Party will demand the fulfillment of the pioneering mission of the State in the realization of Zionism and in filling its functions towards the Jewish people: in securing urgent and free Jewish immigration and its absorption in the country, in the constant development of the settlement enterprises, in reinforcing the defensive force and in uniting the diasporas around Zionist action.

The party will fight for the popular democratic and secular character of the State, for the hegemony of the labor movement in governing it; for the development of the country and agrarian reform; to raise the standard of living of all the inhabitants; for progressive social legislation, to preserve the independence and freedom of organization of the working class and of its political, trade union, economic, social, cultural and educational enterprises. The Party will fight the forces of reaction and aggressive clericalism, to destroy fascism in all its forces— for the achievement of socialism.

The Party will fight for the full equality of rights of all the citizens, Jews and Arabs, and to cultivate relations of cooperation and fraternity between the nations in the State. It will work to promote forces of social liberation within the Arab people and to establish a joint socialist front with the masses of workers, fellaheen and progressive intellectuals within it. . . .

(From the Unity Program, adopted at the Founding Congress of Mapam, ibid., pp. 83-85.)

12 • The Differences Renewed

At the close of the War of Liberation there was room to hope that the new era would be one, if not of peace, then at least of more or less normal relations between Israel and her neighbors. In those years neither Mapam nor Mapai imagined a perspective of permanent tension and the danger of a "second round." Reality, however, worked out otherwise. The days that followed were of "no peace and no war," of economic boycott, infiltrations, threats of vengeance, a race for armaments—a complicated situation and a tense atmosphere. It wasn't easy for a socialist party to maintain a consistent policy of peace in foreign relations and of international fraternity within the State of Israel itself, at the time of military tension and while the country was reinforcing its defensive potential. In their histories, Hashomer Hatsair and Left Poale Zion were equipped to face a test of this kind better than the members of Ahdut Haavoda. Here we find the explanation for the fact that the responses of the L'Ahdut Haavoda members to the complications and tension began to veer more and more toward activism. They did, indeed, continue to support civil equality for the Arab minority within Israel, but were opposed, for the most part, to accepting Arab workers as full members in the Histadrut and to accepting Arabs as members of Mapam, despite the fact that hundreds of Arab workers and intellectuals were knocking at the party's doors. The members of L'Ahdut Haavoda wanted to solve the problem of these Arabs (who were organized within the Arab section of Mapam) by setting up an independent national party of Arab workers that would only be affiliated federatively to the Jewish Mapam. Hashomer Hatsair and Left Poale Zion, on the other hand, wanted a territorial Histadrut and workers' party (that is, to accept Arab members, too, into these socialist-Zionist organizations).

In the days when the inter-bloc "cold war" was beginning and the Soviet Union's attitude toward the State of Israel had deteriorated so far as to return to the anti-Zionist positions of pre-World War II days, the enthusiasm and sympathy for the U.S.S.R. began to wane. These had been quite widespread among large parts of the working public who remembered the historic war of the Red Army, its decisive share in defeating fascism and saving the remnants of European Jewry, the "Gromyko Declaration," the large Jewish immigration from the popular democracies, and the help they gave in arms and volunteers when the State was established. Within the ranks of Mapam, too, two different approaches began to stand out clearly: Poale Zion, Hashomer Hatsair, and some L'Ahdut Haavoda members had a long tradition of a fundamentally positive attitude to the October revolution and of looking upon the Soviet Union as the natural center of the militant international working class, even when its regime showed increasing signs of deterioration that demanded serious and open criticism, and even when the Soviet Union had a distorted view of the Jewish question and the Israeli territorial solution for it. For this reason, despite the bitter disappointment in the temporariness of the "Gromyko Declaration days," the movement's fundamental socialist positions were not shaken.

On the other hand, many of the members of Ahdut Haavoda did not agree with the character of the "balanced and qualified" criticism of the U.S.S.R. by the other part of Mapam.

Throughout their years of public activity the members of L'Ahdut Haavoda had served in key positions in the Hagana, Palmach, Histadrut, Hechalutz, etc. Even after their departure from Mapai, this situation did not change all at once, although Mapai did everything it could to remove them from these positions at the first opportunity. However, during the War of Liberation and more so after its culmination, this process of displacement was stepped up and almost completed.[1] At first, the members of Ahdut Haavoda tended to respond to these acts with ill-considered emotion and it was only with difficulty that the party institutions rejected their demand that the Mapam Ministers resign from the Provisional Government. They were unable, however, to accustom themselves to an extended situation of being in the opposition, or of being a discriminated-against minority far from the focus of power.

In the elections to the Constituent Assembly in 1949, Mapam emerged as the second party, after Mapai (Mapai, 46 delegates out of 120; Mapam, 19). The two parties, with 65 delegates between them, had a clear majority in the Knesset. Ben-Gurion, however, preferred to set up a broad coalition by compromising with the bourgeois and clerical parties and opposed any previous agreement or permanent cooperation between the two workers' parties within the Government. Mapam, which had been represented in the Provisional Government by two Ministers (Mordehai Bentov, Minister of Labor; Avraham Zisling, Minister of Agriculture)

---

1. We can mention here two of the more dramatic examples. Yisrael Galili, who was one of the heads of the Kibbutz Hameuchad, L'Ahdut Haavoda and later, of Mapam, served as head of the National Command of the Hagana, and afterwards of Zahal. The then Minister of Defense, David Ben-Gurion, compelled him to resign in May 1948, at least partly because of the conflict between Mapai and Mapam. (Today Galili is a Minister in the Israeli Government and one of the heads of the Labor Party.) In November 1948, even before the conclusion of the War of Liberation, Ben-Gurion also disbanded the Palmach staff which was headed by General Yigal Allon, also one of the leaders of Hakibbutz Hameuchad, L'Ahdut Haavoda and Mapam, on the grounds that with the establishment of the State and Zahal, there was no longer any need for the separate existence of the Palmach or of any "party army." (Today Yigal Allon is Foreign Minister, Deputy Premier, and one of the heads of the Labor Party.)

voted by a decisive majority not to join a coalition of this kind, and this decision was taken with the agreement of most of L'Ahdut Haavoda delegates to the Party Council. They, however, did not believe that Ben-Gurion could maintain a government without Mapam and thought that the party's days as an opposition in the Knesset would be no more than a short and passing episode. As their stay away from government lengthened, their patience ended and they began to exert increasing pressure to join the government almost unconditionally. They turned the matter of *participating in the coalition into a sanctified principle,* supposedly serving as the touchstone and trademark of pioneering constructivism and Zionist responsibility. Relations between Hashomer Hatsair and L'Ahdut Haavoda continued to grow sharper since Hashomer Hatsair, though it felt it to be both a privilege and an obligation to take part in the Israeli government and did not make a principle of opposition, being very careful in every decision in this direction, was still very far from making a principle of participating in the government and vigorously refused to consider this participation the test of pioneering Zionist constructivism. It insisted on keeping its freedom of maneuverability and liberty to decide by carefully studying the circumstances and the possibilities of continuing the struggle effectively.

There were, therefore, increasingly strong differences between the recently united movements on three important issues: Jewish-Arab relations, the attitude toward the Soviet Union, and participation in the government, and these affected the process of ideological, social and organizational integration of the two sections of which Mapam was composed, each with its own tradition and mentality. When the united party had been established, the existence of "movement sections" had been recognized as a transitory necessity on the way to full integration. However, as these differences deepened, the "sections" stopped being mere remnants of the past and turned into permanent and organized factions. The L'Ahdut Haavoda section, which actually formed only a minority within the united party, and whose members often were divided among themselves in the parity-composed party institutions, began to demand "sectional discipline" of its representatives and to look upon the party as a kind of permanent federation divided equally between the factions, without the right to take any important decisions by majority vote—that is, that the minority section had the right of veto. This trend within the L'Ahdut Haavoda section naturally had its countertrend within the Hashomer Hatsair section, which also felt compelled to insist more on appearing united in discussions and decisions.

The view of the party as an intersection federation and the demand for the minority's right of veto were the results of deepening political differences and of the L'Ahdut Haavoda section's fear of "disintegrating" and turning from an equal partner in the present into a minority in the near or more distant future. This position, however, was also related to the general traditional conceptions within L'Ahdut Haavoda (and its predecessor, Siah Bet) on the organizational questions of the socialist-Zionist party, views which fundamentally opposed any centralism in executive bodies and considered the factional structure of the broad party as almost natural. They had once fought for this concept within Mapai, and they continued to fight for it in Mapam. Now this fundamental organizational concept, mistaken as it was, crystallized even more and became more inflexible and extreme than ever.

The "Unity Front" and the Second Congress

As Mapam's Second Congress, which was supposed to formulate the Party Program and its organizational statutes, drew closer, fronts were formed on the following lines:

The former Hashomer Hatsair, most of the former Left Poale Zion, most of the former "Hebrew communists," a small minority of L'Ahdut Haavoda in the cities and among the new immigrants, as well as some personalities who had joined the united party as "individuals" (General Yitzhak Sadeh, Dr. Moshe Sneh, and others), formed the "Front for Party Unity," which was headed by the former Hashomer Hatsair leaders, Meir Yaari and Yaakov Hazan,[2] and former Left Poale Zion leader, Yitzhak Yitzhaki.

This was confronted by the L'Ahdut Haavoda section and a minority of the Left Poale Zion, called the Erem Group,[3] with only the question of accepting the Arab comrades into the party ranks dividing these two permanent allies.

In the elections to the Congress, in which each of the three groups campaigned with its own program, 564 delegates of the Unity Front were elected, 329 delegates of L'Ahdut Haavoda, and 44 members of the Erem Group. The Congress represented 47,000 members in 200 branches. It adopted the Party Program (the "Haifa Program") partly unanimously and partly by a majority vote. The formation of the organizational statute was left to a special session of the Party Council which was supposed to convene after some time and ratify the statute by authorization of the Congress. The minority's protests and threats notwithstanding, it was decided that in the future, until the eventual integration and disappear-

---

2. Yaakov Hazan, the leader of the Mapam Knesset group, was one of the outstanding founders and leaders of Kibbutz Ha'artzi and the Hashomer Hatsair Workers' Party.

3. The Erem Group included most of the veteran leaders of the World Union of Left Poale Zion (see Chapter 6), among them Moshe Erem, Yaakov Zerubavel, Nahum Nir, and others. Though this group was the permanent ally of the L'Ahdut Haavoda section in most of the disputed issues, it agreed with the Unity Front in supporting the acceptance of Arab members into the ranks of the Histadrut and the party.

ance of the sections, party organizations would be constituted according to the balance of forces of the Congress, and no longer by parity as heretofore. The minority protested in the course of the Congress debate and voted against a whole list of resolutions which were adopted by the majority. Concerning two of these, however, the minority stated that these were two situations that were matters of principle and conscience and on which it could not accept any decision. The *one* would be any attempt to implement the resolution in principle to turn Mapam into a territorial party by accepting the members of the Arab section of Mapam into full membership in the party; the *second,* an attempt by the Party Council, which had been given the task of formulating the organizational statutes, to compel the minority to accept the abrogation of the sections, what the spokesmen for L'Ahdut Haavoda and the Erem Group labeled "Hashomer Hatsair's attempt to take over the whole party."

SOURCES

1. The process of territorial concentration of the Jewish people in Palestine, the state character of Jewish life in Israel, the new status of the Jewish community as a nation deciding the economic, social, political and cultural development of the State of Israel, the problems of the existence and future of the Arab national minority, the national and social struggle for liberation of the Jewish people returning to the country and the masses of the Arab people living in it, their life in common, the unity of the class struggle of the Jewish and Arab workers in Israel—all these will inevitably lead, as has also been proven by the experience of the revolutionary labor movement throughout the world, to the establishment of the workers' organizations in Israel as territorial organizaitons, in whose ranks all the workers of Israel will find their place, without national distinctions, on the basis of international solidarity and of the satisfaction of their specific needs and just national aspirations.

2. The United Workers Party, striving for leadership in the State of Israel, the Jewish people and among the Jewish and Arab workers, must by ideological and political consolidation develop into a territorial party of the working class as a whole, serving as a faithful expression for both the processes of national territorial concentration of the Jewish people and the establishment of Jewish-Arab relations in Israel on the basis of international workers' solidarity.

3. While preserving the Histadrut's functions in immigration, absorption and integration, in construction, the "Hechalutz," education and settlement, combined with workers' trade union struggle, the United Workers Party will struggle to open the gates of the Histadrut immediately to every Arab worker and laborer as members with equal rights.

(From the Mapam Program adopted at the Second Congress, Haifa, May 30–June 4, 1951, published by Mapam, Tel Aviv, 1951.)

... The debate with the "Front" over turning our party into a territorial party of Jews and Arabs had been brought up here. True, the Leninist parties are built territorially, but those parties at the same time also say Jewish assimilation. So long as the Jews are an extraterritorial nation and do not rule their own country, no Zionist party can be a Jewish-Arab territorial party. The Founding Program expressly said: "a revolutionary Zionist party combining class struggle and construction of the country." There was no doubt that a decision on a different party character would exclude those who think that the territorial concentration of the people from all the diasporas of the world requires a party whose Jewish Zionist character is stressed, undisguised. The time for an Israeli territorial party will certainly come, but this will only happen as a result of concentrating millions more Jews in the country, at the time when most of our people will have gathered together in its country. My remarks do not imply any denial of the Zionism of those who are for a territorial party, but the party would not be able to serve as a tool for the fulfillment of this Zionism, since it would no longer be an expression of world Jewry, but a domestic party, the property of all the inhabitants of the territory, at present, and expressing their immediate limited interests, without the Zionist perspective. . . .

(From an article by Y. Tabenkin, "In Defense of our Spirit," *Mibefnm* 2–3, Vol. 18, pp. 101–103, February 1951. This was presented as a resolution by the L'Ahdut Haavoda section within Mapam.)

The party sees the vital need of establishing a revolutionary socialist party among the Arab workers which would recognize the right of the Jewish people to territorial concentration in Eretz Israel and the national and class mission of the United Workers Party and which would be joined by a federative alliance to the United Workers Party. . . .

(From the Bar-Yehuda, Y. Galili, O. Livshitz Resolution in "Towards the Congress of the United Workers Party: Theses for Discussion," published by Mapam, Tel Aviv, 1951.)

If we try to evaluate Mapam's Second Congress according to its place in party history and by the events that took place after the Congress and up to the split, we would have to say that, on the one hand, it demonstrated the growing strength and influence of Hashomer Hatsair and its allies within the party as a whole; on the other hand, it was precisely the signs of this fact and of the approaching acceptance of the Arab members into the ranks of the party, as well as of the end of the fixed sections, that united the ranks of the minority and spurred it to complete its own factional organization—a sort of party within the party, with its own discipline, consultations and institutions. Thus, while the Second Congress gave a clear majority within the party ranks, institutions, and most of the branches to Hashomer Hatsair and its allies of the Unity Front, it also pointed to the failure of the goal of the First Congress—the integration of the uniting forces and the consolidation of a single party.

In this context it may be worthwhile in retrospect to evaluate not only the Second Congress but also the establishment and campaign of the Unity Front before, during, and after the Congress.

1. The Front for the Unity of the Party was set up, according to the intentions of most of its founders, as a means of defense against the process of factional consolidation of the L'Ahdut Haavoda section, and its expressed desire was to turn the united party into a federation of factions giving the minority the right of veto, an aim that threatened to doom the party to stagnation and paralysis from within and to strangle it on the outside. However, after the situation became one of an intersectional struggle for power in the party, the Front's justified demands and motives were not sufficient to prevent mistakes and an escalating series of steps on both sides, as a kind of chain reaction.

2. The establishment of the Front was indeed preceded by the consolidation within the L'Ahdut Haavoda section, but its success in winning a clear majority helped to accelerate this process within L'Ahdut Haavoda and to bring it to completion. It also led those members of L'Ahdut Haavoda, whose hearts weren't in the progressing factional consolidation and polarization, to despair of any hopes of influencing the shaping of Mapam's character and of transmitting some of their own positions and specific movement values to the party as a whole.

3. Precisely because of the Front's success, on the eve of and during the Congress, in guaranteeing itself a convincing majority in the urban branches which were less specifically defined than those in the kibbutzim, many members of the Front began to identify the party as a whole with the Front itself. Its successes in the branches, among the new immigrants and others, seemed to many to outweigh L'Ahdut Haavoda and the Kibbutz Meuchad's growing internal estrangement in the party. It was, however, undoubtedly a fundamental mistake to look upon the L'Ahdut Haavoda faction as only a deviationist and bothersome minority and no more, and not as one of the two essential forces within Mapam, a *fundamental element*, which, as far as the party's character was concerned, couldn't have any "numerical" substitute. There were thus more than a few members of the Front who began to forget that it was a Front for Party Unity and not the party itself.

4. It is not surprising that these circumstances encouraged the growth of sectarian leftist approaches and views on the fringes of the Front. Afterwards it was to become clear that the Front's existence and mistakes made it possible for Moshe Sneh and his colleagues—people who were as far removed as possible from Mapam's fundamental idea of integrating pioneering Zionism and revolutionary socialism—to disguise themselves and hide their real views behind the smoke screen of the struggle "For Mapam and against the L'Ahdut Haavoda deviation."[4]

4. See below.

5. Here, another, more fundamental question arises: for any union to have prospects of success it must be based on at least a minimum of political and ideological proximity. The closer the uniting groups are to identity in views, the closer the unification program, ideological and political, can come to something like a maximum program; on the other hand, a broad union of groups that are fairly close to each other and yet divided in their views must necessarily be based on a minimum program, both ideologically and organizationally.

The main question, therefore, is what conclusions the members of the Unity Front should have drawn when it became increasingly evident that they were mistaken in the hope of drawing the sting of the traditional differences and of the existence of a close identity of ideology. At that time they hoped that by means of ideological struggle and influence, within the patterns of democratic debate, it would be possible to arrest the expanding centrifugal trends and, despite everything, to fulfill the vision of the "single and revolutionary party" at the time of the unification. Today, the question is whether it wasn't a mistake and a lack of realism when they continued to conduct themselves within the party, *even after the radical changes that had taken place since the unification, as if nothing had really changed.* At the time of the unification and in the days that followed, they had justly desired a party that would be united ideologically, socially and organizationally, but perhaps they should have asked themselves once more whether a looser, less consistent and effective basis—ideologically and organizationally—was not preferable to the tragic dismemberment of the pioneering leftist union as a whole.

Ultra-leftist Unrest in the Unity Front

After the Second Congress the party entered a period of growing division and mutual suspicion: fears of Hashomer Hatsair domination and attempts by the minority to exert pressure and threats to leave the party, and countless efforts by the majority to prevent the split, despite the paralysis of the present in order to save the historic prospects of the future. On the other hand, simultaneously increasing ultra-leftist sectarian tendencies within the ranks of the Front detracted a great deal of the efficacy of these efforts. This situation became more critical after the results of the Knesset elections toward the end of 1951, when Mapam lost four of its nineteen seats in the First Knesset, both because of unfavorable external conditions and because of the internal dissension and paralysis. In the light of the results the members of L'Ahdut Haavoda and the Erem Group decided that they had to save the party from "insufficient Zionist activity and sectarian degeneration" by joining the new government at any cost. They had apparently tired of being an opposition minority within an oppositionary minority party. After long and arduous negotiations with Mapai, and after conscientious and responsible consideration, the majority found itself unable to yield to the minority's pressure and voted against joining the government. And so, from the spring of 1952, internal party tension increased sevenfold.

The disappointment over the election results and the dissatisfaction over the *party* paralysis within the party caused by the permanent veto and threats of secession by L'Ahdut Haavoda and the Erem Group may be seen among the causes of the growing ultra-leftist unrest within the ranks of the Front. This unrest now infected the party cadres in the city, some of the new immigrants and young kibbutz members, including even some of the central personalities within Hashomer Hatsair. The ultra-leftists did not understand, or at any rate did not accept, the reasons for the patience displayed by Meir Yaari, Yaakov Hazan, and Yitzhak Yitzhaki, nor their efforts to explore all the possibilities of avoiding a split. They didn't share the care taken by the "historic leadership" to prepare the rank and file, especially in the kibbutz branches, and to leave them without the shadow of a doubt that if, after all, the split did take place, the majority had done everything it could to preserve unity.

It was their responsibility to maintain the unity and spiritual wholeness of the movement, something which was more important than any momentary considerations of profit or loss. When the ultra-leftists' demand for a "strong hand" vis-à-vis the minority was not accepted, they began to charge the leadership openly with "centrism," with an "alliance with the right against the left," and with being too considerate of some central members of Hashomer Hatsair who had always been against the unremitting battle against Mapai and inflexibility toward the L'Ahdut Haavoda within Mapam. However, although in the revolutionary workers' parties in other countries leftist deviations are generally reflected in sectarian actions leading to various tactical, political and organizational mistakes (which are bad enough) in the socialist-Zionist picture, in view of the hostile attitude of the Soviet Union and the Communist movement to Zionism, including all the parties and wings of socialist Zionism, there is always the danger that ultra-leftism will go beyond its emotional shortsightedness or mistaken judgment on problems *within* socialist Zionism and may be infected, or make it easier to be infected, by liquidationary tendencies toward socialist Zionism in general. An ultra-leftist deviation within a socialist-Zionist party may therefore remain only a sectarian infantile sickness, but it can also slide far down the slope of liquidation.

Hashomer Hatsair's traditional attitude toward the Soviet Union was based on the principled support of the October revolution, the proletarian dictatorship and socialist construction in the U.S.S.R., while rejecting the path of the Comintern and leveling severe criticism both against Soviet policy toward the Jewish national minority in the U.S.S.R., toward the Zionist movement and the Jewish community in Palestine, and against the signs of the degeneration that had attacked the Soviet proletarian dictatorship, such as the Moscow trials in the second half of the '30s. This balanced posture began to change toward greater stress on solidarity and identification, toward giving greater trust and reducing criticism to a minimum, during the Russian-German war, when the greater share of the struggle to defeat fascism was placed on the Red Army, when the fate of all mankind hinged upon the results of this struggle.

In those years the members of Hashomer Hatsair hoped that with the defeat of fascism and the removal of the permanent threat of intervention, when the Soviet Union freed itself of the imperialist siege and the necessity to achieve socialism in one country, conditions would ripen to make it possible to correct the mistakes and distortions in Soviet policy. They hoped that its attitude toward the international labor movement, and also toward Jews, Zionism, and Palestine would change. They expected the dictatorship of the proletariate to return to the purity of its early Leninist days and make greater progress toward socialist democracy. These weren't only pious wishes but a forecast and hope based on such important and meaningful phenomena as the disbanding of the Comintern, the establishment of the united Trade Union International, the formation of the "popular democratic" states with the stress on their following a path that was independent and different from that of the Soviet Union. Then there was the historic "Gromyko Declaration," the support given by the Soviet Union and the popular democracies to the young State of Israel's first steps and struggle for existence on the international forum, in supplying arms and training volunteers, in opening the gates of the popular democracies to mass Jewish immigration, etc.

> ... Closing one sixth of the continent to unrestrained capitalist exploitation, the efforts toward building a socialist economy, a plan, on a high level of technical development ... its influence, by its very existence, as a lighthouse lighting the darkness of the suffering workers' life throughout the capitalist system ... all these turn Russia into one of the most important factors deepening the present crisis. ...
>
> ... The Comintern's inability to guide the masses of workers towards the victory of socialism has been made clear, because of:
>
> - The falsification of the principle of proletarian dictatorship reflected in its inability to adapt it to the economic situation of the central capitalist countries and in the danger of bureaucratic degeneration within the U.S.S.R.
>
> - Complete denial of the need to adapt the class struggle to the concrete conditions of every specific country, something that finds its expression in the bureaucratization and centralization eroding the national and international structure of the Comintern;

- The destructive tactics of the Comintern in the colonies.
- Its narrow-minded party politics, most strongly and shamefully expressed in the split in trade union organization that forms the cornerstone of workers' organization and strength.
- The mobilization of the main forces, even in light of the terrible danger of fascism, for war against other workers' parties.
- Denying the national interests of the pauperized Jewish masses, reflected in the criminal war of the Comintern against the liberating Zionist enterprise . . .
> (From the resolutions of the Fourth Enlarged Council of the Kibbutz Ha'artzi, Hadera, Jan. 25, 1933, in "Resolutions and Summations—1927–1935," pp. 41–42, Mishmar Haemek, 1935.)

. . . If the vicious circle of building socialism in one country under conditions of siege is broken, if the proletarian dictatorship regime will succeed in widening its sphere and if Hitler is defeated in the Russian spaces and the nightmare of the danger of intervention is removed for a long time, then the dictatorship will move towards its gradual liquidation and step after step will make way for socialist democracy. The fulfillment of socialism will then go forward with giant steps. We are sure that the war front will forge the second generation of the revolution like steel . . .
> (From Meir Yaari, "The Opening of an Era," theses prepared for the Kibbutz Ha'artzi Council at Mishmar Haemek, April 1942, pp. 51–52; Merhavia, 1942.)

To Hashomer Hatsair's great disappointment, only a few years passed after the end of World War II and the Cold War began and brought an end to most of the hopes, froze at their very start all the positive processes which had begun to appear at the end of World War II and in the early years afterwards. The dictatorship became an even harsher one, the signs of degeneration that had appeared even earlier now were multiplied, and Soviet policy returned to the sectarian positions in the international labor movement and its traditional militant anti-Zionism, leading to the suppression and ultimate liquidation of the remnants of national and cultural autonomy for the Soviet Jews, while physically annihilating its spiritual leadership.[5]

Today we can say, looking back, that when it became clear that the Cold War was not only a brief and transient episode but a protracted era, the objective bases for our hopes began to disappear and we therefore should have returned, as early as the first half of the '50s, to our original position regarding the Soviet Union, based on a balance between support

---

5. At the end of 1948, the Jewish Anti-Fascist Committee, which had taken the place of the Yevsektsia during World War II, was disbanded. Its organ *Einigkeit* ceased publication and the *Emes* (Yiddish publishing company) ceased activity. Almost all the Yiddish writers and many of the members of this Committee were arrested. At the beginning of the '50s, dozens were executed and the rest sent to labor camps.

and criticism. If a re-examination, a new analysis and summation of the objective processes and our subjective hopes was not made then (and was only done some years later, between 1954–1957), this fact finds its main explanation in the following two reasons:

The first is the natural interval between objective events and changes and their reflection in subjective consciousness, always lagging behind the objective facts themselves. In other words: it is easier to forecast the limits and transactions from one historic stage to another, or to understand them afterwards, than to distinguish them in the course of the struggle. In addition, it is difficult for fighters and dreamers to abandon the hopes and assumptions that were reasonable and correct at an earlier stage, when they must become accustomed to the idea that their hopes have been disappointed and their assumptions refuted, and a re-examination, a new analysis and new conclusions are needed.

The second is the fact that the intersectional conflict within the united Mapam, precisely during that first half of the fifties, certainly didn't create the proper atmosphere needed for taking stock and re-examining problems and conclusions to be drawn from the evident changes.

In any case, this re-examination of attitude toward the Soviet Union was not done at the proper time and this helped the leftist unrest.

During the beginning of the 1950s many of the ultra-leftists within Mapam refused to come to terms with the deteriorating relations among the Soviet Union, the Popular democracies, and the world Communist movement on the one hand, and the State of Israel and the Zionist movement, including Mapam, on the other. They considered it so important to stop this fatal process that they tried to explain it unilaterally only or mainly by the sins of the Israeli government's pro-Western policies, innocently believing that "moderating" Zionist terminology, weakening the ties to the Zionist organization (or at least not participating in its executive bodies), even more vigorous opposition to Ben-Gurion's policies, as well as an even more aggressive struggle against L'Ahdut Haavoda and for a revolutionary party worthy of the name, in combination, would help Mapam counteract the process of deteriorating relations between the "world of revolution" and Mapam. Removing the divisions between us and the world of revolution had been put in the Haifa program as an ultimate goal whose attainment depended upon a whole series of conditions, and especially the socialist world's recognition of our full rights to build our enterprise and to choose our socialist-Zionist path. This formulation was now interpreted by the impatient ultra-leftists as an immediate political goal whose impending fulfillment depended merely upon us. In order to achieve this, they claimed that we had to diminish the differences between us and that world, first of all by limiting our differences with the "world of revolution" to the Israeli Zionist sphere alone.

Some of the ultra-leftists did not allow this trend to bring them to the readiness to give up Zionism, pioneering and the kibbutz; there were others, however, for whom, in the course of time, the desire for "integration with the communist world" overcame all restraints and by classifying and limiting their devotion to socialist Zionism, began to mount the liquidationist path. While the ultra-leftists within the leadership of Hashomer Hatsair generally belonged to the first group, the second group, which allowed its ultra-leftism to lead to liquidationism, was represented by Dr. Moshe Sneh, and some of the veteran members of Siah Bet in Mapai who had also left the L'Ahdut Haavoda–Poale Zion and come via Hashomer Hatsair to Mapam, where they belonged to the Unity Front. They also included some Left Poale Zionists among the new immigrants and some dozens of members of younger kibbutzim. However, no matter what their subjective motivations and the ultimate personal and political paths of the ultra-leftists, they all had the same single objective result: at a time when the tragic events, which we will discuss in the next chapter, weakened Hashomer Hatsair and its allies, the ultra-leftism on the fringe of the Unity Front worked to help those within the L'Ahdut Haavoda and the Erem Group who had determined to set up a separate factional organization within Mapam. By pointing at the ultra-leftists and quoting their doubtful comments and formulations and identifying them with the Unity Front as a whole, they succeeded in frightening the rank and file and in convincing them that they had to organize in order to "save the party from the danger of ultra-leftism and liquidationism." Some of the ultra-leftists may perhaps have honestly wanted to serve as a "vanguard within the vanguard" and to spur the Unity Front as a whole to a more vigorous struggle with L'Ahdut Haavoda. Actually, they achieved the very opposite; on the one hand, the L'Ahdut Haavoda section grew stronger with the help of the supposedly ultra-leftist fermentation within the Front; on the other hand, the growing ultra-leftists deeply disturbed the leadership and many of the rank and file and cadres of the Hashomer Hatsair kibbutzim and the urban branches because of its possible effects on the integrity of the movement as a whole.

13 • The Prague Trials—Split in Mapam

Toward the end of 1952, one of the leaders of Hashomer Hatsair and Mapam, Mordehai Oren, was arrested in Prague, implicated in the Slansky Trials, and charged with spying for Western intelligence. On that occasion charges of espionage were hurled at the World Zionist Organization and the State of Israel, as well as against Mapam, Oren's party. These fantastic charges and libels against one of the veteran leaders of the pioneering left in the Israeli labor movement evoked a storm within the Hashomer Hatsair kibbutzim and in Mapam as a whole. What is more, the unrestrained attacks, libels and incitement against Zionism and Israel, accompanied by openly anti-Semitic comments in the Prague court and the Czechoslovakian press, shocked Jews everywhere, both in the Diaspora and in Israel. Politically, however, this was a blow especially to those who had hoped for relaxation in the Soviet-Israeli tension and expected improvements in the relationship between the world of revolution and Mapam in the near future.

The blow was a heavy one for the party, but it was particularly hard on L'Ahdut Haavoda, whose former sympathy for the Soviet Union—based more on sentiment than on principles—rapidly disappeared. The Prague trial was absolutely catastrophic, however, for the ultra-leftists. All their rosy hopes of a close integration in the "world of revolution" exploded. Many of the ultra-leftists felt themselves to be facing an ultimatum like the one the Comintern, in the early '20s, had posed for the Left Poale Zionists: to choose, each on his own, between two worlds. Here some of the ultra-leftists found themselves departed with no retreat and rapidly took the decline of liquidationism. Some of the ultra-leftists at first looked at the Front's, or more precisely, the party's reaction to Oren's arrest and the libels of the Prague judges through the prism of interparty struggle. They found additional proof of coddling of the left in the resolution that was worded so that L'Ahdut Haavoda could accept it. Even though they, for their part, did not believe in Prague's charges against Oren, Zionism or Israel, they still argued over the wording of the resolution, desiring to tone down criticism of the trial, except for its anti-Zionist and anti-Mapam aspects and of those behind it. They also tried as much as possible to hedge their solidarity with the Zionist organization, and were afraid of joining the anti-Soviet chorus, and of the Unity Front's rightward trend toward a reconciliation with L'Ahdut Haavoda.

The Unity Front did not accept the ultra-leftist criticism, and the party council, by a majority of 232 to 49, with 18 abstentions, adopted the resolution expressing solidarity with Oren, defending the progressive character of Zionism, and severely criticizing the instigators of the Prague trial.

> ... The charges levelled against Zionism at the Prague trial are groundless. Zionism is the movement for national and social liberation of the Jewish people. The State of Israel came into being as the product of this liberation movement, organized now for a generation as the Zionist Organization, of which we are an organic part and participate in its Executive. We are struggling to maintain and reinforce the World Zionist Organization that is mobilizing all the sections and classes of our people for the construction of the country, to defend its popular character and democratic structure, to strengthen the national funds and intensify the participation and help of the Jews of the Diaspora in strengthening the State, to expand the development projects and absorption of immigration, to cultivate a movement of volunteering, education and pioneer training among Jewish youth; to mobilize the progressive forces among the Jewish people for aid to the workers' enterprise, and to guarantee the progressive character of the Jewish renaissance and Jewish culture in the country.
> ... Mapam is struggling against the reactionary trends showing their signs within the Zionist movement and against using its name and authority for policies contradicting its nature and progressive mission. The presence of such trends does not give anyone the right to besmirch the progressive content of the liberation movement of the Jewish people, just as the progressive contents of other liberation movements are not denied because of the presence of a reactionary section within them. . . Under no circumstances can a transitory official policy be identified with the essence of the national liberation movement that is striving for national renaissance, for territorial concentration and to build a homeland—a movement of which Mapam is the loyal vanguard. . . .
> Mapam reiterates that according to the best of its knowledge our comrade, Mordehai Oren, who worked on its mission, is innocent of any crime. We are convinced of the purity of his intentions and we cannot conceive of the possibility of malicious activity against the Czechoslovak Republic. Even after what was said at the Prague trial we are sure that only an accidental combination of tragic circumstances led to the charges levelled against Mordehai Oren and we hope for his speedy return to the homeland. . . .
> (From the resolution of the Mapam Council, "Al Hamishmar," Dec. 26, 1952.)

Now not only the leadership of Hashomer Hatsair and of the Unity Front, but also some of the ultra-leftists themselves clearly saw the liquidationist character of the group centered around Moshe Sneh, which in the past had attempted to appear as sentinels of Mapam's ideological purity, at a time when it was really rejecting Mapam's fundamental concept of the synthesis between pioneering Zionism and revolutionary socialism. Now Sneh and his colleagues found themselves isolated, when their former comrades in ultra-leftism remained loyal to Zionism and pioneering and separated from them. Sneh and his comrades attempted to form their liquidationist faction within Mapam (the "Left Section") but this was banned by the party institutions in January 1953. The Left Section refused to disband and Sneh and his comrades were expelled from the ranks of Mapam and established a new organization of their own: the "Socialist Left Party in Israel," which maintained a close united front with Maki.

> The World Zionist Organization and the World Jewish Congress, whose activity is coordinated with the regime prevailing in the State of Israel, endeavor to harness the Jewish people to the imperialist chariot—in absolute conflict with its vital interests, and they serve as tools of the Jewish bourgeoisie, tied to American and British finance capital. The Party therefore opposes participation in the World Zionist Organization and the World Jewish Congress....
> ... The united front of the "Socialist Left" and the Communists will serve as the beginning and foundation for the militant unity of the working class and a broad Israeli popular front. Because of the differences in the historic development of the new parties and their attitudes to the problems of territorial concentration, the question of the unity of the two parties is not on the agenda. However, the two parties are in single common camp—the camp of peace, progress and socialism conducting a historic and fateful struggle throughout the world and in Israel against the war camp, reaction and imperialism. The establishment of the united front between them is therefore necessary and pressing.
> (From the Founding Program of the Socialist Left Party in Israel, March 1953, in "Sources for the History of the Labor Movement in Palestine," Merhavia, p. 78.)

A year and a half later, when the Left Party finally joined Maki, this last logical step met little opposition. Some of its members hesitated to join the openly militant anti-Zionist Maki; some of them abandoned politics, while others looked for a way back to Mapam.[7]

However, even the expulsion of Moshe Sneh and his group from the

---

1. On January 15, 1972, some weeks before his death, Mosh Sneh tried to explain his policy and tactics in his testament:

> I had good reason to believe that it would be possible to stabilize and to strengthen the friendship of the Soviet Union with Israel of the years 1945-1950 (and I knew she would be present in our region as an influential factor), but not on the basis of the Zionist ideology that contradicts the Marxist-Leninist world concept, as conceived by its official interpreters, but on the basis of the practical conclusions, such as immigration, settlement (development), defence, independence, etc. I was trying to go this road, and I said to myself: if I succeed, my whole people will be grateful to me, and if I fail, I shall ask nobody to be partner in my failure. The only thing I regret is that I went too far in denying Zionism totally—which is unjustifiable, neither in theory nor in practice, from no serious aspect whatsoever. This I repent.

(From "Moshe Sneh's political testament," published in "Israel at Peace," No. 4, Organ of the Communist Party of Israel-MAKI, Tel Aviv, April 1972) ranks of Mapam did not close the ultra-leftist episode within the Kibbutz Ha'artzi of Hashomer Hatsair. On the one hand, the subversion by Sneh's supporters within some of the younger kibbutzim had to be stopped; on the other, the ideological debate had to be continued with those members who had not gone as far as Zionist liquidationism and had separated themselves from Sneh and his group, but who still hadn't revised their ultra-leftist differences on the questions of integration (in the Communist world) and on preserving the integrity of Mapam, as well as leftist criticism or Hashomer Hatsair's ideological road. The thorough and extended discussions conducted in all the kibbutzim concluded with the expulsion of the Snehites and with the Kibbutz Ha'artzi's almost total support of its leadership. The ideological discussions were summed up in Meir Yaari's theses to the Kibbutz Ha'artzi Council at Givat Haviva: "Ingathering of Exiles in the Mirror of our Times" (1954). In the chapter on the "Sorry Affair," in addition to debating the question of integration and the internal situation of the party, Yaari also went into two theoretical problems: leftist criticism of the synthesis between pioneering Zionism and revolutionary socialism and Borochov's national theory and its critics.

Even when Sneh was still in the party, many of the ultra-leftists had argued that there was no room to talk of a "synthesis," since such a synthesis implied an *equivalence*, whereas the proper relation of Zionism to socialism should, in their view, be that of a part to the whole. In their eyes Zionism was only one clause in the local program of world socialism. This attack on the equivalence between our inseparably combined historic missions, and the attempt to replace the theory of the synthesis with the theory of the "part and the whole," were what led Sneh inexorably to the clause in the program of his "Party of the Left" which said that "the Party rejects any possibility of a synthesis between socialism and any nationalist ideology, and therefore also between socialism and Zionism. The theory of scientific socialism, the compass for the emancipation of the working class, is also the compass for the emancipation of the peoples, and our people among them, from imperialism." The attack on equivalence and on the concept of "synthesis" developed logically, therefore, into an attack on Zionism itself. These members, who separated themselves from Sneh and disagreed with his liquidationist views, also had to differ with his starting point and to return without reservation to the fundamental idea of Hashomer Hatsair and Mapam: *the full and inseparable integration of pioneering Zionism and revolutionary socialism.*

The debate over Borochov's theory and the corrections which had to be made in light of historic experience since it was first formulated at the beginning of the century was interesting and important in itself. However, the main argument of the ultraleftists had been that Borochov hadn't limited himself to a Marxist analysis of the Jewish anomaly and of the processes working toward territorial concentration in Palestine, but had gone into "foreign territory" in trying to find a Marxist definition for "people," "nation," "conditions of production" and the like, so that the general definitions would fit the extraterritorial Jewish nationality. Though the ultra–leftists (or at least some of them) were compelled to differ with the erroneous assumptions and conclusions of the Marxist and Leninist classicists concerning the Jewish question and its Palestine solution, they denied any right to criticize or to add to the general doctrines of the "world of revolution" including the definition of "nation." It was enough for them that they had to differ with the "world of revolution" (in which they hoped we were very shortly to integrate) on our own specific problems, and they did not want to widen the debate and to increase the divisions by doubts, criticisms and "pretentious" innovations in the field of the general and official theory of that world.

It was this point that was stressed by many of the ultra-leftists when they criticized Borochov's national theory and defended the definition of a nation as enunciated by Stalin. In this manner, these two theoretical discussions of "synthesis" and "Borochov's national theory" merged in the great debate over "immediate integration" (in the Communist world) and became the movement's criteria for the acceptance, in practice as well as in theory, of the "right to a different path to socialism" and the "Israeli path to socialism."

SOURCES

> *Stalin*: "A nation is a stable community, formed in history, of language, territory, economic life and a psychological particularity revealed in a common culture."
> *Borochov*: "A nation is a group of people which has come into being historically, with a common past, and whose economic life has been developed under common conditions of production and whose spiritual life therefore obtained the character of a common culture."
>
> ... It is evident that the conditions of production or the factors for difference of the national economy that Borochov suggests in the name of Marx and Engels are in no circumstances the parochial conditons of production for an extraterritorial people like ourselves alone, just as Borochov's definition of "nation," based on the definitions of Marx and Engels, does not apply only to abnormal nations alone. Borochov's definition of nation and the theory of nationalism, based on Marx and Engels' definitions of the factors, does not deal only with the Jews or only with abnormal nations, but with the dialectical-historical development of peoples, nations and nationalism in general.
>
> ... There is no essential conflict between Stalin's definition of the four criteria for a normal nation and Marx-Engels' and Borochov's definition of the factors for difference or the "conditions of production" of the national economy of peoples and nationism in their dialectical and

historical evolution. Essentially, the two definitions go together. Nevertheless, we cannot accept the *ultimative* character of these four criteria of Stalin's which only recognize normal nations and deny the existence of peoples lacking any one of these criteria. Stalin's four criteria form a clear definition of the *desirable* which we must strive for in order to secure the future and continued existence of our people and in order to liberate an extraterritorial people from its national anomaly. However, they don't fit us or any other exterritorial people to the extent that they form an *unwaivable condition for recognizing us as a people.*
(Meir Yaari, "Ingathering of the Exiles in the Mirror of our Times," pp. 128-129; Merhavia, 1954.)

We are therefore permitted to affirm that from the Marxist standpoint the national theories of Stalin and Borochov do not contradict each other and are also not identical with each other, but rather complement each other. They complement and correct each other in not-unimportant clauses which require coordination and the corrections of mistakes. Now there is no doubt that only Sneh and Maki can continue to argue that Stalin's theory of the nation satisfies them completely and that they don't need it to be completed by Borochov's theory of the nation. On the other hand, all those who reject Maki's liquidationism cannot stand up for Stalin's conclusions denying the existence of exterritorial nations and recognizing only the existence of normal nations equipped with all the four criteria he outlined. All those who say that Stalin's theory of the nation satisfies them must also accept his conclusion that "only that nation is worthy of the name of nation which is marked by a stable community, established historically, of language, territory, economic life and psychological structure revealed in a common culture." Anyone accepting Stalin's doctrine alone inevitably accepts his assumption that only a people possessing all these four criteria are worthy of the name of a people and nation, while a people like our own, lacking such an important criteria as territory, must be denied its national particularity and destined to assimilation and disappearance.
(Ibid. pp. 125-126.)

Borochov's theory of nationalism must sooner or later be accepted by the world of revolution as going together with Stalin's theory of nationalism and as an additional development of the Marxist-Leninist outlook in the field of the national question.
(Ibid. pp. 142-143.)

... This isn't the place to go into a detailed analysis of the other mistaken assumptions in Stalin's work (*Marxism and the National Question*) which have had a very deleterious effect. For example, the "definition of a nation" which this work gives according to "five signs," which only all together, according to Stalin, make it possible to talk of a nation, is not at all verified by the historic experience of the struggle for national liberation in our days. It becomes evident that it is possible for nations to take form, to exist and to struggle, without their having a common language (Indonesia, India, Ghana), or to have a common language

without having a common territory or common economic life (the well-known processes in the Arab East), or to be formed in the course of the joint struggle of the peoples of different countries against imperialism, etc. The metaphysical character of this Stalinist definition, limited to the specific conditions of the national movements in Europe, has been completely revealed when these movements received greater momentum and their historic and economic bases changed. . . .
(From "The Non-Capitalist Path and the National Liberation Movement—Critical Comments on Stalin's Approach," by K. Ivanov; translated from Russian into Hebrew and published in Maki's monthly *Zu Haderech,* no. 12, Tel Aviv, 1964.)

After a thoroughgoing debate, those members who had been attracted to ultra-leftism admitted their mistakes. The Council unanimously adopted Meir Yaari's theses and also by a decisive majority the leadership's recommendation to re-elect these members to the Council of the Kibbutz Ha'artzi and give them another opportunity to reintegrate themselves in the movement's ideological entity.

After Hashomer Hatsair and its allies had overcome the ultra-leftist danger, the Unity Front renewed and even intensified its efforts to come to terms with L'Ahdut Haavoda in order to free the party from its paralysis. Overcoming the ultra-leftism within the ranks of the Unity Front had indeed removed one of the prime factors that had previously prevented intersectional reconciliation, and there seemed to be room for hope to turn a new page in intra-party affairs. The gap, however, had already become too wide and the L'Ahdut Haavoda section could not alter its course, so that all the efforts at reconciliation came to naught. When, after innumerable delays, the majority finally felt compelled to implement the Second Congress' resolutions on the organizational statute and full membership to the members of the Arab Section, the tension between the two sections came to a climax and L'Ahdut Haavoda (and the Erem group) voted to leave Mapam. The direct motive was L'Ahdut Haavoda's decision to publish its own paper, *Lamerhav.* The Unity Front proposed a number of suggestions[1] concerning this but L'Ahdut Haavoda was aware that its new party, after being established, would need sufficient time to prepare for the coming elections to the Histadrut and the Knesset and it therefore rejected all the compromise proposals and refused to accept the decisions of the party council that convened in July 1954, banning the publication of a sectional newspaper. In August of that year the minority finally seceded and re-established the Ahdut Haavoda–Poale Zion Party, with *Lamerhav* as its organ.[2]

2. These included putting out a special paper devoted to internal party debate; a monthly supplement to the daily *Al-Hamishmar,* which would be devoted to controversy, with an editorial board based on parity; opening the kibbutz branches of each of the two sections to speakers from the other group, and the like.
3. Originally as a biweekly and later as a daily newspaper.

The Mapam Council that convened in September 1954 summed up the secession, ratified the party institutions and the organizational statute, and decided to accept the Arab comrades into the ranks of the party and to co-opt them to the administrative bodies.

Thus, all the efforts to prevent a split had come to naught and it took place more or less along the traditional lines. Despite this, even after the split, Mapam did not once more become a kind of revised version of the one-time Hashomer Hatsair Party: in addition to the whole of Hashomer Hatsair, most of the former Left Poale Zion, most of the one-time "Hebrew Communists," some of the L'Ahdut Haavoda militants among the new immigrants, a roup of younger members of the Kibbutz Hameuchad, and some hundreds of Arab members remained in the party.[4]

The achievement, however, did not lie only in the demographic composition of the party after the split, but no less in the fact that thanks to the historic leadership's vigorous stand during the "sorry affair" and to the patience it revealed in relation to L'Ahdut Haavoda, Hashomer Hatsair's unity was preserved. No one doubted that even if mistakes had been made at the outset, in the later stages supreme efforts were made to preserve the great prospects of leftist-pioneering unity within the Israeli labor movement and to prevent the fatal split. Though this achievement was mainly a moral one, it played an important role in helping Mapam to recover after these heavy blows, all delivered within so short a time, to reorganize and to go forward.

SOURCES

. . . Your decision, putting an end to the United Workers Party as a united party, is only the last stage in the long process of breaking agreements. At the time when the Kibbutz Hameuchad was fighting for its very existence in the face of Mapai's splitting, the alliance between the main pioneering forces in the party was broken and the shameful partnership between the Kibbutz Ha'artzi and the Sneh group was formed in order to secure domination over the party. The partnership with Sneh and his comrades not only diverted the party from its mission and isolated it within the working class and the people, but also sowed and cultivated within the party the seeds of intolerance which we had struggled to destroy before the Haifa Congress, at the Congress and afterwards, throughout the history of Mapam. Even after the efforts made at the Congress to bring positions closer, a whole series of fundamental suggestions which we had proposed on defining the

---

4. Some of the leading personalities of the united party did not join Mapam nor Ahdut Haavoda–Poale Zion after the split, either because they didn't feel sufficiently at home ideologically in either of the two rival factions or because they didn't see any justification for the split itself. These included L. Levite, one of the leading theoreticians of the Kibbutz Hameuchad and L'Ahdut Haavoda, and Zeev Abromowitz, one of the veteran leaders and theoreticians of the Left Poale Zion.

mission of the party, were rejected. At the Congress' close, we expressly declared that the fundamental questions had remained in dispute, including questions of principle and conscience. We announced that we would maintain our ties for ideological and political expression within the frame of the freedom of thought that should prevail in the party and within the frame of discipline in action. On the closing evening we announced that we were leaving the Congress worried by the internal situation in the party but would lend our hand to any unifying efforts toward a united party without divisions. . . If the Front had been interested in the same joint goals on which we had united and if it weren't bent on turning the United Workers' Party into an Hashomer Hatsair party, it wouldn't have adopted the splitting resolution and would have responded to our suggestion for joint responsibility for the party. The forces that united in Mapam can only raise their partnership to a higher level without domination or obedience. It is stupidity and irresponsibility to demand of us to agree to be silenced. . . .

(From "Announcement of the Section," presented by Yitzhak Ben-Aharon at the session of the Political Committee of Mapam, and published in *Lamerhav,* Aug. 20, 1954.

. . . However, L'Ahdut Haavoda within Mapam isn't the same as L'Ahdut Haavoda outside it. Their separation from us with the attitude they have recently adopted toward the Soviet Union instead of the attitude adopted at the Haifa Congress, this separation from us with these attitudes on questions of security, on the question of war and peace, that they have adopted recently—these, too, in contradiction with the attitudes adopted at the Haifa Congress—all these are very disturbing. I don't want to be a prophet. I am only analyzing things that we all see. I don't want to prophecy anything bad for them. I had read that in some place Yisrael Galili expressed his opinion that he considers these prophecies inimical and malicious actions. But I would very much want them not to go down the decline. I would like us to be surprised favorably. But if they start out with such equipment and with the bundle of libels expressed in the statement against the party in which they were for six years and more, the question of *quo vadis* poses itself in all its severity: Where are they going?

I have no doubt that between Maki and Mapai there is room for only one party—a revolutionary Zionist party: Zionist in contrast to Maki, and revolutionary in contrast to reformism. Under no circumstances is there space for two Mapams. If they want to be a Mapam like us then the whole split was sheer madness. I forecast that when this party faces the public it will be neither an alternative to Mapai nor to Mapam; it will be an intermediary growth directed mainly against us. A fair attitude on our part won't help. I say that we are not interested in inciting disputes and useless arguments. We are interested in the establishment of decent public relations within the Histadrut, in our relations with Mapai and in our relations with our comrades of yesterday, but the ball is in their hands. I fear that our good will is not going to help and that we have to be ready for difficult days. We shall reveal good will so far as we can, but I am afraid that we won't succeed.

(Remarks by Meir Yaari at a meeting of Mapam's Central Committee, Aug. 18, 1954; Meir Yaari: "Facing Our Mission," published by Mapam, Tel Aviv, 1954.)

14 • The Struggle for Peace and the Sinai War

The elections to the Third Knesset in 1955 brought losses to the two main partners of the government coalition—Mapai and the General Zionists. Mapai lost five seats in the Knesset to the parties of the pioneering left, while the General Zionists gave up seven to Herut. Even though the split had left the large majority of the members and branches within Mapam, Ahdut Haavoda-Poale Zion won the greater victory, obtaining ten seats to Mapam's nine. In the election campaign Ahdut Haavoda had appealed mainly to the large numbers who were complaining of Mapai rule and the Histadrut bureaucracy, without yet going on to a fundamental rejection of Mapai's policies. It had also encouraged chauvinistic sentiments among the younger voters and new immigrants, particularly those coming from the Arab countries.

Mapam's slogan for the election campaign had been: "An end to Mapai's coalition with the Right—For a Progressive Government based on the three workers' parties." In view of Mapai's decline in the elections and the strong opposition within its own rank and file to renewing the coalition with the right, and since the General Zionists also feared that renewing their coalition experiment would weaken them further to Herut's benefit, Ben-Gurion was now compelled to agree to what he had stubbornly rejected in the First and Second Knessets: a center-left coalition with an agreed-upon "fundamental policy" of the workers' parties. Ahdut Haavoda-Poale Zion was represented in the new government by two Ministers,[1] and Mapam also had two Ministers.[2] When the two parties joined the government they at least temporarily solved one of the standing differences between them before the split. In addition, on a number of issues concerning the status of the kibbutz movement and the pioneering youth movements, economic policies and the defense of the standard of living of the masses, the demand for neutrality in foreign policy, and others, the four pioneering-left Ministers found themselves often working together in the coalition.

On the other hand, the more the security situation on the frontiers deteriorated, the more Ahdut Haavoda gave its full support to the group among the Mapai Ministers and Ministry of Defense who favored the idea of a "preventive war" as the supposedly only effective answer to

---

1. Yisrael Bar-Yehuda, Minister of Interior; Moshe Carmel, Minister of Transportation.
2. Mordehai Bentov, Minister of Development; Yisrael Barzilai, Minister of Health.

the provocations and threats of the Arab countries, the increasing number of infiltrations and the escalating arms race that was turning the balance against Israel.

In its activism, Ahdut Haavoda sometimes went so far as to blur the limits between its own propaganda and that of Herut, with the danger which that propinquity held for the education of the youth and of the new immigrants. In contrast to this, Mapam's Ministers and the Knesset faction campaigned for a policy of peace and against "preventive war." Yaakov Hazan's speech in the Knesset in behalf of saving the peace made a deep impression among the Israeli public, transcending party lines:

> ... We still cannot continue to build our national lives in tranquility and in relations of peace, cooperation and mutual aid with our neighbors. We have to go forward with Israel's peace in constant danger, hanging over the abyss itself. That is a peace that demands many sacrifices of us but it is better than any war as long as its continuation does not threaten the very existence of the State and as long as it isn't bought at the price of its sovereignty, the integrity of its borders or its continued development and construction. It is better than war, because as long as it lasts we can continue saving the Diaspora and building the State. This bitter peace is better than war because as long as it lasts there is the hope that it will turn into a true peace without our having to march over the ruins of our lives and the lives of others. . .
>
> If there was anyone who could succeed in proving to me that war was unavoidable, I would inevitably come to different conclusions and I was very much shocked to hear my friend, M. K. Galili's statement that events won't allow us to maintain the peace. How does he know that? War isn't inevitable! Every year of peace is a year of additional possibilities of fighting for peace. What did the prophets of inevitable war tell us last year, half a year ago and three months ago? I am referring primarily to Knesset Member Begin, the one-stringed fiddler who is always playing one tune: "War." From the very beginning of this debate he has always been talking and building everything on two theories: the fallacious doctrine of the "last moment," and the false doctrine of the "right time," and he keeps coming to us with the complaint that we have wasted an opportunity, or with the threat of the "last moment," "zero hour," "we have lost; our strength is declining; if we don't do something today, we will be lost. . ."
>
> . . How shall we maintain our security? Knesset Member Begin suggests that in order to maintain the peace we make war. I know that war brings with it only one thing—war. No war ever prevented war. . . .
>
> Certainly, defense isn't a *policy;* it is a condition for our being able to continue policy. What kind of policy will guarantee our existence, the possibilities of a true peace? The answer is–building faster; training all our forces for construction! To strengthen our defensive ability to deter the enemy, to compel him to weigh once more whether it is worthwhile to attack us; political independence, noninvolvement in any alliances; winning friends and returning friendship to all those who are friends to us; immovably standing up for our rights. . .
>
> (From the speech by Yaakov Hazan in the Knesset, "Al Hamishmar," July 20, 1956.)

In October 1956 Ben-Gurion confronted the government as a whole with the *fait accompli* of the Sinai War. Some of the Ministers were perplexed and hesitated, but ultimately only the Mapam Ministers voted against the last-minute ratification of the operation. Mapam was opposed to the Sinai campaign because it wasn't convinced that the State of Israel was really on the verge of an invasion by Egypt—despite the rampaging fedayeen,[3] Nasser's provocative threats and declarations, and his army's large store of both Soviet and Western arms. Mapam feared armed Soviet intervention in the Middle East, viewing it as an irresponsible and even adventuristic risk for the future of Israel, the Jewish people, and the whole world. Mapam feared that this operation and especially the coordination and cooperation with the Anglo-French Suez War, which was intended only to defend imperialist interests and nothing more, would further increase Israel's isolation in the Afro-Asian world, if not in the world as a whole. It was also clear to Mapam that despite the military achievement, not one of the great questions facing Israel and the Arab world would find its solution.

At the same time, however, Mapam was aware of the repeated threats and the declared hostility of the Arab leaders to the State of Israel's very existence, if a "preventive war" *did* break out. It was this dual character of the Sinai campaign as both a military and political step which should be opposed and a war for national existence which had to be won, that dictated Mapam's conduct at that time; it voted in the government against opening the operation and then assumed part of the responsibility for seeing it to a successful conclusion, with the party reserving the right of criticism in the government, in the Knesset, and in the press. The party continued to struggle within the government and within the Israeli public against any deterioration into activism or participating in any colonialist adventures or international entanglements. Instead, it tried to steer Israeli policy in the direction of a peace initiative, neutrality, and integration in the Afro-Asian world.

In the first session of the Knesset immediately after the conclusion of the Sinai campaign, Mapam General Secretary Meir Yaari made a statement in the name of his party, in which he declared that Mapam was just as convinced then as it had been in the past that peace, no matter how unstable, was preferable to war. However, since his party's efforts to prevent the war had failed and the die had been cast, Mapam had kept faith with the people's struggle for existence and with the defense forces. At the same time, Mapam considered itself at liberty to express its reservations concerning the Sinai campaign whenever or wherever it saw fit. Meir Yaari went on to attack not only the ideology of "preventive war" but also the one-sided condemnation of Israel by both the U.S.S.R. and

---

3. Arab terrorists, the predecessors of present-day Al Fatah.

the United States. These powers had consistently ignored Nasser's provocative threats of war, the infiltrations and fedayeen activities. For tactical and opportunistic reasons they had either directly or indirectly been on Nasser's side; because of these policies those powers had a considerable share in the responsibility for creating the tensions among the Israeli which had served as fertile soil for the growth of the ideologies of despair, of "preventive war."

In the Sinai Campaign the Israel defense forces also occupied the Gaza Strip that had consistently served as the jumping-off point for infiltrators and fedayeen. Removing the Egyptian army from this region could radically change the security situation of the settlements in the Negev. However, if there was any prospect (*prospect*—not certainty!) that the U.N. would acquiesce to Israel's integrating the Gaza Strip within its borders, it would depend on Israel's readiness to absorb the Arab population of the Strip. Together with the refugees from the War of Liberation, the Strip's population came to more than 300,000 (100,000 native inhabitants and 200,000 refugees). Such a partial solution of the painful and troublesome refugee problem, with the help of international financial aid, might perhaps have appealed to certain circles within the U.N. However, when the Mapam and Ahdut Haavoda Ministers demanded a declaration in this spirit, the majority of the government was deterred by the prospect of increasing Israel's Arab minority to 400,000–500,000 and feared the many difficulties that such integration would undoubtedly have involved. When Israel avoided making such a declaration, the demand for territorial integration remained only an empty and futile gesture. Israel was ordered by the U.N. to evacuate the Gaza Strip and the Israel defense forces did so.

The hurried evacuation of the Gaza Strip, without the Government's having made any political or constructive effort worthy of the name to hold on to what had been considered one of the most vital security goals of the Sinai campaign, aroused disappointment and vigorous criticism in the Knesset and the press. The negative effect of the evacuation was heightened by contrast to Ben-Gurion's pompous declarations, at the conclusion of the campaign, "on the annexation of the Sinai Peninsula as part of the Third Kingdom of Israel." This not only aroused vain hopes and false illusions but was an act of extreme political irresponsibility. By blurring the defensive nature of the proclaimed motives behind the Sinai War, it seemed to ratify and strengthen the Arab propaganda of the danger of Israeli expansionism.

> "Eilat will once again be the chief Jewish port in the South, the Straits to the Red Sea will be opened to Israeli shipping, and Yotbat, called Tiran, until 1,400 years ago an independent Jewish Kingdom, will once again be part of the Third Kingdom of Israel." These re-

marks were included in a letter by David Ben-Gurion, the Prime Minister and Minister of Defense, to the Israeli Defense Force unit that had traversed 300 kilometers along the eastern coast of the Sinai Peninsula and was today making its impressive formal dress parade at Sharm a Sheikh, opposite the Island of Tiran at the southern tip of the peninsula and the entrance to the Gulf of Eilat. . . ."

(*Davar,* July 11, 1956.)

. . . The Sinai Campaign, for which L'Ahdut Haavoda–Poale Zion had a considerable share of responsibility, was a correct and necessary action that was carried out at perhaps the very last possible moment. Everything that happened before the campaign and after it only prove how bad our situation would have been without it. Even if mistaken and harsh decisions are taken tomorrow, they will not do away with the gains won by the campaign and the "preventive force" of the campaign will inevitably remain in effect. . . .

(From remarks by I. Bar-Yehuda in the Ahdut Haavoda–Poale Zion Conference, in *Lamerhav,* April 3, 1957.)

. . . The Council ratifies the position of its Ministers in the Government and spokesmen in the Knesset in support of the independent Israeli initiative in the Sinai Campaign that saved Israel from the fate of being a victim of a surprise attack; in the opposition to the Israel Defense Forces' retreat from the defense line of El Arish-Abu Aglielah-Quseima; in the then opposition to the decision to retreat from the Gaza Strip and the Straits of Tiran and to the results of the preliminary negotiations with the American Secretary of State that served as the background to this dangerous retreat.

(From the resolutions of the 9th Council of Ahdut Haavoda–Poale Zion, *Lamerhav,* May 4, 1957.)

. . . The Central Committee of the United Workers Party (Mapam) ratifies the decisions of the Political Committee in its meeting shortly before the Sinai Campaign, which said, among the rest:

. . The military campaign conducted by the Israel Defense Forces with readiness for sacrifice and supreme heroism, was crowned by a brilliant success and won important military gains. The aftermath of the military campaign, however, brought us a very critical political crisis which we had feared and warned against. In one of the most fateful hours of her existence Israel found herself isolated, with even loyal friends revealing their lack of understanding of the siege in which we were found. It was clearly proved that even the most successful military campaign does not in itself hold any solution for the fundamental problems of the State . . .

The Party's Central Committee meeting, at a time of critical political struggle in the U.N., declares the Party's readiness to do its share in bearing the burden of the political campaign. The Central Committee reiterates its view, in the new situation, that Israeli policy must be founded on the basis of neutrality and independence in order for it not to be identified in the eyes of the world with the aims of the colonial powers that are not her own. While firmly resisting pressures and threats against her vital interests it is imperative for Israeli policy to make a supreme effort not to lock the doors to winning the understanding of all those forces deciding the fate of the world, and among them, the countries of the Asian continent engaged in a tremendous struggle to win their freedom and complete independence.

In view of the political pressure being exerted on the State of Israel, the Central Committee of Mapam states its position on the matters on the agenda:

1. We must endeavor to include the Gaza Strip within the State of Israel while guaranteeing the full rights of its inhabitants and a constructive solution of the refugee problem. It should be the Government's task to promote a constructive policy towards the native inhabitants of the Strip. The return of Egyptian rule or the establishment of a U.N. regime in the Strip hold the dark prospect of renewed fedayeen activity and of creating a wide field of activity for warmongers.

Israel's security needs not only do not conflict with a constructive approach to the problem of the refugees and a policy of full equality for the Arab minority—they are rather elements that go clearly together. The struggle in which we are found verifies Mapam's fundamental conception that Israel's interests and positive policies towards the Arab minority complement each other.

2. Guarantees for the freedom of Israeli shipping in the Gulf of Eilat and the Suez Canal are an unshakeable right. Mapam's Central Committee supports the Government of Israel in its firm demand for U.N. guarantees for the freedom of shipping.

3. In view of the threat of economic sanctions the Yishuv must reinforce its preparedness to withstand a siege and to struggle for the fundamental rights of the State of Israel.

4. The Central Committee of Mapam emphasizes again that the striving for a stable peace must be the central effort of Israeli policy. The State of Israel must untiringly demand the opening of immediate negotiations for peace, without any preconditions and guaranteeing the territorial integrity and the just rights of all the peoples concerned. It must guarantee full and real equality of rights to the Arab minority and strive unceasingly to break the circle of hatred surrounding us. [It must strive for] the neutrality of the State of Israel and nonadhesion to any military alliances; for the dismemberment of all the military alliances existing in the region; for the neutralization of the Middle East and its separation from the sphere of the armaments race; for Four Power and U.N. guarantees for the recognized neutral states of the region and the removal of all foreign forces from the region.

5. The Central Committee gives its support to its representatives in the Government and the Knesset in the struggle for the Party's line of policy and affirms Mapam's readiness to do its share in the State of Israel's efforts to break the military siege and guarantee peace. In view of the critical political dangers the Central Committee of Mapam calls the public as a whole to be aware of and ready to bear the burden of the struggle in which we find ourselves at this time.

(Resolutions of the Mapam Central Committee, "On the Problems of the Hour," *Al-Hamishmar,* Nov. 2, 1957.)

15 • Fighting Against Signs of Confusion

In order to frustrate the attempts to isolate it and remove it from the sphere of decision, Mapam decided, even after the Sinai campaign and the retreat from the Gaza Strip, to continue the struggle within the government and not to allow it to be replaced with a right–wing coalition. Nonetheless, the party's position, in a public that was being swept by a wave of chauvinism, was a quite difficult one. What is more, the ranks of the party itself were also affected by a crisis that took on a special character among some of the younger kibbutz members who had been mobilized in the military units and participated in the Sinai Campaign. It was hard for these young people to grasp to the full fundamental political considerations of the party leadership in stubbornly maintaining its loyalty to the policies of peace even at a time of tension and of threats from beyond the border. The attitudes of the younger people (and of not a few veterans) to the Sinai campaign were determined less by analysis and considerations of principle than by Nasser's threats of annihilation and the murderous attacks by the fedayeen that had preceded the campaign, as well as by the sight of the tremendous quantities of Soviet arms (in addition to the Western arms) in Egypt's possession. This last fact, coming after the Prague trial, the libels against the Jewish physicians in Moscow,[1] and the revelations concerning the annihilation of Jewish writers and leaders in the U.S.S.R., dealt a final blow to the former sympathetic attitude toward the Soviet Union. The veteran cadres of the party had been accustomed to this from the period before World War II to the Soviets' militantly anti-Zionist attitude and to their own severe criticism of the Soviet regime (as during the Moscow trials in the second half of the '30s); they were shaken by every one of these blows, but their fundamental views had not changed. Many of the younger members, on the other hand, had known the Soviet Union from the Red Army's heroic battles and defeat of fascism, its rescue of part of East European Jewry from the German death camps, from Gromyko's statement in favor of a Jewish State, the arms and volunteers during the War of Liberation and the mass

1. A libel against nine well-known Soviet physicians, seven of them Jewish, in which they were charged, in January 1953, with having assassinated Soviet leaders, supposedly in the name of the "international world bourgeois nationalist organization," the JOINT; the latter was charged with being an espionage agent of the American intelligence. Stalin's death ended the matter.

immigration from the popular democracies. These were all swept away now by the revelations of degeneration in the Soviet regime, the swing back to the traditional hostility toward us, the arms deal with Egypt, the Hungarian tragedy, etc. Many veterans, as well as young people, found refuge in confusion and in sterile, apolitical cynicism. Only very slowly, by energetic and systematic educational activity and extended discussion in the Kibbutz Ha'artsi, the party and its branches, did the party overcome the crisis and begin to come out of the confusion. This process was summarized in the thesis prepared by the Party's General Secretary, Meir Yaari, to the Third Congress.[2]

Mapam's Third Congress, convened in Haifa in January 1958, represented 32,000 members organized in 242 branches: 88 in the cities, *moshavot* (villages), and temporary immigrant villages (*maabarot*); 72 in the kibbutzim; 58 in Arab villages and towns; and 24 in the *moshavei-ovdim* (smallholders' cooperative villages). The agenda included both theoretical and practical questions such as foreign and domestic policy, problems of economics and immigrant absorption, the revelations of the 20th Congress (C.P.S.U.), the situation of the Jewish minority in the socialist countries, the Arab minority in Israel, the party's status within the government coalition, and its own organizational situation. If we were to summarize the theoretical innovations of this Third Congress as compared with the program adopted at the Second Congress (Haifa, May 1951), we might stress the following points:

1. The concept of "removing the barriers between us and the world of revolution," as it appeared in the Haifa program, had been interpreted incorrectly, both by those outside the party and, during the "sorry affair," among the party ranks themselves. It was now decided no longer to use this misleading term or to engage in prophecies concerning the future, but simply to affirm the links and solidarity with the international revolutionary labor movement.

2. After all the events and revelations since the previous Congress, as far as Soviet foreign and domestic policy was concerned, in addition to the differences over Zionism, the Ingathering of Exiles and the worsening relations between the Soviet Union and Israel and between the Communist parties and Mapam, there was no longer any point in talking of identification with the "world of revolution" in everything except the Jewish-Zionist issue. Mapam, like all other socialist parties, would have to reserve the right to examine the specific actions, the political and tactical moves, and the theoretical innovations in both foreign and domestic policy of the socialist countries and the world labor movement. Mapam's attitude toward the world labor movement would have to be

---

2. These appeared in the form of a book, *The Trials of our Generation*, published by Sifriat Poalim, Merhavia, 1958.

based on solidarity and independence. That kind of attitude was to be considered an inseparable component of the theoretical conception of "different paths to socialism." Mapam's path to socialism leads through the Ingathering of Exiles and, as far as the Israeli labor movement is concerned, it does not recognize any abstract socialism divorced from the Ingathering of Exiles.

> Our growing enterprise in this country, settling its wastelands and expanding the dimensions of immigration, the growing strength of the working class in formation, the increasing strength of the United Workers Party and its increasing revolutionary momentum, intensifying the struggle for world peace and to reinforce the State of Israel's national independence; deepening the solidarity between Jewish and Arab workers—all these will promote the conditions for recognition on the part of the revolutionary international labor movement of our conceptions of the solution of the Jewish problem, and of Mapam as the party that will bring socialism to the State of Israel and the Jewish people, ultimately removing the barriers still separating us from the revolutionary camp of which we are an inseparable part. . . .
> (From the Mapam Program adopted at the Second Congress, published by Mapam, Tel Aviv, 1951.)
>
> . . . The United Workers Party is founded on the doctrine of pioneering fulfillment and class struggle integrated with the construction of the country; on Borochov's doctrine as the Marxist formulation of the solution for the national question of the Jewish people by territorial concentration in the land of Israel and the mission of workers' Zionism; on Marxism-Leninism as a world outlook and the guide for the political struggle of the revolutionary international labor movement.
> (Ibid.)

3. The Haifa Program had used the term "Marxism-Leninism." Among the public at large and even among many members of the party, this term had not been interpreted as a synonym for "revolutionary Marxism" and for the most consistent school of Marxist thought as it had been developed and formulated by Lenin, but rather as the sum total of ideas, policies and tactical moves adopted by the present Soviet regime (ideas and moves, some of which were supported and some of which were rejected with all our power). It was decided to replace this short but misleading term of "Marxism-Leninism" by "the fundamentals of Marxism and Leninism as the theoretical basis of revolutionary international socialism."[3]

---

3. The entire statement reads as follows: "While maintaining our ideological independence based on Zionist-pioneering realization and class struggle integrated with the construction of our country, and on Borochov's doctrine as the Marxist formulation of the solution for the national question of the Jewish people, Mapam will devote itself to undogmatically adapting the fundamentals of Marxism and Leninism as the theoretical basis of revolutionary international socialism, to the conditions of our people and country."

Mapam's unequivocal definition of itself as an independent left socialist party also led to some conclusions concerning the nature of its ties within the international labor movement. Ever since the Third Congress, strong emphasis has been put on cultivating and ramifying these ties—in addition to those existing within the frame of the "Peace Movement," the International Federations of Women and Democratic Youth, and the like. Mapam began to look for informational contacts with *all* workers' parties everywhere, no matter what their international affiliations or domestic policies, but it has been seeking especially to establish ties of friendship and cooperation with leftist socialist parties and groups. In keeping with this, it has established ties in the course of time with the Italian Socialist Party (P.S.I.), the People's Socialist Party (SF) in Denmark, the Pacifist Socialist Party (PSP) and the Political Radical Party (P.P.R.) in Holland, the United Socialist Party (P.S.U.) in France,[4] and with the French Socialist Party,[5] the Swedish and German Social Democratic Parties, the Socialist Party of Austria, the Portuguese Socialist Party, the two socialist parties in Spain (the Socialist Workers' Party and the Socialist People's Party), the Malta Labor Party, the Socialist Party of Chile,[6] the Movement for Socialism (M.A.S.) in Venezuela, the Mass Movement of the Colombian People, the Canadian New Democratic Party (N.D.P.), the socialist parties of India and Japan, large sections of the labor parties in Great Britain and Australia, with the Communist parties of Sweden, Italy, Yugoslavia, Rumania and Cuba,[7] as well as with the Independent Left-Socialist Groups and Committees of Intellectuals for a Negotiated Peace in the Middle East," etc.

The debate at the Third Congress was a very lively one. Some delegates demanded that the party use the term Marxism without the addition of "Leninism," while others opposed changing the concept "Marxism-Leninism" as it has been accepted at the Haifa Congress (the "debate over the hyphen"). In the end, however, the new version ("the fundamentals of Marxism and of Leninism") was adopted by a large majority.

4. In 1969 the P.S.U. changed by majority vote its former fairly balanced approach to the Arab-Israel conflict, took a clear pro Al-Fatah stand and cut off its relations with Mapam.
5. When the old SFIO has been rejuvinated by its merger with the "Socialist Clubs" and the Mitterand Group.
6. When in 1970 the leader of the Socialist Party of Chile, Dr. Salvadore Allende, was elected President of the Republic, Mapam was invited, as the only Israeli party, to attend President Allende's inauguration.
7. In 1958 a Mapam delegation was invited to the Congress of the Yugoslavian Communist Party. In 1968 a representative of Mapam attended the Congress of the Swedish Communist Party. From 1969 on, representatives of the Mapam C. C. frequently visited Rumania as guests of the Rumanian Communist Party. Mapam's 7th Congress in 1967 was attended by a high-ranked Rumanian Communist delegation. Mapam had very friendly relations with the Cuban Legation in Israel, and the Chairman of the Israel-Cuba Friendship League was a member of the Mapam C. C. In 1975 and 1976 frequent talks took place between Mapam and Italian Communist representatives, both in Italy and in Israel.

The Third Congress did not, indeed, bring the debate to an end, but it not only freed many members and groups within the party from their confusion and strengthened the party, it also laid the firm foundation for the educational work within the party itself[8] among the Israeli public, world Jewry, and the International Labour Movement.[9] It shaped Mapam's character as a party of pioneering Zionism, for peace and fraternity of peoples, as an independent left-socialist party sympathetic to the socialist countries but free and even obliged to criticize them on Jewish as well as any other issues—whenever according to its independent judgment the policies of these countries are not faithful to the principles of revolutionary socialism.

SOURCES

....2. In the Soviet Union, the first socialist state, the basis for socialist construction has been laid; the domination of the capitalist minority over the means of production has been eliminated. Capitalist relations of production have been destroyed and the foundations for socialist relations of production have been laid, relations which have persisted for a generation and have become well-rooted. After all the trials through which it has gone, the Soviet Union has attained second place in the world in production; it is competing with the United States in military potential and is destined to compete with it economically as well.

... The 20th Congress of the C.P.S.U. uncovered the manifestations of deterioration within the Soviet regime and the signs of the degeneration which have infected the dictatorship of the proletariat. These disturbing phenomena did not disappear completely with Stalin's death. The most outstanding feature of this process may be seen in the degeneration of democratic centralism that has given way to anti-democratic bureaucratic centralism. Collective responsibility has been replaced by the tyrannical rule of an individual or individuals. The democratic centralism and the collective responsibility which were fully effective in Lenin's time and whose return was announced at the 20th Congress are still waiting for redemption....

(From the Resolutions of the Third Congress of Mapam, Haifa, published by Mapam, Tel Aviv, 1958.)

... 9. After decades of civil equality and the existence of cultural life in the Yiddish language, the Jews have now been faced with manifestations of national discrimination. The Jewish minority has been sentenced to forced assimilation. The spiritual leadership of Soviet Jewry met the bitter fate of physical annihilation. The Jews have been deprived of the right to an autonomous cultural life and up to the

---

8. Since its 3rd Congress in 1958, Mapam has been publishing a theoretical and political magazine (first monthly, later bimonthly) *Basha'ar* (At the Gate), in addition to its Hebrew daily *Al-Hamishmar* (On Guard) and the Arabic weekly *Al-Mirsad* (The Guard), as well as its papers in other languages for the new immigrants.
9. Mapam publishes a *Mapam Bulletin* in English, as well as political commentaries in English, German, Spanish and Italian, to serve its expanding foreign ties.

present day have not been given the free choice of immigrating to Israel, for any who may want to do so. . . .

. . . 17. The tragic experience of Soviet Jewry provides additional verification for the thesis that even the socialist regimes banning national discrimination by law cannot bar the way to serious revelations of anti-Semitism and cannot do away with the Jewish anomaly. It has once more become evident to all that the Jewish question has one and a single solution—the Zionist solution, the Ingathering of the Exiles of our people in its historic homeland . . . We must demand the right of self-determination of national existence for the Jewish minority in the socialist countries and the right of every Jew desiring it to migrate to his country and homeland. In view of bitter and sad experience we must now, more vigorously than ever, demand of all regimes the right of the Jewish people to free migration to Israel. . . .
(Ibid.)

The Third Congress also saw the beginning of another debate that was continued in the Fourth Congress (in 1963), and was not resolved even then, over the question of the proletarian dictatorship. Some of the delegates had concluded from the signs of degeneration that had infected the proletarian dictatorship in the Soviet Union, from the heavy criticism that Mapam had leveled against these phenomena and from the Congress' reservations concerning Marxism-Leninism as an absolute doctrine, that Mapam also had to reject the principle of the dictatorship of the proletariat as the only kind of socialist regime, especially since Mapam had more than once declared that in its view socialism in this country would come to power by democratic decision.

Those delegates who were opposed to this rejection of the dictatorship of the proletariat as a principle raised the following arguments in reply:

First, we have yet to see socialism established anywhere *not* by the path of proletarian dictatorship. There is no doubt that from this viewpoint this Marxist fundamental has passed the most decisive test of all, the test of fulfillment. Second, it has not at all been proven that the degeneration that has infected the proletarian dictatorship in the Soviet Union in the course of the years was an inseparable part and organic result of the dictatorship itself and not the result of specific historic and local situations. Third, today we are witnesses to a very wide variety of regimes all of which are included in the theoretical concept of "proletarian dictatorship," and this variety will certainly increase as more countries begin to build socialism.

Thus, according to this view, the "dictatorship of the proletariat" is not a specific, definite and standard form of political rule but a definition for the *sociological function of the workers' regime* in the period of transition from capitalism to socialism.

Whenever some socialist parties (or fronts) in more countries take over control (in one way or another, depending on specific circumstances and the international and domestic balance of forces, etc.), this new government, in contrast to the various reformist "Labor governments," will have to strive systematically and determinedly, even within a multi-party parliamentary regime, to intervene fundamentally in order to introduce revolutionary changes in economics, education, legislation, government apparatus and the like, and will have to defend this workers' regime and the fulfillment of its declared aims, by all necessary means, against domestic sabotage or foreign intervention.

Summing up: The theoretical Marxist thesis of a revolutionary transition between capitalism and socialism and of the need for a regime under firm workers' control will have to serve, in the future as well, as a guideline for all true socialist policy.

However, as we have said, opinions on this issue were divided and the debate has not ended.

16 • The Israeli Road to Socialism

Hevrat Ovdim (General Cooperative Association of Labor in Israel)

The historic dual role of the Israeli workers' movement—class struggle combined with construction—can also be found in an organizational structure adapted to this role. On the one hand, the Histadrut must fill all the functions of trade unions everywhere, while on the other hand it has the additional and specific task of building the working class and shaping it physically and ideologically, with all that this implies. This includes initiative and action in organizing immigration, education and training, in helping the immigrants to become integrated and to find their roots in the country, culturally and socially, in the villages and in productive physical labor.

The role of the Jewish middle class in this constructive activity was minor and the brunt of the labor of settling the wasteland, of establishing an economy, fostering culture, guarding the border and protecting life and property, fell mainly—and for a long and decisive period almost solely—on the labor movement. The Histadrut's constructive initiative thus has had a double importance—not only building and shaping the subjective human factor of the class struggle as part of the construction, but also actually building the country itself. For this reason, in addition to its trade unions, the mutual aid and social insurance institutions and the Center for Culture and Education, the Histadrut also includes an independent labor economy.

In its second Congress, in 1923, the Histadrut set up the *Hevrat Ovdim* (Workers' Society) as the holding company and legal framework for all its property and enterprises in order to ensure its ownership and control over them. Its task was declared to be "to unite the Jewish Workers in Palestine in all the various working occupations on a cooperative basis." Among its main fields of activity are production, consumers, services, housing, credit and insurance cooperatives, administrative enterprises like Solel Boneh,[1] and the labor settlements.

The cooperative movement has some considerable achievements to its credit but it has also faced problems, dangers and serious crises. The first

---

1. Solel Boneh (Paver-Builder)—contracting company originally established to provide labor for unemployed workers, and now Israel's largest industrial and contracting enterprise.

was the problem of hired labor, particularly in the transportation and hauling cooperatives. A second problem has been the slackening ties between the cooperatives and the Histadrut's authority. A third: in recent years, cooperative activity has been less integrated into the dominant trends and mainstream of Israeli social and economic life, which is taking an ever more clearly bourgeois capitalist character. The Mapaiites heading the Histadrut are guided almost exclusively by the "tested axioms" of bourgeois economics. It is not sufficient at all for cooperative activity to be part of the apocalyptic socialist vision, if it is not organically part of the class struggle, the general trade union and political struggles of the working public and the Histadrut. On the contrary, only such an anticapitalist class struggle can spark energetic cooperative activity, and only such an integration can give the formal attachments of the cooperatives to the Histadrut as a whole real content and moral force. Undoubtedly, the phenomena of stagnation, degeneration and social disintegration shown by part of the cooperatives—alongside their economic successes—can best bring home to us what might happen to the economically successful kibbutz enterprise if its collectivist vision were not inseparably joined to the general vision and struggle for Zionism, pioneering and socialism.

The administrative and cooperative enterprises have played and still continue to play a role of the first order in construction and housing, in road-building, fortifications, and public works and the like; in the establishment of auxiliary industries and supplying the raw materials for these fields; in setting up basic heavy industries; and, in cooperation with government and national and private capital, in establishing and operating services of national importance. At the same time, however, the weaknesses of this expanding branch of the workers' economy have been apparent for many years.

First, the administrative and cooperative enterprises have, in practice, become a tremendous autonomous empire, while their links to the authority of the Histadrut bodies have been very largely only formal. Second, the managements have become bureaucratic, without the workers employed in these Histadrut enterprises possessing any more rights, status, influence, or sense of participation toward "their" enterprises than do workers in capitalist firms. Third, in their quantitative growth, unceasing expansion and branching out, these enterprises have gone beyond the possibilities of planning and efficient management by any single center. Mapai tried to find a remedy for this by breaking up Solel Boneh into three separate sections (in 1953): industry, building and public works, overseas projects and ports. In general, the experience accumulated over many years in this field in our country, as well as abroad, in both the socialist and capitalist countries, may be summed up as follows:

a. Nationalization, or any other means of guaranteeing public ownership, is a step in the right direction, but still only a first step. If the change in ownership does not go together with the democratization of management, the nature of the ownership inevitably is falsified and the public economy loses much of its advantages over private ownership.

b. In fighting against overcentralization and bureaucratic degeneration, decentralization is a proper step, but it alone cannot serve as a barrier to the continued existence of bureaucratic control in a few centers instead of one center. Only decentralization plus fundamental and consistent democratization can do this.

The labor settlements belong to the Federation of Agricultural Laborers, which includes both the hired agricultural workers and the labor settlements. The institution directing the Agricultural Organization—the "Agricultural Center"—is divided into two departments, one for the hired agricultural workers and the other for labor settlements, representing the kibbutz movements and the small-holders' settlements. Numerically, it is true, the kibbutz movement is not more than 3.5 percent of the country's total population; during recent years, the *moshav* (small-holders) movement has been somewhat larger, after having been reinforced by the "immigrants' villages." Nonetheless, in its achievements and objective role in the fields of culture, education, immigrant absorption, security, agricultural production (and most recently, industry, too) the kibbutz movement's importance is far greater than its numerical size, both absolutely and relatively. This is reflected in the large number of kibbutz members in the leadership of the Histadrut and the main parties, out of all proportion to their numbers in the Histadrut or their party membership, and in their leadership status and first-rank moral authority. This phenomenon can be explained by the fact that the kibbutz, by its very nature, has maintained the principle of ideological realization as a fundamental; the kibbutz members live in a collective framework and are subject to its moral and spiritual influences; and they make their living in emancipated labor and maximal economic independence. As a result, the ideology of the movement has been preserved in the kibbutzim, and crystallized in its purity more than in any other sector. And in keeping with this, the wider working public has looked on the existence and growth of the kibbutzim as the consistent fulfillment of the pioneering socialist-Zionist ideology shared by the Histadrut as a whole, and by the traditional parties, even when most of this public does not actually join the kibbutz. The fact that the kibbutz is the fulfillment of the ideology and the values of the Histadrut and the labor parties is what has given it its special status in the leadership of the Histadrut and in every one of its parties. However, unlike the leftist–pioneer parties,[2] Mapai has begun to retreat, ever since the

2. Leftist pioneer parties, or "Pioneering Left," is often used as a collective name for Mapam, the former Ahdut Haavoda (until its merger with Mapam and Rafi in 1968) and the Min Hayesod group (see Chapter 19.)

establishment of the State, from its own traditional pioneering position and is being swept into the capitalist bourgeois stream. Since then, the traditional identity between the party and the kibbutz elements has been gradually altered. As a consequence, the specific weight of the kibbutz within that party has also been declining gradually.

The kibbutz makes a contribution of prime importance to the Israeli working class struggle to replace capitalism with socialism, by providing a prototype of future Israeli socialist society and by concretizing—not in drawing plans but in everyday life—the ways to a solution and the possibility of a solution of the fundamental problems of every cooperative society, questions that are still subject to prejudice, doubts and suspicions. It is sufficient if we mention here such problems as integrating social possibilities and individual personality: collectivism and family; the advantages of collective education while preserving and cultivating the relations between parents and children; the emancipation of women, and the like. The implications and importance of the superiority and greater efficiency of the collective method of production over capitalist private enterprise go far beyond the agricultural sector. The kibbutz movement that is preserving its collectivist principles and, at the same time, prospering economically, is thereby dealing a heavy blow to the prestige of the "irreplaceability" of private initiative and, therefore, contributes greatly to the socialist education of the Israeli working class—in the Histadrut, parties, and youth movements.

It would also be a mistake to view the kibbutz movement apart and separate from Israel's cooperative movement in general, in all its forms. As a pioneering commune, the kibbutz is the highest rung of cooperation in Israel, in addition to all its other pioneering, socialist, political, educational and security functions. From this point of view, it is the decisive link in the whole chain, and its own achievements, growth, stability and enterprise to a great extent determine the character and fate of the cooperative movement as a whole. On the other hand, it would be hard to conceive of the kibbutz existing and prospering in a cooperative vacuum, that is, in a situation in which there were only kibbutzim and a totally capitalist environment in towns and countryside, without any intermediate cooperative stages.

The kibbutz movement is therefore vitally interested in the maximum amount of cooperation among the workers outside its ranks, in the growth and stability of the *moshav shitufi*[3] in an expanding and successful net of *moshav ovdim* smallholders' settlements faithful to cooperative principles. It encourages expanding consumers' cooperation, the links between the

---

3. Moshav ovdim (*moshav*; plural *moshavim*)—cooperative smallholders' village based on individual production and private households. Moshav shitufi (collectivist moshav)—a form of cooperative village, combining collective production (like in the kibbutz) with private households (like in the moshav). (See Appendix III—Types of Villages in Israel.)

producers' cooperatives and the Histadrut, the democratization of the administrative enterprises, etc.

The particularity of Israeli socialism

Despite the essential differences between the kibbutz movement and the moshav ovdim in the village and productive and consumers' cooperatives in the cities, and despite the differences between the workers' economy and the municipal and government enterprises, it is possible, from a certain viewpoint, to include all these sectors in the term "public economy"—that is, not managed by private initiative for the enrichment of exploiting employers. This economy forms a comparatively high proportion, about 47.5 percent, of Israel's total economy. It is also worthwhile adding, in order to complete the picture, that a decisive proportion of the land is nationally owned (92.6 percent). However, these facts are used by each of the workers' parties to reach different conclusions concerning the Israeli path to socialism.

Ahdut Haavoda, during the Third and Fourth Aliya, and afterwards Mapai, looked on the Workers' Society and the workers' cooperative enterprises as the beginnings of the socialist regime that was to be established in Palestine by the constant growth and increasing strength of the Workers' Society, without this process necessarily being accompanied by class struggle or integrated with any political struggle to exchange the capitalist system for a socialist one. The Labor Party of today, at the head of the government coalition, puts its faith mainly in the capitalist mechanisms, in the cult of private initiative and bourgeois economic doctrines; however, whenever the particularity of Israeli socialism is discussed, labor's spokesmen identify the public economy in all its forms with the Israeli socialist society and consider the existence and growth of this economy in itself to be the Israeli way to socialism.

On the other hand, Hashomer Hatsair, and afterwards Mapam, have looked on the large workers', cooperative, and public sector of the country's economy, headed by the kibbutz movement, as a strategic position for the labor movement in its class, economic and political struggle, making it easier for the labor movement, after coming to power, to overcome the difficulties in the transition from capitalism to socialism, and to make that transition as brief as possible. The socialist government of the future would have at its disposal a tremendous lever with which to move the other sectors of the economy from private initiative to ramified forms of public ownership—governmental, municipal, cooperative and kibbutz. In other words, it is not a matter of identifying the workers' and public economies with Israeli socialism, but of *integrating* them in the trade union and political class struggle of the labor movement. It is precisely this combination that gives the Israeli labor movement's path toward socialism its special character. The former Ahdut Haavoda–Poale Zion's positions on this matter are a mixture of different attitudes. Like the former Mapai, it has never been weaned completely from the heritage of Syrkin's utopianism of Third Aliya days—as if the workers, cooperative and public economies must and can serve as the highway for the Israeli economy, without any need for a capitalist stage. If, despite everything, capitalist private enterprise does take hold in the country's economy, it is only because of subjective mistakes, inhibitions and inactions in building and reinforcing the independent workers' economy. At the same time, in view of the unfortunate fact that a class-conflict-ridden capitalist economy has developed, the former Ahdut Haavoda–Poale Zion often argues, like Mapam, for the consistent conduct of the class struggle and for the integration of the construction of the workers' cooperative economy in this class struggle.

In the debate over the shape and future of the workers' economy it became clear that it was the pioneering left that refused to consider the Histadrut enterprises as the end-all and be-all, and that argued for these enterprises to be integrated into the class struggle to change the system. They were the ones who really demanded the expansion of these enterprises while maintaining and cultivating their stated social principles; whereas the "maximalists" of the Mapai school, who identified these enterprises with "our special road to socialism," were actually torn between their youthful inclinations for the utopia of the workers' society as the highroad to socialism, and their later love for the magic of all-powerful private initiative and the truths of the doctrines of bourgeois economics. These conflicts in the present-day Labor Party have become real hindrances to the preservation of the cooperative principles of the workers' economy and have prevented a new momentum to expand these enterprises ever further.

SOURCES AND DATA

COMPOSITION OF THE HISTADRUT

1. Histadrut population at   31.12.1975

Adult members	1,277,500
Working youth	683,400
Total Histadrut population (adults, youth & children)	1,960,900

(56.76% of total population of Israel)

2. Histadrut composition by occupation, in percent, 1947–1977

(not including labor settlements)

Economic Branch	End of 1947	End of 1977
Agriculture & Gardening	3.4	2.6
Industry & Crafts	25.7	23.8
Construction	5.2	5.2
Total Agriculture, Industry, Construction	34.3	31.6
Public works & unskilled workers	6.1	8.0
Transport & Communications	5.1	6.0
Free professions & arts	5.8	0.9
Office workers, public and personal services	25.0	37.9
Total office workers, free professions and services	35.9	38.8
Others *	23.7	15.6
Total	100.0	100.0

* Labor settlements included.

3. The largest trade unions in the Histadrut (end of 1976)

National Union of Clerical and Administrative Employees	120,000	members
National Union of Metal, Electrical an Electronic Workers	100,000	″
National Union of Civil Servants	55,000	″
National Union of Building Workers	50,000	″
National Teachers' Union	50,000	″
National Union of Textile, Clothing and Leather Workers	50,000	″
National Union of Agricultural Workers	45,000	″
National Foodworkers' Union	30,000	″
National Union of Workers in Histadrut Enterprises	28,000	″
National Union of Technicians & Engineers	25,000	″
National Union of Restaurant and Hotel Employees	25,000	″

THE COOPERATIVE MOVEMENT IN ISRAEL

a. Number of Cooperatives 1967–1975

Year	Jewish sector of economy	Arab sector	Total
1967	1,804	159	1,963
1975	1,682	216	1,898

Source: Cooperative Almanac of Israel, 1976–1977, Tel Aviv.

b. Number of Cooperatives by kind (end of 1975)

Kind	Jewish sector	Arab sector
1. *Agricultural Cooperatives*		
Kibbutzim and Kvutzot	239	—
Moshavim	323	—
Moshavim Shitufiim	40	—
Other cooperative villages	45	—
General Agriculture	261	3
Processing & Marketing	77	10
Irrigation Districts	69	118
Agricultural Insurance	5	—
Total Agricultural Cooperatives	1,059	131
2. *Production and Service Cooperatives*		
Production	96	3
Services	69	13
Transporation	21	15
Total Production & Services	186	31
3. *Others*		
Consumers' Cooperatives	22	8
Housing Cooperatives	209	16
Suburban Housing Services	14	—
Credit Cooperatives	35	3
Mutual Assurance	3	—
Mutual and Pension Funds	94	—
Mutual Aid & Savings	32	11
Saving Co-ops (in schools)	—	16
Audit Unions	9	—
Aid Unions	12	—
Miscellaneous	7	—
4. Total Cooperatives in Israel	1,682	216

Source: Cooperative Almanac of Israel, 1976–1977, Tel Aviv.

TYPES OF COOPERATIVE VILLAGES IN ISRAEL

1. *Kibbutz or kvutza* (plural: kibbutzim, kvutzot) are collective villages, governed by the general assembly of all members. All property is collectively owned and work is organized on a collective basis. Members give their labor and in return receive housing, food, clothing and social services. There are central dining halls, kitchens and stores, communal kindergartens and children's quarters, social and cultural centers. Individual living quarters provide personal privacy.

    The kibbutzim are predominantly agricultural, but many run sizable industrial enterprises. There are 235 kibbutzim with populations ranging from 80 to 2,000. Total population–100,000 (i.e. approximately 2.8 percent of the total and 3.3 percent of the Jewish population. Nevertheless the kibbutzim contribute 40 percent of the total agricultural output, and 8 percent of the industrial output). The first kvutza, Degania, was founded in 1909.

2. *Moshav* (plural: moshavim) is a cooperative smallholders' village, based on principles of mutual aid and equal opportunity. Each member has a farm worked by himself and his family, but produce is sold, and supplies and equipment are bought, through central cooperatives. Some farm machinery is owned by the village as a whole. The general assembly elects a council, which approves all transfers of farms and acceptances of new members.

    There are 378 moshavim of various types, with populations ranging from 100 to 1,000. Total population –127,000 (approximately 3.7 percent of the total and 4.0 percent of the Jewish population). The first was Nahalal, founded in 1921.

3. *Moshav shitufi* (plural: moshavim shitufiim) is based on collective production and ownership (as in the kibbutz), but each family has its own house and is responsible for its own cooking, laundry, and child care (as in the ordinary moshav). Work and pay are adjusted to individual circumstances. Like the kibbutz, the moshav shitufi tends to develop industry in addition to agriculture.

    There are 29 moshavim shitufiim, with populations ranging from 60 to 100. Total population, 6,300. The first was Kfar Hittin, established in 1936.

(Jan. 1, 1977)

Structure of the Histadrut

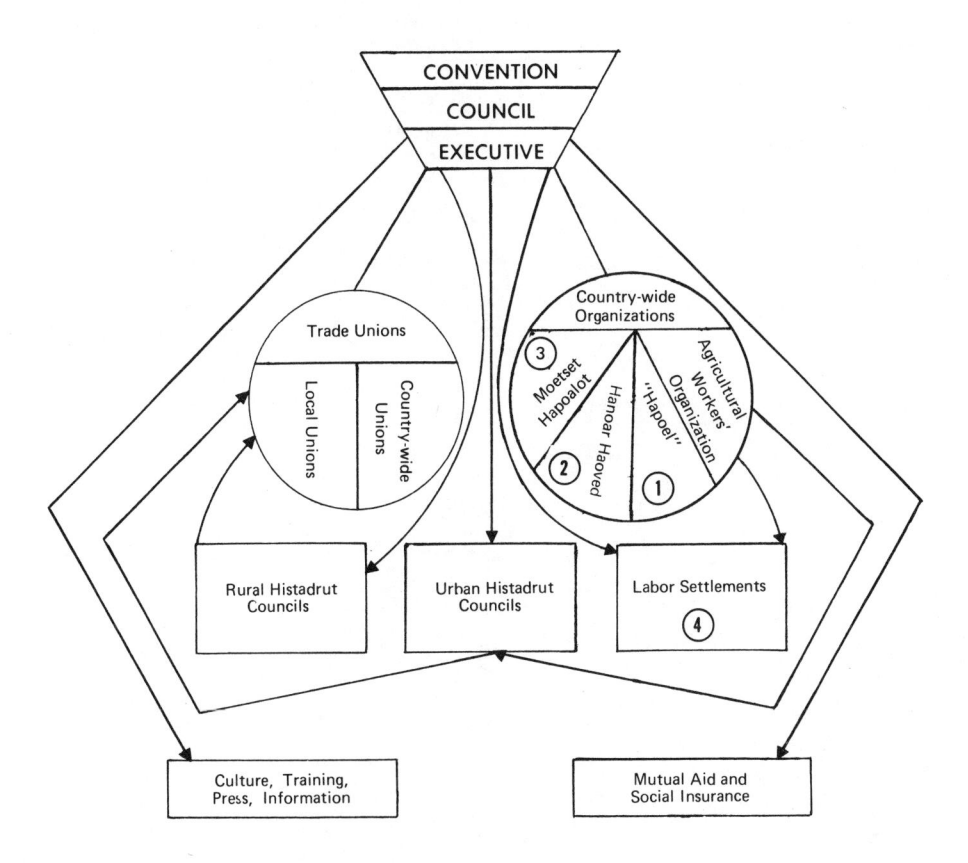

1 Workers' Sports Organization
2 General Federation of Working and Studying Youth
3 Women Workers' Council
4 Kibbutzim and Moshavim

Structure of Hevrat Ovdim

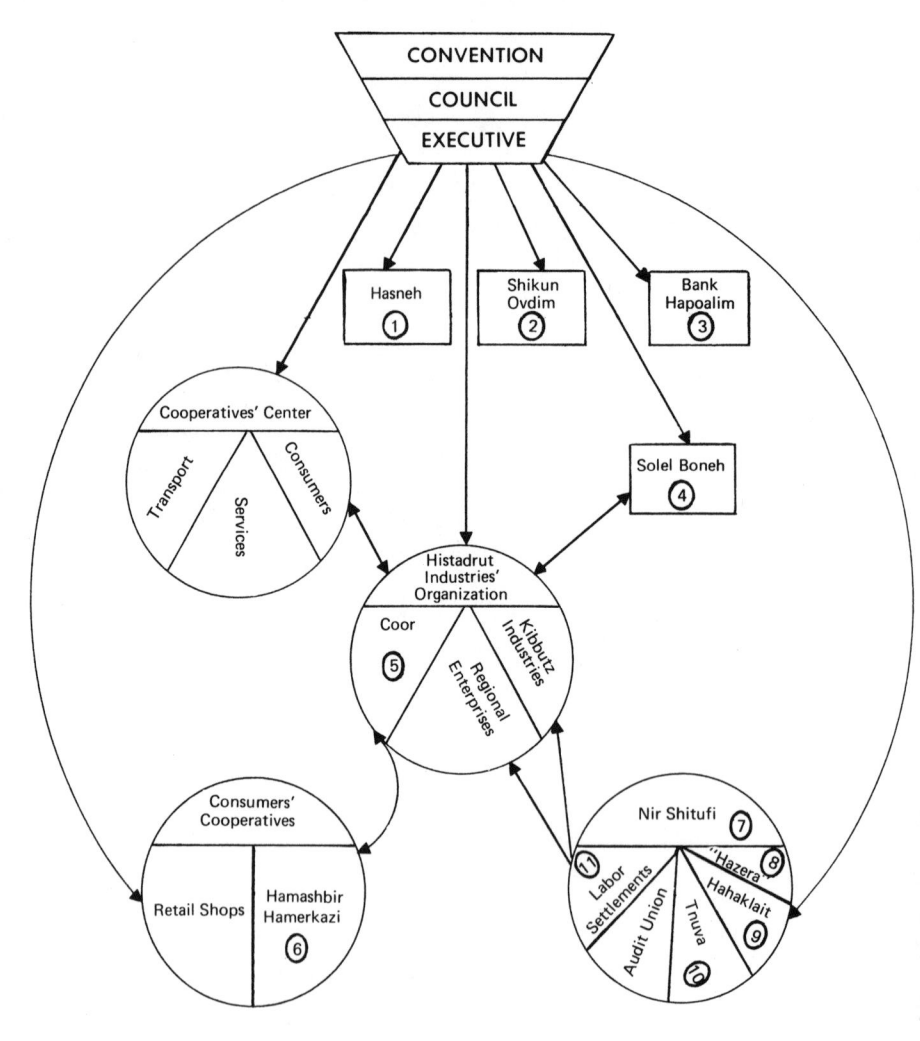

1. Insurance Cooperative
2. Housing Cooperative
3. Workers' Bank
4. Histadrut Contracting Company
5. Holding Company for Industries directly managed by the Histadrut
6. Central Supply Organization
7. Legal frame through which the "Agricultural Workers' Organization" exerts its authority over the affiliated Cooperative and Collective Villages
8. Selected Seed Producers' Cooperative
9. Cooperative Animal Insurance
10. Agricultural Products' Marketing Cooperative
11. Kibbutzim and Moshavim

Mapam Resolutions on the Histadrut

1. The General Labor Federation (Histadrut), which materializes the principle of the unity of functions in defending the hired laborer, constructing its autonomous economy and developing the tools of mutual aid and social insurance, bears the main burden and is the guarantee for worker-pioneering hegemony in the State.

By maintaining this unity of functions in the State, the class and the economy, the Histadrut can play a leading role in shaping Israeli society in its progress toward the formation of a socialist workers society.

2. Mapam calls upon the workers' public to defend the Histadrut's autonomy and inclusive character in order to forge its guiding and militant force at the head of the organized working class; in order to preserve its pioneering character in absorbing immigration and developing the country; in order to secure the freedom of trade union struggle and guarantee the worker his fair share of the national income.

The Workers' Society (Hevrat ovdim)

1. The workers' economy with all its various sectors—including cooperative agriculture in the kibbutz and moshav, producers' and consumers' cooperatives, administered and kibbutz industry, in building, contracting, in finance and insurance, transportation and tourism, medical enterprises and social services—forms a leading factor in furthering the aims of economic planning, of developing basic economic branches, of promoting movement to the development areas and of technological progress, and in providing an example of advanced labor relations.

2. The entrenchment of the signs of the trends toward bureaucracy and technocracy, which betray the vision of building a socialist workers' society in Israel, is the main reason for the decline in the human element and the deterioration of labor relations, and as a result, for the signs of the retreat of the Histadrut enterprises before the private sector in industry and the stagnation in development. In order to overcome these dangers, the workers' society must develop economic momentum and wide social reforms.

The Workers' Society will act:

• To renew the industrial initiative of the workers' economy in general and to encourage the industrial activity of the communal and cooperative settlements.

• To apply Histadrut authority in fulfilling the decisions of the Histadrut institutions concerning workers' participation in the management of Histadrut firms and companies, in their profits and in responsibility for their progress and success.

• To train management cadres coming from the working class and the settlements while encouraging pioneering initiative in strengthening the various links of the economy.

• To develop export initiatives and obtain modern technological know-how, strengthening the Planning Center and organizing the enterprises of the economy into sectors according to specializations.

• To encourage producers' cooperative activity in Jewish and Arab communities, by guaranteeing self-labor, training independent management personnel and deepening internal democracy.

• To maintain effective and consistent supervision by the Workers' Society over the economy's activities and social character by intensifying efficient control, strengthening the Institute for Economic Audit, publishing reports on the economy's enterprises and drawing organizational and economic conclusions from the findings of these audits.

• To secure the government's full share in financing the various branches of the Histadrut economy and in providing organized aid in guiding industry, looking for export markets, obtaining international know-how and encouraging domestic research.

• To guarantee real cooperation among the pioneering and constructive trends and forces bearing the responsibility for the Workers' Society.

Class and Social Struggle

1. Mapam will struggle to defend and promote the rights and just interests of the workers. It will struggle for an economic policy of development and full and productive employment, and for a progressive social policy that will guarantee equality in bearing the burdens, narrow polarity and social differentiation, maintain a decent standard of living and improve the workers' social rights.

2. Mapam will fight against freezing workers' wages or fringe benefits. Mapam sees its urgent task in correcting the injustices suffered by the production workers who are discriminated against in wages and fringe benefits. Mapam will demand that the Histadrut's wage policies be determined in democratic consultation including the shop committees, the Workers' Councils and the trade unions.

3. In order to maintain real wages, Mapam will demand guarantees for price stability and the maintenance of the wage-increment system to provide full compensation for price rises.

4. Special priority for a higher standard of living for the low-income hired laborers and for large families will be secured by a trade union policy that will guarantee fair wages, improved fringe benefits and expanded social security.

5. Mapam will demand the inauguration of fair and equal minimum wages for men and women workers entering into employment. It will guarantee the implementation of the law for equal wages for equal work for men and women in all fields of work.

6. Mapam considers greater efficiency and increased productivity to be vital matters of prime importance for the country's economy. Continued progress in increasing productivity depends upon the cooperation of all the factors of production in raising the levels of management, the acquisition of modern equipment, the intensification of technological know-how, decreasing management costs and blown-up profits.

7. Mapam will demand greater effort and resources in order to expand the system of vocational training and the adoption of urgent measures in order to absorb new immigrants, women, youths and discharged soldiers into productive employment.

8. Mapam will act to integrate the Arab worker within the Histadrut and will struggle to guarantee him wages and social rights equal to those of all other workers in the country, to bring all Arab employed workers into the frame of the Histadrut, to establish Workers' Councils, employment services and mutual aid institutions where the Arab workers live.

9. Mapam will oppose the attempts to organize labor relations by legislation intended to limit the freedom of trade union struggle. Labor relations within the economy must be determined, as in the past, by agreements between the Histadrut and the employers' associations.

Within the Knesset and the Histadrut bodies, Mapam will oppose the proposed law for a cooling-off period for strikes.

For Progressive Social Planning

The Histadrut must be a moving and initiating force in planning and expanding social legislation in the State of Israel and must expand the activities of its institutions for social security and mutual aid.

The Histadrut must work:

• To urge legislation for unemployment insurance.

• To enact a compulsory health law by means of the existing Sick Funds. Mapam will struggle against the deliberate delay in passing this legislation by government bodies.

• To increase governmental participation in the Sick Fund's budget while maintaining the principles of popular public medicine.

• To expand hospital facilities, preventive medicine and mother and child stations.

- To expand legislation for general incapacity insurance and pensions.
- To intensify Histadrut authority over its social security organs in order to increase efficiency, to provide fraternal and inexpensive services, to fulfill the rights of its members and to strengthen social progress.

(From: Resolutions of Fifth Congress of Mapam, published by Mapam, Tel Aviv, March 1968.)

Mapam Offers Principles for Histadrut

Mapam's main conceptions concerning future Histradrut policy were presented to the Alignment Information staff and adopted for the most part.

According to these principles the Histadrut will have to continue its campaigns in the economic and trade union fields. Among the aims guiding these campaigns will be the following:

- Freedom of trade union struggle and freedom of strike, while guarding the Histadrut's authority in formulating labor agreements and opposing all proposals for compulsory arbitration.
- Economic policies that will stop inflation, renew economic growth and guarantee full employment and wages reflecting the workers' just share in the national income; an equitable distribution of the burden.
- The prevention of speculative enrichment, war against black capital, true taxes on capital, control over commodity prices, services and profits.
- Publication of an income tax register; a supplementary tax in addition to the 60 percent marginal tax, to be imposed on recipients of high incomes as a one-time tax on capital;
- A minimum wage linked to 60 percent of the average wage in the economy. Equal wages to women workers for equal work; premiums in production and services in return for increases of productivity; equal fringe benefits to all workers; maintenance at all costs of the instrument of cost of living increments; maintenance of the real value of pensions.
- Deepened democracy in industry by workers and employees' participation in management, responsibility and profits; deepened democracy within the Histadrut by co-opting workers to Histadrut organs;
- Development and expansion of the social security and mutual aid systems: health insurance, pensions for all, based on real wages and separate from the allotments of the National Insurance; narrowing the social gap, an aim that must be a permanent component of policies in the fields of economics, trade union struggle, education and housing.
- Industrialization of the Arab village by Histadrut initiative by creating places of employment near the Arab workers' homes.

(Brit Mapam, published by World Union of Mapam, Vol. 3, No. 8, Tel Aviv, April 1977.)

17 • The Kibbutz Movement

Aims, Trends, Stages

We will outline here the stages of kibbutz development, stressing those aspects vital to an understanding of the history of the Israeli labor movement.

The *kvutza ktana* (small commune), the only form of settlement by self-employing labor during the Second Aliya, eventually ended up in crisis because of its small size, which inhibited the development of the economy, as well as cultural, social, family and personal life. Toward the close of the Second and the beginning of the Third Aliya, this crisis led to the experiment of the *kvutza gdola* (large commune)—the "group of 60" at Kinneret in 1920, and to the *moshav ovdim* (cooperative smallholders' settlement), which were conceived and created by members who left the small commune. The first moshavim were formed in Nahalal and Kfar Yeheskel in 1921.

The Third Aliya brought both the members of the Russian Hechalutz who established the Joseph Trumpeldor Labor Battalion (Gdud Haavoda), and the members of Hashomer Hatsair from Poland, who concentrated in Betaniya Ilit and Gdud Shomriya, with some others joining the Gdud Haavoda. The Gdud Haavoda believed in agricultural settlement and in the "Conquest of Labor," in communal life and in establishing an egalitarian standard of living, with a single treasury for all the Gdud Haavoda groups throughout the country.

The aim:

> To guide the country by establishing a general commune of all the Jewish workers in Palestine.

Principles:

> A. The organization of members in disciplined kibbutzim under the authority of the Histadrut in all matters of labor and defense;
> B. A general fund supplying all the needs of the members;
> C. Domestic production to meet the needs of the members;
> D. To expand the economy and improve working conditions by investing the surplus profits for this purpose.
> E. To reinforce the Histadrut and to direct it toward the aims of Gdud.
> (From the constitution of the Gdud Haavoda al shem Yosef Trumpeldor, adopted at the founding convention at Migdal, 1921.)

Some of the members of Hashomer and of the Second Aliya "large commune" joined the Gdud Haavoda, believing that it could serve as a vehicle for the realization of the idea of the large commune. The meeting point between the two groups was the program for settlement in the Nuris Block at the foot of Mount Gilboa. In September 1921, a Gdud Haavoda group settled in Tel Yosef, and in December of the same year, in Ein Harod—both forming a single common economy.

It did not take long before the two groups—the Third Aliya supporters of the General Commune of the Workers of Palestine, on the one hand, and the Second Aliya partisans of the "large commune," on the other found themselves divided in their views. One point of conflict was the question of the status of the settled kibbutz within the national Gdud as a whole. . . . The members of the Second Aliya considered the development and stabilization of the individual kibbutz as the essential, while the more orthodox Gdud members looked on it as just another one of the groups. They saw no need to give the settled kibbutz any preference over the groups earning their living from wage labor in the cities, on the roads, in the quarries, etc. In keeping with these conflicting views, the partisans of the large commune opposed using settlement budgets for anything but developing the kibbutz farmstead while the heads of the Gdud saw nothing wrong in using them for maintenance and to meet the deficits of the other groups. The first demanded that the demands for stable personnel for the developing kibbutz be guaranteed, while their opponents considered the members of the kibbutz farm to be subject to national manpower organization and to transfer from one place to another according to need and the labor market. Finally, the first wanted wide kibbutz autonomy in planning and management, while the second clung to the principle of a centralized countrywide management for the Gdud as a whole.

There was a second problem involved in the debate—the relations between the Gdud and the party, that is, Ahdut Haavoda, to which a considerable part of the Gdud membership, and particularly the people of the Second Aliya, belonged. The members of the Third Aliya who headed the Gdud Haavoda intended it to have a guiding function, socially and morally as well as politically, in shaping the Histadrut toward a radical spirit and aim. The members of the Second Aliya (and especially the partisans of Ahdut Haavoda) wanted to distinguish between commune and politics and between the Gdud and the party. As they saw it, the Gdud was to occupy itself with the conquest of labor and in establishing agricultural communes, leaving politics to "the Party."

In practice, all these points of conflict were interwoven, and the fissure in the Gdud's ranks continued to grow deeper. The first result was the partition of Tel Yosef-Ein Harod between the Gdud partisans, who remained in Tel Yosef, and the partisans of Ahdut Haavoda and the large commune, who concentrated in Ein Harod and left the Gdud completely. Within the Gdud's groups and settled kibbutzim (Tel Yosef, Kfar Gileadi, Ramat Rachel) the debate over the relationships between the Labor Battalion and Ahdut Haavoda continued and led to increasing polarization. With the Fourth Aliya—accompanied by the petit bourgeois and nonpioneering phenomena, economic crisis, unemployment and closed immigration, etc.—the utopian illusions from the Third Aliya that were still prevalent in the Gdud soon evaporated. Some, led to bitterness by the unsympathetic and sometimes even unfair and hostile attitudes of the Histadrut leadership, sometimes went from justified criticism to doubts about and even the rejection of Zionism. These persons began to reveal sympathy, or at least neutrality, toward the subversions of the violently anti-Zionist and anti-pioneering Palestine Communist Party. Another part of the Gdud was in favor of forming closer links with Hashomer Hatsair, and even joined with it in 1926, in forming the "Kibbutz List" for the elections to the Third Histadrut Congress in 1926. The right wing was composed mainly of members or sympathizers of Ahdut Haavoda who were opposed to the Gdud's appearing or acting independently in the Histadrut or political arenas. In December 1926, the Gdud split into a "Rightist Gdud" (including the three settled kibbutzim) and a "Left-Wing Gdud" that was strongly influenced by "liquidationism" and communist subversion, and which served as the chief base for the left opposition within the Histadrut. In 1927 some of the leaders of the Leftist Gdud (headed by Menahem Elkind) left the country for the Soviet Union, where they formed a commune called "The New Path."

In contrast to this degeneration and disintegration, Kibbutz Ein Harod, after its separation from the Gdud, had served as a center of attraction and unity for various kibbutzim. First, it combined with Havurat Haemek (the Emek group); later it labeled itself the Ein Harod Kibbutz—that is, as a national commune, and not only as a single commune—which was joined in the course of time by groups in the city and colonies, immigrant groups from Hechalutz, Hechalutz Hatsair, Habonim, and other organizations. In August 1927, these kibbutzim and groups, together with the Hashomer Hatsair kibbutz from the U.S.S.R. (now Afikim), organized themselves as the Kibbutz Hameuchad (United Kibbutz). In December 1929, Kibbutz Hameuchad was also joined by the remnants of the Gdud Haavoda—Tel Yosef, Kfar Gileadi and Ramat Rahel. The Kibbutz Hameuchad considered the Gdud's failure to have been the result of three main points: that it had not put the establishment and development of kibbutzim at the center of its activity, with the other groups in the towns and colonies only serving as transition forms until settlement; that it had not given even a limited degree of autonomy to each of the kibbutzim; and third, that at least some elements within it had been looking for some independent political path or mission, and had forgotten that they belonged to *the* party (then Ahdut Haavoda, later Mapai). From now on, Kibbutz Hameuchad's members and groups were composed of Ahdut Haavoda (later Mapai) members and nonaffiliated Ahdut Haavoda voters (with the addition of a small group of Left Poale Zionists taken over from the former Gdud kibbutzim).

As the legacy of the Gdud, however, they did receive the idea that the objective pioneering and socialist-Zionist tasks and imperatives, as well as the organizational ability to fulfill these, were the almost exclusive criteria for the structure and size of the individual kibbutz; they favored "the communal settlement of members of Kibbutz Hameuchad in large and open communities." They stressed the "popular, open-to-all" character of the kibbutz and even declared their belief that in principle there was nothing to prevent the ranks of the kibbutz movement expanding to include all or most of the workers of Palestine.

After a number of years of dispersion and searchings, most of the Third and Fourth Aliya Hashomer Hatsair kibbutzim and kvutzot (smaller groups) came to recognize the need for some common organization, for cooperation and mutual aid, as well as to guide the educational movement in the Diaspora. They also felt the need to formulate their common ideology and to conduct independent political activity within the working class public and the Histadrut, since none of the existing parties were able to satisfy the Hashomer Hatsair Kibbutzim. The recognition of this need took on material form, with the establishment of the Kibbutz Ha'artzi Hashomer Hatsair in Haifa in April 1927. Not having originated in either the majority or minority of the Gdud Haavoda, the Kibbutz Ha'artzi went further than the Kibbutz Hameuchad in learning the lessons of the Gdud's failure. In its "Ideological Assumptions" the Kibbutz Ha'artzi declared that the kibbutz was at one and the same time a way of life with its own autonomous content and a national and class instrument, with both of these aspects inseparably combined, and that, especially in the hostile capitalist environment, organizational ability and initiative, good will and propaganda were not enough to guarantee the establishment of stable kibbutzim; the consciousness of objective imperatives had to go together with training and education, and cultivating the feelings of personal satisfaction of the subjective human element (the "organic kibbutz"). This also led to the need to limit the numerical size of the kibbutz to an optimum that would meet the needs of the developing planned collective economy, but still permit the atmosphere of the kibbutz as a home and of social and personal satisfaction. Another corollary was the need to grant every kibbutz unit a considerable measure of autonomy in order to cultivate the individual's personal identification with the collective. What is more, kibbutz cooperation must go beyond the educational, cultural, social and economic spheres to embrace the ideological and political aspects as well; the absence of collectivism in the last sphere holds the seeds of dissension and of division that could, in certain internal circumstances, lead to the split that had overtaken the Gdud. As a matter of fact, Kibbutz Hameuchad also had a one-party situation (since they were all members or supporters of Ahdut Haavoda and later, Mapai), as had the Hever Hakvutzot (the members and supporters of Hapoel Hatsair and, later, also Mapai, after the union). In this, however, Hashomer Hatsair went further than the other two kibbutz movements. It did not satisfy itself with the unofficial negative attitude of all the movements to a multi-party structure, but also added the positive element of consistently seeking for the maximum amount of collectivism and of joint ideological and political crystallization—"ideological collectivism."

The kibbutz is found on social, political and economic activity. The definition of political assumptions does not imply the organization of a political party, but a frame for uninterrupted ideological activity and consolidation. Kibbutz Ha'artsi's political strength lies in its being an autonomous political trend within the Israeli labor movement.

Kibbutz Ha'artsi's ideological assumptions are reflected in three main principles: (a) Zionism; (b) socialism, and (c) kibbutz.

. . . Kibbutz Ha-artsi, as part of the kibbutz movement in Israel, considers the kibbutz form to be:

1. *The pioneering cells of the new society.* Every kibbutz forms an organic unit. The kibbutz is not be considered only a class or national instrument, since it has its own content as the prototype of the communal society and as an autonomous ideological and political collective. The nature of the kibbutz is derived from its social life in which it strives for the full integration of individual and society in a joint life's enterprise encompassing all the internal and external spheres of kibbutz activity. It permits the maximal development of the individual, endeavors to find a solution for the problems of family, the woman, and education, and makes possible deeper personal and moral relations.

The important tasks of building the kibbutz movement and social life within the organic kibbutz demand particular social and individual pioneering education and training, which must be carried out mainly by the Jewish youth movement in the Diaspora.

2. *The constructive instrument of the Jewish working class.* The kibbutz fulfills the historic constructive role of the Jewish working class, by (a) establishing settlement-enterprises in village and town; (b) the maximum penetration into all branches of production; (c) preparing the class for autonomous economic management.

The constructive activity of the working class is not to be considered the chief solution for the class contradictions; it is the liquidation of the existing regime by means of a social revolution that will achieve the organization of production and economy by the working people on the basis of justice and equality.

3. *The instrument for the absorption of Jewish labor immigraton.* The kibbutz enterprise is founded on the maximal absorption of pioneering immigra-

tion, on making it easier for it to settle on the land and making possible the thorough penetration into all the branches of labor.

4. *The bulwark of the class struggle.* The kibbutz participates in class struggle: (a) as an organic unit of the trade union movement; (b) as a political and ideological collective with a consolidated class positon.

(From "The Ideological Assumptions of the Kibbutz Ha'artsi," adopted at Founding Congress, Haifa, 1927.)

After the establishment of the Kibbutz Ha'artzi and of the Kibbutz Hameuchad in 1927, the *Hever Hakvutzot* (formed in 1925 at a meeting in Bet Alfa) was left mostly with the smaller communes and was not very active. This situation changed only when it was joined, during the Fifth Aliya, by members of the Gordonia Youth Movement (inspired by A. D. Gordon and Hapoel Hatsair, this union took place in the Ramat David Council in 1934). With the formation of Mapai in 1930, two kibbutz federations were affiliated with it, even if only informally—Hakibbutz Hameuchad and Hever Hakvutzot. All the efforts of the leadership of the united party to bring these two kibbutz groups to unification were of no avail, for two main reasons: First, at that time, there were great differences between them in structure, style and tradition. Second, despite the unification of Hapoel Hatsair and Ahdut Haavoda, the tendencies to avoid obliterating the differences between the two original parts were stronger within the kibbutz federations (and moshav ovdim settlements) than among the urban rank and file. Later, during the second half of the 30s and the beginning of the 40s, when the conflicts between trends and factions in Mapai grew more intense, the situation was no longer appropriate for the unification of Hever Hakvutzot with the Kibbutz Hameuchad, most of which headed the leftist opposition faction, Siah Bet.

The Mapai split in 1943–1944 complicated the Kibbutz Hameuchad's internal situation very much. Overnight, the practical single-party situation which had substituted for "ideological collectivity" was ruptured, and a two-party situation was rapidly formed—as in the Gdud before it. The two-party situation eventually led to a split in Kibbutz Hameuchad (at the Givat Brenner Council in 1951) with the large Mapai minority leaving to join with the Hever Hakvutzot to form the new Ihud Hakvutzot Vehakibbutzim (Union of Kvutzot and Kibbutzim). This split caused a great deal of damage—divided kibbutzim, population transfers, and a wave of departures from the kibbutz in general. Eventually, the Kibbutz Hameuchad stood the test heroically and managed to reorganize and regain its former momentum, but the split was a great shock that turned it from the largest of the federations into the third in rank—after Kibbutz Ha'artsi and the Ihud.

There is no doubt that most of the questions that have been in tradi-

---

1. Generally shortened to "Ihud."

tional dispute between the three kibbutz movements—kibbutz structure and size, etc.—have lost most of their force. Within the Kibbutz Hameuchad, the ratio of former youth movement members has increased greatly. In the course of time, specific settlement conditions—available land, water and manpower, have kept the Kibbutz Hameuchad's new communes to dimensions very far from the original concept of the "large and open kibbutz," and closer to those of the Hashomer Hatsair kibbutzim, which had, in turn, gradually expanded. One cannot, therefore, really speak of polar differences between the three kibbutz movements—in the kibbutz field— that could serve as a block to unification of the kibbutz movement. As for "ideological collectivism," both the Kibbutz Hameuchad and the Ihud are indeed still opposed in principle. They have both, since 1951, returned to the one-party situation, broken in the Ihud by some members' participation in the Min Hayesod group and in Rafi (until the recent reunification). In addition, the differences between the Kibbutz Ha'artzi's "ideological collectivism" and the "ideological unity" practiced officially by the Kibbutz Hameuchad since the Givat Brenner council in 1955, though not limited to terminology alone, are certainly not such as to be a decisive hurdle to unity.

The background and basis for increasingly closer cooperation in various fields between the different kibbutz movements undoubtedly exist; in 1963 they led to the formation of the confederative League of Kibbutz Movements.

Increased Social and Political Involvement

The concept of the kibbutzim as socialist islands in a capitalist sea was always correct in principle, and still is; but it does not cover all the aspects of interaction between the kibbutz and society at large. Between the socialist kibbutz and the Israeli society and economy, there were always significant transitory levels of Histadrut economic endeavor, consumer and producer cooperatives, cooperative villages, the government and municipal economic sector, the socio-political area of the Histadrut and the workers' parties. The kibbutz movement served as a spinal cord that projected and guided—the highest rung of a prolific cooperative-socialist ladder. Hence, the image of pure kibbutz socialism facing a pure capitalist environment is an unrealistic oversimplification. But, in the 1950s, this ladder of intermediate stages began to prove unsteady, and the kibbutz found itself in a position of growing isolation.

The kibbutz had two options: either to despair of the surroundings that were receding from it and from its values, and to concentrate on its internal problems; or else to recognize that there could be no long-term peaceful coexistence between the lay and autonomous socialist kibbutz and an entirely alien and hostile environment in which bourgeois reaction, chauvinism, and clericalism would reign supreme, while the workers' movement would be ruled by pragmatism and the tendency to compromise and to surrender—either the complete and final victory of a bourgeois society unable to live with the constant threat and provocation of socialist fortress islands which daily demonstrate the superiority of socialist production and life, and serve as an obstacle to pragmatism, compromise or capitulation of the workers' movement; or growing strength and eventual victory for socialism on a national scale. The latter implied a kibbutz obligation to be more socially and politically involved, to escape the threat of encirclement and isolation—to participate as best as it could in the effort to block the rise of reaction, while securing the continued and uninterrupted development of kibbutz society.

The rise of neo-capitalism gave warning signs and showed growing resistance to these developments. More and more people—not only the left-wing Marxists within the Zionist-Socialist workers' movement, but also considerable sections of the Labor Party—began to understand that a bourgeois government must eventually rule in a society and economy where the private sector, bourgeois values of private initiative, individualist freedom with its central motive of chase after personal riches, standard of living, career and status are constantly gaining power. To be sure, for many years following independence, the Israeli bourgeoisie suffered from having played an infinitesimal role in the creation of the conditions that brought about the foundation of the State of Israel. All the activities and mechanisms of Jewish autonomy in mandated Palestine—whether political, economic or military—were headed by representatives of the workers' movement who almost automatically became the government of the young State. However, many Labor Party leaders and active members recently came to understand that, though the Israeli bourgeois handicap gave their movement a certain head start in which to fortify workers' hegemony and build foundations more solid than the glory of a heroic past, there was, in the long run, still no chance for a labor government to rule over a neo-capitalist society and economy.

In any case, the past was slowly being forgotten; many immigrants who had come since independence knew nothing of it and did not connect what they found in Israel with the workers' movement that created it. And so a large section of the Labor Party also began to recognize the need to rehabilitate anti-capitalist awareness and socialist class-consciousness among the masses of Histadrut and Party members, and the voters—especially the young ones—in the face of the assault by the bourgeois opposition. Pragmatism could be a fatal drug for a labor movement that needed dynamic action. Socialist revaluation within the Labor Party, though not equally intense in all its wings and factions nor as yet expressed in decisive politics, strengthened the wish of a major section of the party to deepen the alliance with its left-wing alignment colleague, Mapam. Naturally, it also revived the power of the affiliated national kibbutz federations, within the party and its internal leadership; and it improved the attitude to the pioneering youth movements, the kibbutz and its specific problems and requirements—within the Labor Party, the Histadrut and the government.

Another fact was becoming obvious. The cardinal problems of Zionist realization—absorption of immigration, integration of Eastern and Western communities, creation of a class of Jewish workers rooted in every branch and grade of production, Jewish self-defense, negotiation and attainment of peace with our Arab neighbors—could not be solved by private initiative and individualist chase after riches at the expense of society in general. The solution of these problems demanded, as in the past, pioneering socialist methods and motivation, through the agency of a united workers' front and a militant trade union organization, with the socialist kibbutz and its values of voluntarism, idealism and collective creativity serving as symbol and center. A bourgeois Israeli government would be not only a blow to the Zionist-Socialist labor movement and working class, but also a tragedy in terms of achieving the Zionist objectives. No wonder, then, that the recent sentiments and processes surrounding the kibbutz have helped in galvanizing its members into overcoming their feeling of isolation. During the first half of the 1970s, the entire kibbutz movement has adopted the slogan of "increased involvement" in shaping the image of Israeli society, including the struggle for a more militant and radical labor movement—a battle which will be decisive for the place, the chances and the future of the kibbutz itself.

This process of increased involvement culminated in the massive mobilization of the kibbutz movement during the Histadrut election campaign of June 1977, shortly after the victory of the Likud in the parliamentary elections: the kibbutz movement virtually saved the Alignment's overall majority in the Histadrut (see chapter 27).

The Pioneering Youth Movements

The ties between the kibbutz movement and the pioneering youth movements in the Diaspora were in existence from the very beginning: the kibbutz trends and national federations came into being as the product and organizational continuation of the immigration coming from these youth movements.[2]

2. This was true for Hakibbutz Ha'artsi—and the World Hashomer Hatsair Movement; for Hakibbutz Hameuchad—and Hechalutz Hatsair–Freiheit and later Dror; for Hever Hakvutzot—and Gordonia, and later for the Ihud Hakvutzot Vehakibbutzim—and Habonim.

It was, however, a much more complicated problem to establish ties between the kibbutz movement and Palestinian Jewish youth. At the time these various kibbutz trends and national federations were taking shape (during the second half of the '20s) a large part of the youth were showing signs of indifference to pioneering activity and the kibbutz, as if they felt that they had done their Zionist duties by the very fact that their parents had brought them to Palestine and that they had grown up in Zion. The vast majority of the youth were unaffiliated or they belonged to the "Scouting Organization," which was attempting to copy Baden Powell's scouting movement in Palestine. Only an insignificant minority belonged to political parties. As for working youth, some were organized in the "General Organization of Working Youth" (formed in 1924 by the Histadrut).

The attempts of the kibbutz to break through this wall of indifference and alienation on the part of the youth did not succeed very much and generally only transient local ties were established. This situation changed only during the economic and psychological crisis that came after the Fourth Aliya. Palestinian Jewish youth began to show signs of a growing social and ideological ferment, indifference giving way to a sense of siege. Immigration, conquest of labor, and settlement, formerly simply accepted as facts which did not depend on the Palestinian youth and did not obligate them to any efforts, were now put into question by the crisis and some sections of the youth began to feel called upon to enter the fray. There was also an awakening interest in the activities and experience of the Jewish youth movement in the Diaspora and even a "discovery" of the kibbutz, in whose close proximity they had been living for years. This ferment and the desire to establish closer ties with the pioneering movement in the Diaspora and its endeavors within the country led to a split in the Scout Organization when the Jerusalem Scout Legion seceded from it in 1926. This led to the formation of the Student Youth Circle in Tel Aviv in 1927, and to its speedy expansion in the *Hugim* (Circles) movement. And it also led, in 1929, to the establishment of the first branches of Hashomer Hatsair in Mikve-Israel and Haifa. It was only when the kibbutz movement's desire to establish contact with the local youth coincided with the searchings and processes of crystallization that were ripening among youth themselves that the situation was ready for the formation of the pioneering youth movements attached to the kibbutz movement, rooted in the reality of the country and able to speak for and educate Palestinian youth.

The Legion of Jerusalem Scouts as well as scout groups in Petach-Tikva, Hadera, and Rehovot united with the Hugim movement in 1930 after a great deal of debate over the links between the United Movement. A year later its name was changed to Hamahanot Haolim (The Ascending Camps) and one of the kibbutz trends. On the one hand, it was drawn to the Hashomer Hatsair kibbutzim, with its youth movement background and style; it was also attracted by the idea of becoming part of the largest and oldest of the pioneering youth movements in the world. On the other hand, Ahdut Haavoda, which was then in the process of unification with Hapoel Hatsair, considered its links with this youth movement of vital importance for its future position among the Palestinian student youth. Berl Katznelson and Moshe Sharett in particular exerted the greatest efforts and influence to prevent the Hugim and the Legion from joining Hashomer Hatsair and finally turned the balance in their own favor. Hamahanot Haolim affiliated itself to Hakibbutz Hameuchad in 1931. There were, however, many leaders and members who did not accept this decision and they joined Hashomer Hatsair, which was in the early stages of organization and forming most of its original leadership.

After the split in Mapai in 1944, Hamahanot Haolim also split: while the majority remained loyal to the leadership of Hakibbutz Hameuhad and inclined toward Hatnua Le'ahdut Haavoda, the minority demanded affiliation with Gordonia, which had been established in 1937 and was affiliated to Hever Hakvutzot and the right-wing majority of Mapai. When this demand was rejected, the minority left Hamahanot Haolim and, uniting with Gordonia, in 1945 established the United Movement which was affiliated to the Hever Hakvutzot and afterwards to Ihud Hakvutzot Vehakibbutzim. In 1959 it also united with the General Federation of Working Youth to form the Organization of Working and Student Youth in Israel.

The first branches of Hashomer Hatsair in Palestine had already been established in 1929 and the national organization was founded in September 1930, when it declared its affiliation with the World Hashomer Hatsair. From its very first, Hashomer Hatsair was compelled to overcome not only parents' resistance to "abandoning their children to the danger of kibbutz fulfillment," but also fierce political incitement conducted against it by bourgeois circles and the schools, as well as the lack of sympathy and almost open hostility shown by Mapai. These hurdles were only overcome very slowly. An additional problem was that of the age composition. The founders of the movement were mainly older youth, upper classmen in the secondary and vocational schools, who had come to the movement, often from the other organizations, through an ideological decision. The task they faced was to bring into the branches younger groups of the optimal educational age. It was also necessary to adapt the educational programs customary in the world Hashomer Hatsair for the specific conditions of the country. It was only after considerable progress had been made in solving these problems that the first regular convention of the Hashomer Hatsair Organization was called in April 1938.

After the establishment of the State of Israel, Hashomer Hatsair helped to organize a counterpart of this within the Arab community—the Arab Pioneering Youth, in 1954. This movement sent training groups to the kibbutzim so that after their periods of training the members could return to their villages to fill pioneering roles there in cultivating the ideas of Jewish-Arab peace and fraternity, in changing Arab society and economy, in strengthening cooperative trends in agriculture, etc.

In its first years and up to the establishment of Mapai in 1930, the General Working Youth Organization (Hanoar Haoved) had been run jointly by Ahdut Haavoda and Hapoel Hatsair, with Ahdut Haavoda wielding decisive influence. After the Mapai split in 1944 an agreement was reached between the two wings, without leaving any room for the other Zionist-socialist parties. (This situation actually continued to exist when Ahdut Haavoda, after the split, was part of Mapam; Hashomer Hatsair continued being excluded from the Working Youth.) This agreement, originally based on parity between Mapai and Ahdut Haavoda–Poale Zion, gradually changed in Mapai's favor. Mapai's control became even firmer after the Working Youth united with the United Movement. In any case, the Organization of Working and Student Youth in Israel serves mainly as a reserve for the Ihud Hakvutzot Vehakibbutzim, as well as for Hakibbutz Hameuchad.

With some reservations, we should also mention here the Scout Organization, which defines itself as general and nonpartisan, without any ties to the socialist-Zionist labor movement. At the same time, settlement groups have been and still are being established within the organization, to set up new kibbutzim or join existing ones. However, since most of these groups affiliated themselves with Hakibbutz Hameuchad, the Scout leadership, which despite its generalness and lack of ties to the labor movement, was under Mapai influence, tended to look askance at Hakibbutz Hameuchad activity, and eventually, in 1950, helped bring on a split in the Scout Organization and the formation of the Pioneering Scouts, affiliated with Hakibbutz Hameuchad, which eventually united with Hamahanot Haolim in 1955.

All these movements have in the course of the years established tens of settlements—both kibbutzim and moshavim, in addition to filling out existing settlements. The existence and growth of these movements have been important for the youth itself; their contribution to the construction of the country and their importance as reserves for the labor settlements became many times greater after the annihilation of the center of the pioneering movements and immigration in Eastern Europe. However, they also have another important aspect: bringing the student youth closer to the labor movement and its parties. The youth sections of the political parties, of course, have important roles and spheres of activity, but for the younger age groups among both student and working youth we cannot imagine a purely party youth organization having the same influence. Wide sections of youth are brought into the labor movement by the long and fundamental method of pioneering education for kibbutz realization.

The National Kibbutz Federations

Federation	No. of Kibbutzim	Population total	%
Hakibbutz Ha'artzi[1]	77	37,000	34.5
Ihud Hakvutzot vehakibbutzim[2]	88	35,900	33.4
Hakibbutz Hameuchad[3]	60	28,500	26.5
Hakibbutz Hadati[4]	13	5,000	4.7
Poale Agudat Israel[5]	2	800	0.8
Nonaffiliated	1	100	0.1
All Movements	241	107,300	100.0

[1] Affiliated with Mapam
[2] Formerly affiliated with Mapai, now with Labor Party
[3] Formerly affiliated with Ahdut-Ha'avoda, now with Labor Party
[4] Affiliated with National Religious Party
[5] Affiliated with Poale Agudat Israel (extreme orthodox)

(*Source*: Cooperative Almanac of Israel 1976–1977, Tel Aviv.)

18 • Reformism and Anti-Reformism in Israel

Revolutionary socialism and its counterpart and rival, reformism, are both starting points, approaches, and methods of solving the problems facing the labor movement in the course of its struggles. In reality, however, there is no such thing as revolutionary or reformist socialism as such; they always appear as a combination of the fundamental approach, the problems they face and the different solutions offered. Since some of these problems are shared by all or most of the countries, while some are specific to groups of countries, or even to one country alone, both revolutionary socialism and reformism always are, to some degree, specific to every individual country. In defining some specific party in any single country as reformistic or revolutionary-socialist, we are referring to the theoretical and methodological common denominators uniting it with other parties in other countries. The fact of the particularity of every party compels us to make a concrete analysis of the problems it is facing and to examine the possible solutions. It is because of this that we here in Israel cannot conceive of the existence of any reformistic or revolutionary socialism per se, divorced from the context of our socialist-Zionist problems, while the existence of these special problems does not deprive the concepts of "reformism" or "revolutionary socialism" of their real content or soften the conflict between these two rival paths, a conflict which will decide the fate of socialist-Zionism.

Since the establishment of the State, the membership of the Histadrut has grown from about 200,000 to nearly two million (about 56 percent of the total population of Israel). Objectively, it may be said that the labor movement forms a larger share of the general public than ever before. The attainment of national independence also immeasurably increased the potentialities for attracting and absorbing immigration, for development and settlement, and concomitantly, the objective need to stimulate and activate the pioneering and subjective forces to meet all these expanding potentialities and growing needs. The inevitable conclusion, therefore, is that after the attainment of national independence, the Israeli labor movement faces tasks no less vital and responsible than those of the pre-State era. The Histadrut, the workers' parties, the kibbutz movement and the pioneering youth movements will still have to take the lead in building the country and governing the State. There is no contradiction between the need to establish governmental frameworks and institutions and the Histadrut's own independence as a labor and pioneering movement. As in the past, but now on a much higher plateau, it is the task of the national and governmental bodies to help the independent pioneering forces; now, too, as in the past, they cannot replace or inherit these pioneering forces. This is indeed the logical conclusion, but it is here that the central historic interest of fulfilling Zionism and building the country comes into conflict with the nature of Israeli reformism. Mapai (now the Labor Party) in the State of Israel has been the organic continuation of Mapai of the 30s and 40s; however, in view of the greater responsibility it bears as the largest party and the governing party, these older reformist contradictions have now assumed far more serious implications. In the absence of national independence and the instruments of government, Israeli reformism was *compelled* to cultivate class autonomy, with all the values, forms and frameworks that autonomy involved, as well as to support the independent activities of the pioneering and kibbutz elements even when the principle of class autonomy and the radical socialist views held by most of the pioneering and kibbutz elements were not in accordance with the reformists' own views. However, with the establishment of the State, Israeli reformism was able to free itself gradually of these contradictions from the past and applied itself systematically and persistently to implementing David Ben-Gurion's old idea of "from class to people."

It was, of course, not an easy matter to free themselves all at once from the past, both because many of Mapai's cadres and members found it difficult to cut themselves off from the ideals and slogans they had nurtured so long. These ideas are also popular among large sections of the public and the youth both in Israel and abroad, and Mapai has been careful not to make an official and open break with the slogans of the past. And yet, there is no concealing the fact that the kibbutz movement affiliated with Mapai has been declining in its relative importance within its own party, nor that the kibbutz movement has been a permanent target for all attacks by Ben-Gurion and his followers. To this we might add the elimination of the "workers stream"[1] in the educational system, to be made part of the "general stream"; the fact that pioneering youth movement activities were banned for years in the schools and that there have been various attempts to divorce the Histadrut of its cooperatives, indus-

1. An autonomous and authorized system of schools run under Histadrut auspices. It was established in 1925 and existed until 1954, when it was abolished by the Mapai majority in the Histadrut and integrated with the "general system." (On the other hand, an autonomous system of religious schools is still in existence!) At the time of its elimination the Histadrut system numbered 1,847 schools with 140,000 pupils and 6,500 teachers—50 percent of all Israel's children and 70 percent of all immigrant children.

trial enterprises, medical organization (Kupat-Holim), and the like. In a word, there is a growing trend to do away with the supposed "duality" between governmental jurisdiction and workers' and pioneering independence. This conflict between workers' and pioneering autonomy and the cult of the State (etatism), faith in the omnipotence of the bureaucracy, has been one of the most fundamental axes around which the debate between Mapai and the pioneering left has revolved. Within Mapai itself many members have been torn for years between loyalty to their party and their feelings of being part of and sharing the views of the pioneering left and most of the kibbutz movement. The resistance to the anti-pioneering and anti-Histadrut trends was undoubtedly one of the main motives and sources for increasing oppositional unrest within Mapai which came into the open during and following the "Lavon Affair."[2]

The cult of the State and the faith in the omnipotence of the bureaucracy are what led David Ben-Gurion and his supporters to the conclusion that the World Zionist movement formed a superfluous barrier between the State and the Jews in the Diaspora, introducing harmful divisions and making it more difficult for our representatives to mobilize the support of all sections of Jewry for Israel. The pioneering left parties, on the other hand, as well as that part of Mapai for which the late Moshe Sharett was the most characteristic spokesman, believed that the State isn't "Zionism after fulfillment." They believe that the State should not be viewed as the substitute for Zionism, but rather as an advanced stage in the historic process of achieving Zionism, as one of the most important and precious instruments in promoting this process and bringing it to fruition, an inseparable part of the whole process. The greater part of the task of Ingathering of the Exiles and of settling the country is still ahead of us and the task of mobilizing and training the pioneering reserves among the Jews of the Diaspora and Israeli youth is still one of prime importance and devolves mainly on the Zionist and the pioneering youth movements.

In the sphere of economic and trade union policies, the compromises with coalition parties from the bourgeois right and the adoption of the remedies of bourgeois economics led to policies of nondemocratic taxation, wage freezes, systematic attacks against wage increments, in the process depriving the trade unions of their functions and militant spirit. The wage freeze, generally maintained most strictly toward the lower wage levels, not only has led to lowering the standards of living, to inequality and mass suffering, but actually contradicts the basic Zionist task of productivization, of promoting a transition to physical labor. These reformistic economic policies also primarily affect the new immigrants who have mostly come from the countries of the Middle East and

---

2. See Chapter 20.

North Africa, and have disturbed the process of integration between the occidental and oriental sections of the Jewish population.

In contrast to these policies of adaptation to bourgeois economic theories, presented every few years (in 1951, 1962 and 1966) by Mapai as a "new economic policy," Mapam has demanded the inauguration of a pioneering regime that would imply striving for productivization and full employment, wage and tax policies that would guarantee equality in bearing the burden and the maintenance of a decent standard of living. It also demands greater planning in investment and manpower policies; the total mobilization of national and public capital and guiding private investment capital to meet the needs of integration, production and development; energetic war against speculators; price and profit controls; the encouragement and expansion of the autonomous workers' enterprises, the public and governmental sector and the labor cooperatives; and the encouragement of the pioneering and kibbutz forces that are the best guarantees for the fulfillment of these goals. In this struggle Mapam often found an ally in the Ahdut Haavoda–Poale Zion Party.

In the parliamentary sphere, Mapai has generally preferred a coalition with the right to any united front with the pioneering left parties. Only its inability to obtain an absolute majority in the Knesset or to guarantee the participation of the General Zionists (later the Liberals) in the coalition compelled it from time to time to bring the left, or part of it, into the government. In order to liberate itself from this necessity, Mapai has been working persistently to change the present electoral system of proportional representation to one of regional majority elections in order to obtain the absolute majority it could not obtain by present democratic methods, and thus free itself of the need for the left. Mapai's many concessions to the clerical parties are at least partly to be explained in this context. Though the vast majority of Mapai's leadership and cadres is not religious, the party has been arguing for years that we "must not split the Jewish people and separate the Jews of the Diaspora from the State over the attitude toward religion." They also claimed that they didn't want to push the traditionally religious immigrants from the Arab countries into the arms of the religious parties. For these reasons they claimed the need to make such far-reaching concessions to the religious circles as making such matters as marriage and divorce and the ban on public transportation on Saturdays and holidays, etc., exclusively religious functions. In order to avoid dispute with the religious parties Mapai has assiduously avoided giving the country a constitutional law, satisfying itself instead with specific fundamental laws in various fields.

The pioneering left parties did not at all underestimate the fact of the religious traditions maintained by a large part of the immigrants and therefore never declared a militant *kultur kampf* against religion or religious institutions. They have, however, vigorously opposed the imposition of religious laws and practices on the nonreligious part (actually the majority) of the population.

In foreign policy, Mapai's consistently one-sided Western orientation has led to a gradual retreat from the principle of non-identification that the State of Israel had proclaimed in its early years. The adherence to the Eisenhower Doctrine, Israeli arms sales to Western Germany,[3] talk of a Paris-Bonn-Jerusalem axis, and unreserved support for French policies on Algeria and nuclear tests in the Sahara have been some of the landmarks on this dangerous road.

Undoubtedly, the Soviet Union's one-sided support of the Arab countries in their dispute with Israel, as well as the vital necessity of obtaining up-to-date weapons for the Israeli Defense Forces in view of the large quantities of both Russian and Western equipment flowing to the Arabs, have been factors reinforcing that trend, though these factors are not an excuse or justification for policies that are in crying contradiction to the primary interests of the Jewish people, dispersed as they are among both world blocs, or of the State of Israel that sees its future in integration into the Afro-Asian world. On this question, the Israeli labor movement is divided, with the Labor Party on the one side and Mapam—and to some extent the former Ahdut Haavoda–Poale Zion as well—on the other. It may be, however, that the increasing ties between Israel and the countries of Africa and Asia with their anti-colonialist feelings and neutralistic views will begin to impel the Israel Foreign Ministry toward modifying it traditional pro-western links.

In the sphere of *Israeli-Arab relations*[4] a considerable section of Mapai

---

3. The Israel government's adherence to the Eisenhower Doctrine in 1957, the shameful affair of the arms deal with the neo-Nazi West German Army in 1959, the hesitant and conflicting attitudes toward the German scientists working in the Egyptian arms industry in 1964, as well as the establishment of diplomatic ties with Bonn shortly after the stoppage of German military aid, in 1965, all led to serious parliamentary and governmental crises.

4. During the first half of 1965 the debate centered mainly about three issues:

(a) *The Jordan waters:* In light of the decision of the heads of the Arab states to divert the sources of the Jordan, the "activists" of various kinds demanded a preventive military action, while Mapam demanded a vigorous political campaign to prevent the diversion: the Prime Minister, the late Levi Eshkol, adopted a middle position of issuing threats of military action (for deterrent purposes) in the event the political campaign did not succeed.

(b) *Statements by President Habib Bourguiba*: The President of Tunisia came out in favor of negotiations for a peaceful solution of the Israeli-Arab dispute but did not elicit an appropriate response from the Israel government. Mapai and Ahdut Haavoda tended to play down the importance of these statements, whereas Mapam considered them a rare opportunity to develop a peace initiative.

(c) *Israeli reprisal raids into Jordanian territory:* Mapam was opposed to these raids that followed Al-Fatah sabotage activities in Ramat Hakovesh and Afula, stressing that all the possibilities of political activity had not been exhausted and these reprisals served to reunite the divided Arab camp and to isolate Bourguiba.

(the later Rafi leaders like D. Ben-Gurion, M. Dayan, S. Peres and others) were partisans of "activism" and looked upon the reinforcement and appropriate equipping of the Israeli Army—something that all of us agree to be a prime necessity in itself—as a substitute for political initiative toward negotiations on peace and the conclusion of a peace treaty. The repeated declarations of our readiness for peace and for direct negotiations have undoubtedly been positive and desirable, particularly when they are compared with the Arab threats of war and annihilation and their stubborn rejection of any negotiations on peace. At the same time, if these declarations had gone together with a neutral foreign policy and support for the aims of the colonial peoples for liberation, the open disavowal of a future "preventive war," a more flexible and constructive attitude toward the solution of the refugee problem and toward the Arab minority in Israel, these declarations would have had much more weight, been much more influential, and held greater prospects. Even if it could be argued that the rulers of the Arab countries did not care what Israel's policies were, this was not true for the African and Asian countries in whose area Israel wanted to integrate and who might be the most hopeful mediators between us and the Arab countries. For the latter, the kind of policies Israel adopted were of great importance.

In this sphere of Israeli-Arab relations, Ahdut Haavoda–Poale Zion was closer to the views of Ben-Gurion, Peres and Dayan. Mapam, therefore, generally was compelled to stand alone against the activist trends that put the stress on military solutions in its struggle for an inclusive and consistent policy of initiatives for peace. Within Mapai there was a wide circle that rejected "activism" and military substitutes for political solutions. This circle's weak point lay in its avoidance of an open ideological debate and its failure to combine its criticisms of "activism" with a demand for a general revision of Israeli foreign policy in the direction of neutrality.

As far as the attitude toward the Arab minority in Israel was concerned, Mapai had been responsible for the main supporter of the policies of military administration, justified by security considerations, in view of the open continuation of the state of war with the Arab countries, attempts at espionage, infiltration and the like. Almost all the other parties in the Knesset, however, left and right alike, had begun to question these arguments. Israeli public opinion was increasingly coming to the view that security problems on the border areas could be solved by the regular laws and security forces, without the need to exempt all the affairs of these areas (for the Arab inhabitants alone) from the jurisdiction of the appropriate governmental departments. Military control actually went so far as to intervene in municipal elections and the election of village councils, to interfere with the political activities of the other parties (except for Mapai), and to exploit the need for permits to travel to work for Mapai party interests. The administration also tended to rely on the conservative and even reactionary elements among the Arab public and to patronize groups ready to support Mapai for their own opportunistic reasons, just as they had always supported governments in power in the past. (Here we find the explanation for the "Arab Lists" affiliated with Mapai.)

Mapai's stubbornness in defending the military administration may be explained, first of all, by the general pessimism characteristic of Ben-Gurion and his followers concerning the prospects of Israeli-Arab peace, and their inclination to view increasing military strength as a surrogate for a policy of peace initiatives. Secondly, the military administration, with its exclusively Mapai composition and unlimited authority, provided Mapai with an opportunity to dominate the Arab sector.

However, although in the early years of the State Mapam fought a lone battle against both the military administration and the Communist slogan of "separation from the State," these views gradually came to be adopted by wider circles of the public which began to cooperate with Mapam in the "Jewish-Arab Association for Peace and Equality" (beginning in 1956). On the parliamentary level, Mapai found itself on the defensive on this issue and found itself compelled to make concessions from time to time.[5] In December 1966, the military administration apparatus was eliminated, in keeping with one of the conditions for Mapam's joining Levi Eshkol's coalition (February 1966). The liquidation of the military administration apparatus was an important and perhaps a decisive step forward, but still only a *first step,* and the campaign to do away with the military administration itself, with its content, spirit and nonsecurity interference in the life of the Arab community will have to continue.

Another aspect of Mapai's attitude toward the Arab minority was its permanent refusal to open the gates of the Histadrut to the Arab workers, some of whom were organized in the Communist-dominated congress of Arab workers and others in the Palestine Workers' League that was affiliated with, but not part of, the Histadrut. Here, too, Mapai was compelled to retreat one step after another until Mapam's consistent struggle over many years finally bore fruit, and early in 1960 the road to full membership in the Histadrut was opened to Arab workers.[6]

On the international labor front, Mapai has always been part of the

---

5. The parliamentary campaign against the military administration came to a peak when five bills to do away with the military administration were presented in the Knesset (by Mapam, the Liberals, Ahdut Haavoda–Poale Zion, Herut, and Maki). These bills were voted down by the narrow majority of 59 to 55, by the votes of Mapai, the religious parties, and two of the Mapai-patronized Arab Knesset members on February 20, 1962. On a second occasion, on February 10, 1963, the military administration was saved by a single vote (57–56).
6. Arabs had been admitted to the Histadrut-affiliated trade unions since 1953.

right wing of the world labor movement and of the (Second) Socialist International, with its anti-Communist bias preventing it from distinguishing good from bad in the socialist countries, causing it to uncritically (and unrealistically) admire western capitalism, dressed up as the "Free World," and worst of all, detrimentally affecting the government's foreign and domestic policies.

Israeli reformism's attitude toward the "unity of the labor movement" is a chapter in itself. On this issue, Mapai continued the bad traditions of its old Ahdut Haavoda forerunners, both in mystically sanctifying the slogan of unity and in its intolerance toward the views of other parties or lack of respect for their ideological contributions. There were even attempts to impose unity by force by posing the ultimatum of either full unity or total noncooperation, and by rejecting in principle the idea of a united front that could exhaust the possibilities of joint practical activities while respecting the integrity of the separate political groups so long as differences in principle continued. While they sanctified the slogan of unity, the Mapai leaders always accompanied this with intolerance toward minorities within their own party, as the fate of Siah Bet and later of Pinhas Lavon can prove. Mapai's struggle for unity has always been associated with a policy of splitting other pioneering and workers' groups in which it did not form a majority. Classic examples of this latter trend were the dismemberment of the Palmach in 1948, even before the war had ended and at considerable risk to the State's security, and the split within the Kibbutz Hameuchad in 1951 when the Mapai minority in this large kibbutz movement seceded.

We have listed above some of the many and serious points of dispute between left and right in the Israeli labor movement. At the same time, we must remember that objective circumstances as well as the pressure of the pioneering left and of part of its own rank and file often compelled Mapai to adopt constructive and more or less correct policies despite the erroneous principles and points of departure. Despite these differences, therefore, there remained a wide field for cooperation in the spheres of security, immigration, integration, settlement, etc., and for a united front between the pioneering left parties and Mapai within the Histadrut, the Zionist movement, and even the government. It has therefore been the task of the pioneering left to combine the anti-reformist struggles with efforts to establish a unified front with Mapai in order to exhaust all the possibilities of intensifying the efforts for national and social liberation.

SOURCES

Pioneering versus etatism

The call for Israeli city youth to go to settlement so that the country wouldn't remain desolate lost a great deal of its importance when the State began to establish the immigrant settlements. Happily, the sombre prophecies of the failure of these settlements have proven false. The country isn't desolate and the desolate areas (south of Beersheba) require special irrigation arrangements for them to be cultivated. In the same way, in Central Galilee appropriate land arrangements are needed in order to establish Jewish settlements.

I don't think that the youth, born in Israel, haven't gone to settlement because they saw settlement being carried on very well without them. Youth hasn't gone to settlement because they wanted and found an easier life in the city. The process of settlement, however, hasn't stopped and agricultural production hasn't fallen behind. In addition, the most appropriate area that the government had for the absorption of immigration was agriculture. The State had the land, water and capital, the knowhow and planning needed in order to settle the immigrants in agricultural villages. These three factors—immigrants needing to be absorbed, the desolate soil and the Yishuv's ability provided by the State, joined together and even if Israeli youth didn't go to settlement, the country didn't remain in its desolation.

(From an article by M. Dayan, "The Crisis of Pioneering," in *Haaretz* Sept. 25, 1959).

If there is something that is a contradiction in itself, it is the term, "State pioneering." There is, of course, pioneering, *for* the State, but there isn't any pioneering *by* the State. The State can't make itself change its own character. The State has to fulfill social functions and we can only hope that it will succeed in this, but it doesn't have the function of creating pioneering by compulsion. If you impose on the State a function which it can't and doesn't have to take on, you aren't increasing the status of the State but only blurring its real nature and turning it into a fuzzy conglomerate. The State must be a reality with a character of its own and not be given a character not intended for it.

It is self-understood that there are very important and very basic functions which are filled by the power of the State, but the State doesn't have the function of making personal decisions; where there are personal decisions, you don't need State power.

This is one of the greatest confusions that could be created and that could have currency among the public; pioneering rests on a permanent decision and not on any subservience to power or on any actions because of that subservience.

(From remarks by Prof. N. Rotenstreich, at the Hulda meeting, *Min Hayesod,* No. 50, May 14, 1964.)

In place of the former triangle of pioneering settler, worker, and devoted public servant, a new triangle is beginning to appear—the successful man, the bureaucrat and the politician who often rules the public more than he serves it. These three, despite differences between them and despite the differences in their sociological origin, objectively march hand-in-hand and point to the fundamental change taking place in Israeli society.

(From an article by P. Lavon, "Across the Barriers," in *Min Hayesod,* Amikam Publishers, Tel Aviv, 1965.)

State, Zionism and the Zionist Organization

Zionism, whose history begins with the First Zionist Congress, lost the ground under its feet with the loss of European Jewry, and became superfluous with the establishment of the State. However, that Zionism that feeds on the perpetual springs of the Eternal People and completely and unreservedly identifies itself with the historic struggle of the Jewish people to secure its existence wherever it was, to implement its redemption in its homeland and its messianic mission to the world, that Zionism now has two goals which are not inferior in value and prospects to everything Zionism did in the last fifty years: to maintain and intensify the attachment of the Jews in the Diaspora to the eternality of Israel and the spiritual values of the Jewish people and to stand at the side of the State in its messianic mission to carry out the full and complete redemption.

(From a speech by Divid Ben-Gurion, "The Aims of Israel in our Days," *Davar,* Jan. 25, 1954, published in the fifth volume of his *Vision and Path,* Am Oved Publishers, Tel Aviv, 1959, p. 57.)

" . . . After the establishment of the State, the dangerous illusion began to become prevalent amongst us that the State could do everything and that it was an omnipotent force. Some of its leaders became more and more intolerant of any independent and initiating force among the people, within the State or outside it. They don't want partners, only subjects. That would be a serious process for any well-established state, all of whose members, or the vast majority, live within its borders. It is ever so much more a dangerous process for our young State, and especially for its younger generation, which does not understand that we are a State which has everything except the people itself.

Without the Zionist movement as its loyal and equal partner among the Jewish people, the State of Israel would be threatened by the danger of political, social and cultural degeneration. If the Zionist movement and its organization didn't exist, it would be necessary to create it now.

The State of Israel also needs the Zionist movement as a political partner; not only as an auxiliary force, but as an important factor in shaping policy; our policies cannot only be those of a little state in the Middle East. They have to be policies representing the vital interests of the Eternal People, dispersed between the East and the West, whose very existence determines its policies—for peace, independence, non-identification and neutrality.

(From an address by Y. Hazan at the 25th Zionist Congress, in *Al Hamishmar,* Dec. 30, 1960.)

Changing the Electoral System

... The system of proportional elections existed in the Yishuv [Jewish community] before the establishment of the State and may have been justified in the Mandate period. This system was also introduced into the State of Israel by the Provisional Government out of intellectual inertia and has become, as experience has proven, a burden for the State and its democratic character. This system actually prevents the people from electing their representatives directly, hands over the choice of Knesset members to party nominating committees, weakens the representative's ties to his voters, promotes exaggerated and harmful divisions, sows unnecessary disputes among the people, cultivates communal isolation, undermines government stability, cultivates an irresponsible opposition, leads to frequent crises, lowers the prestige of democracy in Israel, and weakens the State internally and externally. In order to ensure the direct election of their representatives by the people, to strengthen the representative's ties to his voters and to give preference to national interests over those of sectarian groups, blocs and communities, a system of regional elections like those practiced in England and the other veteran democracies must be introduced in Israel. Only regional elections can guarantee both a responsible government and a responsible opposition, and will make it possible for the citizen to choose his representatives in the Knesset directly.

(From the Mapai Program to the Third Knesset, 1955, published in S. Rehav, *Parties in Israel,* Givat Haviva, 1958, p. 60.)

... Despite the present argument between Mapai and the General Zionists—actually a pre-elections argument—the majority party in the Histadrut is planning in the future to continue the line of rejecting workers' solidarity and renewing the alliance with the reactionary bourgeoisie as the program of regional majority elections testifies. This program that has been suggested by Mapai and included in its program for the elections to the Histadrut and the Knesset is aimed at removing the pioneering workers' parties from the stage in order to tighten the alliance and stabilize the division of power between power-hungry reformism and the profit-hungry reactionary bourgeoisie. ...

(From Mapam's Program to the Third Knesset, 1955, Ibid. p. 64.)

... There are only a very few things on which I have intervened in Israeli domestic policy. What I have tried to explain in my books and articles is that British democracy isn't simply a two-party regime, and Israeli democracy isn't only a multi-party regime. Democracy is a way of life on which both the regimes are founded. I think, however, that the true relationships between our democracy and Israel's will be destroyed if her multi-party system is replaced by Britain's two-party regime. I remain convinced that a two-party system happens to work well for us at this moment; we have won the elections. But I am not at all sure that this system is always to our advantage, or if it would still be to our advantage if three parties were operated. This system works mechanically at the cost of arbitrarily distorting the democratic vote.

(From a farewell broadcast by R. Crossman on the BBC, published in *Al Hamishmar,* Jan. 11, 1964.)

Wage rises or wage freeze—Two views.

Too large wage increases above increased productivity may perhaps give some temporary satisfaction but disappointment sets in when the worker finds that a general rise in prices has set in as a result. This rise in prices damages the foundations of our economy, our financial stability and possibilities of exporting. When this "cycle" is completed our situation as a whole and as individuals may be worse than before. This country needs price stability. That was our policy in the past and we shall make efforts to maintain it in the future as well because it is good for the worker, good for the State and good for exports. It is impossible, however, to maintain that stability when the wage raises are exaggerated. We have to stop this vicious and useless circle of wage raises and rising prices chasing each other.
(From speech by Finance Minister Pinhas Sapir, at the 10th Congress of the Histadrut, *Davar,* Jan. 7, 1966.)

The Mapam delegation will not support the suggestion for trade union policy for 1967–1968 that was ratified by the votes of the Alignment [Mapai and Ahdut Haavoda] in the Trade Union Department since, in our view, it is an unbalanced and one-sided policy that does not meet the needs of the workers, evades problems that are particularly vital for the production workers and the weaker strata, and therefore also does not serve the interests of the economy.

The Alignment's proposals do not offer the working public any prospect of improving their situation in the future and it is doubtful whether they can even maintain what exists.

We have presented the Executive Committee with another resolution that is balanced, more in keeping with principle, and also answers the concrete needs of the workers and the economy.

1. A fundamental principle behind any progressive and stable trade union and social policy must be the elimination of unemployment and guarantees of employment for anyone seeking it. We must point with satisfaction at the improvement that has taken place in the employment situation in recent months. At the same time it is becoming clear that in 1968 there will also be about 25,000 unemployed. The Histadrut must demand of the Government and of all the other factors in the economy that they use all the means at their disposal in order to guarantee full employment. The development budget must not be cut in order to avoid overintense economic activity. This important and vital matter is not reflected in the Alignment resolution.

The Alignment resolution links guaranteed employment to frozen wages—something that we reject both in principle and in practice.

2. Our resolution also stresses the matter of making the economy more efficient and of raising productivity. We see in that a central goal that must provide a firm economic base for the State and the starting point for a higher standard of living for the population of the State in general and for the working public and laboring strata in particular. We call upon the working public to lend a hand and not to avoid accepting the responsibilities involved in advancing the economy and making it more efficient; but this effort must be a general one—of all the factors in production: management, workers and government. We reject imposing obligations upon the workers alone.

It is surprising that this point is lost in the Alignment resolution. The Alignment resolution also contains an unclear clause that is liable to confuse accepted concepts, such as the demand to "raise output above the measured norms". When norms are fixed the worker is interested in obtaining premiums and in any case tries to raise output above the norms. Otherwise the premium payments lose all their point.

3. a. Under the *wage* clause we propose that in January 1968 wages be raised in those branches and enterprises in which the wage policies and labor agreements concluded in 1967 were not implemented. There has recently been improvement in production and employment even in those branches whose situations were especially difficult in 1967. Even textiles have shown improvement in orders and employment. There are some textile sub-branches which could have supported the limited wage increases even in 1967.

The Alignment resolution on this clause is unclear and speaks of continuing negotiations; a clearer and more decided posture on the part of the Histadrut could guarantee workers their wage rises.

b. We suggest demanding a wage rise in January 1969 in keeping with increased output in 1968.

There are clear signs that in 1968 the economy will overcome the difficulties of the crisis and that production will increase and there is no reason to deprive the workers of their raises.

It should be pointed out that in 1967 industrial output went up by 2 percent. According to the statement by the Advisor to the Finance Minister, Mr. Moshe Zandberg, as published in *Davar* on 10.12.67, 1967, showed an increase in industrial productivity of an estimated at least 10 percent per workday. There are grounds to assume that this process will increase and grow stronger in 1968.

(From speech by Mapam representative, Shmuel Cohen, at meeting of Histadrut Executive Committee, Dec. 31, 1967, from the minutes of the meeting.)

. . . One of the central questions in the debate on how to renew the impetus of economic development is the question of the role of wages in this process. Some argue that in this country wages and wage policy form a central and decisive factor. On the other hand, some argue the opposite. We believe that even though it is obvious that wages are not necessarily the vital influencing factor, it still has a great deal of weight in this field. For that reason the focus of our activities in the coming period is to be on maintaining the continuation of the economic stability that has been achieved.

Those who believe that the only aim of trade union policy is to guarantee higher wages are mistaken. Additional income for workers does not necessarily involve changes in the wage-scale. We all know the phenomenon of workers' real income not increasing despite high wages. Trade union policy makes it possible to increase income by the returns on savings or as a result of professional advancement. Progress on both these levels is to the benefit of the workers and economy alike.

Such a resolution on our part will contribute towards continuing to maintain economic stability and, together with the cost-of-living

increment agreement, will make it possible to maintain the workers' real income....
>(From the booklet by Yeruham Meshel, *Trade Union Policy*—1968/69, Tel Aviv, published by the Histadrut.)

... In light of the positive changes in the economy, and in order to secure the continuation of the economic upswing and greater employment, and considering the special security needs, the Histadrut has decided on the principles of its trade union policy for 1968–69, as follows:

1. In order to maintain the stability of the economy, the stability of prices—and security of employment, there will be no changes in the wage scales of all the branches of the economy in the years 1968–69, and the collective agreements will be extended for two more years unchanged.

2. The Histadrut will demand the continuation of the cost-of-living grants to workers earning up to I£ 12,500, and will insist on these being increased....
>(From Resolutions of Executive Committee of the Histadrut, Nov. 31, 1967, ibid.)

Policy for 1970–71

Mapam has recently formulated clear principles in the fields of trade union and social policy. We have been struggling *now* over the Alignment's Program for the Histadrut elections and over the formulation of a wage policy towards renewing the labor agreements for 1970–71.

Our suggestions are as follows:

1. Wage increases in accordance with the growth in national output and in accordance with the situation of the industry and the social conditions of the workers. Wages in services will rise in keeping with the average increase in the productive branches. A floor and ceiling for the wage raises will be fixed in order to leave room for the trade union to negotiate and to struggle for their demands in keeping with the possibilities.

2. Starting wages on entering employment in the productive branches to be increased and equalized with the starting wages in services in order to stop the gap between production and services and to guarantee the production worker at least a minimal decent existence.

3. Implementation of the equalization of benefits between day workers and salaried employees (after the equalization in vacation and family allowances) will go on to separation pay, rest-homes, seniority, inclusive pension and the like.

4. To double the allowance for workers' children (the first three children) from I£12.50 monthly to I£25, while also raising the monthly grants for large families (from the fourth child and onwards). In this way real additional income will be guaranteed for low wage-earners with large families.

5. The Government and Histadrut will guarantee that the rising wages do not lead to higher prices and indirect taxes and thus become

absorbed by employer's profits. Price stability is to be maintained as well as the system of automatic cost-of-living increments as a brake on price rises and a means of preserving the real value of wages.

6. To accelerate and expand the process of democratization within the Histadrut and the trade unions that was begun with the 1968/69 elections to the Agricultural Workers Union, the Food Workers Union, the Government Employees Union and the Army Workers Union, to include all the trade unions in which elections have not yet been held. The election dates will be adhered to strictly, with the election to the Histadrut and the trade unions taking place on a single fixed date once every four years. The Histadrut and the trade unions will be given the appropriate authority and means in order to carry on their functions in all fields of work. A fitting place will be guaranteed workers from the shop in the general and administrative organs of the trade unions.

7. The freedom of trade union struggle and the strike will be guaranteed. The Histadrut will oppose all legislative intervention into labor relations and the suggestions from the right concerning compulsory arbitration, strike bars and the like. . . .

(From: "Mapam on the Trade Union Struggle," by Naphtali Ben-Moshe, published by Mapam, Tel Aviv, 1969.)

Present-day Relations Between Mapam and the Histadrut

One of Mapam's outstanding representatives at Histadrut Headquarters, Naphtali Ben-Moshe, when interviewed on present-day relations between Mapam and the Histadrut, made the following statement:

". . . Today, we can honestly say that no decisions are taken within the Histadrut central bodies without Mapam's agreement. The first reason for this is the fact that the Labor Party by itself does not have a majority and needs Mapam's support. Histadrut Secretary-General Jeruham Meshel also knows that he cannot allow himself or the organization he heads to become a rubber stamp for government policy and that he must go along with the workers he represents. In doing this, his policies come close to those of Mapam. And third, though this is a factor which cannot be measured exactly, the active role which Mapam's representatives fill within the Histadrut indubitably gives them a measure of influence beyond their numerical weight."

(*Brit Mapam*, Vol. 3, No. 4, December 1976, published by World Union of Mapam, Tel Aviv.)

Against Preventive War

Israel will defend her sovereignty, territorial integrity and rights with her strength lying in defense and the deterrence of aggression. The Political Bureau warns against trends of thought and activist views which see the solution of the water problem in a preventive war, by exploiting some "propitious moment" for a military decision. A military solution cannot solve the complex political problems. Israel must, therefore, strive for a peaceful solution.

(From Resolutions of Mapam Political Bureau March 3, 1965, in *Al-Hamishmar*, and *Bashaar*, Nos. 65–66.)

Mapam has said: Water—yes; war–no. There is no doubt that this saving formula deserved a copyright without any competitors. It preached to the Government of Israel to exhaust all the political means in order to frustrate the diversion of the Jordan's sources without war... We have never denied the need to exhaust all the possibilities of political means and have done so on many occasions. However, one of the decisive cards in dealing with the problem was the eventual possibility that if the political efforts failed, Israel would prevent the diversion by military force, if she found no other way. Anyone asking the Government of Israel to undertake in advance to deny her right to use our army in order to defend our waters and borders, our right of shipping and the lives of our citizens, sentences all our political efforts to failure in advance.

(From an address by Ahdut Haavoda leader Yigal Allon, at the Kibbutz Hameuchad Council in Alonim, in *Lamerhav*, July 18, 1965.)

Mapam Peace Program—1965

Our Peace Program must be composed of the following clauses:

1. Immediate negotiations on a solution for the refugee problem, on the assumption that when peace is attained, a minority of them will be absorbed within the borders of Israel and the majority will be rehabilitated in the Arab countries with the aid of a development program to be financed by international forces, the State of Israel, and the neighboring countries.

2. An immediate agreement on bilateral nuclear non-proliferation as a full step towards general disarmament and the neutralization of the region.

3. An agreement on the aim of a federal connection between the neighboring countries and Israel while preserving her full sovereignty.

4. As a first and decisive step towards this federative connection, the State of Israel will strive for economic cooperation with the State of Jordan regardless of the political regime prevailing in it. Only cooperation in equality with Israel can guarantee Jordan her full independence, the exploitation of the Dead Sea, two-thirds of which belongs to Jordan, while the third in our possession already brings our State's treasury tens of millions of dollars. We must guarantee Jordan a free outlet to the sea. All these are liable to open a new era of peace with the undisturbed development of the State of Israel and of the State of Jordan. It cannot be decided in advance at what stages the ties between the two parts of the natural geopolitical unit called the whole of Palestine will be tightened and made permanent.

5. First of all, we must abolish the Military Administration and inaugurate a regime of equal opportunity to all the citizens, free of exploitation, discrimination and fear. This equality guaranteed the Arab minority in Israel will serve as the dependable security that in-

stead of the danger of irridention and of a "fifth column," they will be a bridge to understanding and peace between ourselves and our neighbors.

Summing up, if in the Middle East region our national and social struggle for liberation becomes integrated in the national and social liberation struggles of the neighboring countries; if atomic non-proliferation and general disarmament replace the feverish armament race; if the neutralization of the region takes the place of the competition between the powers; if economic cooperation and mutual cultural fertilization replace the economic boycott and the dependence on others' good graces, then the ingathering of the exiles will be secure and fulfilled and the socialist State of Israel will flourish as an equal member of a federation of the Middle Eastern nations."

(From "Between War and Peace," by Meir Yaari, *Al-Hamishmar*, April 16, 1965.)

"The following is a summary of the Prime Minister's remarks on the main points of his answer:

Solving the refugee problem: We cannot accept Mapam's formula that within the framework of peace, an agreed and definite number of refugees be accepted within the borders of Israel. If the Israel Government adopts this slogan, it would be false to itself and making declarations which it had no intentions of keeping, or would be opening the door to the destruction of the State. No serious refugee problem in modern history has been solved by repatriation. What Mapam's formula means is the readiness to absorb in the State a considerable number of people who left at their leaders' orders in order to return after its destruction. . .

The answer to Bourguiba: Without mentioning the President of Tunisia by name, Eshkol rejected the argument that Israel should have immediately responded to the recent peace declarations. "It isn't the task of the Israel Government to give anyone good marks for his remarks or to adopt an attitude in detail towards any suggestion, especially since it isn't directed at the Government and does not come directly from the States bordering on Israel."

Atomic nonproliferation: Mapam's Peace Plan contains a clause discussing "bilateral nuclear non-proliferation as a first step towards general disarmament." There is no State in the Middle East that has nuclear weapons. The conclusion from that, according to Mapam's proposal, is that we must disarm ourselves of weapons we don't have and leave to the future to deal with the weapons which offer a real threat to Israei.

Federative ties: Another clause in Mapam's Peace Plan talks of federative attachments between the neighboring countries and the State of Israel, while preserving its full sovereignty. That is a thing and its opposite, since in federation the member bodies give up a certain measure of their sovereignty. In addition, in federation there would be the problem of movement for all citizens; in our situation that would mean agreeing to allow the refugees to return by the back door. . . .

(From reply by Prime Minister L. Eshkol in Knesset political debate; summary in *Davar*, May 20, 1965.)

The "Military Administration"

We rule out the Military Administration as Jews concerned about the future, the existence and the security of the State of Israel as a Jewish State. We rule out the Military Administration as socialists. But I say that if we were convinced that the existence of the Military Administration was a guarantee for Israel's security, we would become its supporters, because the thing that precedes and determines our national and social struggle, that guarantees our very ability to build here a just human society, is our national Jewish existence, the existence of the State of Israel. That is our moral, Zionist, national and socialist test.

However, since we are convinced that the Military Administration does not serve the security of the State of Israel and contradicts the fundamentals of justice and law, we reject it both as Jews and as socialists. We reject it in our loyalty to the Jewish people and its moral heritage, and in our loyalty to our socialist vision. The Military Administration does not guarantee the security of the State of Israel. I am convinced that the opposite is true; it harms it and endangers it; it harms all of us as Jews; it is an embarrassment for a large part of us as socialists.

The proposed law we are bringing to the Knesset is intended to abolish the Military Administration without ignoring the security problems that are liable to arise in connection with that and giving answers to those problems.

Certainly, the economic situation of Israel's Arab citizen has improved very much. But not only we, but all peoples, and the Arabs too, do not live by bread alone. What is more—the more bread there is, the greater the feelings of social and political deprivation and the greater the protest against them.

The discrimination against part of Israel's citizens, the right that the majority has taken for itself to impose on the Arab minority a Military Administration with a whole system of legal discriminations, must also damage the moral image of the majority responsible for all these. That, too, is a valuable security asset. Democracy, the feeling of equality and just legislation and law, are indivisible. This discrimination expressed in the Military Administration is a cancerous growth threatening the very existence of Israeli democracy, the foundations of justice and law and of liberty in the State of Israel as a whole.

That is not all. Everybody knows, and I could mention innumerable examples of this—that the Military Administration is utilized not only for security matters. It interferes with all the affairs of the Arab citizen; it leaves him no rest anywhere; it humiliates him everywhere. Everywhere he is compelled to apply to it; if it likes, it will answer him, if it doesn't—it won't. There is no law or court of law. It is the concern and desire of the Military Governor that counts. What is it that motivates, directs and guides the desire of the Military Governor? We have learnt that it isn't always the concerns of the State of Israel's security; not always general military problems, but unworthy party considerations which have nothing to do with the problems of security. The problems of security are exploited for party interests.

There is no way to correct this situation except by abolishing the Military Administration while providing all the arrangements needed to maintain the security of the State by its legal tools—the army, the frontier police, the police, civilian laws and courts equal to all.

(From an address by Y. Hazan in Knesset, February 20, 1962, in explaining Mapam's proposal to abolish the Military Administration, *Divrei Haknesset* 33, p. 1327.)

The Arabs of Israel

(Resolution adopted at 7th National Congress of Mapam, June 1976)

Mapam is the only Socialist-Zionist party which realizes the principle of brotherhood in its organization. As a Jewish-Arab party it will continue its long struggle for the integration of Israeli Arabs into the life of the State and oppose any manifestation of discrimination against them. Mapam was in the vanguard of the struggle for the abolition of the military administration in Arab-populated border areas of Israel, and for the admission of Arabs into the Histadrut as members with full rights.

The integration of Israeli Arabs has been hampered from the beginning by difficulties arising from the continuous state of belligerency as well as by an erroneous policy on the part of the Government. But despite the difficulties and obstacles, the condition of the Arab population has gradually improved and the standard of living has risen, although the gap between this sector and the majority of Israeli Jews has not yet been closed. Israel should adopt a consistent policy aimed at accelerating the process of integration.

Recent events have made the public and the Government aware of the urgent need to deal with the problem of relations between the Arabs and Jews of Israel and to make changes in the present policy. Measures should be adopted to solve the problems of the Arab population and comprehensive plans be drawn up for their implementation.

Development and Industrialization

The development plans of various regions will take into account the needs of the Arab citizens by allocating land reserves to ensure the growth and development of Arab and Druze villages.

(a) No Arab lands shall be confiscated except in exchange for land of equal value or payment in lieu equivalent to the full value of the land and only where the confiscation is linked with a development plan for the benefit of the population as a whole.

(b) The elected representatives of the Arab citizens shall be fully involved in any framework for planning and implementation of development projects in their areas, and in any committee set-up to determine compensation for expropriated property.

(c) Development of agriculture, which is a major source of livelihood in the Arab sector, shall be promoted by ensuring sufficient quotas of land and water, variety of crops and increased mechanization.

(d) A plan for industrialization of the Arab sector shall be drawn up and implemented, the master plans for the villages shall be completed, and building land for this purpose shall be released by the

Israeli Land Authority.

(e) Villages not yet linked to the national electricity grid or lacking asphalted approach roads shall be supplied with these vital services.

(f) The network of clinics and mother-and-child health centers shall be completed, health centers set up in the large villages and mobile clinics in small villages and Bedouin-populated areas.

Civil Equality

(a) Full equality shall be guaranteed to all Israeli citizens irrespective of nationality or religion, with no legal or administrative discrimination, in accordance with the progressive democratic character of the State.

(b) All citizens shall be entitled to children's allowances from the National Insurance Bureau, on an equal basis and equal rate.

(c) All demobilized soldiers shall be entitled to the same rights by virtue of their military service (grants, housing, education, employment, etc.)

(d) The rate of government grants and loans to Jewish and Arab local authorities shall be equal.

(e) The establishment of local councils shall be completed, with smaller villages and Bedouin centers integrated into regional councils.

(f) A just solution shall be assured to the problem of Bedouin lands in the Negev.

(g) A plan for absorption of Arab college graduates into professional and administrative posts in the government and Histadrut will be worked out, in order to correct the shortcomings in this regard.

(h) Assistance on an equal basis shall be available to provide housing for young couples.

Education

(a) There shall be a comprehensive reform of the educational system in the Arab sector. Arab experts shall participate in the planning and implementation of this reform.

(b) The network of agricultural and vocational schools shall be extended.

(c) Budgetary allocations shall be guaranteed for speeding up construction of extra classrooms needed by Arab schools.

Youth

Everything necessary shall be done to guarantee the successful absorption of Arab youth into all areas of Israeli life, with special attention to the education and integration of Arab girls. The link of Arab youth to their national culture shall be cultivated.

Ikrit and Biram

Mapam reiterates its demand (of many years) that the Government of Israel allow the uprooted inhabitants of Ikrit and Biram to return to their villages immediately.

19 • The "Ben-Gurion-Lavon Affair"

From the expulsion of Siah Bet from Mapai in the '40s and up to the events of the Ben-Gurion–Lavon affair at the beginning of the '60s, Mapai hadn't had what might be called a left wing or left opposition. The feelings of discrimination and uneasiness sensed by the Mapai kibbutz movement had also not yet been given any general ideological expression or crystallized into anti-reformist criticism. On the other hand, Mapai was divided by a conflict between what might be called the "traditional" (or "conservative") Mapai elements and an explicitly militantly revisionist and pragmatic trend which considered even the party's traditional fundamental bases, or its differences with the bourgeois right, to be outmoded. This trend raised the banner of "activism" as regards the Arabs, all-Israeli "etatism," the cult of "efficiency," the "unity of all men of action, ability and goodwill," and the like. They also revealed an attitude of skepticism and cynicism toward the Zionist movement, the kibbutz movement, the special mission of the Histadrut, the party system, and the rules of parliamentary democracy.

The conflict between these two trends in Mapai was distorted by the labels of "old-timers" and "younger men" given each of them, respectively, though the "younger men" like Dayan and Peres, who were entrenched in the Ministry of Defense, and among some of the officers, were supported by an old-timer like Ben-Gurion, while some of their most vigorous opponents were found in the kibbutzim and especially among the younger members of the Ihud Hakvutzot vehakibbutzim as well as among officials of the Histadrut and the veteran leadership of Mapai.[1]

> ... The speaker called for a wage freeze until the State succeeded in curing the economy and demanded the reduction of the costs of production in order to compete with foreign markets. He listed the various channels of pioneering, which were not only in going to the kibbutz, but also in the Army and many other spheres. Dayan raised the possibility of firing 5,000 clerks employed in the government, the Jewish Agency, the municipalities and other places in order to save the State 20 million pounds. . . . The head of an enterprise who employs more workers than are needed is a careerist while the one satisfied with the minimum of workers or clerks is doing pioneer work.

1. The center of opposition to the "younger men's" campaign for domination at the height of the "affair" was within the "Younger young circle," which served as the nucleus for the formation of an ideological group of members within Mapai and afterwards became the Min Hayesod group.

At the beginning of his speech, Dayan pointed out that today he and Shimon Peres are spoken of as the "younger generation" and that isn't true. On the other hand, he asked whether the Israeli youth who crawled among thorns and rocks with rifle in hand, who passed the test of planes and warships in the War of Liberation and the Sinai War, understand the problem of the Jewish people less than do those who have been sitting for twenty years on the fifth story of the Histadrut headquarters or other places.

(From a report in *Davar,* Dec. 29, 1958, on Moshe Dayan's speech before a Mapai meeting in Jerusalem.)

... Thousands of young people are organized in the Party and tens of thousands in the Histadrut but this group doesn't represent the younger generation in Mapai and the Histadrut. It doesn't represent the younger generation in the kibbutz because the young person in the kibbutz doesn't have trust in its path. It doesn't represent the younger generation going into building or shops and factories. It doesn't represent the younger generation in the youth movements of the Party and the Histadrut. It doesn't even represent itself because in every matter of fundamental value the opinions of the members of the "younger men's group" are as divided as the "old-timers." The question is: What is this group's desire and function? There isn't any joint platform. There isn't any real desire and ability to investigate together the critical problems of our time. There isn't any understanding of the fundamental questions of the working public. Don't we have to draw the conclusion that the only thing uniting these people around one flag is the desire—legitimate in itself—to win positions and to enter the higher levels of government leadership by exerting pressure rather than by organic hard work?

... For months the Party and the Histadrut have been undergoing an unending bombardment by Comrade Moshe Dayan on a series of subjects on all of which he has borrowed from the ideas of others. I doubt whether he had the time or the patience to examine these ideas thoroughly before throwing them to the public.

..."The youths crawling between thorns and rocks" aren't in anyone's pocket. They are free youths to whom it isn't easy to sell false goods. Throughout all the years the youth have participated in the elections to the Knesset and the Histadrut and to the municipalities and have voted according to their conscience and understanding. They have fulfilled their duty to the homeland in every time of trouble, but didn't give up their rights to be free citizens and to decide on the matters of the state and working class according to their own understanding. The attempt to oppose these youths to the people on one story or another of some building or other is a cheap one and I am sure that the better part of the youth will reject it out of a sense of civil responsibility for Israeli democracy.

... Perhaps it isn't an accident that only yesterday, in a talk with a *Ha'aretz* reporter, a member of Moshe Dayan's group—Aharon Remez—said that he "was convinced that the broad public was tired of and sated with party cynicism." He, Remez, "believes in Ben-Gurion's leadership and thinks that if Ben-Gurion could succeed in working in a government with people who didn't belong to parties and who were experts, Israel would attain some fine achievements." If Aharon Remez did accidentally reveal a glimpse of the secrets of the theories and philosophies developing in this group, then the matter becomes even more serious. If it is true that these remarks by Dayan and Remez reflect the trend of this group, then it is the responsibility of every responsible public figure to warn against it and to call on the members of the party not to lend their hands to the implementation of these aims which, no matter whether they originate in social infantilism or crystallized ideas, in both cases pose a serious danger for the Party, the Histadrut and the State of Israel.

(From address by P. Lavon at a Mapai meeting in Tel Aviv, according to *Davar*, Jan. 4, 1959.)

This struggle, with its factional, tactical and personal aspects, more than once took dramatic form, as when David Ben-Gurion left to settle at Kibbutz Sde-Boker (in 1953), leaving Moshe Sharett as Prime Minister, with Pinhas Lavon as his Defense Minister. Ben-Gurion ultimately came back to power, first as Minister of Defense, by deposing Pinhas Lavon, and then as Prime Minister, with Moshe Sharett resigning. The epilogue to those events came with the open split in the Mapai leadership in 1961-1962, following what has been labeled the "Lavon Affair." This began when Pinhas Lavon began a public campaign to clear his name of false accusations concerning his supposed responsibility for the "Security Scandal"[2] of 1954, as a result of which he had been compelled to resign. At the same time, some of the factional and personal conspiracies of those days began to come out in public and cast a dark shadow over the methods used by the "younger men" in their struggle and over their veteran patron. When Lavon finally won rehabilitation by a Ministers' Committee (including three members of Mapai) and its conclusions were ratified by the Government (on Dec. 25, 1960) this aroused the anger of Ben-Gurion and his followers and they demanded that the decision be revised and Lavon be deposed from his position as Secretary General of the Histadrut. Their demands were partly fulfilled only when Ben-Gurion resigned from the Premiership on January 31, 1961 (according to law, the government as a whole resigned with him) and when he threatened not to return to office again. Only then the Mapai Central Committee yielded and by a vote of 60 to 40 percent decided to ask Pinhas Lavon to resign (on Feb. 4, 1961). The opponents were headed by Moshe Sharett and Nathan Rotenstreich. Revising the rehabilitation itself depended on Mapai's partners in the coalition and Ben-Gurion was therefore unable to obtain it.

2. This concerned a number of acts of violence said to have been committed in Egypt by the Israeli intelligence in order to "harm the relations" between the U.A.R. and the United States. These relations had improved at that time. The instigators of these acts were revealed and led to some tension between Washington and Jerusalem. Pinhas Lavon, who was then Minister of Defense, repeatedly claimed that he had not given the order for these acts and that his signature had been forged.

The vengefulness displayed by David Ben-Gurion and his followers and their punishment of the man who had fought for and won rehabilitation aroused a wave of protest within the Israeli public, even among many who were closer to the views of the "younger men" than to those of their opponents in Mapai. The general public was disturbed not so much by the ideological debate or the factional fighting within Mapai as by the revelation of the moral degeneration and the "leadership cult" which broke down all the accepted norms of democratic practice, as if everything was moral and permissible in order to defend the honor and status of the ruling party and its leader. Wide circles actually began to fear for the security of the democratic regime itself, with the danger of a dictatorship of one kind or another looming on the horizon.

True, the "younger men's" opponents within Mapai had been more than a little responsible for their party's reformist policies. They had been among the most bitter antagonists of the pioneering leftist parties and even today they are still very deeply rooted within Israeli reformism. Nonetheless, in the struggle we have described above, they undoubtedly represented a more progressive stand than did their younger rivals.

Those who were counted among the "young men of Mapai" à la Dayan and Peres were not a uniform ideological and political group and almost every one of its leaders represented a shading, stress and style of his own. However, the variations and differences were much more striking among their opponents. Here, four main groupings could be listed:
    a. the Tel Aviv bloc
    b. the Haifa bloc
    c. the veteran leadership
    d. the Min Hayesod group

The Blocs—in Tel Aviv and Haifa—competed for influence in the party and their share in party positions.[3] Their opposition to the "younger men" was distinguished mainly by their interest in holding on to their positions in the face of the "younger men's" onslaught and demands. The ideological element was kept in the shadow, though the desire to maintain the status quo as far as status and influence were concerned fitted in with a tendency to maintain the status quo in Mapai's traditional ideas, slogans and style of propaganda. Because of their activity in the Histadrut institutions, the members of the "Blocs" were also close to the working public and this, too, kept them from rushing towards revisionist and liquidationist innovations like their "younger" rivals. For the most part, however, they were loyal to Ben-Gurion and vied in this, too, with their "younger" rivals.

---

3. The Tel Aviv bloc was headed by Shraga Netzer, the key man in the party apparatus. The Haifa bloc was headed by the late Haifa Mayor Abba Houshi and the present Minister of Labor Yosef Almogi.

The group of *veteran leaders*[4] was also united in its opposition to the "younger men" by the desire to maintain its status and authority in the Mapai leadership. In contrast to the Blocs, however, their ideological opposition to the innovations of Dayan, Peres, and their friends took pride of place. Within this group, too, there was a wide range of shadings in the degree of their independence and daring to oppose Ben-Gurion or his "activist" policies, his stresses and methods, his conduct in the "Affair," and the like. This group had a great deal of influence in the Ihud Hakvutzot Vehakibbutzim, in the cooperative smallholders' settlement (moshav) movement, among the Mapai-affiliated intellectuals, in the Knesset faction, and even among a certain part of the "Blocs."

The fourth group was that of the *"Min Hayesod."* When the "Affair" and its aftermath brought the interfactional strife to a dramatic tension, some of the traditional antagonists of the "younger men" were drawn forward to take up positions and views far transcending anything they had thought in the past. This group, headed by Pinhas Lavon and Prof. Nathan Rotenstreich, gathered around the bi-weekly "Min Hayesod" (From the Roots) and fought a bitter battle for the very right to publish the paper, with their opponents among both the "younger men" and the "bloc" attacking it as "factional activity" opposed to the party resolutions of the Kfar Vitkin Party Congress in 1942 banning factions.

The views of the Min Hayesod group were composed of a mixture of sharp criticism of the systems of bureaucratic and antidemocratic degeneration within their own party, and of traditional Mapai positions and prejudices concerning the pioneering left. The group accompanied its condemnation of the liquidationist trends among the "younger men" and its struggle against the bureaucracy, as well as its critical analyses of the image of the new Israeli society, with a series of positions on immediate problems that were close to those of the pioneering left parties. These included the criticism of the Ben-Gurion–Peres German policy, opposition to the policy of concessions to the religious parties, the demand to abolish the military administration in the border regions, more or less clear reservations concerning the idea of "regional elections," wage freezes, compulsory arbitration, and the like.

On the other hand, harking back to the doctrine of A. D. Gordon and the spiritual world of Hapoel Hatsair, the Min Hayesod group was opposed to Marxism and was completely alien to Mapam's balanced attitude to the Soviet Union—of supporting the fundamentals and condemning the symptoms of distortion and degeneration. The group was also skeptical about Mapam's demand for a foreign policy based on neutralism and initiatives for peace.

4. Moshe Sharett, Levi Eshkol, Golda Meir, Zalman Aranne, Mordehai Namir, Pinhas Sapir, Aharon Becker, and others.

As far as the situation of the Israeli labor movement was concerned, the members of the group favored the "inclusive unity" of the three workers' parties, one based on broad autonomy for each of the united movements, and with a united kibbutz movement at its center. On this issue, as in some of the others mentioned above, the Min Hayesod group was closer to Ahdut Haavoda–Poale Zion than to Mapam.

The biweekly *Min Hayesod* was the meeting place for a rather limited number of hard-core supporters, as well as a much wider circle of Mapai members who defended the right of the group to exist and demanded that Lavon and his colleagues be restored to the party and their places in the leadership. The Min Hayesod group enjoyed the support of a certain part of the Ihud Hakvutzot Vehakibbutzim, young people and intellectuals They also had some support among Mapai cadres in the Histadrut and local workers councils and party branches—especially among people originating from Hapoel Hatsair or the Gordonia Youth Movement abroad. The lines of demarcation, however, between the different groups were often blurred; this is true for many of the supporters of the veteran leadership and the blocs, but it is equally true for the veteran leadership and Min Hayesod sympathizers.

When David Ben-Gurion resigned from the premiership and this task was given to Levi Eshkol, it soon became evident that Eshkol was not merely a "substitute." Though he didn't ignore the political and party factor that was called "David Ben-Gurion at Sde-Goker," he began nonetheless to shape the image of his government and policies as he saw fit, in his own style. This was a deliberate and flexible policy, and within certain limits, a rather independent one. Now the members of Min Hayesod as well as many of the other people who wanted to reverse the expulsion and the aftermaths of the "Affair" understood that the proper time had come. It had been clear that as long as Ben-Gurion headed the government and Mapai he would not backtrack and return Lavon to party activity and leadership. The Min Hayesod group therefore began to demand more vigorously that the injustice be remedied, and when it saw that Eshkol was hesitant to do so (for fear of appearing to provoke Ben-Gurion and of damaging the already troubled domestic tranquillity of the party), it had no alternative but to issue Eshkol an ultimatum: it called for a countrywide meeting of the members and sympathizers in the Hulda forest, and even threatened to leave Mapai. (It was obvious that such a secession would mean their contesting the elections for the forthcoming Histadrut Congress.)

At the last moment, Eshkol prevented this secession by sending a personal letter to the chairman of the Hulda meeting (on May 1, 1964) in which he announced that the expulsion discussion belonged to the past and no longer had any practical validity for the present or the future.

I have recently talked a great deal with comrades regarding the matter about which I want to write now, a matter which I know is particularly close to you, to many members and large parts of the public.

This is what I would like to say:

a) The Mapai Central Committee in its session on February 4, 1961, decided at my recommendation that under the prevailing circumstances in the State and the Party, Pinhas Lavon could not serve in the Party's name as the General Secretary of the Histadrut. Following this decision, the Executive Committee of the Histadrut convened a meeting on February 9, 1961, in which Pinhas Lavon announced his resignation from his post.

b) I have raised these matters which belong to the past in order to tell you and your close friends that on various occasions I have expressed my opinion that I considered all this history, and that this decision today no longer has any meaning at all;

c) The possibilities are open to you and your close friends to return to regular activity within Mapai and its institutions as members with equal rights and obligations, responding to its demands and ready to take on missions in its name and with its authorization.

Be sure that my comrades and I will lend all our help and influence towards this. I add and call on you and other comrades to lend your hand to strengthen Mapai by the path of free discussion in a comradely style.

I hope that this statement will deepen the comradeship in our midst, will help to clear the air in the party and will be a factor for greater unity within the labor movement as a whole.

With loyal comradely greetings,
Levy Eshkol

(From *Davar*, March 5, 1964.)

True, the promise implied in this statement was a vague one and wasn't enough to satisfy the more sophisticated participants in the Hulda meeting. At the time, however, by sending the letter, Eshkol helped divide the radicals from the moderates and inevitably the former had to give in to the latter and restrain themselves for the time being.

While Eshkol's letter prevented a secession on the left, it aroused a storm on the right and Mapai was in a furor. Before sending the letter to Hulda, Eshkol had secured for himself the backing of the veteran leadership, the decisive part of the Ihud Hakvutzot Vehakibbutzim and part of the bloc, especially in Tel Aviv. Ben-Gurion's supporters, headed by the "younger men" and part of the bloc (mainly Haifa), attacked Eshkol and condemned the letter both because of its contents and for "undemocratically circumventing the party institutions that had previously voted for the expulsion and which alone were authorized to rescind this decision, if they so desired."

In the course of the ensuing debates, meetings, declarations and counter-declarations, exchanges of letters with Ben-Gurion, and the like, Eshkol didn't retract his letter, but froze its implementation, to the disappointment of the more naive members of the Min Hayesod group. At this stage, at least, the maneuver had gone well; Min Hayesod's secession was prevented and the frontal confrontation with Ben-Gurion's adherents was put off.

As the negotiations went forward between Mapai and Ahdut Haavoda–Poale Zion for a "dual alignment" that would include a joint list for the Knesset elections, the Histadrut Congress and the municipalities, it seemed as if this broader framework would solve the problem of "annulling the expulsion and bringing Pinhas Lavon and his friends to activity," if not immediately in the Mapai institutions, then, at the first stage, at least in the broader framework of the Alignment. In any case, this was one of Ahdut Haavoda–Poale Zion's stated demands in the negotiations and even Levi Eshkol favored a solution of that kind.

On this issue, however, both the Tel Aviv and the Haifa blocs joined the "younger men" in uncompromising opposition to any reconciliation with Min Hayesod. In the meetings of the Mapai Secretariat during the second half of October, it became completely clear that Eshkol could not succeed in forcing his opposition on "annulling the expulsion" and of reintegrating themselves actively in Mapai. Without waiting for a formal decision by the Mapai Central Committee in the Alignment, a meeting of Min Hayesod cadres voted to secede from Mapai and to set up the Min Hayesod movement (Tel Aviv, July 11, 1964).

SOURCES

A group of members of ideological activity has been organized among the members of Mapai and its sympathizers because of their critical attitude toward the party's handling of the "Affair" and its aftermath and later expanded its frame of discussion to all the problems of Israeli society. The Israeli labor movement must come to grips with the problem of the imbalance between implementation and values and between methods of action and ideological and moral content...
(From the Introduction to the *Min Hayesod Anthology,* Amikam Publishers, Tel Aviv, 1962.)

... We have to stress and stress again that our fundamental aim is to attain a socialist society. We reject the path of bloody social revolution but we cannot rely only on the objective processes of development by their own force leading to the formation of a society which we can view as the realization of the social aspirations of the labor movement in this country—tens of years ago we created the *fact* of a society that was mostly pioneering and socialist without knowing that we were "talking poetry." Today we are strengthening the capitalist sector in the Israeli economy and singing songs of praise to the socialist idea. Socialism cannot be realized without fundamental changes in the social character of economic activity. *Without a socialist economy there is no socialist society.*
(From "Beyond the Barries," by Pinhas Lavon, p. 74.)

. . . The great man, the leader of the party, needs the apparatus and depends upon it. He knows the faults and sins of the apparatus but can never lift his voice against it. He will never fight a struggle against the negative characteristics he knows and recognizes. The great man depends on the apparatus and needs it, while the apparatus needs the great man. It needs the aura of fame surrounding the party leader. . . .

(Ibid., p. 90.)

. . . We dare not—and we are talking of the labor movement as a whole—be in a hurry to despair of Mapai as a workers' party. I know, no less than you, all the distortions and the internal dangers found within that party, but at the same time I must say—and I don't say this for export—Mapai is still the greatest fortress of the laboring and working forces in this State. The moment we reach the conclusion that its value has ended—not numerically, but qualitatively and ideologically, I fear that we will stand before an empty space that even the Soviet astronauts couldn't fill.

And therefore any thinking about the future of Mapai must be based on the assumption that this party still—and let us hope, for many years—serves as a national and social, a working and constructive force, in the last analysis, despite the distortions and despite the deviations from the just path. We must not pray for splits and we must not throw the existing forces on the scrap heap. What we have to do is to look for the Archimedes' point that can bring a cure not by force of numbers, but by force of its quality, loyalty and ability to achieve.

(From address by Pinhas Lavon of Ahdut Haavoda-Poale Zion convention, in *Lamerhav,* Dec. 9, 1962.)

. . . The question facing us in this context is this: What path should the United Workers Party [Mapam] take? If it cannot serve as a realistic political alternative and if its prospects for growth are generally conceded to be limited, how can it contribute its share towards renewing the strength of the labor movement and changing the line-ups in Israeli social life? Do Meir Yaari or his comrades know any other way but that of uniting the Israeli labor movement? True, that path involves certain dangers. Let us assume for a moment that Mapai will degenerate completely and become a kind of copy of the Social Democratic Party in Germany before Hitler or of Guy Mollet's Socialist Party in France today. Would Mapam be the one to profit in that event, or would it be those forces that are hostile to us from both a workers' and Socialist point of view? Would Mapam then be able to clear its conscience by the argument that others were supposedly responsible for this fatal development?

True, the suggested unification involves some danger. Mapam's idyllic existence—to the extent that it still prevails—will be disturbed. Its members and leaders will have to contest other views that will flow with great force in the united party. If the aim isn't to set up an order of "all our friends" but a political party, then the only way to try to correct the fatal development of the labor movement is the path of uniting the three workers parties into one party that will undoubtedly be full of passions, clashes and conflicts, but will at least be able to open a new page in the history of both the State and the movement.

It is self-understood that such a unity cannot come about on the basis of organizational or ideological uniformization. Such unity would have to leave a great deal of room for organizational frameworks and to guarantee a minimum program that would not try to be all-inclusive, but would give a minimum of security that the united party would be faithful to the fundamental line uniting the vast majority. If you don't answer this question or if you satisfy yourself with raising proposals that aren't completely realistic, you are running away from the front on which the labor movement is fighting and where its fate for the next generation will be decided. . . .

(From Pinhas Lavon, "The Lacks in Meir Yaari's Theories," No. 23, Apr. 4, 1963.)

The Lavon group, that is, the group now gathering around the biweekly *Min Hayesod*, never considered the possibility of fighting outside its party's framework. That is the truth and the group never hid this from the world. From this viewpoint, it never received itself or its members.

Pinhas Lavon voiced this same truth to Ahdut Haavoda at its last convention. We, on the other hand, never deluded ourselves concerning the nature of this group, its potentialities or aims. If there *really* appeared to be a possibility for an alternative in that direction, we would tend towards it and seize it. We have to thank comrade Pinhas Lavon for taking on himself the thankless task of duelling with the Mapai leadership, but without deluding people of his aims and the limits he had set himself.

Today Lavon and his comrades are questioning the existence of the Military Administration. They revolt against the lurking dangers to Israeli democracy and they stand up in defense of the pioneering elements in Histadrut activity and leadership. Pinhas Lavon has not, indeed, criticized his own international orientation, but in their paper members of the group reveal commendable courage as an undefined trend within their own party. More than once they have faced the threats of punishment without flinching. They were ready to pay the greatest price for their freedom of expression and it can also happen that one day they will find themselves unwillingly outside their party. There is no doubt that in such an event we wouldn't be too exacting in clauses and subclauses and would invite them at least to establish a united front. Meanwhile a situation of neither peace nor war prevails between them and their party and for the time being they are content with expressing themselves independently. We can understand the Lavon adherents' loyalty to their party even under the present circumstances, but they are turning their trouble into a blessing and recommending to others to follow their path. . . .

(From Meir Yaari, "Between Vision and Reality," pp. 1–11, *Merhavia*, 1963.)

The 35 years of Mapai's existence saw great and important achievements. However, the internal developments of the recent past revealed serious symptoms of crisis, conflicting with its ideological content, its historic path, the fundamentals of comradeship, the possibility of influencing the party, the labor movement and the Histadrut.

The members of Min Hayesod saw in Mapai the embodiment of the principles of Socialist-Zionism, national redemption, the image of an original Jewish labor movement and the expression of great moral and spiritual forces working to create a laboring people as the free creator of a socialist economy and society.

The members of Min Hayesod were among the founders of Mapai, among its veteren members, the builders of the labor settlements, the cadres of the Histadrut and the labor movement, the thinkers and theoreticians of the Jewish labor movement, the teachers of and emisaries to the youth. The internal developments within Mapai, however, led this well-rooted and constructive section of the Jewish labor movement to the sense of deep crisis since the situation within Mapai contradicts the content and nature of the fundamental values and the possibilities of maintaining these in daily life.

These are the signs of the crisis:

1. The party has been emptied of its spiritual life and the apparatus has replaced the idea. The apparatus has won exclusive control and there is growing competition between power groups over positions, with politicians dominating the public instead of serving it;

2. The elected party institutions have been voided of content and deprived of the possibility of free discussion and decision on the important questions deciding the shape of our public life;

3. In most cases, the positions of public representatives have been taken over by an oligarchic stratum concentrating all the powers of implementation and mocking values;

4. The equality between members of the same party has been destroyed, the limits between the permissible and the forbidden in our lives have been blurred, and "one man's" dictates have become an accepted and normal way of life;

5. The party leadership has ceased to guide and teach the movement and has practically become the satellite of a self-appointed apparatus that is paralyzing any initiative by the leadership;

6. The campaign for this year's elections to the party congress was exclusively a contest between blocs and persons for positions of control and was completely lacking in any content of ideas on anything concerning views and principles. This election campaign was not preceded by any theoretical discussions on the fundamental problems of the party, the labor movement, the Jewish people, the State and Israeli society;

7. Boycott and ban have turned from weapons aimed against one member to a regular way of life employed by the party daily against every group or individual daring to question the actions of the apparatus;

8. The link between principles and everyday policies has been ruptured, the party now works according to pragmatic responses divorced of any ties to the system of principles in which the party believes;

9. From an independent labor movement building a socialist workers society, the Histadrut has turned into the stronghold of pressure groups with special interests and into a satellite of government policy, and thereby lost the possibility of shaping an economic and social policy meeting national and workers' interests;

10. As a result, the nature of Israeli society is being distorted and

capitalism, cultivated by the Histadrut's weakness and by a workers government, is taking power and is the chief beneficiary of national and public funds. The quantitative and qualitative weight of the workers' enterprise has been declining, the social and ethnic gap is growing, and the reason for the particular and specific existence of Israeli society is disappearing;

11. Ever since the Hulda meeting we have been hoping for some change in this path. Though the Prime Minister's letter contained only the very minimum promises and guides towards correcting the distortions, we wanted to see in it a door to change. However, the contents of the letter sent to the Hulda meeting were retracted after one or two days.

We also hoped that the negotiations to establish a new alignment in the labor movement by way of an alliance or federation and with autonomy for all its parts—would lead to a change. In our sense of responsibility for the fate of the labor movement and especially for the success of the alignment, the Min Hayesod group abstained from presenting any demands concerning its integration and place in the alignment. Because of these considerations, we turned to Mapai and demanded our right to exist as a countrywide ideological section within its framework.

Not only did we receive no response to the demands themselves, but it became clear to us in the course of contacts with the Prime Minister that in his view, one of the conditions for the alignment's success was our agreement to waive any representation or appearance of Min Hayesod as part of the new alignment either in Mapai or in Ahdut Haavoda. It became clear beyond any doubt that not only had the boycott and ban not been removed within Mapai, but they were even going to be extended to Ahdut Haavoda as a condition for the establishment of the alignment. The practical conclusion and true aim of the position is that Mapai prefers the Min Hayesod group not to be present within its framework as an active force.

For these reasons the meeting proclaims the establishment of the Min Hayesod movement.

This movement will be independent, not part of the existing frameworks in the labor movement and will see as its aim the realignment and reunification of the workers' parties in this country.

(Statement by founding meeting of the Min Hayesod movement, Tel Aviv, July 11, 1964, in Min Hayesod, 62–63.)

It is generally agreed that no one will be found to blame the members of Min Hayesod on seceding from Mapai for having been overhasty or for not having tried to exhaust to the full all the possibilities of remaining within Mapai as members in equal standing. For almost four years, Pinhas Lavon and his comrades were banned and boycotted by their party only because the Mapai leadership yielded to David Ben-Gurion's ultimatum that he was not prepared to sit in one place with Pinhas Lavon. Prime Minister Eshkol recently delivered an emotional address that was full of sympathy for the Lavon group, but he was not ready to do anything to guarantee their rights within the party. Now, when the group has finally drawn the inevitable conclusions from its intolerable situation, Levi Eshkol puts on an injured and insulted look—

and protests against the splitting activity. The secession of the Min Hayesod group has created a new situation. This situation involves new possibilities and conclusions. Conditions have been created for a pioneering socialist alignment, faithful to the fundamental values of the Israeli labor movement. The test now is mainly that of Ahdut Haavoda. . . .

(From an editorial in *Al-Hamishmar,* Sept. 11, 1964.)

20 • Ahdut Haavoda and Mapam

If we try to sum up the main differences that divided Mapam and Ahdut Haavoda–Poale Zion, we could list the following:

1. As a result of the development it had undergone since the Second Aliya, Ahdut Haavoda was, to a great extent, a pragmatic party; that is, it created an illusory conflict between "program" and "reality." It didn't put great store, like Mapam, on a crystallized social theory, a detailed organizational statute or definite principles guiding its political steps and tactics.

2. Ahdut Haavoda–Poale Zion had never given up the idea of "inclusive unity" and wanted Mapam to come into Mapai, even if only in stages, together with Ahdut Haavoda itself. By this joint action, Ahdut Haavoda hoped to secure for itself greater freedom of maneuver in Mapai. This would also free Ahdut Haavoda of the danger of the opponents of unification with Mapai within its own ranks from moving over to Mapam. Mapam, on the other hand, did not believe in the possibilities of unification with Mapai, especially given the existing course of development; the one-time failure of Siah Bet within Mapai only reinforced Mapam's belief that *proximity of views* (though not necessarily identity of views) and a *joint minimum political program,* together with organizational democratic guarantees, were an unalterable condition for the success of any unification. Instead of uncontrolled factional fighting within the party and its internal paralysis (or one trend taking power and compelling the others to disappear), Mapam preferred to explore all the possibilities of real cooperation in broader frameworks and on specific issues. In any event, the existence of such cooperation and the resultant proof of Mapai's good will, respect, and tolerance for other groups would have to precede any notion of higher stages of cooperation. Here we see the old debate that had been conducted between Hashomer Hatsair and Ahdut Haavoda from the Third Aliya onward over the conception of unity, either in its Mapai metamorphosis of repeated attempts to impose unity by force, or in the form of the identification of "inclusive unity" that had been consistently promoted by Ahdut Haavoda throughout its history. The members of the former Siah Bet never freed themselves of their loyalty to that idea of "inclusive unity"

even when circumstances, temporarily, as they thought, deprived it of any immediate political actuality.

The example of Ahdut Haavoda clearly shows how real an influence a movement principle can have, even when, temporarily, implementation has to be put in the freezer. For Siah Bet within Mapai the principle of inclusive unity was a factor preventing its own ideological consolidation; after Siah Bet was pushed out of Mapai, the dogma of "inclusive unity" seemed to Tnua L'Ahdut Haavoda to be an alternative to Mapam's demand for the unity of the left. Loyalty to this principle also affected the ability of the L'Ahdut Haavoda section within Mapam to view the party as an alternative to Mapai. After its secession from Mapam, this same principle was used as the theoretical justification for hesitating to establish closer connections with Mapam. Afterward, it led to the "dual alignment" and ultimately to unity with Mapai in the Israel Labor Party.

3. Though Ahdut Haavoda shared a great deal of Mapam's criticism of Mapai's policies, it did not, like Mapam, consider changes in these policies to be a precondition for the possibility of the political and organizational unity of the Israel labor movement. With all its criticism of Mapai, it conceived of a kind of coexistence of socialists and non-socialists, pioneers and anti-pioneers, democrats and anti-democrats in the united labor movement. In its view, the anti-worker and anti-pioneering line dominant in Mapai was indeed a danger and should be criticized, but nonetheless it had to be considered a legitimate element and one of the components of the workers' party, a kind of "erring brother" of the pioneering left in the united family.

It is not strange, therefore, that Ahdut Haavoda never looked on the course and struggle of the pioneering left as an alternative to Mapai— that is, an independent theoretical and political system extending over the whole front facing the policies conducted by Mapai, but viewed it rather as a corrective. (The only alternative Ahdut Haavoda was willing to envision was the whole united labor movement facing the bourgeoisie.)

In addition, since any political party's struggle has a natural tendency to take on the character of an "alternative," Ahdut Haavoda was suspicious of the very existence of party organizations which were liable to artificially inflate differences far beyond their real differences, and thus stabilize polarities that were liable to hinder the attainment of "inclusive unity" or to threaten its existence after it was attained. Here we can find the basic explanation (apart from tactical considerations or degrees of proximity to either Mapai or Mapam) for Ahdut Haavoda's refusal to accede to Mapam's suggestions of *pioneering left union.* In the special circumstances of 1947–1948 it had appeared to the members of Ahdut Haavoda that unity with Hashomer Hatsair could serve as a step towards the achievement of inclusive unity, but in light of their experience in the years that followed, they became convinced that the face-to-face confrontation of Mapai and the pioneering left could objectively sharpen the contest between them, and this conflicted with their basic concept and their forecast of "inclusive unity."

Mapam, on the other hand, did not believe in the above "coexistence" in a socialist and pioneering workers' party. Its struggle was aimed at the labor movement's overcoming the reformist and anti-pioneering illusions and trends. That aim could only be achieved by giving unequivocal alternative solutions instead of those proposed by Mapai, otherwise there was no prospect of convincing the working class that the struggle was a vital one for it, and that it was possible to conduct other policies. Besides, the prospects of convincing them of this would increase in the measure that the proposal of an alternative path went together with the construction of a broad and united alternative force that would give the alternative path real prospects of implementation. Summing up, we see that there was an ineluctably logical link between the concept of inclusive unity and Ahdut Haavoda's policies of "corrections" to Mapai policy, just as there was a link between the concept of an alternative and Mapam's demand for the unity of the pioneering left.

4. Ahdut Haavoda thought that participating in the government coalition was the criterion for pioneering constructivism and bordered on being in opposition on principle. Ahdut Haavoda's adherence to the coalition as almost a matter of principle (despite crises from time to time) very seriously limited the momentum and freedom of maneuver of the pioneering left as a whole. Mapam, on the other hand, saw many important advantages in participating in the government but also could conceive of situations in which the balance of advantages and disadvantages would be such as to obligate it to go over to the opposition, without this undermining in the least Mapam's constructive contribution to building the country.

5. Ahdut Haavoda was fundamentally opposed to accepting Arabs into its ranks and instead attempted to set up an affiliated Arab Labor Party. In the 1959 elections, this party won only 4,000 votes; in 1963 Ahdut Haavoda no longer presented the Arab list and instead asked the Arab public to vote for it directly. It didn't win any response and the number of its Arab votes decreased even further. In contrast, Mapam, after Ahdut Haavoda's secession, had accepted Arabs into its membership and party institutions and since 1951 its faction in the Knesset always included an Arab member. In the 1959 elections its Arab votes were almost doubled as compared with previous elections, and in the elections to the Fourth, Fifth and Sixth Knesset, it received around 10 percent of all the Arab votes. In the 1959 municipal elections, Mapam almost tripled its votes as compared with the previous election, and since then, its representative, Abdul

Aziz Z'ubi, has been serving as Vice Mayor of Nazareth.[1] Mapam had 20 representatives in Arab municipal councils, compared with three who might be considered to be affiliated with Ahdut Haavoda (though in the 1965 elections the latter appeared as part of the Alignment and not independently). In cooperation with the Hashomer Hatsair educational youth movement, Mapam helped found an Arab Pioneering Youth Organization (in 1954) and opened its kibbutzim to groups of trainees formed by that organization. Mapam also took the initiative in establishing the Jewish-Arab Association for Peace and Equality in 1956, and the Middle East monthly *New Outlook*. Ever since the establishment of the State of Israel, Mapam has headed the public campaign to abolish the military administration, to accept Arab workers into the ranks of the Histadrut and the political parties, and in general to guarantee the Arab minority its full civil and national rights and genuine integration in the country's life and economy. It publishes an Arabic weekly (*Al-Mirsad— The Guard*), established an Arab book-publishing enterprise, and for a number of years also actively assisted in publishing a literary and political monthly, *Al-Fajr (The Dawn)*,

6. In contrast to Ahdut Haavoda's pessimism over the possibilities of peace initiatives, and its inclination toward quite activistic retaliations, Mapam believed in the possibility of peace and the need for peace, though the party was keenly aware of the security problems and was concerned to equip and train the Israel defense forces as effectively as possible. Mapam rejected "preventive war" on principle as well as in practice and demanded untiring initiatives for peace. This latter demand was organically linked to the demand for a neutralist policy and support for the struggles of the colonial peoples for liberation.

> . . . Sometimes there is room for a relatively large operation and sometimes a pinprick in the enemy's back by a small unit is sufficient; sometimes on the other side of the immediate border, and sometimes in the capital itself. Sometimes restraint is desirable, and sometimes a "hit and run" strike is necessary. And we shouldn't exclude the possibility of driving the invader out of the occupied parts of the country, if security needs require this. . . .
> (From address by Yigal Allon in Knesset, January 2, 1956, in *Divrei Haknesset*, 19, p. 691.)

> . . . True, this shaky peace, this peace in which we are living, is better than any war, but even those who believed that we could maintain this shaky peace are coming to the recognition that there are forces around us and in this world which will not permit this peace to exist.
> Once more, we say in unequivocal fashion: In replying to these

---

1. When, in the municipal elections of November 1965, seven Mapai representatives, seven Rakah, and one Mapam representative were elected, Mr. Z'ubi served for a number of months as Mayor, in addition to being a member of Knesset.

attacks against us, we are not at all obligated under all circumstances to defend ourselves from inside the "fence" of the State; we must not allow the enemy to feel secure that always and under all circumstances we will always go back to where we came from. We don't think that it is possible to keep the struggle limited in time and targets. We have no choice of not defending ourselves for fear that war will break out; if we don't defend ourselves it will certainly break out. Our defense, even when it is liable to involve us in war, is better than a lack of action leading to surrender and defeat. . . .

. . . The Iraqi Army has nothing to do on the banks of the Jordan and the Yarmuk, just as no other country has anything to do on the banks of the Euphrates and the Tigris. If we have to confront the Iraqi Army it is better for this confrontation to take place on the Jordan rather than in Jerusalem or Kalkilya. The difference between an army entering eastern Jordan or western Jordan isn't an essential one; it is only a difference of time; it is still impossible to get to the West of the Jordan without first being on its east. We cannot, therefore, be quiet about this danger, even if there has been a retreat held up, since no one can know if this plan won't come up again and be implemented. Members of Knesset: the present time is loaded with very critical events. Let us arm ourselves with strength, wisdom and courage.

(From address by Israel Galili in the Knesset on October 16, 1956, *Divrei Haknesset,* 21a, p. 85.)

. . . The serious repercussion of the Israel Defense Forces operation at Samoa led to the beginning of a kind of stock-taking. There was a growing awareness within the public and the government that not every attack and every case can be answered in full force and the circumstances, the conditions, implications and political connections must be considered very carefully. It has become completely clear that the world—friends and enemies alike—refuses to agree to operations like Samoa. The world won't agree and isn't prepared to agree that because of an attack on three of our soldiers—who are the whole world for us, and for whose loss there is no consolation or replacement—Israel must retaliate on an almost warlike scale with the mobilization of forces and the application of power out of all proportion to what happened before that. The world as a whole will ignore our just cause and sentence us to harsh isolation and defeat, politically and even more, morally.

Inevitably, we say that between the choice of giving up the right of self-defense and sitting with folded hands, or crushing operations involving the danger of a military conflagration, there are transition stages and intermediate levels of defense and activity.

. . . Yigal Allon's declarations put things in distorted proportions. What is more, they are a kind of competition with Moshe Dayan who only recently also at a meeting of Rafi cadres warned the Government against the experiment of retreating from the methods of reprisal that were forged during Ben-Gurion's governments.

Here, indeed, Yigal Allon is stretching out his hand to Moshe Dayan. The "activistic" philosophy rejects all intermediate stages and any examination of dimensions and proportions. For the philosophy of "activism" there is only one reprisal—everywhere, every time. "Bang and we're finished!" That is the slippery path leading directly to the "beginning of failure." That is, incidentally, also the philosophy whose victory is perhaps desired by all those elements in the Arab countries which do not see any outlet except by an immediate direct contest, in the hope that the marginal attacks will involve the Arab countries in war against Israel. . . .

(From "The Plotters Abroad and the Underminers Within," by Nikanor in *Al-Hamishmar,* Dec. 20, 1966.)

The "activistic" propaganda that won Ahdut Haavoda–Poale Zion its surprising success in the 1955 elections betrayed them when they tried to use it again in the elections of 1959. Ahdut Haavoda–Poale Zion lost three of its mandates, while Mapam succeeded in holding on to its nine despite the poisonously chauvinistic atmosphere prevailing during the election campaign. The new government had one Ahdut Haavoda minister (Yitzhak Ben-Aharon: Transport), and two Mapam ministers (Mordehai Bentov: Development, and Israel Barzilai: Health). The defeat aggravated the continual debate within Ahdut Haavoda, and in many branches an increased number of members were going over to Mapai, without waiting for the conclusion of the debate going on in the party institutions.[2]

As the elections to the Fifth Knesset (the "Affair elections") drew near, in August 1961, Mapam suggested establishing a joint list based on parity with Ahdut Haavoda–Poale Zion, but the latter turned the offer down, both for tactical and, apparently, also more fundamental reasons.[3] Ahdut Haavoda believed that since it was the party between Mapai and Mapam, by going alone it would win the votes of Mapai members and sympathizers who would refuse to vote for the party this time—in protest against Lavon's expulsion. In addition, they were apparently also moved by the fear that the formation of the suggested joint list would create a new situation that would hinder their process of drawing closer to Mapai.

In these elections, Mapai, together with its client Arab lists, lost six of its 52 mandates. However, though the pioneering left parties increased their votes considerably, they were unable, appearing separately, to convince the electorate that they could be a real alternative to Mapai. Mapam had added about 6,000 votes since the 1959 elections and Ahdut Haavoda 5,000 (this time, unlike 1959, without a separate Arab list). Since Ahdut Haavoda had the largest number of surplus votes, it won an added seat (eight all told), while Mapam's surplus was not enough to give it the added tenth.

After the elections, Mapam, Ahdut Haavoda, the Liberals (union of

---

2. Something similar happened to the L'Ahdut Haavoda section in the period between the Haifa Party Congress and the secession from Mapam, when a number of the section's urban cadres became impatient and left Mapam to join Mapai.

3. Ahdut Haavoda made its agreement conditional on the participation of the Lavon Group. Since Lavon made it clear he wasn't even considering such a possibility, this condition was tantamount to a rejection.

General Zionists and Progressives who had united just before the elections) and the National Religious Party agreed to negotiate with Mapai for the renewal of the coalition, on two main conditions. The first was that the new government be composed according to the size of the coalition parties as reflected in the elections—that is, that Mapai would no longer have an absolute majority in the government. This demand was aimed at guaranteeing that all important matters be discussed and decided by the whole government instead of in the smaller circle of Mapai ministers or Ben-Gurion's confidants, as in the past.

The second demand was formulated as a result of the lessons of the security scandal of 1954 and of the Lavon–Ben-Gurion affair as a whole. The security services had to come under the real supervision of both the government and the Knesset's Foreign Affairs and Security Committee. Mapai, however, ultimately succeeded, with the aid of the National Religious Party, in splitting the Four Party Club; the only joint negotiations left were those of Ahdut Haavoda, and Mapam with Mapai. Since in the smaller coalition (along the lines of the former coalition) there was no avoiding a Mapai majority, the main aim of the negotiations, as far as the pioneering left parties were concerned, was to secure programmatic guarantees for the progressive elements of the new government's policies, and guarantees for the rights of the minority against arbitrary use of majority decisions.

Throughout all the turns and twists of the extended and wearisome negotiations on the composition of the new government, the two parties maintained very close contact and a maximum amount of coordination in their positions and demands. Finally, they presented Mapai with ultimatums over guarantees for the maintenance of the workers' real wages, the maintenance of the status quo in religious affairs, the abolition of the military administration, the rights of the Knesset Committee on Foreign Affairs and the Security Committee to appoint committees of inquiry in certain circumstances, and freedom of vote on arms deals with Germany. It was here, at the final stage of the negotiations, that Ahdut Haavoda's representatives broke down, practically yielded on all of these issues and, rupturing the united front with Mapam, joined a coalition composed of Mapai, the National Religious Party, Poale Agudat Israel, and Ahdut Haavoda, all of which together had the narrow majority of 68 of the Knesset's 120 members. In so doing, it did Mapai and the "younger men's" campaign for power an incomparable service: Ahdut Haavoda not only extricated them from the dead end into which they had come in their attempts to form a government not in accord with the election results, but also gave them, after their defeat in the elections, the largest majority Mapai had ever enjoyed in the government (eleven of the sixteen Ministers, most of them belonging to the "younger men" or other Ben-Gurion adherents). Worst of all, however, by joining the coalition in the given circumstances, Ahdut Haavoda served the cause of Mapai propaganda intended to quiet the opposition within its ranks and to restore the prestige of Ben-Gurion and of the "younger men" after its precipitous decline during the "Affair." Mapam refused to follow Ahdut Haavoda on the road of concessions and considered itself obliged, this time, to choose the role of opposition.

> We can only adopt a position toward the new government on the background of the events that preceded a critical political crisis that led to the premature dissolution of the Fourth Knesset and the earlier elections to the Fifth Knesset.
> This wasn't an ordinary government crisis; it didn't originate in an argument over some detail or other of domestic or foreign policy. It broke out as a result of the serious attacks on the very foundations of Israeli democracy. The crisis aroused a public storm whose like had not been known throughout the years of existence of the young state. It drew in parts of the public that had until then been indifferent to politics. It aroused the Israeli youth which until that time had kept apart from active political life. Everybody understood that the battle this time was a fundamental one over the foundations of our political life and the existence of democracy in Israel.
> ... The government that has come into being in this way is worse than its predecessor. Is that why we went into the great battle—one in which there were hardly any differences between us and Ahdut Haavoda—in order to establish a government in which Mapai would have more ministers than it had ever had in any Israeli government until now? Is that why we went into the battle—to intensify the divisions within the Israeli left, and all this without Ahdut Haavoda being able to show that its achievements in the field of government and the promises of its progressive workers' character outweighed this loss?
> This government contradicts the results of the elections. Mapai came out of the elections weaker; it goes back to the government stronger. The left maintained its strength; it goes into the government divided and weak. All these also cancel all those achievements won in the extended negotiations, first by the four parties and then by the two parties. This government doesn't promise either stable government or stronger foundations for Israeli democracy. It only deepens the social and moral crisis. We shall vote against it.
> (From address by Yaakov Hazan, in Knesset *Al-Hamishmar*, March 11, 1961.)

For both Mapam and Ahdut Haavoda their kibbutz movements served as the source of moral and intellectual inspiration and the political and organizational backbones. The relative importance of their kibbutz movements as well as the nearness of their views on the roles of the Zionist movement, pioneering, the pioneering youth movements in the ingathering of the exiles and building the country, on neutrality, the defense of parliamentary democracy and workers' autonomy, etc., all could have provided a firm basis for the two parties to coordinate their positions and work together despite the differences separating them.

... Mapai, with Mapam and Ahdut Haavoda, could have formed a bloc of workers parties, but, as we can see every time anew, it is dreaming of a dictatorship under the mantle of democracy, while Mapam and Ahdut Haavoda, with their unnatural division, make this task easier for it.

... By regional elections it wants to wipe out both our parties together. Since both parties defended themselves against this aim of liquidation, Mapai's aims continue to deepen the divisions in the working class. The only answer to this aim is the greater unity of our two parties. On the other hand, I am in favor of cooperating with Mapai on every agreed-upon issue. But we all know that in order to make effective cooperation with Mapai possible, Mapam and Ahdut Haavoda have to unite. ... Every time that Mapam and Ahdut Haavoda came together, Mapai began to conduct negotiations worthy of the name with them, while it only tried to profit when they were separate. ... I believe with all my heart that Ahdut Haavoda's and Mapam's appearing together in the Knesset, in the Histadrut and the public in general is a vital matter, especially since the two parties have a common natural mission.

(From remarks by Meir Yaari in an interview in *Davar,* June 1, 1961.)

21 • Debating the "Alignment"

The basic problem occupying Ahdut Haavoda-Poale Zion in its last years of independent existence was that of its relationships to Mapai and Mapam. Despite its proximity of views to Mapam in many spheres, only very few of the leaders and cadres of the Ahdut Haavoda-Poale Zion Party supported the idea of pioneering-left unity as proposed by Mapam. The main debate within the party evolved around the question whether the gradual unification with Mapai—via the "alignment"—should be made conditional on Mapam's participation, or whether to move towards such unity even without Mapam. While some of the Ahdut Haavoda leadership came out clearly for the *dual alignment* with Mapai, their opponents rallied around the slogan of either threefold unity or the status quo.

In May 1962 one of the outstanding Ahdut Haavoda leaders, Yitzhak Ben-Aharon, resigned from the government, among the rest because of differences with his colleagues over the pace and way of further unification with Mapai. His colleagues' attempts to convince him to return were to no avail and he was not even appeased when the party convention[1] repeated the traditional appeal for "inclusive unity".[2]

> In its previous convention, in its program for the Fifth Knesset and in written and verbal speeches, the Ahdut Haavoda-Poale Zion Party has brought up the need for a new alignment of the Israeli workers and its program for the inclusive unification of the socialist-Zionist trends in the Israeli labor movement. Mapai and Mapam, each for its reasons and arguments, have rejected this program. Mapam has even avoided cooperating with Ahdut Haavoda and Mapai in the Israeli government, while within Mapai there are trends towards revising socialist and pioneering values and the distortions from the viewpoint of internal democracy have become even more pronounced.
>
> Social and political occurrences in Israel, however, the dangers from abroad, the needs and tasks at home and the goals of the labor movement in view of capitalist development, give this program of ours special importance. The political unification of Israel's workers is a demand of the hour and it can arise on the basis of a joint socialist-Zionist program, the recognition of the right of independent ideological groups to exist, and a democratic way of life and discipline in action.
>
> The Party will work to fulfill the program as a whole and the convention states its recognition that our own struggle for Ahdut Haavoda-

1. September 12–15, 1962.
2. Pinhas Lavon was a guest speaker at the convention and made an address in favor of inclusive unity.

Poale Zion's path and greater strength, together with the cooperation of the workers parties in the Histadrut and the State, hold the main prospect for the unification of the labor movement.

("For a New Alignment in the Labor Movement in Israel," in "Resolutions of the 1962 Convention of Ahdut Haavoda-Poale Zion," Shfayim-Tel Aviv, September 12-15, 1962; published by Ahdut Haavoda-Poale Zion, Tel Aviv, 1962.)

A few months later Yitzhak Ben-Aharon came back into politics by publishing a lengthy article which contained an emotional and closely detailed appeal to the Israel labor movement as a whole:

I suggest:
1. The immediate establishment, by the free will and decision of the workers parties, of a union of the socialist workers in Israel, centered around the three workers parties and the socialist religious workers, on the basis of an agreed program of action for this decade, the acceptance of a majority decision in implementation, the freedom of ideological organization and the freedom of expression. All the builders of this union will undertake to maintain its existence for at least two terms of the elected bodies in the State, the Histadrut and the Municipalities. Its wholeness, the most certain guarantee for the change, is a function of the triple union but the veto right to end this course as a whole should not be left to any one factor alone.
2. The union and all its member organizations, sections and individuals will publicly undertake an economic, social, political and security program of action for the current decade. It will devote itself to its implementation and bear unlimited responsibility (without any limited liability) for all the hardships and sacrifices that this program will impose on individuals and the public.
3. The union will not recognize within itself any fermentation or any faction whose distinguishing marks reflect or serve special professional, communal or economic interests; on the other hand, it will not take any majority decisions on any theoretical and ideological matters subject to differences unless the subjects of the controversy themselves desire this.
4. The union will present its list to the elections to the Knesset, the Histadrut and the municipalities on the basis of an agreed-upon ten-year plan for all the fields in which it appears and its elected representatives will form a single group with discipline in action and individual freedom of opinion at home and abroad. The factions of the founding bodies in the Knesset, the Histadrut and the municipalities will unite immediately.
7. Meetings of all kinds and at all levels, as well as discussions, organs of expression and the like, of all the recognized organizations and sections within the union will be open to all the members of the union—in keeping with the matter and the level of the meetings; thus the central committees and secretariats of the sections will be open to the members of the secretariat of the union, and so on. All secret discussions and consultations contradict the strength and welfare of the union and membership within it.

8. The institutions of the union will be composed—for the first term—in accordance with the relations of forces in the Knesset, the Histadrut and the municipalities; for the second term—on the basis of proportional or personal elections—according to the subject, the place and the prevailing conditions. It would, however, be in conflict with the welfare and charter of the union to remove talented persons fit for missions because of the sectional relations of forces.

9. The union will maintain a daily paper and will publish journals for ideological and operational discussions on the basis of freedom of opinion and loyalty to its program. Every section and any member or group of members will be free to maintain weeklies or any other periodical publication, but not to maintain an independent daily newspaper. (The reasons for this, as I will explain further on, are mainly economic, though I do not intend to hide the unifying educational aim.)

13. An alliance of the kibbutz movement will be formed immediately, with the aim of bringing about the full and unreserved unification of all the existing national kibbutz organizations, including the Religious Kibbutz. . . .

(From "Courage to Change—Before Too Late," by Yitzhak Ben-Aharon, in *Lamerhav* Nov. 1, 1963.)

After some brief hesitations, the Ahdut Haavoda-Poale Zion Party adopted Ben-Aharon's plan with some minor changes and opened discussions with Mapai and Mapam on the New Alignment in the Labor Movement. This time, Mapai revealed a tendency to agree to the existence of factions within the suggested united party—as a transitional stage on the way to full union, on the basis of Ben-Aharon's suggestion of "majority decision in implementation." On the other hand, its spokesmen completely ignored Ben-Aharon's minimum program and especially rejected any demand to change the new economic policy.

Mapam's representatives did not consider themselves authorized to give the Ahdut Haavoda spokesman a final answer, since the party was on the verge of its fourth convention. Nonetheless, they didn't leave their interlocutors with any doubts about Mapam's disbelief in the practicality of any unity, federative or other, with Mapai and suggested, as the only realistic program, a reunion of the pioneering left parties which would also influence the pioneering and clearly socialist section within Mapai and help it toward independent crystallization.

Mapam's Fourth Congress instructed the party's Secretariat to renew the negotiations with Ahdut Haavoda–Poale Zion and to propose a union of the left at any level or any form that the other party desired, and also to work out a joint minimum political program to serve as the basis for such a union. Ahdut Haavoda–Poale Zion, this time too, rejected any suggestion of a pioneering left union, explaining that, as far as it was concerned, there were only two possible unions: the one *they* preferred was a *federative union* (according to Ben-Aharon's program) *of all three parties:*

Mapai, Ahdut Haavoda–Poale Zion, and Mapam. In the event that Mapam refused to take part in such a union, the only other possibility was a union of Ahdut Haavoda–Poale Zion and Mapai alone, as a first stage toward inclusive unity.

David Ben-Gurion's resignation from the premiership in June 1963 (according to the law) led to the resignation of the government as a whole. The formation of the new government was entrusted to the Minister of Finance, Levi Eshkol. In keeping with the decisions of its Fourth Congress, Mapam declared its readiness to open negotiations on the formation of a new coalition headed by the three workers' parties, based on a new fundamental program that would be decided upon in negotiations. Mapai completely ignored this proposal but Ahdut Haavoda demanded that Mapai invite Mapam into the coalition, and that Mapam join the coalition on the basis of the former fundamental program (that is, the one that had been adopted by Mapai, the religious parties and Ahdut Haavoda alone and which Mapam had then not considered as enabling it to join the former coalition, toward the end of 1961.) Mapam's Central Committee rejected this proposal as baseless and on the following morning (June 25) Levi Eshkol presented his new government, with the same party composition as the former one, to the Knesset.

The change in the premiership soon began to show signs of certain changes, both in the style of the government's internal activity (more cooperation and information, limits to the authority of the Deputy Ministers, something that affected first and foremost the Deputy Minister of Defense, Shimon Peres, and limited his old practice of reaching into the province of the Foreign Ministry, etc.), as well as in the style of foreign policy. The latter was revealed in greater restraint in reprisal activities, more emphasized reservations concerning Bonn while highlighting its responsibility for the activities of German scientists who were building Egyptian missiles, reiterated expressions of the hope and desire for improved relations with the Soviet Union, further relaxation in the operation of the military administration in the Arab-populated border areas of Israel, etc. True, this was not a *political* change, but still it was a *change* in style, climate, and emphasis. This change also was reflected in the Mapai Congress that convened a few months later as the third session of the 9th Congress, in October 1963. The Congress' deliberations and resolutions did indeed prove once more that Mapai had not moved away from its traditional reformist positions. At the same time, however, its self-confidence seemed to have been shaken; the increasing strength of the "normal" capitalistic trends in shaping Israeli society led a considerable part of the leadership and active members to some concern over the party's status and future within the system that was crystallizing and which the party inevitably did not reflect and represent, neither from the viewpoint of its economic and class basis nor from that of its social superstructure and values. This concern was unequivocably reflected in the Congress' deliberations. The greater use of the term "socialism" as compared with former years may perhaps be explained somewhat by the fears of many in the Mapai leadership that the party's position would be harmed and its domination shaken if they didn't succeed in time to draw a clear line of demarcation, using socialist landmarks, between itself and the bourgeois capitalist sector that was more and more shaping Israeli society. Another partial reason for this use of socialist slogans and definitions may be found in the desire to prepare the ground for the negotiations on the dual alignment with Ahdut Haavoda–Poale Zion.

However, no matter what the reason, the ultimate results and conclusions were the same: Mapai remained a reformist party as before; its differences with the pioneering left had not disappeared or even decreased essentially. The deliberations of the Congress did not reveal any definite opposition forces to take up the struggle for a change within Mapai, in politics and economics. At the same time, however, the formulations, the style and the climate *did* change, and for the better.

This beginning of change was enough to encourage Ahdut Haavoda to renew its initiative concerning a new alignment (inclusive or dual) and in December 1963 the representatives of the three parties met. The Mapam representatives stated at that meeting that they did not consider such a "triple alignment" to be practical, but it was decided to begin negotiations on Mapam's joining the government.

These negotiations extended through January and February but ultimately failed, despite some early progress, since Levi Eshkol saw no possibility of meeting Mapam's ultimate minimum demands for the elimination of the housing slums, increased grants for large families, increased development budgets for the Arab village, a declaration of the aim to abolish the military administration in the future, and appropriate representation in the government in accordance with the party's strength. By a majority of 301 to 16, with 55 abstentions, the Mapam Council voted on February 22, 1964, that "conditions had not been attained nor the basis established for participation in the government."

> Following the resolution of the Fourth Congress, which once more stressed that it considers Ahdut Haavoda-Poale Zion as the potential partners for an alignment in the labor movement towards a real change in Israeli society and greater resistance to the dangers threatening us at home and abroad, Mapam turned to Ahdut Haavoda-Poale Zion with the proposal to establish a joint front in the Knesset, the Zionist movement, the Histadrut and the local authorities. To our sorrow, this appeal was not accepted and, instead, the Ahdut Haavoda-Poale Zion Party raised the suggestion of establishing a "new alignment" by forming a federative union of the three Zionist workers parties that would

be based on an agreed-upon program, the obligation of discipline in implementation, while preserving the ideological and organizational autonomy of the parties.

This suggestion of establishing a "new alignment" in the form of a federative union, while it apparently grants the two minority parties ideological and organizational autonomy, in practice would lead to their elimination in favor of the dominant line in Mapai, and we therefore reject the program for a "new alignment."

Despite some sounds of criticism that were heard at Mapai's last Congress, it has still not come to any modifications in its economic, social and political policies—a move that would serve as a guarantee for a change and real movement along a clearly workers' and pioneering line in achieving Zionism and building socialism in Israel. So long as such change does not occur in Mapai, any form of union between the three Zionist workers parties beyond their cooperation in the State government, in the Histadrut and the Zionist movement, could lead to the self-denial of the other parties. Only deepening the cooperation and basing it on a minimum program of action in equality and mutual respect, can pave the way for greater unity in the Israeli workers movement in all its parts, while maintaining each party's character and specific mission.

The immediate union of Mapam and Ahdut Haavoda–Poale Zion could also lead to a change within Mapai, towards preserving the pioneering values, removing the distortions that have been revealed in society and striving for the realization of socialism in Israel.

Faithful to the resolutions of the Congress, we shall continue to fight to maintain the true cooperation among the three Zionist workers' parties.

The Council once more calls on the Ahdut Haavoda–Poale Zion Party to help establish the pioneering left front as the alternative in the Israeli labor movement.

(From the Resolutions of the 17th Council of Mapam, February 21, 22, 1964, *Al-Hamishmar,* Feb. 23, 1964.)

Another Mapam application to Ahdut Haavoda–Poale Zion, in April 1964, for a pioneering left union was rejected again, and from then until September 1964, intensive negotiations were conducted between Ahdut Haavoda and Mapai for a "dual alignment" between these two parties in the course of which the parties drew closer in their positions. These efforts were concluded by the two parties presenting a joint list for the elections in the Knesset, the Histadruft and the Municipalities on a previously agreed-upon election platform.

At the outset, Ahdut Haavoda had indeed desired to *separate the parliamentary and Histadrut spheres* and to keep its independence in the Histadrut elections, where it had generally been closer to Mapam than to Mapai on most issues in dispute. This, however, was something to which Mapai could under no circumstances agree, for fear of losing its narrow majority in the Histadrut; the desire to protect this majority by Ahdut Haavoda support had actually been one of Mapai's main motives in the negotiations for this "new alignment." They ultimately came to an agreement, therefore, on a joint list of candidates and program, but maintaining the separate factions as a transition stage after the elections, though these were obligated to maintain continuous coordination, consultation and cooperation between themselves.

> ... The Alignment factions will guarantee the Histadrut a democratic leadership, able to initiate and implement, and will work together under the obligation of consultation in order to fulfill the working program and the promises given the voters.
> ... The principle of collective responsibility will be maintained in the Knesset and the government. The factions of both parties will form a single faction working and adopting obligatory decisions according to the joint platform and fundamental program. In the Knesset Ahdut Haavoda–Poale Zion will keep the same rights to an independent position that it had in the Fifth Knesset (on such questions as Germany and the like). Alignment Deputies will be called to the Knesset platform and written in the Records as: "Member of Knesset so-and-so, of the Alignment-Ahdut Haavoda–Poale Zion" or "Member of Knesset so-and-so, of the Alignment-Mapai—has the floor."
> During the period of existence of the Alignment, Mapai will not exercise its strength in the Knesset in order to abolish the system of proportional elections and to replace it with a system of regional elections. This principle was one of the premises in the negotiations from the very first meeting and everybody knew that it couldn't be deviated from in any way.
> The new Alignment will have to find a solution for the problem of the Min Hayesod group and the members of this veteran group must find their expression within the united alignment. If the alignment does, indeed, arise, it is destined to reveal tremendous sources of creative energy among the youth and the new immigrants and renew the alliance between the labor movement and the intellectuals.
> The Alignment will be in effect from the time of its signature until the end of the term of the Sixth Knesset with the aim of extending it and this possibility will be examined toward the end of the term of the Sixth Knesset.
> The Alignment will not be aimed against Mapam; the approaching election campaign will be aimed first of all and mainly against the forces hostile to the labor movement and towards the aim of pioneering and socialist change in Israel.

A second bone of contention was the question of *regional elections*. Mapai for years has had an explicit resolution to campaign within the electorate and the Knesset to replace the system of proportional elections by a system of regional elections, whereas Ahdut Haavoda, like Mapam, was strongly opposed to this change. The negotiators for Mapai were ultimately compelled to yield on this issue, at least temporarily, and to declare that during the period of the agreement Mapai wouldn't exercise its strength in the Knesset to change the electoral system. On the matter of a "joint program," Ahdut Haavoda–Poale Zion did not obtain most of what it wanted, especially in the social and economic spheres; according to the suggested agreement it was compelled to accept the majority decisions of the combined faction in the Knesset.

The negotiations aroused internal debates within both parties. Within Ahdut Haavoda–Poale Zion, most of the leadership, headed by Yitzhak Ben-Aharon, Yigal Allon, Yisrael Bar-Yehuda and Yisrael Galili, were in favor of signing the alignment agreement. An important minority, however, headed by Yitzhak Tabenkin, Zev Tzur, Y. Rabinowitz, Benny Marshak and Moshe Erem, were against a "dual alignment" (*any* alignment—either with Mapam or with Mapai) and wanted either a "triple alignment" or the status quo—that is, the independent existence of Ahdut Haavoda–Poale Zion while continuing to campaign for a "triple alignment" and "inclusive unity." These argued that the dual alignment with Mapai would deepen their differences with Mapam and bar all future prospects of bringing it into the alignment or unification they wanted. On the other hand, they were concerned over the status and future of their own movement if this had to find its place alone, without Mapam, in the dual alignment and later in the united party, face to face with the Mapai majority about whose intolerance and domineering trends they had no illusions.

A parallel argument also went on within Mapai. While Levi Eshkol had initiated the negotiations with Ahdut Haavoda–Poale Zion and spoken in favor of the dual alignment, Ben-Gurion and the "younger men" had their open reservations concerning the Eshkol-Galili agreement on the alignment. First of all, they considered it only a poor substitute for real unity; second, they would have preferred the alternative of a "turn rightward"—that is, an agreement with the Liberals against Herut, on the one side, and against the pioneering left, on the other. Third, they looked on an alignment of this kind as changing the balance of forces within the party in Eshkol's favor, and in any case, as weakening the position of Ben-Gurion himself and of the "younger men." For these reasons, they campaigned against Eshkol and the alignment by claiming that it should have been the duty of the negotiators with Ahdut Haavoda–Poale Zion to stand firm on Mapai's right to work for a change in the electoral system even during the period of existence of the alignment. If Ben-Gurion's demand had been met, it would have meant killing the new alignment from the start and terminating the negotiations between the parties on this subject.

Another serious hurdle on the way to the successful termination of the alignment negotiations had been the question of Min Hayesod. Ahdut Haavoda–Poale Zion had promised this group when it was still within Mapai that the establishment of an alignment would have to include a solution for the problem of bringing Pinhas Lavon and his colleagues back into party activity. However, since Mapai had replied that this was intervening in its own domestic affairs, it rejected this demand and thus the members of Min Hayesod had been compelled to leave the party. Ahdut Haavoda–Poale Zion wanted to keep its promise at least *within the framework of the alignment;* the Min Hayesod movement should either be allowed to join the alignment as a third party or, if the movement agreed to combine with Ahdut Haavoda–Poale Zion, Pinhas Lavon and his comrades would be brought into the alignment and the joint list of candidates as Ahdut Haavoda–Poale Zion representatives.

However, this demand, with its two alternative possibilities, was rejected by Mapai on November 15, 1964. Levi Eshkol was compelled to yield on this to firm opposition of the bloc as the only way of winning its support for the alignment. This decision put the representatives of Ahdut Haavoda–Poale Zion in a very delicate position since the choice before them was either to keep their promise to Min Hayesod and thereby give up the alignment, or to break that promise and to create the paradoxical situation of establishing an alignment with Mapai, not only without Mapam but even without the members of the Min Hayesod who were their allies within Mapai. Such a development was a dangerous one, promising the Ahdut Haavoda–Poale Zion leadership battles and severe crises within their own party and in the Kibbutz Hameuchad.

Despite the vigorous opposition of David Ben-Gurion and the "younger men" (Moshe Dayan even resigned from the government on November 5, 1964), Levi Eshkol managed to obtain the support of the larger part of the bloc. Bloc members, despite their admiration for and loyalty to Ben-Gurion's leadership, were concerned most of all to secure Mapai's majority in the Histadrut and looked on the dual alignment as a reasonable possibility of achieving that. By a vote of 182 against 8, with 24 abstentions, the Mapai Central Committee ratified the proposal to establish the alignment with Ahdut Haavoda–Poale Zion, on November 15, 1964.

SOURCES

1. We view the establishment of a pioneering Socialist Zionist Workers Front as the need of the hour, something that is necessary to stop the dangerous developments in Israeli society and economy threatening to destroy all our achievements up to now. This front is vital to renew the momentum of the working class in building and deepening all those foundations of our life guaranteeing our advance towards the construction of a socialist society in the course of continuing the ingathering of the exiles and by establishing a pioneering regime in Israel.

Such a workers' front can only arise on the common basis that already exists and already today unites those who are establishing it. The value of any such program will be tested if it will obligate its founders in practice as well as theory, and not serve only as a collection of slogans, generalized definitions and declarations without anything real behind them.

We are confident that between us and Ahdut Haavoda there does exist such real unity on a series of fundamental social, economic and political problems, making it possible to establish such an alliance or front at once.

We are not aiming at negotiations to renew party unity between us nor at a minimum program of unification. We are aiming only at summing up all those views we actually share. We intend to erase from the program we are suggesting everything that the members of Ahdut Haavoda do not agree that we are united on. We are prepared to add to this program any point which may have been forgotten or not stressed enough on our part. We are confident that the agreement that remains after all this will be sufficient to serve as a firm basis for the establishment of a joint front. . . .

3. The establishment of such an alliance will encourage those forces close to us within Mapai as well, and these are first and foremost the groups centered around the Min Hayesod group. This can be the beginning of a wide-ranging change in her internal composition. This could lead to far-reaching conclusions concerning the ways to unite the labor movement in Israel.

4. We are prepared to discuss any form of organizing the alliance between us which will be grounded on mutual and obligatory decision in all the agreed-upon fields and on full autonomy in all other fields.

(From "Foundations of a Joint Program for the Unification of the Pioneering Left," *Al-Hamishmar*, April 30, 1964.)

After having heard the report on the negotiations with Ahdut Haavoda, the Central Committee affirms that the basis has been created for an alignment of Mapai and Ahdut Haavoda–Poale Zion, that will include the following clauses:

A. The Alignment will be established between Mapai and Ahdut-Haavoda. Members who in the course of the establishment of the Alignment will move from one of the parties participating in the negotiations to the other will not be included in the joint list except by mutual agreement.

B. The government level: the two parties will appear in the elections to the Knesset with a single list according to a joint platform and will operate in the Knesset as a single faction according to an agreed-upon program. In those clauses in which the coalition agreement gives Ahdut Haavoda the right to abstain from voting in the Knesset, this right will be maintained in the new Alignment.

C. The municipal level: a united list and a united faction will be established in all the municipalities and local councils that will operate according to joint platforms as a joint faction.

D. The Histadrut level: The two parties will establish a single list for the elections to the Histadrut, the local workers' councils, the trade unions and the Working Women's Council on the basis of an inclusive and joint program. It will appear with a joint and obligatory platform. Within the framework of the Histadrut the two parties will maintain separate factions. The Central Committee instructs the negotiating committee to continue the negotiations with Ahdut Haavoda and to decide on all the matters concerning the Histadrut level in order to ensure the alignment being established on the basis of an inclusive and joint program. The joint platform will strive to win a majority within the working public in order to guarantee the Histadrut a majority able to make decisions and carry them out.

4. Changes in the electoral system: Since the parties are divided in their views on the system of elections to the Knesset that is desirable for Israel, they are free to express their views on this matter as they like.

From the establishment of the alignment and up to the termination of the Sixth Knesset both parties will not take any initiative to change the electoral system to the Knesset and will not join any other party in such initiative except if there is mutual agreement on this between the two parties. This rule will be effective for the period of the existence of the alignment.

The two parties will continue to conduct a joint clarification of this subject before the close of the term of the Sixth Knesset. If agreement is not reached as a result of this clarification, both parties will be permitted to suggest changes in the electoral system before the close of the term of the Sixth Knesset in order to allow both parties to consider their course.

> (Resolutions of the Central Committee of Mapai, on the Alignment, *Davar*, Nov. 16, 1964.)

1. The Council of Ahdut Haavoda decides to mobilize for the election campaign as an independent force—with its full path, values and banner—with the platform and list of Ahdut Haavoda–Poale Zion.

2. The Council instructs the party institutions to open negotiations with the Min Hayesod group in order to clarify the programmatic and public possibilities of appearing jointly in the elections to the Histadrut.

> (Minority Resolution on the "Alignment" at the Ahdut Haavoda–Poale Zion Council, *Lamerhav*, March 9, 1965.)

Note: The resolutions of the Council in favor of a "dual alignment" with Mapai were adopted by a majority of 202 votes against 59 who supported the minority resolution; 140 abstained.)

The majority in the Ahdut Haavoda–Poale Zion Council did not heed the dramatic, last-minute call of its venerated leader, Y. Tabenkin, and ratified the resolution of those supporting the establishment of a "dual alignment" with Mapai. There is no need to bring up once more every one of the arguments against the establishment of the 'Alignment.' That was done better by the spokesmen for the minority of the Ahdut Haavoda–Poale Zion Council, whose arguments were generally the same as Mapam's. We can only wonder that as an alternative to the "Alignment" the Ahdut Haavoda minority wanted to clarify the possibility of joining together with 'Min Hayesod', while ignoring Mapam, though it saw fit to stress that in its positions, especially on the questions of the labor movement, it was immeasurably closer to it than to Mapai. The partisans of the Alignment in Ahdut Haavoda–Poale Zion stressed the aim of unity in their approach. However, it is a fact that while striving for the Alignment, the conflicts within Mapai and even within Ahdut Haavoda–Poale Zion are increasing and these parties are not going towards the alignment with united ranks. In this situation, we cannot assume that the 'Alignment' will add any strength to the labor movement, but from the preparations for it the *right* drew the inspiration to forge an anti-workers front. Unfortunately, both the 'alignments' are the same in that not principles but *accounts* decide their course. Because of these accounts, the majority in Ahdut Haavoda lent its hand, de facto—to renewing the expulsion of Pinhas Lavon and his group . . .

(From "Ahdut Haavoda Has Crossed the Rubicon," an editorial, *Al-Hamishmar,* March 10, 1965.)

To those who are aiming honestly for the unification of all the Zionist workers' parties in the responsibility for the State and the Histadrut, we must say: There is another way to unite the workers' parties in responsibility for the people, the State and the working class, besides the path of giving up political independence and surrendering to the majority, now taken by the leadership of Ahdut Haavoda. We, too, are eager for unity and are not happy about division. But Mapai's path and all that has been taking place within it make it necessary to go towards unity on the basis of a programmatic agreement between equals; an agreement that will promise the maintenance of a pioneering workers' regime while striving for communal, social and national equality and the preservation of democratic freedoms, the maintenance of a regime that will keep us from sliding down the slope of liberal capitalism. This unity too must be reached by stages, but they do not lead to liquidation of the forces joining it, but to developing and strengthening them. It may be that this is a longer road but it promises the fulfillment of Zionism and socialism in our country. We stubbornly offer this choice to Ahdut Haavoda and the Min Hayesod group. Will it yet find a heeding ear?

(From "The Other Choice," Meir Yaari, *Al-Hamishmar,* Jan. 15, 1965.)

. . . We are meeting today, the representatives of the Eretz Israel Workers' Party (Mapai) and the Ahdut Haavoda–Poale Zion Party in order to establish the Alignment for the Unity of the Workers of Eretz Israel.

Striving for the complete unity of the Israeli workers movement, this Alliance is being established first and foremost between our parties and it is aimed at uniting all the workers' parties in a single camp for the fulfillment of an inclusive and agreed-upon program of action.

. . . The Alignment for the Unity of the Workers of Eretz Israel will encourage the Government of Israel to persevere in its efforts for Israel's sovereign independence and domestic freedom, to strengthen peace in the world, friendly relations with all peace-loving countries to avoid extending its hand to any aggressive aim or alliance against any country whatsoever, for mutual relations with the countries that have been liberated from colonial domination, in loyalty to the principles of the Charter of the United Nations.

The danger from the side of the forces hostile to the workers' movement has increased recently with the establishment of the extreme right bloc, bringing together the interests in enrichment and the exploitation of others, of the General Zionists and the aspirations for adventurism originating in Herut, in order to break the power of the workers' movement. The Rightist Bloc formed by Herut and the Liberals is striving to deprive the worker of his national and social achievements, to terminate the autonomy of the Histadrut, to move it from the pattern of its function, and to pave a broad road for the satisfaction of exploiting capitalist interests.

The increased unity of the workers of Israel will increase the daring and strength in repelling the forces of the right, whose aims threaten the vital needs of the masses of the people and the goals of national renaissance and construction.

The Alignment for the Unity of the Workers of Eretz Israel calls on every man and woman in Israel, on the youth, on all the partisans of creation, democracy and progress, the members of the parties, and the non-party people—to lend their hand in strengthening the State and reinforcing the position of the labor movement among the people, to support the Alignment for the Unity of the Workers of Eretz Israel so that it can take its place in the forefront of the nation and the State in achieving the goals of the morrow.

(From "The Statement of the Alignment," *Lamerhav*, May 20, 1965.)

22 • Split in Mapai

Although the Mapai Central Committee clearly supported Levi Eshkol's proposals, it was also clear that this decision was not the end of the chapter. First of all, by barring the way to the Min Hayesod group's integration in the Alignment, the ratification of the Galili-Eshkol agreement by the Ahdut Haavoda–Poale Zion Council was left in question. Second, when the resolution in favor of the Alignment was passed, David Ben-Gurion resigned from the Mapai Central Committee and announced that he would appeal the decision before the coming party convention. Third, Ben-Gurion asked the Secretariat of his party to demand that the government set up a "judicial committee" to investigate the "Affair" of 1954 as well as the legality and procedures of the Ministers' Committee ("Committee of Seven") that had investigated the Affair in 1960 and cleared Pinhas Lavon of responsibility. The demand was evidently aimed directly at Levi Eshkol, who had been one of the heads of the Committee of Seven that Ben-Gurion now wanted to investigate. Bloc members who had been compelled to abandon Ben-Gurion in voting for the Alignment now tended to support his demand for a committee of investigation, either because they agreed with the demand itself, because they accepted Ben-Gurion's leadership in general, or because they wanted to compensate him for their vote on the Alignment. At the same time, they understood that accepting the demand would be tantamount to deposing Levi Eshkol from the party leadership and the premiership, and they therefore formulated a compromise suggestion according to which the activities of the Committee of Seven would not be investigated, but only the 1954 Affair alone. Levi Eshkol, however, did not consider this distinction to be a compromise, since it was the Committee of Seven that had investigated the 1954 Affair, and even if only the Affair were reopened, it would be equal to a vote of nonconfidence not only against the Committee, the government and the Knesset, but also against himself personally. At this stage he decided to present the President with his government's resignation (Dec. 24, 1964) in order to make the members of the bloc, the Moshav Movement and the Ihud Hakvutzot Vehakibbutzim make a clear decision between himself and Ben-Gurion. In this, indeed, he succeeded: despite all their admiration for Ben-Gurion, the members of the bloc were not ready to risk the shocks and dangers connected with Eshkol's departure, in view of the approaching elections and of the dangers of the "younger men" increasing in strength in the party leadership and the government. The Mapai Central Committee, on December 17, 1964, decided unanimously to ask Levi Eshkol to form a permanent government to be headed by him. A decisive majority (124 to 61) also ratified the Secretariat's suggestion "to leave the matter of establishing an investigating committee to the sole decision of the members of Mapai in the Government." As a result of these decisions, the old coalition government was re-established on December 22, 1964, with the same composition as formerly.[1]

> The Secretariat recommends to the Central Committee and the Knesset faction to decide to give our comrade, Levi Eshkol, the task of forming the permanent government which he will head.
> (Resolution adopted unanimously by Mapai Central Committee, Dec. 16, 1964.)
>
> The question of setting up the investigating committee is left to the sole discretion of our comrades in the Government.
> (Resolution of the Secretariat, adopted by Mapai Central Committee, 124 to 61.)
>
> The Central Committee recommends that our comrades in the Government accept the demand for the investigation of the 1954 Affair.
> (Resolution proposed by Central Committee member M. Surkis; won only 61 votes against 124 who voted for the above resolution of the Secretariat.)

There is no doubt that, in this, Levi Eshkol won a second victory over David Ben-Gurion and the "younger men" (in addition to the Central Committee's vote in favor of the Alignment.) The intra-party struggle, however, continued even more vigorously toward the party convention set for February 16. Though the subject of the various battles was different and specific, there was still very clearly a close link between reopening the Affair and the vengeful and uncompromising attitude toward the Min Hayesod group on the one hand, and opposition to the Alignment on the other. In view of Ahdut Haavoda–Poale Zion's formal undertaking to end the depositions within the Alignment, it was clear that the boycott against Min Hayesod was an attempt to explode the Alignment even before its establishment. The common denominator for all these battles was Ben-Gurion's and the "younger men's" nonacceptance of Eshkol's leadership when the latter no longer was content with the role of caretaker but began to shape his (Mapai) policies according to his own views, adapting his style of talk and action to the changing new circumstances.

Ben-Gurion and his followers were particularly afraid of the changing balance of forces between the rival Mapai factions by establishing the

---

1. At the meeting of the new government on December 27, 1964, Dov Joseph's suggestion to set up a new committee to investigate the 1954 Affair was voted down by all the Ministers representing all the parties, with the exception of Minister Yosef Almogi.

Alignment, and of Eshkol's personnel policies barring the way for the "heirs apparent" to the leadership that Ben-Gurion had destined them for. *The Mapai that was consolidating and taking form under Eshkol's leadership, in growing cooperation with Ahdut Haavoda–Poale Zion, looking toward full unity with them and in the course of this weakening the power and influence of the "younger men," was a completely different Mapai.* It was not, indeed, so different as to satisfy the consistent pioneering left that remained loyal to its principles and historic mission, but it already no longer matched the tastes and desires of Ben-Gurion and his "younger men." In preparation for the convention, both rival camps made supreme efforts to win the support of the delegates who had been elected before the deterioration in inner-party relations. At the convention, which took place on February 16–19, 1965, there were dramatic clashes between Moshe Sharett, Levi Eshkol and Golda Meir on the one side and David Ben-Gurion on the other. Despite its bitterness, the debate took on a personal character and was an open battle over leadership and control rather than an ideological and political dispute. Still, it was Moshe Sharett who made a great speech in which he drew a clear line of demarcation between honor and respect for Ben-Gurion's personality and achievements for the State and his party, and the "leader's cult" whose damage and danger Sharett unfolded to the convention's delegates.

In the end, Eshkol's supporters were triumphant, but still Ben-Gurion succeeded in winning 40 percent of the votes on the issues of the Alignment and of reopening the "Affair." This 40 percent included the "younger men," the Haifa bloc, part of the Tel Aviv bloc, and a considerable number of delegates from the development towns.

Once the convention had made its decisions, Levi Eshkol was rid, at least for the time being, of the need to continue to deal with the Affair and now the way was also clear to complete the negotiations with Ahdut Haavoda–Poale Zion for the establishment of the "Alignment for the Unity of the Workers of Israel" which was finally signed in Haifa on May 19, 1965, though the ceremony was boycotted by the opponents of the Alignment in Mapai and Ahdut Haavoda–Poale Zion alike. The minority did not accept the convention's decision and continued to work to undermine Levi Eshkol's leadership. The step they took now was to demand that Ben-Gurion be put at the head of the candidates for the Knesset. When this demand was not met, Ben-Gurion began a frontal attack against Levi Eshkol, stressing how he had been disappointed with Eshkol and had come to the conclusion that the latter was not fit to be Prime Minister. Eshkol's counter move was his demand of members of the government who agreed with Ben-Gurion on this to draw the conclusions and resign. And indeed, this situation left Shimon Peres and Yosef Almogi with no choice but to tender their resignations from the government (May 21, 1965).

Among the landmarks in the factional organization of the minority we might list the mass meeting in Avihail on May 26, 1965, a meeting that was called by Ben-Gurion, the architect of the Kfar Vitkin[2] statutes that had banned all factional organizations. Most of the speakers rejected the demands for a split that were made during this meeting and concentrated on the demand for the convening of an extraordinary convention that would discuss and decide on who was to head the list of party candidates for the Knesset and be the head of the Government after the elections. The Mapai Secretariat, however, rejected this demand, relying on the party constitution's ruling that the matter was within the jurisdiction of the joint decision of the party's Central Committee and its caucus in the Knesset. The majority came to the meeting of the Central Committee and the caucus with a compromise suggestion whereby David Ben-Gurion would head the list of candidates, while the premiership after the elections would be given to Levi Eshkol. In two stormy sessions of the Central Committee and the Knesset caucus, the minority rejected this suggestion and insisted on its demand for convening the convention and, in any event, that David Ben-Gurion be chosen as both head of the list and Premier-to-be.

The suggestion for a convention was voted down in a secret ballot by 167 to 155; after that Levi Eshkol was voted (again by secret ballot) Mapai's candidate for the head of the government after the elections to the Sixth Knesset. His candidacy received 179 votes (63.5 percent) while Ben-Gurion received 103 (36.5 percent). Before the voting, a letter from Ben-Gurion was read, in which he said that he would not allow himself to be put at the head of the list ahead of the candidate for the premiership.

Once the decision had been taken in the Mapai Central Committee, the question arose within the ranks of the minority of how they were to continue their struggle—as an opposition within the party and the institutions, or as an independent organization outside Mapai. This debate, concluded over tactical considerations and different estimates of the balance of forces, trends of development and prospects for success, was not a little due to the varied composition of the minority itself. Side by side with the "younger men" and their associates, there were also many others, such as the Haifa bloc, certain circles within the moshav movement and in the Ihud Hakvutzot vehakibbutzim, and others. The Ihud supported Ben-Gurion, in addition to reasons of personal sentiment, primarily because they believed that his leadership and place at the leadership of the party were important and even necessary for Mapai's prospects of success in the coming election trials. That is why they were prepared to support Ben-Gurion's demands (sometimes even against their own convictions, without deciding on the merits of the issue in itself). Their main

---

2. Avihail is situated in close proximity to Kfar Vitkin.

point of departure in supporting Ben-Gurion and becoming involved in the minority within the party was, therefore, the desire to strengthen Mapai and improve its prospects of success. It is not surprising, therefore, that most of them were ready to agree to Ben-Gurion's demands to reinvestigate the "Affair," while more than a few differed with him on his uncompromising opposition to the Alignment. The same fears of Mapai's entering the campaign without Ben-Gurion at its head, or of his possible departure from the party if his demands were not met, also made them ready at last to swallow the few concessions that Eshkol had made to Ahdut Haavoda–Poale Zion in order to establish the dual Alignment— all in order to protect the party's ruling position in the Histadrut, the municipalities and the State government. The idea of secession from Mapai and setting up a competing minority list was, therefore, in contradiction to the point of departure and aims of some of the leaders of the minority.

In any event, the internal debate within the leadership of the minority during the second half of June was ultimately decided in favor of appearing separately in the elections. Only part of the minority accepted this decision and even Moshe Dayan[3] maintained some reservations concerning it for various (apparently tactical) reasons. Seven members of Knesset, headed by Ben-Gurion, Peres and Almogi, formed a separate caucus calling themselves the "Workers of Israel List" (Rafi), on July 12, 1965.[4] Their claim that establishing an independent list for the elections did not mean their leaving Mapai was, of course, unacceptable to the party institutions who were ultimately compelled to decide, after difficult considerations and tactical measures that lasted throughout July and half of August, that anyone appearing in a separate list or giving it his support thereby removed himself from the party.

The most charactersitic feature of the bitter polemics between Mapai and the dissidents was the absence of any ideological-political basis, and they were conducted almost purely around the argument of "breaking unity and internal democratic decisions," and "preferring justice and truth to the sanctification of frameworks and procedures." The absence of any ideological differences was stressed particularly by the Mapai spokesmen, both because the split really hadn't taken place on account of such differences or even on account of differences of style and stress, as had existed in the united Mapai, and besides, because of two tactical considerations. One was the central propagandistic aim of Mapai to isolate the dissidents from the masses of party members and supporters

3. It was only at the last moment before publication of the list of candidates for the Sixth Knesset that he agreed to be included in the Rafi List.
4. After a great deal of discussion, the members of Rafi decided to appear independently also in the elections to the Histadrut and the municipalities. On July 30 they began to publish a weekly, *Mabat Hadash* (A New View).

and voters by convincing them that the secession was unjustified and illogical; the second consideration was the vital need to unite the party and to hold on ever tighter to those who in the past had been doubtful and wavered between majority and minority, and especially those many members of the minority who had at least temporarily chosen not to join their dissident comrades.

This split and the secession of part of the liquidationist right wing did not result in making Mapai more pioneering, worker-oriented or socialist. On the other hand, now there was on the political scene an independent, new, active and demagogic group, which was devoted to "pure etatism" and was a sworn enemy of the parliamentary democracy in practice. It is not surprising that as a result of the schism, Mapai tended toward greater internal unity or, more precisely, the process of formation of opposition forces struggling for pioneering and socialist renewal within Mapai was held up or put back, at least temporarily, especially among those groups that might have been influenced by Min Hayesod. Their bitterness and former criticism were now overshadowed by their support for Eshkol in his fateful conflict with Ben-Gurion.

This trend also had its effects within Mapam. There were some members who argued that a Rafi election victory would compel Mapai to yield to the dictates of the dissidents; such a victory would also constitute a serious threat to the democratic regime within the State of Israel. They, therefore, concluded that Mapam had to suggest going along with the Alignment in the elections or at least in a mutual nonaggression pact. There were others, however, who believed (and their view ultimately prevailed) that only by appearing independently and consistently could Mapam serve as a countervailing force to the pressures on Mapai from Rafi outside and the Rafi sympathizers within. If there were a danger to democracy, Eshkol could rely on the full support of an independent Mapam.

> ... Perhaps all that Mapam is doing, is to read what the Alignment does first. One way or another, it would be worthwhile changing the order of priorities. The best thing would be if we could turn all our force against the rightist bloc and the Ben-Gurion group. It will be hard to do this as long as the quarrels with the Alignment parties are going on in full force. It might be useful if Mapam were to initiate discussions with the heads of the Alignment with the aim of cutting down, limiting and maybe even stopping—during the election campaign—the inter-party struggle. Perhaps it is possible to reach an agreement which would make possible debate on the theoretical level in the journals, seminars and study circles, while hostile publications would be banned in the daily papers and the platforms of election meetings. In any case, it is worthwhile investing the effort that will make it possible for Mapam and the

Alignment parties alike to direct their full forces against the rightist bloc and Ben-Gurion's group.
   (From "Responsibility Before All," by A. Reiner, *Hotam*, No. 10, July 7, 1965.)

In order to protect democracy and workers' hegemony we declare that when the hour of trial comes we shall be prepared to help a government that is built around workers' parties. That hour of trial will only come after the elections and if we come out of them strong enough for the government to need our cooperation. Those who are too much in a hurry now, four months before the elections, to give up our own independence and unity in order to come to Eshkol's help, not only will be abandoning our own independent mission but will also be unable, in the hour of trial to provide any help for anyone worthy needing it.
   (From an article by Meir Ya'ari, "A Happy Page in a Sad Chapter," *Al-Hamishmar*, Sept. 7, 1967.)

23 • The Elections of 1965

The 1965 election campaign to the 10th Convention of the Histadrut on September 19 and to the 6th Knesset and the municipalities on November 21 was conducted under the sign of the split in Mapai. The party constellation in the Histadrut elections was different from that of the elections to the 8th and 9th Conventions when the campaign had been waged mainly between Mapai, Mapam, and Ahdut Haavoda–Poale Zion. The electors now had to choose not only between the Alignment (Mapai, Ahdut Haavoda and The Religious Worker) and Mapam, but also the Rafi dissidents from Mapai, and Gahal (the Herut-Liberal party bloc).[1]

After its great pretensions, the election results brought Rafi great disappointment (80,000 or 12 percent of the votes) and forecast the limits of its hopes for the Knesset elections. By the use of social demagogy, Gahal was able to exploit the bitterness and discrimination prevailing in a wide section of the working public as a result of Mapai's economic and trade union policies; its first appearance in a Histadrut contest brought it a surprising almost 100,000 votes, or some 15 percent. This number, of course, included an estimated 5–7 percent of the Histadrut membership who had been Herut supporters even before but had given their votes to other parties in the Histadrut elections. However, even the additional 8–10 percent was still enough to worry all those who were concerned for the Histadrut's socialist-Zionism.

Mapam won a small gain of about .5 percent and obtained 19.5 percent with about 95,000 votes. This rise gave hopes for an additional seat in the coming Knesset. The Alignment fell sharply from 72.45 to 50.89 percent[2] and only with difficulty maintained its absolute majority. This

---

1. The second half of 1962 saw a vigorous debate within the Herut movement over the question whether to confine its activities within the working class, as in the past, to its own National Workers Organization, or also to organize its members and supporters within the Histadrut as a separate faction. The Herut convention at the end of January 1963 decided in favor of forming the Blue-White faction within the Histadrut. This would campaign to de-politicize the Histadrut, to have it give up the red flag and abandon its socialist vision. At the same time, following the split in the Liberal Party, in March 1965 the Liberal Labor movement within the Histadrut also split into the Liberal faction and the Independent Liberal faction attached to the Liberal and Independent Liberal parties, respectively. As the elections for the 10th Convention drew nearer the Histadrut institutions refused to authorize the participation of the Blue-White faction in these elections, since its platform was opposed to the principles of the Histadrut; this dispute even reached the courts. However, when the Blue-White faction combined with the previously authorized Liberal faction, the united faction no longer needed any special Histadrut authorization and there was no longer any legal possibility of preventing its participation in the elections.
2. Some attempted to comfort themselves in that, by adding Rafi's percentage, the picture

was a decisive defeat but this fact urged it on to supreme efforts, by all the methods of propaganda, money and pressure at its disposal, in the Knesset campaign. These efforts also apparently coincided with some second thoughts among the electorate; Gahal's surprising achievement in the Histadrut elections and the dangers to Israeli democracy that might ensue from some possible cooperation between Gahal, Rafi and the religious parties led many who had not voted for the Alignment in the Histadrut elections to decide that Eshkol had to be supported as the lesser evil. Many middle-class voters also were deterred by the prospects of a deadlock and the resultant parliamentary confusion, and preferred the stability supposedly offered by the Alignment to the shocks attendant upon a rightist victory.

The Alignment thus emerged from the Knesset elections with gains that were indeed only relative (45 seats or 36.74 percent[3] compared with 50 seats—41.31 percent in the Fifth Knesset) but which in the given circumstances were impressive and unexpected. Rafi had to remain satisfied with ten deputies; the Independent Liberals lost two; Gahal, one; the National Religious Party, one; the Communists, one; and Mapam, one (from nine to eight.)[4] Meanwhile, the onslaught of the right had been repulsed and Israeli democracy was saved.

We should not ignore the real dangers that threatened Israeli democracy and the free and secular character of its society. It would have been enough for three seats to be transferred from the secular left to the religious right, for labor no longer to be able to establish a government without the religious parties; that is, without accepting their conditions for participation. The secular labor camp would then have faced the choice of agreeing to

became brighter, but such a combination had no real significance and was questionable even "purely" statistically. The fact remained that Mapai alone no longer had an absolute majority in the Histadrut and was now only a third.
3. According to previous agreement, these were divided into 36 for Mapai and nine for Ahdut Haavoda–Poale Zion.
4. Between the elections to the Histadrut and the Knesset, Mapam lost about 15,000 votes (actually more, since in the Knesset elections it also received some thousands of votes from Arabs who were not members of the Histadrut.) Some of these lost voters were persons who agreed with Mapam's economic and trade union policies without accepting its policies on Jewish-Arab relations, neutralism, and its confirmed secularism. Many of these were won over to the appeal to "support Eshkol against Begin and Ben-Gurion." This explanation is reinforced by the results of the municipal elections in which Mapam won 13,000 more votes than in the Knesset.

Mapam lost other votes to the Haolam Hazeh–New Force list, some of whose slogans were similar to its own: peace initiatives, the abolition of the military administration, against religious coercion and certain anti-democratic laws—though these slogans were not part of an inclusive pioneering Zionist and socialist program, as in Mapam. On the contrary, they were combined with such almost fascist ideas as: condemnation of the "rotten party regime," "the war of the generations" (young against old), and derision of "Diaspora fund-raising Zionism." The fact remains that Olam Hazeh–New Force slogans appealed to thousands of voters, most of them young, Jews as well as Arabs, and helped it win a seat in the Knesset.

increase the degree of religious compulsion or of allowing parliamentary chaos and a political victory for Rafi and all the others who were working to change the electoral system.

The young Israeli democracy also continued to face the danger of a turn rightward. Rafi had not yet decided on the direction it was going to take and was still standing at the crossroads between the possibility of returning to Mapai or of going further to the right and coming to an agreement with Herut. Menahem Begin's (temporary) departure from the Herut leadership might have made such a step easier. In such an event, the danger of a rightward turn would have taken on frightening proportions. True, even then the right would have come short by six to ten seats of its hope for power by parliamentary means. There was, indeed, room for concern over the ceaseless earthquake shaking the political life in Israel, and which has been a source of constant danger. Meanwhile, the elections came to an end and the older, continuing problems returned, such as the composition of the government coalition and the development and mutual relations between the labor parties.

In the coalition negotiations begun after the elections, Mapam, in keeping with its declared position, worked hard to reach a positive conclusion, as it had in the past. This time, however, there were additional motives and even favorable circumstances. At the beginning of the election campaign, Mapam had declared that while maintaining its full autonomy, it would be ready to lend its support to the defense of democracy. The elections had, indeed, held up the right's bid for power, but in view of the dangers which still threatened Israeli democracy, the establishment of a progressive government with a stable majority and built around the socialist-Zionist parties seemed more imperative than ever, on condition, of course, that a minimum coalition program could be achieved as a basis for such a government.

On the other hand, Rafi's secession, Mapai's decline, and greater dependence on allies (especially in the Histadrut, but on other levels as well) made Mapai itself more amenable in negotiations. Thus, in contrast to the past, it conducted them with clearly positive aims. To this, we could add that the stated opposition of the Independent Liberals to any further religious legislation aided Mapam more than a little in frustrating the traditional aims of the National Religious Party to widen the scope of religious legislation with every new government. This resistance helped restrain Mapai's tendencies to make further concessions in this field, and the religious status quo was strictly kept.

After extended negotiations the fundamental policy of the five-party coalition (Alignment, National Religious Party, Independent Liberals, Mapam, and Poale Agudat Israel) was decided upon and Levi Eshkol was able to present his new government to the Knesset. Mapam received the Ministries of Health and Housing (Y. Barzilai and M. Bentov, respectively); Ahdut Haavoda–Poale Zion received the Ministries of Labor and Transportation (as formerly, Y. Allon and M. Carmel) in addition to a Minister without Portfolio—Y. Galili (later Galili became Minister of Information).

> The Council has heard the report by the delegation to the coalition negotiations and determines that the negotiations brought some achievements, though the party's demands have not been completely satisfied.
> The Council resolves, after studying the situation in the State and the Labor movement, to authorize the delegation to bring the negotiations to a positive conclusion, on condition that the Party be guaranteed its fitting status in the government's activity and in the distribution of functions within it.
> The Council agrees that a letter will be sent to the Prime Minister reiterating Mapam's demands concerning the freedom of trade union struggle and the abolition of the linked mortgages.
> The Council affirms that the contents of the address by the Minister of Finance, P. Sapir, at the Histadrut Convention, were not in keeping with the fundamental program and working program of the new government as these were agreed upon in the coalition negotiations.
> (Resolutions of Mapam Council, adopted by a vote of 168 to 50, *Al-Hamishmar* Sept. 1, 1966.)

Rafi did not join the coalition, in keeping with its unwillingness to accept the premiership of Levi Eshkol. (As we recall, this opposition to Eshkol as premier was one of the reasons for the minority's secession from Mapai.) The election results left the party in a blind alley. If it had succeeded as it had hoped, it could have swayed the balance between a right-center and left-center grouping. In such an event, it could have had the choice of being an active force in forming a right-wing parliamentary majority or of dictating terms to Mapai for reunion. By using the threat of joining the right wing and with the help of Ben-Gurion's many admirers within Mapai, it might have succeeded in dismissing the Knesset and even in changing the electoral system.

On the other hand, if its defeat in the elections had been an even greater one, it would have been compelled to come back to Mapai unconditionally. However, since it neither won an impressive victory nor suffered a crushing defeat, it did not take any far-reaching decisions, hoping that there would be further divisions within Mapai or the Alignment, and that Mapai might have to bring Ben-Gurion or his close aides to power because of some political or military emergency. Perhaps, if Rafi's hopes of gaining an impressive number of votes from the middle class had been fulfilled, this might have accelerated its evolution from an extreme right wing of the labor movement to a bourgeois "non-class" party with some anti-democratic features and dangerous technocratic and etatist trends. These expectations, too, were not fulfilled, and its 80,000 Histadrut votes also formed most of its votes for the Knesset. In addition, the failure of the campaign to win over the middle class increased the influence of the party's supporters and cadres in the labor settlements (especially within the Ihud Hakvutzot Vehakibbutzim) and this helped brake the party's transition from the labor movement to the bourgeois center and right. This necessarily led to some conclusions concerning the attitude to Rafi by other workers' parties. There was no point or logic in pushing Rafi into the arms of the bourgeois camp. Mapam, for instance, despite its vigorous opposition to Rafi, attempted to avoid any feelings of vengefulness and supported Rafi's full participation in all local or national Histadrut institutions, in any workers' coalition in the local municipalities, and the like.

Mapai, in turn, faced two central problems. The first was that of drawing all the political and ideological conclusions from Rafi's departure by holding on more firmly to its working class basis and its socialist-Zionist and pioneering sources. Even if the bourgeois right's bid for power had been repulsed this time, the psychological circumstances that deterred a large part of the middle class from handing over power to the right should not be considered to be basic and perpetual phenomena. On the contrary, in view of the growing "normal" capitalist trends in Israeli economy and society, Mapai had reason to be concerned over its own status and future in a system of which by its very nature it could not be the most consistent representative, both because of its own economic and class base and because of its social value superstructure. In the long run, the new bases and ideological superstructures coalescing in Israel would inevitably also find their natural representatives in a bourgeois government of one kind or another. Mapai could not try to keep the bourgeois right from power only by administrative means, tactics and propaganda tricks.

This problem became more critical in view of the troubles of the Israeli economy. These troubles were an inevitable result of Mapai's irresponsible economic policies. The crisis they forecast was not inevitable. The Israeli economy could have been saved only by extensive long-range planning, by deepening and expanding the progressive socialist elements, by reinforcing the government-public and the independent workers' sectors in the economy, and by a just distribution of the burden of curing the economy among the population as a whole. Mapai, which was most responsible for the trends of Israel's economic development, was likely to be attracted to the idea that we could escape the crisis by deepening the capitalist trends and imposing most of the burden on the workers and the most depressed classes.

Mapai's second test (inseparably connected with the first) concerned the relationships with the other socialist-Zionist trends, that is, whether it would succeed in freeing itself from the tradition of intolerance toward other groups, as cultivated by Ben-Gurion and his disciples, and whether it could, instead, adopt A. D. Gordon's precepts of "allowing others too to live—as they like and in their own way." Only if Mapai showed itself capable of accepting a situation of ideological pluralism within its own ranks, within the Alignment with Ahdut Haavoda–Poale Zion and in its attitude toward Min Hayesod and the labor movement as a whole, was there any prospect of expanding and deepening the united front in the labor movement. Meanwhile, the dramatic events surrounding the secession of Ben-Gurion's minority and Mapai's consolidation around Levi Eshkol in defense of the party's very existence overshadowed and temporarily put a halt to the internal conflicts.

Ahdut Haavoda–Poale Zion could have played an important role in promoting the desirable changes with Mapai as its partner in the alignment. It could have done this by withstanding the liquidationist trends within its own ranks and standing firmly for its own path and aims even within the Alignment. Unfortunately, events showed that Ahdut Haavoda–Poale Zion did not pass this test, and by merging with Mapai disappointed the hopes that been put in it.

Mapam's key problem was to overcome the gap between its influence on the trade union and Histadrut level and its narrower influence in the general political field. This problem was not only limited to the loss of thousands of votes between the elections to the Histadrut and the Knesset, though this spotlighted the problem. As a matter of fact, even Mapam's gains in the Histadrut elections (an increase by one-half percent) were not in proportion to its activity in the Histadrut and trade unions, the leading role it played in the struggles for wage increments and fringe benefits and the wide popularity it enjoyed in working class circles. Facts had shown that Gahal, in the Histadrut, had won not only the support of its regular members and supporters and also thousands of votes more from the traditional supporters of the Alignment and the independent liberals, but even opposition voters whose views on the questions of trade union struggle and the role of the Histadrut were close to those of Mapam and who had even sympathized with it between elections. Still, when the hour of decision came, these were unable to withstand the onslaught of social demagogy and chauvinist and religious incitement of Mapam's rivals, mainly Gahal.

These facts showed that Mapam had succeeded in winning the support of masses of workers in the Israeli union and economic struggles, but still had to find effective ways of winning the masses over to its fundamental ideas and its political program on the role of pioneering, Jewish-Arab relationship, neutralism and a secular society. These ideas were absorbed with even greater difficulty within the "Second Israel"—that part of the working public that was growing in numbers, though the trust a militant socialist party earns by its loyal day-to-day struggle must eventually win it the support of at least part of that public under its trade union influence—for the political struggles as well.

There is no denying the fact that the proportion of Mapam's voters in the cities and towns, in comparison with its Kibbutz Artzi members, has been constantly increasing from one election to the next. Many of these voters had been attracted by the vision and enterprise of the Kibbutz Artzi, but there was also a growing number that saw Mapam as a party that had proved its loyalty to the class struggle of the hired laborers, to the security and welfare of the State and to its Zionist and socialist vision.

But, as we have said, this was only a part of this public, and in addition, even its support was not based on ideological identification but on personal ties and trusts. For that reason it proved not to be stable but subject to changes in complicated political situations. The solution for this problem was to be found in the large long-range investments of manpower and means, in cultivating cadres, particularly among the Oriental communities themselves, so that they could carry on activities within these communities.

As for the problems involved in Mapam's joining the government, we will mention only one here: how to guarantee that participation in government and the attendant collective responsibility would not curtail the party's liberty to expound its views freely and publicly even when they were different or even in opposition to those of the government as decided by the majority of its ministers. In any case, experiences did show that Mapam *had* been able to maintain its freedom of expression intact even when participating in the government.

As a pioneering workers' party, Mapam's natural place was in participating in deciding the fate of the State and the working class. Mapam was not tied to its seats in the government, and when it had not been able to bear responsibility for the dominant policies, it had gone over to the opposition.

> However, I do not want to hide our own special contribution. If this government declares in its fundamental policies that it will strive for a more just distribution of the national incomes by increasing the share of the deprived sectors: if the Prime Minister declares that within a year the apparatus of the Military Administration will be abolished; if the government proclaims a daring campaign to liquidate the slums; if the government intends to respect the right of the organized workers' freedom to engage in trade union struggle and if it undertakes to secure the real value of wages and wage increments in keeping with prices and the higher cost of living; if it promises to guard the freedom of conscience and the status quo in matters of religion so as to preserve the rights of both the secular and religious publics in our State, in mutual

respect, then it is clear to all that the party which I have the honor to represent here had a share in shaping the appearance of this government.

(From the speech by Meir Yaari in the Knesset on presentation of new government by Levi Eshkol, *Al-Hamishmar*, Jan. 13, 1966.)

24 • The June 1967 War and Afterwards

The War of June 1967 in itself is not part of the subject matter of this book. This discussion examines how the war was reflected in and affected by ideological and political developments within the Israeli labor movement and its various parties and trends, as well as the war's effects on the situation and struggles of the Israeli workers.

During May 1967 it became increasingly clear that war between Israel and the Arab states was inevitable. While the government still insisted on exhausting all the hopes that the Great Powers would prevent the war by opening the Tiran Straits and influencing the Egyptians to pull back their forces massed on the Israeli border, the reactionary bourgeois right found the time propitious to undermine, and even to attempt to bring down, Eshkol's government. They demanded that the government be replaced by a "Cabinet of National Unity" and that Eshkol resign from premiership or at least give up the Ministry of Defense, backing up their demands with hysterical cries that the government was weak and hesitant, that the Army was not ready for its fateful role, and that the country had no leader and Minister of Defense worthy of the name. There were growing demands that Ben-Gurion and Moshe Dayan be brought back into the premiership and Ministry of Defense and that Gahal be co-opted into the government.

Within the government coalition itself the National Religious Party ministers played an active role in trying to impose these demands, even threatening to resign and create a governmental crisis in the midst of the national emergency. Under their pressure, a first compromise was offered—making Labor Minister Yigal Allon Minister of Defense and offering Moshe Dayan a key role in the Army command. This was, however, opposed not only by Gahal and Rafi, but also by part of Mapai, which preferred Dayan over Allon, not only for personal reasons but because of the different views the two men represented.

Finally, a few days before the outbreak of the war, the coalition was expanded into a "Government of National Unity" with Moshe Dayan receiving the Defense portfolio and Menahem Begin and Yosef Sapir (the heads, respectively, of the Herut and Liberal Party sections of the Gahal bloc) joining the cabinet as Ministers without Portfolio. Thus, when war broke out, culminating in Tsahal's (Israeli Defense Forces) speedy and unprecedented victory, Moshe Dayan was able to enjoy the full benefit of the praise and publicity for an achievement that had actually been carefully and diligently prepared under Levi Eshkol's leadership by the Chief of Staff, Yitshak Rabin.

The Israeli Jewish community had not had the slightest doubt that in May and June it was standing on the verge of annihilation and that the war was a war of defense *par excellence*. In Israeli eyes the war was more like the War of Liberation of 1948 than the controversial Sinai War of 1956. In contrast to the latter, the June conflict was not a preventive war intended to stem a worsening balance of forces in view of a future danger, but a reply to *an immediate and present danger*—the threatened onslaught by the neighboring states.

At the conclusion of the War there was also general agreement that there could be no returning to the status quo ante of no peace, non-recognition, economic boycott and blockade of Israeli shipping, as well as to the situation of borders that were almost indefensible because of their topography, length, and proximity to Arab bases. There was also agreement that Jerusalem would not again be a divided city cut up by political boundaries and military strongholds in which there was no free access to the historic and religious sites. All this meant that hardly anyone conceived of Israel's willingly taking the suicidal step of evacuating the areas occupied in the course of the defensive war without a full and official peace treaty, including secure and recognized borders, as well as freedom of shipping in the Suez Canal and the Tiran Straits. On the other hand, most members of the government, as well as responsible political circles encompassing a wide range of parties, understood that although the refugee problem had been caused by the Arab invasion of 1948 and the Arab threats of war in 1967, it still was a humanitarian problem of prime importance as well as a hurdle to peace; it was therefore generally agreed that a solution to the refugee problem would have to be included in any peace treaty.

These assumptions were shared by most of Israeli public opinion, the government, and almost all of the parties, including the Israel Communist Party, Maki. Among the dissident groups were the mostly Arab Communists in the neo-Stalinist Communist Party, Rakah, who parroted the Soviet and Arab charges that Israel was the aggressor in June 1967 in the service of American imperialism, and that it has to return to the status quo ante, without any direct negotiations or a peace treaty, and that Israel had to return to its former borders and even redivide Jerusalem and give Jordan back "its part." Similar views were expressed by a small group of Jews organized in Matspen (Compass).[1] For the latter, however,

1. Matspen (official name: Israeli Socialist Organization) was expelled in 1962 from the (then still united) Israeli Communist Party. Its main slogan is "De-Zionization of the State of Israel" (i.e., cutting off its ties with world Jewry) as a precondition for Arab-

these views were not inspired by Moscow nor intended to serve Russian interests, but were rather "independent" results of some Jewish masochistic guilt complex and an anti-colonialist romanticization of the Arab Third World side to the dispute.

However, despite the high degree of assent on those questions (with only Rakah's and Matspen's dissent), from this point onward, views began to differ sharply. On the one hand, part of the Israeli public, including the afternoon press, the bourgeois right-wing parties, large sections of the National Religious Party and even a section of the Labor Party, were infected by chauvinistic and expansionist ideas (for which, perhaps, the same kind of "psychological explanation" could be found as for the Arabs' refusal to negotiate with Israel). These views add up to the argument that the present cease-fire lines were the best security borders possible and that no peace negotiations, peace treaty, or the like, could be trusted even if the Arabs agreed to them. For these as well as for historical, religious, or other reasons the liberated areas were not to be returned, now or in the future. Some of the partisans of the latter view have established the "Land of Israel Movement," nicknamed the "Greater Israel Movement," or "Movement for an Undivided Israel." True, all these people and circles—in the "Movement" and out of it—were only a minority in the Israeli public and government, but they were an extremely vociferous minority, winning a great deal of press attention, both in Israel and abroad. Since the anti-annexationists often preferred to be rather silent to keep peace in the coalition or within their own parties, or for reasons of foreign policy and diplomatic considerations, the erroneous impression has often been gained that the expansionist chauvinists (in the common political slang, the "hawks") form a majority within Israel.

In fact, the majority in the government and in the Israeli public preferred peace and secure, mutually recognized borders to territorial conquest; they did not desire to annex populated areas or to compel another people to become part of Israel, which would thus cease being a Jewish state and become unable to perform its function of inspiring world Jewry and in solving its national problem. They also were interested in bringing to an early end the continuation of Israeli military control over the occupied territories, aware that even the most "enlightened occupation" must lead to demoralization.[2] Though only very few conceived of evacu-

---

Israeli peaceful coexistence, blaming Zionism and Israel alone for the conflict and war. The slogan "De-Zionization" was shared by Uri Avneri's Ha'olam Haze List (founded 1965 as a non-Zionist and non-socialist "anti-establishment" group).

2. Knesset Member Yitshak Ben-Aharon, at that time Secretary-General of the Histadrut and one of the outstanding leaders of the Israel Labor Party, hit the nail on the head with his statement that "Labor Zionism never assumed the possibility that the Jewish people in its state would rule other peoples. In this discussion no one had said that we can be the Arab population's elected government. The greatest optimist in our midst believes that we can be an enlightened, moderate government and that there can be Israeli

ating the administered territories without negotiations or a signed peace treaty, the majority was prepared to give back most of the territory as part of negotiations and a peace treaty that would include some vital border rectifications for reasons of security.

Just like the annexationists, however, the anti-annexationists were divided into differing approaches, emphases and tactical courses. Some argued that as long as there is no sign of readiness on the Arab side to come to an agreement on secure and recognized borders, it would be a mistake on our part to declare our readiness to give up territories, or at least to specify what border rectifications would be the minimum to which we could agree, since then the Great Powers would rush in to exert their pressure on Israel to accept some compromise between this minimum and the extreme Arab positions. Also, they argued, such an official declaration on the part of the government would lead to deep divisions within the public and to a split within the coalition government,[3] probably even within the Labor Party itself—without being able to recompense this psychological shock by showing some real achievement concerning peace.

To this, the spokesmen for Mapam and part of the Labor Party replied that even if these considerations were not unfounded, it was still desirable to say something positive and precise in order to overcome the doubts entertained by the Arabs and world opinion that the State of Israel was at all ready to give back most of the territories in return for a peace treaty. It is Israel's task, they argued, to destroy this erroneous impression and to convince the Arabs and Israel's friends throughout the world that there *is* room for negotiations and that the Arabs have *real prospects* of receiving back most of their territories in the event of negotiations and a peace treaty.

After the War of June 1967 people were sometimes impressed by some few Israeli individuals or marginal groups who believe they can obtain peace by accepting the position of the Arab side, or of its Soviet patron, and claim that *any* agreement, even if reached by the imposition of the

---

rule supported by the Army." He did not say that there could be enlightened Israeli rule which would be supported by the Bible, Jewish morality and socialist-Zionist values. He concluded his remarks by saying that the political solution would be redivision of the country, from the desert to the sea, into two states—Jewish and Arab (*Davar*, Feb. 2, 1973).

3. Even after the resignation of the Gahal ministers from the cabinet (April 8, 1970), there remained another coalition partner, the National Religious Party (represented by three ministers), which did not omit a single opportunity of listing its opposition to any peace settlement based on withdrawing from the occupied territories (in particular from Judea and Samaria). When its fourth party congress met in the beginning of March 1973, "... the most important decision adopted by the convention—by unanimous vote—committed the N.R.P. ministers to walk out of the government coalition, should it decide on withdrawal from 'parts of the Land of Israel, our ancestral heritage.' This was taken to refer to Judea and Samaria, but left the question of Sinai open. . . ." (*The Jerusalem Post*, April 3, 1973).

Great Powers, and even without the formulation of a peace treaty and the like, could guarantee the peace. Thus, the question of security loses its importance, and it becomes possible to evacuate all the territories wholesale, to return Jerusalem to its former divided state, with one half going back to Jordanian rule. Those who are impressed by such views, however, ignore one fundamental fact—that the prospects for peace do not lie in making it abstract, but in a concrete agreement between the *real* Arabs who form the Arab (including the Palestinian) national movements, and *real* Jews—that is, with the Jewish national movement, Zionism, and a State of Israel whose whole *raison d'être* lies in fulfilling Zionism. Individuals and minority groups certainly can contribute to some ultimate agreement, but not by divorcing themselves from, or even attacking and calumnating the historic goals motivating the Israeli collectivity—Zionism, construction of the Jewish homeland, etc. By such an approach they are not only incorrect on these issues but also make their contribution completely irrelevant to the cause of peace. What is more, by linking the correct slogans of peace initiatives and anti-annexationism to an attack on Zionism, they only add grist to the mills of chauvinism. It is only by proving in words and deeds that initiatives for peace are closely and concretely linked to security, and that chauvinism and annexationism are in contradiction to both the essence of Zionism and the real needs of the Jewish State, that dovish minority groups can play a pioneering and hopeful role. This leads us to the role and aims of the dovish Israeli Left as both socialist and Zionist—*to convince the Jewish people that concern for security and the efforts for peace are inseparable.*

After the war, the Israeli public has been split in regard to the so-called Palestinian Entity. There should be no doubt regarding two issues: first, that the war cannot be brought to an end without negotiations and a settlement of the border issues and additional defense arrangements (including the possibility of partial agreements, such as for the reopening of the Suez Canal) *between Israel and the Arab States;* and second, that a genuine and stable peace cannot be achieved unless it is based on dialogue and agreement between the "two main players on the stage," i.e. *the Israelis and the Palestinians.* Such dialogue, however, and particularly agreement between these two, is so delicate and intricate a matter that any success in it would be inconceivable so long as the war continues, and before the revolutionary fact is established of negotiations and some kind of settlement between Israel and at least Egypt.

In the first years after the war, there have been strong inhibitions among the Israeli public, including the political leadership, about recognizing the Palestinian people as a potential partner for negotiations and agreement over a stable peace in the region, largely on account of the character and declarations of the "official" Palestinian representative bodies, i.e., the leadership of terrorist organizations who repeatedly declared that they did not recognize the Jewish people nor the State of Israel and aimed to wipe out this state. Toward the late sixties and early seventies, however, these inhibitions have been gradually overcome and a steadily increasing number of Israelis were recognizing the vital importance of the Palestinian aspect of the problem and of any comprehensive and stable solution to it. Similarly, many came to regard the Palestinians in the administred territories as a potential bridge between Israel and the entire Arab world, and to realize that Israel should encourage similar reactions and conclusions being reached by increasing numbers of people in the West Bank—*by granting them the right of assembly and political activity in the administered areas, insofar as this does not endanger security.* In other words, Israel should foster in the West bank the belief in the possibility of a political solution reached through negotiations and peace agreement. On this issue, too, Mapam found itself in agreement with many supporters and leading personalities of the Labor Party and the Independent Liberals. Mapam and those close to its views held the opinion that in a peace agreement, in peaceful coexistence between the State of Israel and a Palestinian-Jordanian state to the east, in secure and mutually recognized open borders between the neighboring states, and in economic cooperation—leading eventually to the perspective of a confederative link between them (at such time as both sides seek such a solution on the basis of equality and of their own free will)—that all these represent a faithful and contemporary interpretation of the party's former aim (as advocated before 1948 by Hashomer Hatsair) for a bi-national solution. In others words, the correct expression of the idea of bi-nationalism would be a "bi-state" solution within one joint historic homeland.[4]

As far as the Arab terrorist organizations are concerned, the Israeli Left is bitter against those leftists in various countries who have given up a dialectical and specific analysis of the aims, methods and objectives that these organizations fill, in favor of an abstract and superficial "anti-colonialist" romanticism, by drawing mistaken analogies between Al-Fatah and the Algerian and Vietnamese liberation movements. In those countries, terror was used against a foreign invader and conqueror, whereas the Arab organizations are fighting a neighboring people. *There,* they fought for liberation, while *here,* they are against any coexistence

---

4. There is a striking similarity between this classic Mapam formulation and the following resolution, adopted by the Central Committee of the Israel Labor Party's "Young Guard":

". . . Two peoples live in the historic land of Israel, on both sides of the Jordan—the Jewish and the Arab peoples; and there is room for two states—a Jewish and an Arab state . . . Agreement on a durable peace between the two peoples can be realized only through mutual concessions. Only by such a peace agreement would it be possible to realize the national and political aspirations of the Arabs living in Jordan and on the West Bank, who regard themselves as Palestinians. . . ." (*The Jerusalem Post; Davar,* March 21, 1971).

and national equality, not in order to liberate the territories that have been occupied by the Israeli Army since June 1967, but in order to prevent any negotiations, any political settlement, the implementation of Security Council Resolution 242 of November 1967, and to prevent "the danger of peace"—in a word, their aim is to liquidate the State of Israel and, on its ruins, to establish a "democratic Palestinian state, with equality for all religions, as part of the Arab homeland." It need hardly be added that in this caricature of an "anti-colonialist struggle" they are not destroying the State of Israel but the only real and concrete hopes for the evacuation of the occupied territories, for the reunion of the two parts of Jordan with its Palestinian majority, and for the solution of the tragic problem of the Palestinian refugees. By fighting against peace they are perpetuating both Israeli domination over the occupied territories and the refugee problem.

> Article 1. Palestine is the Homeland of the Palestinian Arab people and an integral part of the Great Arab Homeland, and the people of Palestine is a part of the Arab nation.
> Article 6. Jews who were living permanently in Palestine until the beginning of the Zionist invasion will be considered Palestinians.[5]
> Article 20. The Balfour Declaration, the Mandate document, and what has been based upon them are considered null and void. The claim of a historical and spiritual tie between Jews and Palestine does not tally with historical realities and with the constituents of statehood in their true sense. Judaism, in its character as a religion of revelation, is not a nationality with an independent existence. Likewise, the Jews are not one people with an independent personality. They are rather citizens of the states to which they belong.
> Article 21. The Palestinian Arab people, in expressing itself through the armed Palestinian revolution, rejects all plans that aim at the settlement of the Palestinian issue or its internationalization.
> From "The Palestinian National Covenant, July 1968, Articles of the Covenant," quoted in *The New York University Journal of International Law & Politics,* Vol. 3, No. 1, Spring 1970.)

Of course, when people talk about a Palestinian national movement (or any other national movement), the question immediately arises whether this is really a positive and progressive nationalism or an aggressive and reactionary chauvinism. If the Palestinians want to struggle for the national Palestinian character of the state in which they are a majority (what is called Jordan today), for the solution of the problem of the suffering and dispersed refugees, they can achieve both these positive national objectives (which are organically interrelated) only by striving

---

5. An official commentary to the Covenant (p. 51 of the documents of the National Council, 1968) states: "The aggression against the Arab nation and its land began with the Zionist invasion of Palestine in 1917. Therefore, the meaning of 'removal of the traces of the aggression' must be the removal of the traces of the aggression which came into effect at the beginning of the Zionist invasion, and did not emanate from the war of June 1967 . . . ."

for peace and coexistence with the neighboring State of Israel. In that case their movement and struggle would deserve the support of the left throughout the world—including Israel. If, on the other hand, despite occasional conflicts with the reactionary government in their own country, the spearhead of their struggle is directed against the neighboring people and its sovereign national state, that is to say, if it is looking and struggling for a "great and whole Palestine" by annihilating the State of Israel, this movement is *not* progressive at all but represents, instead, the aggressively chauvinistic and reactionary trends within the Arab world and the Palestinian people. In that case it does *not* deserve the support of the left in Israel nor elsewhere. On the contrary, any failure to criticize it severely, or any support given it, is a disservice to the future of Palestinian nationalism, to peace and socialism in the Middle East. The lack of any such examination and dialectical analysis of Arab (or Palestinian Arab) nationalism is one of the grave sins of part of the left in various countries, who are prepared to "fight against colonialism" to the last Israeli Jew and Palestinian Arab.

Mapam, which had always considered it one of its tasks to build a bridge between the socialist-Zionist left and the socialist left throughout the world, intensified its activities among leftist parties and groups throughout the world in the period before the war and especially afterwards, as part of the campaign for a stable peace. Among its achievements in that period we can mention initiating Jean-Paul Sartre's and Simone de Beauvoir's visit to Israel shortly before the war, as well as the statement of outstanding French intellectuals against the dangers of Israel's annihilation, and demanding that all the disputes be settled by negotiations; and after the war, initiative and help in forming committees of left-wing intellectuals for a negotiated peace in the Middle East—in France, Belgium, Switzerland, Argentina and Chile. Similar activities were also carried out by other parties and organizations in the Israeli labor movement: by the Histadrut among the trade unions; by Mapai and Ahdut Haavoda–Poale Zion (later united as the Israel Labor Party) among the various socialist and labor parties within the Socialist International; by Maki among certain communist parties; by Mapam, Ahdut Haavoda–Poale Zion and Maki together, by means of the Israel Peace Council—among the peace councils abroad.

Following the Six-Day War, some striking changes occurred in the attitude of the Israeli working class toward socialism. The attitude of the right wing of the labor movement to the Soviet Union was a negative one from the start, refusing to see any connection at all between the U.S.S.R. and world socialism. Instead, they found socialism to be expressed by social-democracy and the various labor governments, particularly the Scandinavian pattern of social-democratic government. The left wing of the Zionist workers' movement, on the other hand, whose attitude to the Russian October revolution has always been a positive one, was marked mainly by its bitter criticism of the Soviet Union's attitude toward Zionism, its national discrimination towards Soviet Jewry, and more recently its hard policies on the Israeli-Arab dispute, the revelations of anti-Semitism, etc. These criticisms have only slowly and with a great deal of heart-searching also gone over to more general aspects of Soviet policies, because of the deeply rooted tradition in the left wing to identify socialism with the Soviet Union and the popular democracies, rather than with the watered-down right-wing reformism of large sections of social democracy. The quantitative growth in Soviet hostility toward the Jewish people, Zionism and the State of Israel (and toward the socialist-Zionist left), on the one hand, and the criticisms of these on the other, inevitably took on a new qualitative form in the course of time. At the same time, general Soviet policies—both domestic and foreign, and toward the world communist movement—have provided so many heavy and unshakable proofs of the failure of the Soviet path to socialism as to lead the socialist-Zionist left to a comprehensive rejection of the Soviet pattern of socialism. That began as an evolutionary process and became a revolutionary crisis with the cynical and brutal Soviet hostility during the June 1967 war in the Middle East and the invasion of Czechoslovakia in August 1968.

The problem, however, is much deeper and more serious than it appears from the changing formulas of the left party institutions. The thesis that socialism is not to be identified with the Soviet path is not accepted among younger people without rich political experience (even within Mapam and its kibbutzim), who have carried most of the burden of the Six-Day War and the Yom Kippur War. For these age groups the disillusionment with the Soviet Union and the accumulated hatred of the Soviet warmongers, munitions suppliers and shyser lawyers defending the abortive Arab attempt at genocide, the Arab refusal to negotiate peace with Israel, and Palestinian terrorism, often is expressed in disillusionment with socialism in general. This is all the more true since, unlike young socialists in other countries, they do not have the choice of transferring their "disappointed love" for the Soviet Union to some other form of world communism, be it China, Yugoslavia or Cuba, because of the unfortunate fact that in playing up to the Arab rulers and vying for influence among them, China has been trying to outdo even the Russians, while Yugoslavia, with whom Mapam had good relations up to the Six-Day War, had its own reasons for giving unreserved support to Nasser's war adventures (in contrast, Mapam's relations with the Rumanian Communists are very good). At that time, Fidel Castro had not cut diplomatic ties with Israel and his attitudes toward the Middle East dispute have been marked by moderation, but the "Tri-Continent Movement" with its seat in Havana one-sidedly accepted Arab propaganda, thus making it very hard for young Israeli socialists to express their admiration for Fidel Castro and Che Guevara.

To all this we could add that the fact that considerable sections of the independent and non-communist left have joined the Soviet attacks on Israel (although "completely independently") inevitably leads Israeli socialists (even the most radical) to the feeling that they have been betrayed by the World Left in all its sections. This feeling, of course, contributes a great deal toward lowering the value of internationalism among Israeli workers, breeds ideological confusion and apolitical apathy and even cynicism and doubts about socialism in general. This atmosphere, in turn, makes it harder for the Israeli Left to fight against rightist trends and the manifestations of chauvinism fed by the feeling that "in this world everybody looks out for himself, nobody is going to help us, they are all ready to sacrifice us for their own global strategy, and we can therefore depend only on our own strength, our army, on the security borders we are holding now" (etc.).

It is here that the Israeli Left expects greater understanding and solidarity on the part of international left-wingers and progressives; greater help in its struggle within the Israeli public, the world labor movement, and world public opinion in general.

SOURCES

Text of Security Council Resolution No. 242 (Nov. 22, 1967)

The Security Council, expressing its continuing concern with the grave situation in the Middle East, emphasizing the inadmissability of the acquisition of territory by war and the need to work for a just and lasting peace in which every State in the area can live in security, emphasizing further that all member States in their acceptance of the Charter of the United Nations have undertaken a commitment to act in accordance with Article 2 of the Charter,

1. AFFIRMS that the fulfillment of Charter principles requires the establishment of a just and lasting peace in the Middle East which should include the application of both the following principles: (1) Withdrawal of Israeli armed forces from territories occupied in the recent conflict; (2) Termination of all claims or states of belligerency and respect for and acknowledgement of the sovereignty, territorial integrity and political independence of every State in the area and their right to live in peace within secure and recognized boundaries free from threats or acts of force;

2. AFFIRMS further the necessity (a) for guaranteeing freedom of navigation through international waterways in the area; (b) for achieving a just settlement of the refugee problem; (c) for guaranteeing the territorial inviolability and political independence of every State in the area, through measures including the establishment of demilitarized zones;

3. REQUESTS the Secretary-General to designate a special representative to proceed to the Middle East to establish and maintain contacts with the States concerned in order to promote agreement and assist efforts to achieve a peaceful and accepted settlement in accordance with the provisions and principles in this resolution;

4. REQUESTS the Secretary-General to report to the Security Council on the progress of the Special Representative as soon as possible.

The Case for a "Greater Israel"

The Six-Day War has opened up a new and decisive era for the people and the State of Israel. The Jewish nation has come into the possession of its reunited and undivided territory. We have as little right to reject the gift of victory as to abandon the State of Israel.

We hold ourselves committed to the integrity of our country. That is our responsibility towards the generations to come, and no Israeli government, however constituted, is entitled to surrender any part of this territorial integrity which represents the inherent and inalienable right of our people from the beginnings of its history.

Our present boundaries are a guarantee of security and peace and open up unprecedented vistas of national, material and spiritual consolidation. Within these boundaries, equality and freedom, the fundamental tenets of the State of Israel, shall be the share of all citizens without discrimination.

The two prime endeavors on which our future existence depends are immigration and settlement. Only by means of a great influx of new immigrants from all parts of the Diaspora can we hope to build up and establish the Land of Israel as a unified national entity. Let us regard the tasks and responsibilities of this hour as a challenge to us all, and as a call to a new awakening of endeavor on behalf of the people of Israel and its land.

The undersigned hereby dedicate themselves to the fulfillment of these tasks and responsibilities, and will do all within their power to bring their active implementation by the people as a whole.

(From "The Land of Israel Movement, Statement of Principles.")

Statement by French Intellectuals

The undersigned French intellectuals, who believe that they have shown that they are friends of the Arab peoples and opponents of American imperialism, and without adopting all the policies of the Israeli leaders, affirm that the State of Israel is now proving a clear desire for peace and calm.

It is incomprehensible, whatever the moves of the Great Powers, that part of public opinion considers as self-evident Israel's identification with an imperialist and aggressive camp, and the Arabs' with a socialist and pacific camp; that it forgets at the same time that Israel is the only country whose very existence is in question, that every day threatening proclamations are coming from the Arab leaders.

Under these circumstances, we call upon democratic public opinion in France vigorously to reaffirm:

1. That Israel's security and sovereignty, obviously including free passage in international waters, is a necessary condition and starting point for peace;

2. That this peace is possible and must be assured and affirmed by direct negotiations between sovereign states, in the mutual interest of the peoples concerned.

Mme. S. de Beauvoir	P. Vidal-Naquet	V. Jankelevitch
MM. A. Lwoff	D. Mayer	J. P. Kahane
L. Schwartz	MM. J.-P. Sartre	J. Madaule
C. Roy	Etiemle	P. Picasso

Mapam Political Committee on West Bank Problems

Among the developing trends in West Bank public opinion, the following are outstanding: The strengthening of Arab-Palestinian national consciousness; the prevalent recognition by the public that the future depends above all on peaceful relations and cooperation with Israel, without being annexed by Israel; rejection of the position and methods of the terrorist organizations, especially after their failures in all campaigns; disappointment with all-Arab guardianship, especially since Nasser's death; expressions of opposition to the renewal of the Hashemite rule in the West Bank in its former shape; and the achievements of Israel's policy in the West Bank since 1967, the "open bridges" policy, maximal non-interference in internal affairs and the encouragement of economic prosperity.

In view of the above, the reawakening of new political thought on the West Bank, especially among educated young people, should be positively evaluated.

There is, therefore, justification for freedom of organization and freedom of expression on the West Bank, on condition that they will involve no harm to Israel's security.

Israel must work for the economic and social rehabilitation of the refugees, must initiate comprehensive action to do away with the refugee camps, mainly through large-scale housing projects. The re-unification of families must also be enlarged and encouraged.

It must be made clear, both abroad and at home, that Israel is for peace without annexation for its own sake, and for agreed and recognized borders of peace and security.

The Political Committee expresses its opinion in favor of the right of self-determination of the West Bank Arabs, and repeats its opposition to civilian settlement in the occupied areas, which is liable to raise obstacles on the way to peace; along with this, Mapam favors security settlement, in accordance with the needs of security.

(*Al Hamishmar*, Nov. 11, 1971.)

A PLAN FOR JERUSALEM

Mapam leader Ya'akov Hazan recently proposed some ideas for Jerusalem's future.

A unified Jerusalem as the capital of Israel but divided into boroughs giving broad autonomy in social, cultural and educational affairs to its Arab inhabitants in those boroughs in which they form the majority was suggested in a plan for the future of Jerusalem proposed by veteran *Mapam* leader M. K. Ya'akov Hazan to the party's Political Committee.

In the struggle for peace, Mr. Hazan said, the question of Jerusalem's future will be one of the most if not *the* most difficult questions to be faced. Jerusalem is liable to be the most dangerous hurdle in our path towards peace, but it could also be a powerful lever in breaking out of the circle of isolation closing in on us and it could help us in deepening support and sympathy for our struggle for Israel's future and security and for the realizaion of Zionism. The essential details of Mr. Hazan's plan are outlined below:

• Unified Jerusalem is the capital of Israel;

• The municipality will be divided into boroughs in which the Arabs will be guaranteed social, cultural and educational autonomy in those boroughs in which they are a majority;

• Jerusalem's Arab inhabitants will be able to choose between Israeli citizenship and citizenship in the Arab state east of Israel. All of them, including those who choose non-Israeli citizenship, will retain the right of active and passive participation in the elections to the boroughs and the municipality of Greater Jerusalem;

• The Old City will be declared a City of Peace for the three religions; a religious council of the three religions will be established to be responsible for the management of this city in protecting its religious and cultural character and in maintaining the religious sites;

• The main religious sites of Islam and Christianity will be guaranteed a status of extraterritoriality;

• The state of Israel will be responsible for the maintenance of law and order in the Old City;

• The Temple Mount will be granted extraterritorial status; the Moslem members of the Religious Council will be responsible for its management;

• If Jewish religious authorities accept Rabbi Goren's view that there is a place on the Temple Mount where Jews are permitted to worship, this area will be withdrawn from the extra-territorial area and will be set aside for worship by religious Jews;

• A Law of Jerusalem will be enacted, as one of the state's fundamental laws, establishing Jerusalem's special status;

• If an Israeli-Arab confederation is established, the capital of this confederation will be in Jerusalem, governed by the confederation authorities and not be either of the states composing it.

(*Al-Hamishmar,*
Jan. 1, 1976.)

Mapam's Attitude toward the Soviet Union

... The Soviet Union is continuing its great power policies in our area, which are accompanied by the encouragement of Arab hatred towards Israel, and an anti-Israel and anti-Zionist campaign, which is an anti-Jewish campaign, being carried on by the Soviet union and some of its allies. The invasion of Czechoslovakia by the Warsaw Pact armies has deepened the crisis of confidence in the socialist movements in the world and in Israel. Being loyal to the socialist vision, we will struggle against distortions and we will deepen our belief in the victory of socialism, which is indivisable from humanism, democracy and the freedom of man. ...

(From the Proclamation adopted by the 2nd Session of the 5th National Congress of Mapam, Tel Aviv, November 1968.)

... We must, as must any socialist, learn the lesson of the historical development in the U.S.S.R. with respect to the continuation of the struggle for the realization and building of socialism. Different paths befitting the conditions of each country lead toward socialism with adherence to only one uncompromisable goal: the ending of the capitalist regime (the version of revolutionary socialism), and not merely its improvement (the reformist version). Different paths means anything from parliamentary methods to conquering the state by force, whenever no other way is left open. However, Mapam maintains that the socialist regime will be instituted through honoring the law and human rights, freedom of expression and argument, freedom of criticism, and struggle for different paths to realizing socialism, for freedom of political organization according to the principle of political pluralism, and for the right to frustrate any attempt to overthrow the new regime by force.

The carrier of the struggle for socialism is the party, uniting theory and political praxis. It is required to be an example of socialist democracy in its internal life, to be constructed on a wide workers' base, and to win over allies from among youth and intellectuals for progress, peace and socialism. With the October revolution, great hopes were kindled in the world and the vision of socialism united many of the best humanist intellectuals and workers. Our movement saw itself as part of this great socialist and humanist world despite our clearly emphasized reservations in different areas of life. These reservations were not restricted to Jewish and Zionist matters alone. We supported the building of socialism in the Soviet Union, but we criticized the lack of democracy, the restrictions on freedom of thought and the dictates to the world workers' movement. During the Second World War, our criticism limited itself to Jewish and Zionist matters only, in light of the Soviet Union's role in the anti-fascist front, its role in saving the Jews of Europe, and its political and military support of the Jewish State at the time of its establishment and during the War of Independence. The expectations and the assessments of changes in the internal regime of the Soviet Union, which were aroused during the Second World War, were disappointed. The hope for a change in attitude towards Zionism and the rights of Jews in the Soviet Union was also not realized.

The victory of the Soviet Union in World War II did not change its internal regime even though it put an end to the justification for the original deviations from democratic foundations on the grounds of the siege imposed on the Soviet Union and the establishment of socialism in one single country. The continuation of the policy of impingement on human and national rights, and the rights of the Jewish nation and all that occurred in the fatal policy towards Soviet Jewry, the policy of the Soviet Union in the Middle East, and finally, the case of the repression of Czech socialism through the invasion of Czechoslovakia— all raised anew in their full severity the reservations about the Soviet Union in our time.

Mapam expresses solidarity with the forces struggling against enslavement, racism, and national oppression, and against fanning the flames of war in the world, and with the forces fighting for socialism in the world. The Czech Socialist renaissance and the buds of an awakening favoring democratic change in the Soviet Union and in other countries raise the hopes for democratic socialism in the world. . . .

(From the Resolutions of the 22nd Council of Mapam, Tel Aviv, November 1971.)

25 • The Struggle for a United Workers' Front

Immediately after the Six-Day War negotiations for the unification of the labor movement were initiated from two sides: from the right, by Rafi (which had split away from Mapai in 1965), and from the left by Mapam. Despite the fact that one of Rafi's leaders, Moshe Dayan, had joined the government at the last moment in order to become Minister of Defense, Rafi's prestige had declined with the war. For two years its favorite argument had been that Eshkol's government was indecisive, was neglecting the army, etc. The war proved how empty these arguments had been. Rafi was therefore compelled to turn to Mapai (which has been allied for the last two years with Ahdut Haavoda in the Alignment) and to suggest reunification.

On the other hand, Mapam feared the workers' hegemony over the government was being lost and that the military and political emergency would be exploited by the right in order to establish a bourgeois, reactionary regime. Mapam therefore suggested to the two Alignment parties to establish a federated party with Mapam, based on a "common minimum program" with full autonomy for Mapam within a broad Labor Party. Ahdut Haavoda, which was afraid of losing its position in a joint party including Rafi, decided to speed up full unification with Mapai, in order to present Rafi with a *fait accompli* and thereby to prevent Mapai from making any concessions to Rafi at Ahdut Haavoda's expense.

That section of Mapai that was vigorously opposed to Rafi also did its best to speed up the negotiations with Ahdut Haavoda in order to achieve unification before the negotiations with Rafi began. Ahdut Haavoda and that same part of Mapai (which included leaders such as Party Secretary Golda Meir, Foreign Minister Abba Eban, Finance Minister Pinhas Sapir, and Prime Minister Levi Eshkol) also welcomed Mapam's initiative and despite their many fundamental differences with Mapam would have preferred a "triangular" union leftward (with Mapam) to a rightward triangle with Rafi, for ideological as well as for personal and party reasons.

It very soon became evident, however, that a considerable segment of

Mapai's cadres and its members in the administrative bodies (some said one-third, others estimated even one-half) preferred reunion with Rafi to all other unions; not only to union with Mapam but even with Ahdut Haavoda with which Mapai had been joined in an Alignment for two years.

Alignment leaders told Mapam that they were not free in this and that there could be no union without Rafi if Mapai's own unity was not to be threatened. They turned to Mapam with the suggestion to join Mapai, Ahdut Haavoda and Rafi in forming a quadrilateral union, something which fitted in both with their own fundamental conception of all-embracing unity as well as with the present situation.

Meanwhile, the Rafi-oriented wing in Mapai had prevented any immediate unification with Ahdut Haavoda even though negotiations had ended in full agreement. At their demand it was decided that unification with Ahdut Haavoda would only be implemented simultaneously with the unification with Rafi.

When Rafi applied to Mapai immediately after the war, it had hardly raised any conditions for unity. However, after it learned how strong and aggressive the pro-Rafi wing in Mapai was, Rafi began to raise its price and to bring up new conditions, most of them organizational in character: the division of influence in the future united party; in its representation in other organizations and in the party and government leadership; the change-over from the present system of national proportional elections to a regional majority system that had been one of Rafi's main planks since the split from Mapai, etc. In short, Rafi had fixed its sights on the speedy conquest of the new united party and of the government leadership with the help of its growing number of allies within Mapai itself.

In the course of negotiations with Rafi, Mapai had been compelled by the pressure of its own pro-Rafi wing to offer various organizational concessions, all of which went beyond what had been previously agreed upon between Mapai and Ahdut Haavoda, and at the latter's expense. This naturally strengthened the opposition within Ahdut Haavoda to union with Rafi. Several times the negotiations with Rafi seemed to have ended in deadlock and Rafi apparently had broken off the negotiations, mainly under the pressure of Ben-Gurion, who had declared his opposition to union so long as Eshkol was head of the government.

Parallel with these developments between Mapai and Rafi there have been discussions within Mapam concerning the proposal by the leaderships of Mapai and especially of Ahdut Haavoda, for "rectangular unity." However, such participation in a party including Rafi contradicted all of Mapam's long-standing conceptions of programmatic unity based, if not on an identity of views, then at least on their proximity, and which become realistic only when the various parts of the labor movement are in the process of drawing closer. Under certain circumstances Mapam had to consider and even to examine the possibilities of such unity (within a federative framework guaranteeing full autonomy) with Ahdut Haavoda and Mapai, with the latter carrying on its struggle with Rafi not only on the organizational plane but on that of principles and values as well.

The Formation of the Israel Labor Party

It was clear that Mapam could not accept programmatic unity based on a proximity of views and a rapprochement with non-socialistic Rafi or with a party including Rafi. However, in addition to this principled approach, there was a concrete political aspect: after the Six-Day War was over it soon became evident that the war, the emergency and the military victory had not ended the traditional differences between right and left in the Israeli labor movement, in the field of economics as well as in the attitude toward the fraternity of peoples and initiatives for peace. Mapam soon found itself in the midst of an intensifying struggle against the annexationist wing in the labor movement and the Israeli public in general, and against the unauthorized annexationist statements by some ministers who were creating the misleading impression abroad that they were expressing the views of the government and the Israeli public.

A detailed analysis of the possibilities of Mapam's influencing the proposed, new, four-sided united party proved that it would be able from time to time to choose partners in struggle but that in any such struggle its minority status would be "secure." On questions of security and peace it would be in a front with part of Mapai, against the semi-Rafi'ites in Mapai, Rafi and Ahdut Avoda; on economic questions and trade union struggle—in a front (perhaps) with Ahdut Haavoda against Rafi and a large part of Mapai, etc.

In concluding these deliberations, Mapam's Central Committee decided (on September 29) that under the given circumstances unification was impossible and unrealistic. Unification with Mapai and Ahdut Haavoda had to be dropped, while unification including Rafi did not even come into question. At the same time, the party Secretariat was authorized to examine whether conditions were favorable for the establishment of a united front, either of four parties, if the rightward unification was not to take place, or between Mapam and the new party, if it did. If this unification of Mapai with Ahdut Haavoda and Rafi took place, the Mapam Secretariat would have to see how it came about: If it was on the basis of Mapai submission and Rafi's domination, it was very doubtful whether the united front was realistic. If it appeared that there were grounds for negotiation, it was clear that a condition for the establishment of such a front would be a guarantee of an agreed-upon program of action, Mapam's freedom of existence and freedom to appear independently in matters of fundamental differences. If it appeared that there were prospects of obtaining such conditions, the matter would be brought to the Central Committee and decided by the party's convention.

In the voting in the Central Committee, two-thirds voted to authorize these conditional negotiations for the establishment of a united front; one-third voted against such authorization and suggested waiting for developments and the rediscussion at a later stage.

Rafi ultimately made its own calculations and, despite the opposition of Ben-Gurion and a small minority, decided to unite with Mapai and Ahdut Haavoda–Poale Zion even though their conditions were not accepted. It was decided that the question of leadership in the united party as well as the premiership in the next government would be put off until after the Knesset elections in October 1969. The first convention of the united party which, in the summer of 1969, would ratify the list of candidates and the platform for the elections to the Histadrut, the municipalities and the Knesset, would still be formed by agreement; that is, it would not be chosen in general elections by the membership of the party, but set up according to agreement: Rafi, 21.5 percent; Ahdut Haavoda–Poale Zion, 21.5 percent; Mapai, 57 percent. The party would be run by a general secretary (first Golda Meir, and later Pinhas Sapir) chosen from Mapai, assisted by two other secretaries from Rafi and Ahdut Haavoda-Poale Zion, respectively. After the elections to the Knesset, a party congress would be convened, after general elections, which would choose the party's new governing bodies and also decide on the issue of the premiership.

In agreeing to this compromise, Rafi hoped that even within the existing situation it would find allies among the Mapai representatives who had often supported it in the past, and thus would be able to continue its campaign to conquer the united party, even if only at a slower pace during the first year. And so, in January 1968, the Israeli Labor Party was founded by the reunification of the historic Mapai as it had existed before the splits of 1944 and 1965.[1]

Mapam's Fifth Party Congress

The Congress convened in Tel Aviv from March 20 to 23. From the report presented it was revealed that the 787 delegated to the Congress represented approximately 32,000 members in 133 branches: 73 kibbutzim of Kibbutz Artzi (380 delegated), 60 city branches and dozens

---

1. Only nine of Rafi's ten members of the Knesset joined the Labor Party. Ben-Gurion stayed out and continued to maintain a one-man faction in the Knesset.

of cells (407 delegates); 118 of the delegates were women; 39 were Arab members; 13 were members of Moshavei-Ovdim.

The Congress' agenda was devoted in the main to discussions on security and peace, unity of the workers' movement, Mapam's path in the socialist workers' movement, and rules for the election of party institutions.

Mapam's peace program was ratified by an overwhelming majority. However, a small minority presented a resolution that disagreed with it primarily on two points: (1) the minority demanded that the main partner in peace negotiations must be the Palestinian Arabs and not the Jordanian government exclusively; (2) although the minority supported direct negotiations for peace in principle, it nevertheless emphasized the possibility of alternative means of negotiations as well. The majority did not accept these amendments since it saw any questioning of the state of Jordan as a representative partner in negotiations on peace, boundaries, refugees, etc. as creating an additional obstacle to the opening of negotiations at all. As for direct negotiations, it was emphasized that the majority resolution also interpreted this demand flexibly, not as direct negotiations from beginning to end but recognizing the possibility of preparing direct negotiations and the face-to-face meeting of both sides in order to sign an official peace treaty, and the mediatory role of the UN Envoy in preparing the ground for such a meeting.

Another amendment asking to strike out the clause, "confederative ties between the states of Israel and Jordan," was also defeated. This amendment did not want to commit Israel in advance to any tie or any specific form of tie, especially since the entire matter of peace and any kind of cooperation with Jordan seemed far distant. The majority, on the other hand, insisted on including "confederation" in the resolution because it is a perspective whose emphasis has an educational value for both Israelis and Palestinians and serves as a clear alternative to all the open and camouflaged annexionist perspectives and plans.

On the question of the United Front, two motions were presented to the Congress: one, the majority's motion, that requested that authority be granted to the party institutions to continue the negotiations with the Israel Labor Party to create a united front on the parliamentary and municipal levels; as far as the trade unions and the General Federation of Labor (Histadrut) were concerned, Mapam should demand either the right to appear independently in such elections or a satisfactory programmatic agreement upon which joint election lists could be formed, directed against the anti-socialist wing of the General Federation of Labor (Gahal, etc.) and which could serve as an equivalent to appearing independently. The institutions of the party would bring the results of the negotiations before a second session of the Congress. On the other hand, the minority motion opposed any negotiations for a united front since it feared that this would limit Mapam's existence and freedom of independent action and would be nothing but a transitional step toward complete party amalgamation, as occurred in the case of Ahdut Haavoda.

As for the analogy with the alignment between Mapai and Ahdut Haavoda, speakers for the majority replied that this comparison ignored the differences between Ahdut Haavoda's and Mapam's approaches to the question of unity with Mapai. As early as the time of the Third Aliya, Ahdut Haavoda had been in favor of the full political unity of the labor movement within one broad "class party," while Hashomer Hatsair (and afterwards Mapam) had never sanctified political unity as such, at any price and under all circumstances. Ahdut Haavoda had split from Mapam and established the alignment with Mapai, since it considered that to be a clear, official and decisive step toward the fulfillment of its aim of unity with Mapai. Mapam, on the other hand, had not believed in the past, and still does not believe that unity with Mapai is possible or necessary, or that a reasonable minimum program could be formulated for the two parties that would make unification possible. Mapam did not, therefore, view the proposed alignment as a "first step" (as Ahdut Haavoda had), but as a "correct step." Any analogies or hasty conclusions drawn from the fact that the first alignment ended in unity would be unfounded, unless they were accompanied by real analyses of the differing approaches of both Ahdut Haavoda and Mapam on this subject.

In addition, spokesmen for the majority emphasized that there was no conflict between party independence and a united front. On the contrary, a left-wing socialist party acting within the framework of a united front ensures itself a more direct approach to the masses and will be closer to the sources of vital security and political decisions concerning negotiations for peace, the future of the occupied territories, etc.

After a debate in which about 100 delegates, Jews and Arabs, rural and urban inhabitants, participated, the majority motion was adopted by a vote of 64.5 to 35.5 percent. However, the matter was not settled by this vote since the final attitude of many delegates who voted in favor of granting authority to conduct and complete such negotiations would be determined by the results of the negotiations: if the Israel Labor Party were not to agree that in the framework of a united front Mapam would be assured of the right to appear independently in the Histadrut elections (or a satisfactory programmatic agreement) they were to oppose the suggested united front in the second session of the Congress.

Resolution adopted concerning the Israeli Workers' Movement

1. The political and security campaigns which the State of Israel has been involved in since the Six-Day War require the consolidation of the Zionist-Socialist workers parties for the struggle for security and peace, for the advancement of the process of the Ingathering of the

Exiles, for the preservation of a progressive economic regime, and for a guaranteeing of the hegemony of the worker and pioneering forces in the State.

A common appearance in the Histadrut is possible, if a program can be agreed upon, which will suitably cover the basic principles of our independent appearance in the Histadrut and the Hevrat Haovdim (Workers' Economy).

Mapam will preserve its ideological, political and organizational independence.

2. The Congress empowers the institutions of the party to negotiate with the Israeli Labor Party on the basis of the preceding points. The results of the negotiations will be brought before a special session of the Congress.

(Mapam Bulletin, Tel Aviv, 1968.)

The Minority Resolution

The Congress resolves under the present circumstances not to negotiate the question of the establishment of a front or an alignment with the Israeli Labor Party, and calls for an increase in cooperation in the workers' movement in the areas of the government and the State, the Zionist Movement, the Histadrut and the municipalities, and it is ready to enter into pacts with the Zionist-socialist parties.

In light of the establishment of the Israeli Labor Party, Mapam emphasizes the necessity of the continuation of its special mission and its complete ideological and organizational independence, along with its independent appearance in all of the election campaigns in order to advance the struggle toward its goals:

The realization of the Ingathering of the Exiles by means of a pioneering regime; the integration of the class struggle with the up-building of the land; striving towards the realization of socialism through democratic means; the guaranteeing of peace, security, and the brotherhood of nations; the strengthening of ties with the forces for Socialism and progress in the world and among the Jews in the Diaspora.

During special circumstances, Mapam will weigh the possibility of appearing together with the Israeli Labor Party during decisive public campaigns.

(Ibid.)

Following the decision by the Mapam Party Congress, negotiations began between the two parties to examine the possibilities of establishing an alignment between them, while allowing each to preserve its full-party independence. The greatest difficulty in the negotiations was encountered on the Histadrut level, since the Labor Party was vigorously opposed to Mapam's appearing separately in the Histadrut elections or maintaining a separate faction within the Histadrut after the elections.

After tiresome negotiations, it was finally agreed that there would be a single slate for the elections, based on an agreed-upon platform; as for the faction after the elections, in those areas where views were not diametrically opposed, all the members elected would form a single faction, while in controversial areas (mainly wage and trade union policies) there would be an obligation for consultation, but if this were unfruitful, Mapam's delegates would form a separate faction and vote independently on these issues. When the results of the negotiations were brought up for ratification by the second session of the party congress (November 1968 in Tel Aviv), they were accepted by the same majority as in the first session and Mapam's governing bodies were authorized to set up the alliance between the two parties.

The large majority of the opponents of the alignment accepted the democratic decision of the party congress; there were some few who announced their resignation from the party, and a small group headed by Yaakov Riftin and Eliezer Peri (once leading ultra-leftists in Mapam and the Kibbutz Artzi in the 50s), left Mapam and formed an Independent Left Socialist-Zionist Alliance.[2]

Labor Party threatened by schism

The ratification of the alignment agreement by the Labor Party met vigorous opposition by the former Rafi'ites and some of their allies in the Labor Party; they knew that the formation of the alignment would alter the balance of forces against them. Since the decisions on foreign policy and security would be taken within the framework of the alignment and its parliamentary faction, Rafi's hopes of winning a majority in any one of these institutions would decrease to the point of despair.

Their opposition, however, was to no avail and the agreement was adopted by a large majority. The same thing happened when Rafi desired to pass a resolution changing the Labor Party's first "agreed-upon" convention into an elected one. In both cases it became evident that some of the former Rafi'ites were now taking an independent stand, without accepting "factional" discipline. The hopes of winning wide support from some parts of Mapai were also disappointed.

It thus began to become clear to the ex-Rafi leaders that it was doubtful whether their earlier hopes of taking the party by storm from within

2. Mapam argued against this group that it was characterized not only by its sectarian opposition to the idea of the United Front, but that also in contrast to other opponents of the alignment, its leaders have still not freed themselves of their traditional pro-Soviet complex. That is why they hesitated to come out with a clear and unequivocal condemnation of the invasion of Czechoslovakia and of the Soviet Union's war-mongering policies in the Middle East. Another splinter group, even less significant than the above, which also seceded from Mapam in protest to the Alignment, has been called Siach (Israeli New Left), differing from the Riftin-Peri group mainly in age and by its far more critical attitude to Soviet Russia. Towards the 1969 Knesset elections both groups joined ranks with a group of university lecturers and with some others to set up the "Peace List" which was, however, heavily defeated: 5,138 votes—only half of those required for winning one seat in the Knesset.

would ever come to pass. In view of these gloomy forecasts about their prospects within the united party, they began to concentrate more and more on a direct appeal to the public outside the party, with their central slogan: "Dayan for Head of Government." By exploiting Moshe Dayan's wide popularity and his image as a "young, energetic, efficient leader type," they developed a vociferous publicity campaign in the newspapers, began to collect signatures for a petition, etc. They were especially suspicious of the veteran Mapai leadership's desires to push Yigal Allon forward in order to groom him as Levi Eshkol's heir to the premiership, and thereby to block Moshe Dayan's path to the top. When Eshkol appointed Allon to the position of Deputy Premier, this brought on a serious crisis within the party and Rabi's threats of secession. The party leadership was not deterred, however, and chose Yosef Almogi, a Rafi leader who had moved away from his friends, to fill Allon's vacant position as Minister of Labor, and Almogi accepted. Another crisis broke out with the death of Premier Levi Eshkol: the competition between Moshe Dayan and Yigal Allon which could have split the party was avoided only when Golda Meir yielded to pressure and accepted the position of Head of the Government despite her age and poor health.

When the date for the prearranged party convention drew near, a party census was taken that revealed Rafi's weakness even more, so that Pinhas Sapir felt free to offer to make the first convention an "elected" one. Now Rafi was compelled to oppose this and to insist on the agreement. The convention itself was held in August 1969 and was marked by the repercusions of the debate going on in the political committee of the Alignment and its platform committee, mainly over foreign policy and security matters as well as on policies in the occupied areas. In all these debates a clear front was formed with Foreign Minister Abba Eban, Labor Party General Secretary Pinhas Sapir, the Mapam represenatives and others, on the one side, and Rafi leaders Moshe Dayan and Shimon Peres, on the other, with the Ahdut Haavoda–Poale Zion representatives supporting Dayan on some important issues. Moshe Dayan raised most of the issues that were the center of the debate when he (1) demanded that the term "agreed-upon borders" be eliminated from the proposed platform, (2) demanded that the platform specify the security borders that Israel would demand whenever there were negotiations, (3) opposed accepting the Security Council resolution of November 1967 as a basis for negotiations and agreements with the Arab countries, and (4) demanded that Israeli law be applied to the occupied territories, that these territories be integrated into Israel's economy, and that the temporary security holdings be turned into permanent rural and urban settlements.[3]

---

3. After Mapam's Council heard a report of the platform negotiations and summed up the concessions and achievements of the joint platform, and after it was assumed that during the

At the same time the ex-Rafi'ites presented a series of organizational demands in order to increase their own representation within the party institutions and to secure their positions in the Knesset and the new government. These demands, which smacked of blackmail, coming as they did just before the elections, plus the differences in the political committee and platform committee, raised tension to fever pitch and the ex-Rafi'ites openly began to threaten to leave the party if their demands were not met. The matter became even more serious with David Ben-Gurion's announcement that he would contest the elections with his own list—"The Continuers of Rafi." When the Labor Party bodies demanded of the ex-Rafi'ites in its own ranks that they disavow this list, they declared they could not consider openly attacking Ben-Gurion even when they didn't agree with him. At most, they could in a positive fashion call for votes for the Alignment—if their demands were filled. Eventually, their main organizational demands *were* filled. As for the political differences, they did not, indeed, win out on the main issues, but some attempt was made to meet them halfway and reconcile them, against Mapam's opposition, by agreeing to allow them to express their territorial demands as a kind of "oral doctrine," though not as part of the written platform itself.

When the former Rafi'ites convened on August 17, 1969, for the important decision on whether to remain with the Labor Party or secede, Moshe Dayan decided the issue by speaking against schism. He argued that more could be obtained from within, and that without any certainty of obtaining an absolute majority to replace the Alignment, the danger of schism would outweigh its prospects. By a vote of 39 to 6 with 6 abstentions, it was decided to remain within the Labor Party; and at least for the time being, the threat of schism was removed.

This danger of schism, however, and the blackmail on the verge of a difficult election campaign could not help but leave residues of bitterness and tension on the relationships between Moshe Dayan and Shimon Peres, on the one hand, and Abba Eban, Pinhas Sapir, and especially Mapam, on the other. Mapam also resented the concessions that had been made to Dayan for the sake of Labor Party unity, despite the opposition of Mapam and even of some of the Labor Party's own leaders. The dissatisfaction was strengthened by the fear that world public opinion would look upon the platform adopted as not only an election instrument for purely domestic purposes, but as a semi-official document, and would pay less attention to the concessions Dayan had made than to those he had obtained. These latter included the oral doctrine specifying the strategic borders that Israel

election campaign the Party would maintain the right to speak for its own peace plan, the platform was ratified by a vote of 247 to 58, with 22 abstentions. The platform was adopted by the Labor Party convention, at the same time. This still was not a final vote, since the most controversial issue, that of the occupied areas, was still open; it was understood that an agreement would be reached on this as well.

would demand during negotiations, even though they had never been voted by the government, and the formulation of the clause on settlement in the areas occupied by the Israeli Army.

Mapam was particularly concerned over this latter clause, which had been written by the Labor Party leadership as a last-minute concession for the sake of party unity, and which speaks of permanent urban and rural settlement. In Mapam's eyes this clause must inevitably be interpreted as reflecting a policy of establishing faits accomplis and as such contradicting the fundamental Alignment and government policy of open options and negotiations without any conditions. Criticizing this opportunistic compromise, Mapam published its own views on this sensitive issue, views that were quite close to those of Abba Eban and Pinhas Sapir.

> The Central Committee ratifies the paragraphs in the Alignment's platform for the Knesset on foreign policy, security and policies in the territories, while rejecting the clause on civilian as well as military settlements in the paragraph on policies in the territories that was adopted by a majority vote in the Political Committee of the Alignment.
>
> Mapam continues to support military settlements wherever they are required by the needs of Israel's security.
>
> Mapam will continue to appear in public in accordance with this position and the clause in the fundamental policy of the outgoing government: "Israel will persist in its readiness to conduct negotiations without any pre-conditions from any side—with any of its neighbor states—in order to conclude a peace treaty. In the absence of a peace treaty, Israel will continue to maintain the situation as it was at the time of the cease-fire and will reinforce its position in view of the vital needs of its security and development.
>
> This policy of Mapam is in keeping with the needs of Israeli security and foreign policy and its strivings for peace by negotiations, without any preconditions.
>
> (Resolution of Mapam Central Committee, *Al-Hamishmar*, Sept. 29, 1969.)

Mapam considers its main achievement in formulating the Alignment platform to be the unanimous acceptance of the formula of "negotiations without prior conditions." And, indeed, when some weeks later Abba Eban addressed the General Assembly of the U.N., his speech centered around that formula.

> ... Let me make clear Israel is prepared to negotiate without prior conditions of any kind. It does not seek advance accceptance by Arab governments of its own proposals. And the word "non-negotiable" is not a part of Israel's vocabulary. You ask: "What can be discussed and proposed in these negotiations?" I answer: "Everything." You ask: "What is excluded from discussion?" I answer, "Nothing!" In the negotiations we shall, of course, define where our vital and indispensa-

ble interests lie, but once negotiations begin, the participants must commit themselves to its fortunes. Their task will not be merely to state positions, but also to try to bring them into harmony. . .
(From A. Eban's address to the U.N. General Assembly, *Jerusalem Post*, Sept. 21, 1969.)

Decline of the Alignment

The uncertainty that prevailed up to the very last minute whether Rafi would remain in the united party or leave worked more than a little to slow down the Alignment's momentum in its campaign before the Histadrut elections. This naturally caused the Alignment leadership some worry over the election results. These fears actually were realized. In the 1965 elections the parties who were now joined in the Alignment (the Mapai–Ahdut Haavoda alignment, Mapam and Rafi) had together won about 77 percent of the votes; now the Alignment obtained only 62 percent. The "Religious Workers," who had in 1965 appeared together with the Mapai–Ahdut Haavoda Alignment, now appeared independently (though in affiliation to the Alignment) and won another 3 percent—making the total 65 percent, or a loss of 12 percent. All the leftist splinter lists (the two Communist parties, Haolam Hazeh and the ex-Mapamites) received together only 6 percent.

The parties that benefited from decline of the Alignment were the rightist parties in Gahal, the Free Center (ex-Gahal), the Independent Liberals, and Ben-Gurion's State Party. The last-named party, appearing before the electorate as the "Continuation of Rafi," played a considerable role in the Alignment's decline since its 4 percent took some of the votes that had previously been given to Rafi. Some of the Rafi leaders were actually charged with having played unfairly on both sides: after having guaranteed themselves their representation in the Alignment list, they either actively or otherwise encouraged their peripheral supporters to support Ben-Gurion's competing party.

However, the 65 percent promised the Alignment a stable majority, even in the event that Rafi broke away in the future. (It would then depend on Mapam's continued support.)

Many reasons have been deduced for this decline of the Alignment. It is clear, however, that in addition to such reasons as the meagre participation in the elections (only 65 percent of the potential votes—the lowest proportion in the history of the Histadrut), Ben-Gurion's competition, and the like, the main reason in the declining popularity of the Labor Party and its leadership was due to growing bureaucracy, reformistic practices in trade union affairs, and the stupid use of the law (mobilization, disciplinary trials, etc.) against striking workers.

Despite the vigorous debates within Mapam over joining the Alignment, the decisive majority of those who had voted Mapam in former elections now gave their votes to the Alignment, though without being able thereby to prevent the decline. The question Mapam now faced was whether its participation and resultant influence within the Alignment, in conjunction with its own independent actions, would be effective in giving the Histadrut back its image of a militant, constructive, democratic, dynamic and popular workers' organization.[4]

In the elections to the Seventh Knesset and the municipalities on October 28, 1969, the Alignment improved its situation as compared to the Histadrut (due in no small extent to the large turnout of voters—more than 80 per cent). This improvement was not sufficient, however, for the Alignment to win the same strength that its component parties had had in 1965 separately. The Alignment lost seven seats: the former Mapai, 33 instead of 37; Ahdut Haavoda, eight instead of nine; Rafi, eight instead of nine; and Mapam, seven instead of eight, for a total of 56 instead of 63 of the Knesset's 120 seats.

These lost seats went to Gahal (two), to the National Religious Party (one), Ben-Gurion's State List (three), and the Haolam Hazeh-Koah Hadash (one). The gains made by Gahal and the National Religious Party were minimal considering the situation of military tension (only a few days before the elections Arab terrorists laid bombs in some houses in Haifa and caused civilian casualties among women and children). The biggest winner was Ben-Gurion, who expanded his one-man list into a party with four seats in the Knesset. What this really meant was that Rafi had increased its strength from ten to twelve—eight in the Alignment and four in Ben-Gurion's independent but essentially Rafi list.

After the elections the problem of setting up the new coalition government arose. Gahal, which had been represented in the previous government since the crisis of May 1967 by two Ministers without Portfolio and without accepting responsibility for the fundamental program of the government, now demanded to be included in the government as full members. It asked for a number of Ministers in keeping with its Knesset strength and even participation in formulating the fundamental

---

4. After the electoral failure in 1969, the Labor Party leadership had drawn the correct conclusion by putting at the head of the Histadrut a dynamic and rather independent personality like Yitshak Ben-Aharon. Since his appointment as Secretary-General, he had succeeded in regaining some of Histadrut's autonomy from the government, as well as some of its lost credibility and popularity among the workers.

In his efforts to that effect, Ben-Aharon enjoyed large support by Mapam, whilst his own party has been split on this issue, its leadership being torn between satisfaction with the growing popularity of Labor-dominated Histadrut, and resentment of Ben-Aharon's equivocal criticism and often even outspoken opposition to the party's and the government's economic policy and decisions.

After the Histadrut elections of September 1973, Ben-Aharon saw no choice other than to resign from office, accusing outstanding leaders of the Israel Labor Party of having waged against him what he defined as a "systematic ousting campaign."

program of the new government. This demand was vigorously opposed by Mapam, which opened a wide campaign within the Alignment itself, in the press and in public meetings. A considerable part of the Labor Party was also opposed. The great difficulty, however, was that the National Religious Party without whom the Alignment (with its Arab lists and the Independent Liberals) had only a narrow majority of 63, insisted on Gahal coming into the government. By this the National Religious Party hoped to win support for its demands for permanent urban and rural settlements in the West Bank. It also expected that in a broader coalition including Gahal it would play a more important role in the center than it could in a coalition composed mainly of the workers' parties and the Independent Liberals. Moshe Dayan, incidentally, supported Gahal's entrance for the same kind of reasons. If the Alignment had won a decisive majority in the elections it could more easily have withstood these pressures, but its losses in the Knesset and even more in the municipal elections gave the National Religious Party and the Rafi'ites a better bargaining position than ever.

When, despite Mapam's opposition and the differences with the Labor Party, Gahal's participation in the coalition became a fact, Mapam was faced with a bitter dilemma: either to join Gahal in a programmatic coalition with an increased right-wing trend, or to go over to the opposition and break up the united front with the Labor Party. The latter choice also meant giving up the possibilities of obtaining first-hand information and of exerting influence in the spheres of security and foreign policy, and of strengthening the already tight majority in the government favoring the moderate and deliberate policies of Foreign Minister Abba Eban.

Finally, the party decided almost unanimously (both pro-Alignment and anti-Alignment elements) to continue to be part of the national emergency government but without participating in the coalition or accepting responsibility for the fundamental program, and to designate two Ministers without portfolio (Yisrael Barzelai and Victor Shem-Tov), in other words, to be part of the government in the same status that Gahal had enjoyed from May 1967 to the recent elections.

On December 15 Golda Meir presented her new government to the Knesset and this new government, with 14 Labor, six Gahal, three National Religious, one Independent Liberal, and two Mapam Ministers, was ratified by the Knesset.

> The Political Committee of the Alignment resolves to open negotiations to form a new government on the basis of the fundamental program of the outgoing government, with all the parties represented in the Government of National Unity, and to give Gahal representation in keeping with its parliamentary strength.
> (Resolution offered by Prime Minister Golda Meir, adopted by a vote of eight to four, *Davar,* Nov. 4, 1969.)

The Central Committee affirms that the State of Israel's security situation demands the continuation of the emergency government, and Mapam's participation within it.

The Central Committee ratifies the stand taken by its representatives in the Political Committee of the Alignment and in their talks with the leadership of the Labor Party—the rejection of the programmatic coalition with Gahal. Mapam sees in the establishment of a coalition with Gahal a serious deviation from the historic path of the labor movement and a threat to the workers' hegemony in the State and to the primary and progressive character of the government. Even if it supposedly accepts the fundamental program as a whole Gahal does not give up its aim to replace the workers' majority government with a right-wing alternative. Such programmatic agreement and additional concessions to the religious parties can undermine the ideological and political consciousness of the working class and weaken its ability to fight against the capitalist and chauvinistic right.

Mapam's Central Committee resolves to join the government that will be established on the basis of an emergency government accepting responsibility and the duty of discipline only in the field of security, foreign policy and the budget. Mapam's disagreement concerning permanent settlement continues, as it has until now. In keeping with this position, Mapam's representative will serve in the government, by its initiative, with the status of Ministers without portfolio.

(Resolution of Mapam Central Committee, *Al-Hamishmar,* Dec. 10, 1969.)

This decision was changed at the meeting of the Mapam Central Committee (July 15, 1970) by a vote of 92 to 60, and the two Mapam Ministers (Victor Shem-Tov and Nathan Peled, who was elected at the same meeting to be Mapam's second Minister, after the death of Israel Barzelai) accepted the responsibility for the Ministries of Health and the Absorption of Immigrants. The majority argued in behalf of its suggestion to reverse the previous decision—that the government of Golda Meir recently adopted a number of Mapam demands, such as the renewed announcement that Israel accepts the Security Council resolution of November 1967 and is ready to conduct peace talks according to the "Rhodes formula" (that is to say, a combination of indirect negotiations, mediation and direct negotiations in the concluding phase). It also contended that in recent months a change had occurred within the Labor Party and the Doves had become stronger, and Mapam's nonparticipation in the government coalition placed a superfluous barrier between Mapam and this part of the Labor Party. That is particularly unfortunate at the present time when the Labor Party and Gahal are drawing farther apart—and the affinity between Mapam and the bulk of the Labor Party's leadership is increasing, and as a result, the changes of putting an end to the damaging coalition between the Labor Party and Gahal are improving.

On the other hand, the minority argued that by joining the coalition

Mapam would not be promoting the changes of a stronger and more flexible peace initiative and a discontinuance of participation with Gahal on the part of the Labor Party, but would check them, whereas Mapam's demonstrative nonparticipation in a coalition with Gahal increases the ferment within the Labor Party.

This controversy lost much of its relevance, when the Israeli Cabinet decided, a fortnight later, to respond to the American peace initiative ("Rogers Plan"), and that decision led to Gahal's resignation from the Cabinet (August 4), thus putting an end to the existence of the controversial "Government of National Unity." . . .[4]

Doves vs. Hawks

Since there didn't seem to be any real signs that the Arab countries would agree to negotiate with Israel, and Israel's leadership, for its part, didn't formulate any new ideas or initiatives to break the deadlock, the internal political debate within Israel began to center more and more on the question of the policies to be adopted for the occupied territories. The hawks argued that the limitations of "temporariness" should be abandoned, that all the barriers between Israel and the occupied territories be removed, that Israeli inhabitants be permitted to buy land and to establish Jewish settlements, and that they be integrated into Israel's economy. In short, they wanted Israel to adopt a policy that its opponents called one of "establishing *faits accomplis*," or "creeping annexation."

The doves, on the other hand, while they favored the economic and social development of the territories, were opposed in varying degrees of force and consistency to any step (and especially to any combination of steps) that smacked of annexation or could be interpreted to be annexation. They also insisted that the territories continue to be viewed as a pledge for peace and that all the options be kept open for the hoped-for eventual peace negotiations.

In preparation for the elections scheduled for the fall of 1973 (the Histadrut in September, the Knesset in October), the various parties of the right (Gahal, the Free Center, the State List) united to form the National Liberal Union (Likud). Within the labor movement the approaching elections aroused an intensified internal debate within the Israel Labor Party, Mapam, and the Communist Party (Maki).

Within Mapam there was the continuing and even intensified argument between the partisans and opponents of the Alignment with the Labor Party. After a heated argument, the party's sixth convention in

5. After a heated discussion, Mapam decided at its Sixth Party Congress (Tel Aviv, December 1972) to continue in the Alignment, while at the same time preserving its independence. After the resignation of 75-year-old Meir Yaari from the post of Secretary-General of the party, he was succeeded by Meir Talmi (of Kibbutz Mishmar Haemek).

December 1971 had decided by a vote of 68.5 to 31.5 percent to continue within the Alignment while strictly maintaining the party's independence.

Maki was split by differences over the line to be taken towards the government and Mapam, on the one hand, and the various anti-establishment splinter groups, on the other. The party's majority, and mainly the comrades and pupils of the late Dr. Moshe Sneh, supported criticizing and applying public pressure on the government in order to push it forward towards a policy of peace initiatives. The minority, headed by Ester Vilenska, charged the government with "hawkishness," with opposing negotiations for peace and with expansionism. The Maki majority viewed Mapam and the dove wing of the Labor Party as their potential future allies, despite their criticism of Mapam for belonging to the Alignment. The opposition, on the other hand, didn't believe in the perspective of any such leftist coalition and looked for a surrogate by establishing a Left Forum composed of all the leftist groups between the Alignment and Rakah. In Maki's 17th convention in April 1972, Sneh's disciples decisively defeated Vilenska's group, which didn't obtain the support of more than 20–21 percent of the delegates. When the elections drew closer, Maki decided to unite with a new leftist socialist-Zionist group named "Blue-Red," to form a new list: "Focus" (Moked). The opposition, headed by Ester Vilenska, defected and joined with the Haolam Hazeh group and the New Israeli Left to form "Meri" (the Israeli Radical Camp), headed by M.K. Uri Avneri, despite his declaration that he wasn't a socialist and no mention of the word socialism in the list's program.

The Labor Party was also subject to a vigorous debate with, for the first time, most of the leading personalities of the party leadership dissenting from Moshe Dayan's hawkish emphasis and criticizing him openly. However, as the elections drew closer and in view of the right-wing parties' unity and aggressiveness, Moshe Dayan's influence increased (as did that of other members of Rafi in the Labor Party), and he threatened to "sit on the fence" or even worse. In the end the party's leadership yielded and united on what was called the "Galili Paper," which was a compromise with Dayan and included many concessions to his views. The Paper revolved about a program for expanded Israeli activities in the occupied territories during the coming four years, with a view to establishing economic facts and settlements to a degree far beyond what had been accepted, and agreed upon on this subject within the government and the Alignment. Mapam reacted vigorously and declared publicly that it considered the Paper to be a "private document" of the Labor Party alone, not obligating the Alignment as a whole, and that in the course of the election campaign it would openly express its criticisms of and disagreement with this document.

In the Histadrut elections (September 1973) the rightist Likud didn't register any gains over the previous elections (22.7 percent). The Alignment declined slightly (together with its allied Religious Workers it obtained 62.56 percent as compared with 65.17 percent in 1969). The Independent Liberals gained; the Communist lists more or less maintained their strength, while the Black Panthers, participating for the first time in Histadrut elections, won 1.63 percent of the votes.

SOURCES

The Charter of the Israel Labor Party

A. Recognizing that the Israel Labor Movement is united in its historic task of achieving the greatest possible concentration of the Jewish People in its Land and in its vision to establish a free Workers' Commonwealth in the State of Israel, at the dawn of a new era in the life of the nation and the State, hereby is established the unity of the workers of Israel, by Mapai (the Israeli Workers' Party), Ahdut Haavoda–Poale Zion (Unity of Labor–Workers of Zion) and Rafi (Israeli Workers' List), according to the mutual agreements which were adopted and endorsed by the authorized bodies of the three merging parties.

B. The united body will be called: The Israel Labor party (Mifleget Haavoda Hayisraelit).

C. The Israel Labor Party will serve the nation, the State and the working public.

D. The Israel Labor Party will be based on the following foundations:

1. A renewed drive for immigration and the creation of suitable conditions for the absorption and integration of the new immigrants.

2. An endeavor to attain the social, pioneering and national aims of the State of Israel and its people, now and in the future, in the spirit of the heritage of the Jewish people, the vision of Socialist Zionism and the values of the labor movement.

3. The representation of the working people in Israel and activity on its behalf and in its service in the central and local governmental institutions of Israel, among the Jewish people, in the Zionist Movement, in the Histadrut and in the international labor movement.

4. The safeguarding of the principles of freedom of thought, expression and discussion, while preserving unity of action and the implementation of majority decisions according to normal democratic procedure.

E. The Israel Labor Party will work for the affiliation of workers parties, as well as of groups and individuals which will adhere to its fundamental program...

... The contract was signed in Jerusalem, capital of the State of Israel, today, Sunday, January 21, 1968.

Signed by veteran members of the movement, and members of the secretariats of the three uniting parties.

(Published by the Israel Labor Party, Jerusalem, January 1968.)

The Alignment—Israel Labor Party-United Workers Party

Statement of the Alignment of the Israel Labor Party and the United Workers Party.

The Israel Labor Party and the United Workers Party (Mapam) has today established an alignment between them in united Jerusalem, the capital of Israel.

Israel's political and security situation since the Six-Day War requires the unity of the Zionist-Socialist labor parties—to ensure the future of the Jewish People, to strengthen the security of Israel, its persistent struggle for peace and the development of the country, to increase immigration and absorption, to create a strong and progressive economic regime and fortify the hegemony of labor and pioneering forces in the State and among the Jewish People.

The forces that are today joining together in the Alignment established the Histadrut and Hevrat Ovdim half a century ago, built settlements, impressed their character upon the "Hagana," stood at the forefront of the fighters during the period of the Holocaust and resistance, laid the foundations for the establishment of the State of Israel, and since then until the present have been fulfilling a vital and leading role in the life of the country.

The Alignment looks forward to implementing the tasks imposed upon this generation and to realizing the vision of national and social redemption.

The Six-Day War brought about a fundamental change in the life of the people and the State. The wonderful victory of the Israel Defense Forces in the war, which was forced upon us, has increased the opportunities, although there still are many dangers.

This time of emergency makes it essential for the combining of forces in order to face the trials of our time.

Faithful to the Zionist-Socialist vision, the Alignment will be in the forefront of the political and security struggles to strengthen the State, its security and its peace, to advance the concentration of the majority of the Jewish People in its land, to encourage immigration from all countries and its productive absorption; to strengthen the democratic-parliamentary regime of the State; to ensure full equality for all its citizens; to establish a society of workers in Israel; to safeguard the social achievements of the workers and the masses of people; to realize the principles of national and public ownership of natural resources; to settle the desolate parts of the country; to plan the State's economy, development and industrialization; to foster science and technology; to encourage the productive initiative of all sectors of the economy, while continually striving to reduce the social gap; to strengthen and expand the labor economy; to ensure full employment and a decent standard of living for all, paying special attention to the under-privileged classes; to increase pioneering realization in building the economy, in agriculture and industry; to raise the cultural standard and to foster a modern manner of life; to maintain the independent mission of the Histadrut and strengthen its authority.

The Alignment calls upon all the workers in Israel—those in the security front, new immmigrants, youth, scientists and artists, members of the free professions and all lovers of democracy and progress—

to lend a hand in strengthening the State, in uniting the people, and fortifying the status of the labor movement in Israel!

(From Israel Labor Party, Bulletin No. 3, Tel Aviv, February 1969.)

The organizational structure of the Alignment

A. The name: the Alignment-Israeli Labor Party-United Workers' Party.

B. The parties of the alignment will preserve their ideological and organizational independence.

C. Each party will discuss all subjects it sees fit within its own framework.

The representatives of the two parties will be free to convince each other in all joint forums without being obligated to vote *en bloc* according to prior conclusions of each one of the two parties.

D. The number of representatives of each party in the elected and executive institutions in which the Alignment participates will be determined according to the existing relationship of forces between the parties in the Knesset, Histadrut and local governments at the time the Alignment was formed.

E. Each of the two parties will decide on its representatives in the lists for the elections and elective and executive institutions.

F. The Alignment will maintain an administration that will make a common plan of action for the two parties in the framework of the Alignment. The administration will direct the activity of the Alignment and supervise the coordination between its central and local branches. The administration will convene at fixed intervals.

Each of the parties of the Alignment will be able to raise important problems in the administration with the aim of insuring preliminary talks and the possibility of discussion.

The Administration will bring the contents of its discussions to authorized institutions in which both parties participate for decision and the decision will be made there on all matters included in the Alignment agreement in a democratic way. The Administration is not a decision-making and voting institution.

G. The numerical composition of the administration of the Alignment will be based on a 6 to 9 ratio.

H. The Alignment will also have joint activities in the local branches of the parties which will be coordinated and implemented by the secretaries of the branches.

I. The Political Committee will serve the Alignment as a framework for discussion and decision on political matters.

Representation in it will be in accordance with the relationship of forces in the Knesset and its decisions will be made democratically, except for matters which, in accordance with the Alignment agreement, Mapam preserves the right of appearing independently. The Committee will convene at regular intervals.

J. The Labor Party and Mapam will establish an Economic Committee according to rules that they shall determine between them.

K. The Alignment will only be extended to include other parties or public bodies with the approval of both parties.

(From the "Declaration of the Alignment," published in Mapam Bulletin No. 13, March 1969, Tel Aviv.)

26 • The Earthquake of '73 and Its Aftermath

The short period of time between the Histadrut elections and the elections to the Knesset was interrupted by the invasion of the Syrian and Egyptian armies (on October 6). This event, of course, not only put off the Knesset elections to December 31, but also caused deep shocks and far-reaching changes in public opinion and the political scene and put its impress on the election campaign in November and December of 1973. The rightist opposition, united in the Likud, charged the government and the Alignment with responsibility for the "military blunder" that made possible the preliminary successes of the Syrian and Egyptian armies from the sixth to the eighth of October, as well as the heavy losses suffered by Zahal. (The "blunder" charge centers mainly about the government's failure to mobilize the reserves in time in view of the tremendous enemy military concentrations on the borders, and on Zahal's failure to take the military initiative as in June 1967.) The opposition also attacked the government and the Alignment for accepting Security Council's Resolution 338 on the cease-fire, for accepting Dr. Kissinger's six-point program, and for its agreement to participate in a peace conference in Geneva on the basis of a possible territorial compromise.

However, though the Likud made its all-out criticism of the "military blunder" its main election plank, the doves argued that in addition to the organizational, technical and military mistakes that were now being investigated both by the Army itself and a civilian committee of investigators, it was precisely the mistaken assumptions and misleading conclusions of the hawks, at least partially emanating from the right-wing camp itself, which had served as the psychological and ideological ground for these mistakes. As examples, the doves could list some of the following assumptions:

— the Arab armies and soldiers are still as inferior to ours as they were in the past;
— time is working on our side;
— the world powers, world public opinion, and in their wake the Arab countries, too, even if not officially, will slowly come to terms with the fact of the Israeli occupation of Arab land and with their factual annexation to Israel;

— the Arab leaders won't dare to start a war and take the risk of another defeat;
— if another war does break out we will pretty much be able to repeat the lightning war of 1967;
— the Great Powers are interested in a detente and in neutralizing each other militarily; they won't intervene in such a lightning war (or at least not at a too early stage) and wón't prevent us from winning a clear-cut victory;

All these assumptions and expectations were disproved in October 1973 and revealed to be mistaken and false. This fact, however, did not prevent the right-wing and chauvinist Likud from trying to exploit the widespread bitterness over the "blunder" and the great losses, in order to profit at the polls.

Among certain circles, some of them inimical to Israel and some simply lacking in information, as well as among an insignificant minority within Israel itself (a minority itself splintered into different groups and factions), the charge was often made in the past that "the government of Israel and the Israel Labor Party are ruled by hawks." (For that reason, too, they considered Mapam's alignment with the Labor Party to be a "fatal mistake." This charge was based mainly on the government's refusal to accept the demand to return to the *status quo ante,* that is, to agree to evacuate *all* the occupied territories and to accept the June 4, 1967, borders, and on the Israel Government's demand, in return, for recognized, secure and defensible borders. It was often argued against the demand for "defensible borders" that in the era of modern warfare, with the massive use of airpower, long-range artillery and rockets, there is no longer such a thing as a defensible border, and that in our days there is no longer any protection between security and geography or topography.

We find, however, that the same events of October 1973 that exploded the hawks' arguments in their faces also unequivocally proved the invalidity of these last supposedly dovish arguments. If the starting point of the Syrian-Egyptian invasion had been the borders of June 4, 1967, the Syrian armor might have overrun the Galilee and perhaps gotten as far as Haifa even before the Israeli High Command succeeded in mobilizing the reserves, in holding up the invasion and in going over to a counteroffensive. In such an event any American or international guarantee would have proven to be meaningless and useless. After October 1973 the demand to evacuate the whole Golan Heights is a demand for national suicide, pure and simple, and it doesn't matter if the demand comes from ill-intentioned enemies or from innocent friends who aren't well versed on the facts of the situation.

For this reason, the essence of the conflict between the hawks and the doves in Israel lies in the fact that the hawks favor annexing the occupied territories to Israel and oppose returning any "liberated" territories, while the doves are striving for a compromise in which Israel will agree, as part of a formal and unequivocal peace treaty, to return *most* of the occupied territories and to retreat to mutually recognized and secure borders; that is, to borders that are defensible.

The Elections of December 1973

The polarization between doves and hawks has shown its signs within the ranks of the Israel Labor Party, too. Minister of Security Moshe Dayan has lost status since October 6, as have also his colleagues in the hawkish right wing of the party. A considerable section of the general public and of the party, too, consider Dayan to bear the brunt of responsibility for the military mistakes, and to share responsibility with the Minister Israel Galili, the Prime Minister's closest adviser, for the unreality and immobility of Israel's foreign and security policies in recent years. One section of the party's General Committee wanted Dayan and Galili removed from their positions in the leadership, even before the elections; specifically, they wanted them removed from the top of the party's list of candidates.

This latter demand was presented formally as the demand that the list of candidates be reopened, that is, that it be possible to present new lists of candidates in place of those that had been put together before October 6. Unfortunately, this demand, if accepted, would have meant, because of formalistic and technical reasons, putting off the elections to a still later date. Such a postponement, even if it gained popularity among the electorate, would have exposed the Labor Party to heavy pressure to establish a broad coalition as a "National Union Government," with the argument that the old government no longer had a legal or moral mandate to make any far-reaching decisions. Such a coalition would have led to immobilization and complete political paralysis, would have prevented Israel's participation in the Geneva peace conference, or at least deprived Israel's delegation there of any possibility of maneuvering or of revealing any dynamic peace initiatives.

The Labor Party's Central Committee, in its session at the end of November 1973, decided by a large majority against postponing the elections and against the idea of a national union government after the elections. However, since it didn't want to take the risk, a few weeks before the elections, of a split and the possible departure of Dayan's group from the party, it was also compelled to put off the problem of composing the new leadership and government to after the elections. Mapam and the doves in the Labor Party stated that in their views there would be no room in the coming government for the hawks or the semi-hawks in general, and for Moshe Dayan in particular.

Ever since the October War not only Mapam but also many members of the Labor Party Central Committee had demanded the annulment of the "Galili Paper" and the revision of the Alignment's election platform in a more consistent dovish direction.

The Labor Party's Central Committee, meeting in the beginning of December, did not, indeed, agree to drop the Galili Paper formally (in order to guarantee the party's unity towards the elections, but a committee composed of representatives of all the main factions of the party presented the Central Committee with a new document, adopted by the Committee as a whole, and containing 14 principles. This new document, even though also a compromise, was essentially of a dovish character and stressed Israel's readiness for peace negotiations, for peace initiatives and territorial compromises, while, of course, guaranteeing defensible borders. The Galili Paper, though not annulled, has been put on ice, the doves declaring that it is dead, and Dayan's supporters that it is still alive. It was in an emphatically dovish tone that the Alignment conducted the election campaign, in the face of the rightist Likud's attacks, and it was in the same spirit that Israel's Foreign Minister, Abba Eban, made his address at the opening session of the Geneva Peace Conference on December 21, 1973.

The election to the Eighth Knesset, held on December 31, 1973, faced the Israeli voter with a difficult dilemma. On the one hand, he wanted to express his bitterness and protest over the establishment's mistakes in general and those of the sixth of October in particular, by voting against the Alignment. He didn't, on the other hand, want to endanger the attempt being made in Geneva to finally reach some political settlement and perhaps even the beginnings of peace. Bringing the Likud to power would have ended any such hopes. Since these two desires—to punish the Alignment and to explore the possibilities of peace—neutralized each other, the elections didn't lead to any clear decision or to any change in administration. The Alignment suffered a slight decline (51 instead of 56 of the Knesset's 120 seats); the Likud gained somewhat (39 instead of 32). In the municipal sphere the Alignment preserved most of its positions, except for Tel Aviv, where the administration passed into the hands of a coalition headed by the Likud instead of by the Alignment.

The religious parties declined appreciably in favor of the Likud (the National Religious Party obtained ten instead of twelve seats; the Torah Front, (five instead of six). The Independent Liberals maintained their strength (four), as did Moked (Focus), which kept the one seat its Maki members had held previously. Rakah went up from three to four, while most of the smaller lists, some of them older ones and some new, didn't receive the 1 percent minimum necessary for representation in the Knesset, crushed as they were by the duel between the two big camps, and their specific programs and stresses overshadowed by the decision between the attempt at peace and the perpetuation of war.[1] Such was the fate of Meri (Haolam Hazeh and allies), as well as of the Black Panthers who had won some success in the Histadrut elections but appeared in the campaign for the Knesset divided into two factions, both of which were crushed.[1] A new phenomenon on the political scene was the "Movement for the Citizen's Rights" headed by Mrs. Shulamit Aloni, who had left the Labor Party some months before the elections because of personal and organizational differences, as well as disagreement with the party leadership over matters of legislation and domestic policies, though not on foreign affairs. The "Movement" won three seats in the Knesset, mainly at the Labor Party's expense—a protest vote without desiring to move too far away. The "Movement" apparently also took some of the traditional votes of Ha-olam Hazeh. From its inception the "Movement" has demonstrated a certain measure of proximity in views to the Independent Liberals and they considered to draw closer and to establish a joint parliamentary bloc.

The election results made it possible for the Alignment to form a government with a stable majority (Alignment, 51; Independent Liberals, 4; National Religious Party, 10; the Alignment-affiliated Arab lists, 3; and the Movement for the Citizens Rights, 3. This time, however, the renewal of the traditional coalition came up against great difficulties. With the parliamentary decline of the Alignment's strength, the National Religious Party's relative weight increased and led it to increase its pressure for concessions in legislation, the educational system, and domestic and foreign policies. Since the National Religious Party also has a strong hawkish wing (especially opposing any possible territorial concessions on the West bank of the Jordan), and since the Labor Party also contains the same kind of hawk minority, even after the re-establishment of the coalition, the new government had to expect great difficulties in freely exerting influence over the negotiations in Geneva and over the policies of peace and the readiness for territorial compromises.

Finally, after tiring negotiations and dramatic crises, Golda Meir was able to present the Knesset, on March 10, 1974, with her new government, composed of the Alignment, the National Religious party, and the Independent Liberals. This Coalition Cabinet, however, didn't last longer

1. This also seems to explain the decline of the religious parties in favor of the Likud.
2. During the election campaign in the beginning of 1977, the Black Panther Movement disintegrated completely. One group joined the Democratic Movement for Change; another, Rakah; some, Moked; and the rest split into two groups. The one called itself "Zionist Panthers," whereas the other formed other groups—"Liberty, Workers' and Slum Dwellers' List." However, none of them succeeded in winning a seat in the Knesset or the National Congress of the Histadrut. (See Chapter 28.)

than a month. On April 11 the Prime Minister submitted her own and her colleagues' resignations. The Cabinet crisis emerged in the wake of the interim report of the "Agranat Inquiry Commission," appointed by the government to investigate the causes and responsibility for the "blunders" on the eve of the October War. This interim report, issued on April 1, put the blame exclusively on the Chief-of-Staff of the Israel Defense Forces and on the Chief of Intelligence, without commenting on the parliamentary responsibility of the Defense Minister. The public, however, refused to accept this artificial separation between the Chief-of-Staff's and the Defense Minister's responsibility, and demanded General Dayan's resignation or dismissal. The left-socialist Mapam, which had put forward this demand even before the publication of the interim report, was now joined by the majority of the Labor Party, whereas Dayan's own Rafi faction expressed its loyalty to and solidarity with their leader. Since Dayan refused to resign, and Rafi threatened to vote against the government, in case Dayan were to be dismissed, Golda Meir saw no choice other than to submit her resignation.

Another reason for that dramatic step was what Golda Meir referred to as "a ferment which can't be ignored." This ferment manifested itself in a variety of protest groups. Their activities and spokesmen were recruited from among young people who in the past had been "political innocents"—mainly ex-soldiers and Army officers. These groups demand a radical removal of the whole "old establishment," and in particular the dismissal of all the statesmen and personalities who have been, in one way or another, involved with the "blunder" of October 1973. Within the Labor Party this popular wave has been reflected in the struggle for democratization of party life, internal electoral reform and rejuvenation of the party leadership.

After Golda Meir

After the resignation of Golda Meir's Cabinet, two alternatives remained: one, to decide on holding new elections in the autumn, with the outgoing Cabinet acting as caretaker government until then; the other was for the Labor Party immediately to appoint Golda Meir's successor, and for the President of the State then to call on him to form a new Cabinet.

After long dicussions, the executive of the Labor Party decided at its meeting on April 21–22, by a majority of 283 to 170, in favor of forming a new Cabinet. Following that decision, the executive was obliged to elect its nominee for the premiership. The most popular candidate for the task, who would have been accepted by nearly all sections of the party as the natural successor, was the Finance Minister, Pinhas Sapir. However, Sapir refused and all efforts to change his decision were in vain.

From a long list of candidates, the final contest was held between Information Minister Shimon Peres and the Labor Minister, Yitshak Rabin. Shimon Peres, one of the Rafi leaders, could rely on the support of his own faction, as well as a section of the former Mapai. General Yitshak Rabin, the architect of the Six-Day War victory and later Israel's Ambassador to Washington, had been scarcely involved in internal party politics but enjoyed the support of the Ahdut Haavoda faction, as well as that of many former Mapai members. For the first time in Israel's history, the Premier-designate was not to be nominated by his predecessor or some "inner ring," but to be elected by secret ballot at a meeting of the party executive. Yitshak Rabin won by a narrow majority of 298 to 254 (54 to 46 percent), and was afterwards elected unanimously as the Labor Party's nominee for the premiership.

The close vote at the ballot came as a surprise, since Rabin had been openly recommended by Pinhas Sapir, the "strong man" of the former Mapai and present Labor Party. This surprise support for Peres may have come from all kinds of ideological, factional and personal motivations on the part of the executive members. It might also be explained, however, by the dilemma faced by the former Mapai (which forms the bulk of the Labor Party executive): should it elect a man like Rabin, who has good chances of improving the image of the Labor Party in the eyes of the electorate and of the younger generation in particular, or should it elect a man like Shimon Peres, who has considerably richer experience in home and party politics? An additional consideration might have been desired to maintain party unity by a demonstration of goodwill, as manifested in a massive vote for minority leader Peres.

For obvious reasons, Mapam could not interfere in the internal discussions and decisions of its Alignment partner—the Labor Party. Nevertheless it had been made quite clear to the Labor Party that selecting the Rafi leader, Shimon Peres, as Premier-designate would mean putting an end to the Labor–Mapam Alignment. On the other hand, Yitshak Rabin could rely on Mapam's support, as long as he would not yield to pressures exerted by the Likud, the National Religious Party, or the rightist and hawkish Rafi wing of his own party. Such a firm stand, however, could not be taken for granted, especially since the many votes won by Rabin's rival, Shimon Peres, at the party executive, secure him a key position in any Israeli Cabinet. As expected, the efforts of reconstituting the outgoing coalition were in vain, since Mapam and the Independent Liberals vetoed any further concessions to the National Religious Party, the latter being scared of a party split and of a walkout of its "radical" (that is, fanatically orthodox and nationalist) youth. The National Religious Party's decision to stay out of the government turned the scales within the Alignment in favor of forming a "small coalition," composed of the Alignment (54), the Independent Liberals (4) and the Civil Rights Movement (3), a solution that had been favored from the beginning by Mapam and the Independent Liberals.

However, Rafi was completely opposed to the solution of a small coalition, which was the opposite of its official slogan of a "National Unity Government." In addition, the Labor Party executive has been split over the issue of including or not including Shulamit Aloni's civil rights movement in the Cabinet. Golda Meir and her close supporters made it quite clear that they would resent such an inclusion, because this would shift the government's political line sharply in a dovish direction. At the same time, this would block the way for the National Religious Party to rejoin the Cabinet at a later date. Needless to say, Rafi wholeheartedly shared Golda Meir's resentments and misgivings. In order to avoid a showdown with Golda Meir and her supporters, the Labor Party leadership tried hard to form a coalition of 58 (Alignment and Independent Liberals). However, the Independent Liberals refused to join such a minority government and insisted on including the civil rights movement as well. When the Labor Party executive met on May 19, it could no longer evade a clear-cut choice between the formation of a government based on the support by 61 Knesset members or setting up a "National Unity Government."

With an overwhelming majority of 302 to 36 (six abstentions), the executive authorized Yitshak Rabin to form a Cabinet, including the Alignment, the Independent Liberals, and the civil rights movement. The resolution left the door open for the National Religious Party to join the coalition at a later date. A Rafi motion to open talks with the Likud in order to form a national unity government was voted down by 262 to 48, with eight abstentions. Only then was Yitshak Rabin able to form his Cabinet and to present it to the Knesset, winning a vote of confidence of 61 to 54, with five abstentions (June 3, 1974).

The "coalition of the sixty-one" did not last longer than half a year. The Rafi wing of the Labor Party made every possible effort to "correct the too-dovish character of the Cabinet" by including the National Religious Party. The latter was split on this issue. While the young leadership, with its chavinist inclinations and Likud sympathies, vigorously opposed the return of the government, the old leaders were eager to do so and they overruled the opposition by a 60–40 percent majority. The Prime Minister announced that the co-option of the NRP into the existing Cabinet was to be carried out on the basis of the coalition program as agreed to when the government was inaugurated; on the other hand, he promised the NRP that new elections would be held when negotiations regarding territorial concessions on the West Bank reached the stage of final decision. Mapam, which after the elections had vetoed the inclusion of the NRP in the coalition on the latter's terms (essential changes in the status quo on religious issues), now agreed to the co-option, mainly in order to secure a broader parlimentary basis for the Cabinet. Shulamit Aloni's civil rights movement, however, left the coalition and joined the opposition (November 1974).

27 • The Economic Background (1966–1976)

The Policies of "Economic Slowdown"

The coalition government headed by Levi Eshkol that was formed in January 1966 was immediately faced with a number of critical problems, first in the economic sphere and then, increasingly, in the military sphere.

In 1964 the Israeli economy had reached a peak in overexpansion distinguished by spiraling incomes and prices and, as a result, rising consumption and imports. As the inevitable consequence, a rapid increase in the foreign trade deficit made it necessary to bring an end to this overheating. As a matter of fact, the problem went beyond the immediate specific situation and demanded structural changes in order to effect a large-scale expansion in exports by increasing labor productivity and lowering costs of production, as well as by transferring investment capital, credits, and manpower from less important and efficient plants, industries and services to primary production branches and export industries.

How was this change to be effected? On this, opinions were divided, especially between Mapai, backed by bourgeois economists, and Mapam. Mapai wanted to effect the change by freezing wages and ending the system of wage increments linked to the cost-of-living index, cutting investments and credits for non-export industries, reducing government outlays and especially the development budget, by far-reaching limitations in the building industry, and by closing down industrial plants, even when this meant temporary unemployment. This program's partisans also hoped that considerable unemployment would help raise productivity and cut down consumption. Mapam, on the other hand, argued that structural changes should be effected mainly by a planned expansion of the national product, and by transferring capital and manpower to preferred industries. This, Mapam claimed, could be done without freezing wages, depriving workers of their cost-of-living increments or lowering their standards of living. It also did not need the whip of unemployment. Instead, the standard of living and purchasing power of the masses could be protected by maintaining the system of cost-of-living increments and stabilizing prices, by firm control over middlemen and importers, and the like. The emphasis, Mapam said, had to be put on planning and efficiency in industry, by expanding the public and Histadrut sectors of industry, imposing taxes on the wealthy, encouraging exports, and an employment policy guiding workers into preferred industries.

However, even some of the partisans of Mapai's program shared Mapam's view that the timing of the proposed drastic program was a serious mistake. Instead of effecting the structural changes during the upswing, this had been put off from time to time for various reasons (of which election considerations were not the least important. The program was actually put into operation when immigration began to dwindle, leading to a cut-down in building activity and spreading unemployment in this field. Some of the program's supporters also argued, with Mapam, that the new program should have been meticulously planned in advance so that the additional cut-downs in building and the closed plants would coincide with the establishment of new plants or the expansion of the preferred ones which could absorb the displaced workers with the help of the expanded development budget. In actuality, the policy of economic slowdown was put into operation at an inappropiate time without providing other places of employment or working out new projects. Its chief result, therefore, was an alarming rise in unemployment, reaching—in January 1967—a peak of 116,000 workers (12 percent of the total labor force). The unemployment struck hardest at the building workers, among whom were large numbers of new immigrants and Arab laborers and the less permanently established lower echelons of industrial workers. The housing program to eliminate the slums (one of Mapam's chief social demands on joining the government) was cut, and there was a rapid decline in the standard of living and mass purchasing power. Ultimately, the slow-down policy created a new economic crisis and a crisis of faith marked by feelings of insecurity and a drop in morale.

When Mapam's alternative program was rejected and the government began the harsh implementation of the slowdown policies, voices within Mapam began to demand that the party leave the coalition—either immediately or after posing an ultimatum to change policies and to stop the growing unemployment. The majority of the party rejected these demands and decided that in time of crisis it was Mapam's task to defend the unemployed and potentially unemployed—within the government, in order to apply pressure for an unemployment insurance law, to try to stop the precipitate closing of plants and to accelerate the planning and establishment of new plants or the expansion of existing ones—in short, to adopt a policy of "slowing down the slowdown." At the same time Mapam began a wide-scale propaganda campaign on these issues in the press and in the shops. Despite its participation in the government, it took its place at the head of demonstrations organized by workers' committees in the plants and among the unemployed.

After the war of 1967, Israel's economy recovered slowly, as it had after previous depressions, as in 1952-1953, when Israeli economy had to face severe unemployment and a decline of the GNP; but in the second half of 1954 the economy had begun to recover and to enter a stage of expansion that persisted up to 1965. In the period 1961-1966 the GNP increased at an average yearly rate of 8.6 percent, and during 1967-1972 it grew roughly at the same pace (9 percent). The value of industrial production increased at an average yearly rate of 11.4 percent in the 1961-1966 period, whereas during 1967-1972 the real yearly increase came to 11.9 percent. Unemployment went down again (in 1968) to the 1965 level—54,000, or 6 percent of the total labor force (excluding eastern Jerusalem). However, even if the war was over, the unrest on the borders, the "attrition war" with Egypt, etc., going on, and the warlike atmosphere continued and had its curbing impact on trade union activity and labor disputes. Only in the summer of 1970 was the cease-fire with Egypt renewed, and on the frontiers relative quiet was established. Following this, the latent social tensions in Israel's society came again to the fore.

Social gaps and tensions

Many of the social and economic problems that had been overshadowed and put off for future treatment because of the tense security situation before the 1967 war and during the "war of attrition" have surfaced and even exploded, when the tension on the borders has somewhat subsided. We are not concerned here only with the wage-freeze, but also with the shortage of housing for young couples, slum clearance, and the need for greater and more intensive efforts to close the social gap dividing the Jewish communities from the East and the West. The last named problem, in particular, is a delicate and complicated one. On the one hand, there is no discrimination in Israel, neither on the part of any official, public or political organization, nor on the part of the vast majority of those coming from the West against the members of the Oriental communities. On the contrary, the need for integration is widely understood and accepted as one of the elementary postulates of the Zionist idea and Israel's security. On the other hand, however, objective conditions have led to a situation in which there *is* a social gap, and in which many of the members of the Oriental communities *are* discriminated against and suffer deprivation as compared to members of the western groups.

Among these objective conditions we could list the nature of the societies and economies of their countries of origin in the Middle East and North Africa. The heritage they bring with them also reveals itself later in Israel, reflected in low levels of education, the lack of technical traditions or training, large families, indescribable housing conditions, and life on the fringe of poverty. However, even if the discrimination is not the result of any intentions but only of objective situations, it is felt psychologically as deprivation *by intention*, as "ethnic (or communal) discrimination." The same holds true when they meet the new immigrants from the Soviet Union or the Western countries: when they see new and modern houses being built near their own slums, it is only natural that envy and discrimination are felt. As far as they are concerned, it doesn't make any difference that these houses are built by the mobilized resources of world Jewry for the specific purposes of absorbing immigration.

Rational explanations or expressions of goodwill won't help here. This delicate and complicated problem can only be solved by concentrated actions on two levels. The first, by giving budgetary priority to solving the problems of these communities, by providing cheap housing projects adapted to the size of the large families, by additional educational activities, occupational training, etc. The second, by an unremitting struggle to raise the wages of the lower-earning groups which are composed mainly of members of these Oriental communities (and Arab workers). One step in this is the compulsory minimum wage linked to the average level of wages in Israel. The wage-freeze, official or unofficial, hits first of all at them and their possibilities of developing and overcoming the heritage of the past, and at any real prospects of their integration with the members of the other communities. The social and ethnical tensions were the background for the formation, in 1971, of the Black Panther group (after tentative starts in 1970). The group was formed by members of the Oriental communities who decided to "protect against ethnical discrimination" and who put violent demonstrations at the base of their propaganda and activity. At first it seemed to some of the marginal leftist groups that these violent communal manifestations would provide them with the mass basis they were lacking. It soon became evident, however, that these hopes were unfounded. Large sections of the Oriental communities came from Arab countries in which they were persecuted minorities and they still often bear anti-Arab sentiments. In addition, the somewhat *Lumpenproletariat* mentality that is characteristic of many of them makes them facile objects of reactionary social demagogy: against "the (Ashkenazi) establishment," against the better-established organized workers, against the "rich Histadrut" or the "luxuriously" modern kibbutzim. In other words, at the present time the Oriental communities form an unexhausted reservoir of candidates for the Gahal chauvinism and social anti-establishment demagogy in which Herut's propagandists in particular have been specializing for over a generation. The integration of the members of the Oriental communities within the ranks of the Israeli working class and labor movement is not something that can enjoy immediate success by dubious alliances with reactionary communal groups; it must be an extended process of education, conviction and the fraternity of joint economic, social and political struggles.

And still, despite all the primitivism of their views on complex social problems as seen through the crooked mirror of "communal discrimination," or "communal organization," fairness compels us to admit that the Black Panthers' spectacular and sometimes violent activities served to make the Israeli public—the press, the government, the Histadrut, the municipalities and the parties—see the seriousness of the problem with the accumulation of bitterness and attendant dangers of a social and communal explosion. Most important it became clear that no considerations of security, of budgets or long-range economic planning, no matter how reasonable or justified in themselves, could stand in the way of immediately and seriously confronting the social problems that the Israeli public had long become accustomed to put off in favor of other priorities—security, immigration and integration of the new immigrants, etc.

Along with the Black Panther demonstrations, young couples invading new apartments, and the like, there has also been a rising wave of strikes, generally without trade union sanction. The common denominator for the demonstrations, invasions and strikes alike has been their nonpolitical character (generally being rather purely communal or purely trade-unionist in character). They don't point, at least at present, to any radicalization toward greater class consciousness or toward socialism. This may be explained by the fact that despite the social troubles, the extended state of emergency on the borders as well as on the military, political and international fronts continues to keep alive within the broader Israeli public a sense of national and interclass solidarity which still overshadows the social and political differentiation and antagonisms. This process is certainly true for the Arab countries as well; in any case, it holds good for Israel. From this aspect as well, in addition to all the others, peace is vital for the labor movement in Israel and for the Middle East as a whole, if the processes of social differentiation and progress are to take on their full force.

As might have been predicted, a radical change of mood occurred as a result of the October War. As following the Six-Day War and again during the war of attrition in the late '60s, everybody was once more aware of the national emergency, and the feeling of national solidarity again became paramount. It looked as if the process of mounting social tension and escalating class struggle was again leveling off. This became quite apparent in the results of the Knesset elections held on December 31, when social issues proved to have no appeal. The Black Panthers, who had scored a remarkable success in the Histadrut elections on September 11, failed to receive even one single seat in the new Knesset. The same holds true for the first half of 1974, when Israelis had other troubles to worry about, such as the war of attrition on the Golan Heights or the murderous attacks—mostly affecting women and children—carried out by terrorists from across the Lebanese border.

And, yet, it was an inexcusable mistake, a dangerous illusion, to think that the tackling of social problems could again be postponed indefinitely by alleging considerations of security or budget priorities. After all, during the last years not one of the problems we mentioned earlier has been dealt with seriously, let alone solved. Good intentions and plans that existed before the October War have again been shelved.

Trends and Processes in Israel's Economy, 1972-1976

The years 1975-1976 may be regarded as a somehow exceptional period in the development of the Israeli economy, which had to face difficulties of unprecedented severity. Most salient of these is the tremendous balance-of-payments deficit, which has reached $4 billion. Yet in other fields, too, difficulties arose: economic growth slowed down and in 1975 nearly came to a standstill (only 0.4 percent increase in the GNP). Prices went up large percentages per year, budget deficits amounted to billions of pounds, and allocations for development and social services (such as education, health, housing, etc.) had to be reduced. True, during the same period considerable achievements can be registered in agriculture and in a number of industries (especially so in the technologically advanced ones, such as metals and machinery, transport equipment, electrical equipment and electronics, chemical products, etc.). Lately, a remarkable increase in tourism has become notable, as well as in a number of export branches. In spite of these desirable phenomena the overall picture is a rather gloomy one, and there are already repercussions in the social-economic field as well as in the political and security arena (a growing dependence of Israel upon the United States and a shifting of the balance of economic strength between Israel and her Arab neighbors to the disadvantage of the former).

After the October War tension has not reduced in the area and Israel had to devote to her security needs much larger sums than before the war. We may quote here the following data: In 1972 security expenditure amounted to I £6.2 b. Owing to the war the amount nearly doubled in 1973 to 12.2 b. Yet this increase continued after the war, too, to the tune of I£16.5 b in 1974 and 26.5 b in 1975, i.e., within four years security expenditure grew nearly four- and fivefold at current prices, and even taking into account inflation, security expenditure has doubled in real terms over these years. The relative share of security in the GNP, too, has risen sharply: from 21 percent in 1972 to 32.6 percent in 1973; 35.4 percent in 1975 and 47 percent in 1976. Moreover, imports for security accounted to $555 m. in 1971 and decreased to $490 m. in 1972, but then came a leap to $1,253 b. in 1973 and $1,846 b. in 1975. These figures include direct imports of security items only and, adding indirect import items (i.e., imports for locally produced items), we arrive at a total of $2,4 b. for security imports. This ever-increasing load of security expenditure exerted a most negative influence upon the overall economic situation, and it may be stated that, of the $4 b. current deficit in the balance of payments for 1975, no less than $2.5 b., about 60 percent, are due to security expenditure. This enormous increase also caused ever-growing current budget deficits which, in turn, accelerated inflation. It also absorbed a large proportion of human and material resources (workers, raw materials, etc.) and limited the development of production and exports. So we can see that Israel's increasing security efforts during the last years were the dominant factor that loomed large over the economic development as a whole and severely aggravated the "conventional difficulties" such as those originating from the enormous price rises during the years 1973—1976 on the world market for everything Israel has to import (and other difficulties as well).

One of the most serious problems of Israel's economy and politics is her growing dependence upon American aid. In 1972 Israel received U.S. grants to the amount of $60 m. If we deduct this sum from the total capital transfers for that year—$1,055 b.—Israel had at her disposal nearly $1 b. from the United Jewish Appeal, transfers of various institutions, German reparations and private capital transfers. This was enough to cover 90 percent of the current deficit so that dependence upon American aid was very limited indeed. In 1975 the picture was very different: The current deficit amounted to $4,037 b., as stated, while capital transfers, apart from American grants-in-aid, had risen only slightly, to $1,091 b. There remained a gap of nearly $3 b. to be covered by the U.S. government grants or loans, and loans from other sources. The growing dependence upon American assistance in the form of grants or loans is shown in the following figures, where U.S. aid is compared with the total amount of long- and medium-term capital imports into Israel (in $ billions):

Year	U.S. aid grants & loans	Total capital imported	U.S. aid as percentage of total capital imports
1969	0.054	0.659	8.2%
1972	0.262	1.777	14.7
1975	1.855	3.256	57.0

Source: Bank of Israel Report for 1975.

Inflation is certainly not a phenomenon typical of Israel's present economy only, but on the other hand, it is one of the main components of that economy. Over the last years and especially so since 1973, inflationary pressure has been mounting in Israel. The consumers' price index rose by 20 percent in 1973, by 39.7 percent in 1974, and by 39.3 percent in 1975, while in 1970-1972 the average yearly rise had been no more than 10.3 percent. Price rises in Israel have been accelerating over the last years and what happened may well be termed galloping inflation. This tendency has continued in 1976, with a rise of nearly 38 percent. The rise in wholesale prices of industrial products as well as in the input for housing construction was even steeper than that of consumers' prices.

One of the most important parts (though only one of them) in the price inflation of these last years is attributable to the ever-increasing amount of "black capital" that continues to accumulate and to exert pressure on the markets of goods, services and property of all kinds. In spite of tax reforms carried out, the government has not succeeded in curbing this phenomenon. It is a fact that, while the government has managed to increase the collection of corporation tax, collection of income tax from individudal nonsalaried earners is lagging and the arrears are very large. The share of nonsalaried earners in the total amount of income tax collected decreased from 17.8 percent in 1972 to only 13.7 in 1975.

Over the last years social problems and tensions have been mounting; we speak of income distribution and social differentiation of salaries, poverty, etc. In this field we may mention a number of salient facts:

a. The average monthly wages index per full-time worker rose from $153.2 in 1972 to $359.8 in 1975 (1965 = 100). Nominal wages thus rose two- and three-fold. As the consumers' price index also rose two- and three-fold over the same period, real wages have remained constant over the whole period, while production per worker in the Israeli economy rose by 10.4 percent. In other words, wage earners received no reward for increased productivity, while profits continued to grow apace.

b. According to the Bank of Israel Report for 1975, the share of wages and salaries in the total income derived from economic activities in Israel remained constant: 58.9 percent for the years 1968-1972, and again 59 percent in 1975. On the other hand, manpower surveys show that wage and salary earners made up 76.3 percent of the total gainfully employed as against 73.5 percent in 1968-1972. This means that while the percentage of wage earners in the economically active population has risen, their share in the national income has not; or in other words, each individual wage earner's slice of the national "cake" has diminished.

c. Data also indicate a growing differentiation of incomes between wage earners, when incomes of the two lowest cohorts decreased from 8.1 percent of total wage earners' income in 1971 to 7.3 percent in 1974, while the two upper cohorts increased their share from 38 percent to 39.2 percent.

Owing to financial difficulties, the government drastically reduced vital welfare services such as housing, education, health etc. In 1972 there were 89,400 Jewish families living under conditions of overcrowding (more than two persons per room) and in 1975 their number still stood at 75,800 families or about 400,000 persons.

These are only a few features of the complexity of contemporary Israeli economy, but as a complementing background chapter they may serve their purpose.

Divergent Approaches

The government tried to overcome the above specified grave problems and difficulties (such as drastic deterioration in the current balance of payments deficit, galloping inflation, stagnation of economic growth, increasing dependence upon the United States, widening of the social gap, and inequality in wage and income levels, etc.) by slowing down economic activity. Practically this "cooling down" was aimed at reining in the expanding demand for local consumption, so as to reduce imports and to freeze resources for a rapid increase of exports. In order to stop the galloping inflationary trends the government applied a number of measures such as a considerable reduction of building acitivites (both public housing and various non-housing projects); curtailing of government development budgets and of important public services; reduction of subsidies; a policy of keeping down wages; limiting cost-of-living allowances to 70 percent of the index rises, etc. These measures no doubt slowed down drastically economic growth in Israel, but as to the question of whether they achieved their main goals, opinions differed, and the official economic policy has been subject to heavy attacks both from the right and the left.

The traditional approach of the bourgeois parties—from the conservative right to the liberal center—maintained that the way to heal the economy and solve its problems was to give maximum freedom and encouragement to private capital and initiative. In their view such freedom and encouragement would help to improve the efficiency of the economy and increase the ability of Israeli products to compete in foreign markets, thereby causing an increased flow of capital to Israel. Their remedies suggested are—at present as in the past—wage freeze, uncontrolled prices, obligatory arbitration in labor disputes (anti-strike and anti-sanctions legislation, etc.). The bourgeois conception of solving the economic problems adds up to "low taxes and a small budget," that is, reducing social services, preaching belt-tightening (which means in effect tightening the belts of the weaker strata and widening the social gap). And last but not least, the bourgeois conception of a "sound economic policy" implies a "reasonable" number of unemployed.

The traditional approach of Mapam (and part of the Labor Party) has always been based on the assumption that strengthening the productive base of Israeli economy, comprehensive economic planning, expanding and consolidating the public sector of the economy (that of the Histadrut and that of the state), and mobilizing the resources of the economy in order to achieve its required goals are indispensable for solving problems and for progress toward economic independence. The way to check the strong inflationary pressure is first and foremost to absorb surplus money and pass it over in the hands of the public—by means of a compulsary loan and taxes on individuals with large incomes, on corporations, etc. Rejecting the bourgois remedies partially adopted by the government, such as stagnation, "controlled unemployment," curtailment of social services and considering enrichment, private capital, index-linked bonds, etc., a taboo—Mapam's alternative suggestions add up to the following:

—Controlled renewal of economic growth;
—Increased efforts to step up exports and to reduce nonvital imports;
—Increased absorption of excess liquidity from the well-to-do through more efficient tax-collection and elimination of tax evasions; a capital gains tax, a land improvement tax and a property tax on financial holdings;
—Better efficiency and maximum savings in public services and in government budgets, including the defense budget—the largest item of public expenditure;
—greater efforts to improve the structure of economy through giving priority to production branches that contribute to exports or replace imports;
—Stress should be laid upon the development of technologically advanced industries that have the best chances for increased exports;
—In order to make a start in narrowing the social gap, budgets for social services (housing, education, health, welfare) ought to be increased, prices of basic consumer goods be frozen and indirect taxes (including value-added tax) not be raised;
—The Histadrut (representing the interests of the working and underprivileged masses) ought to be consulted during the preparatory stages of any economic planning and shaping of policy.*

According to the official economic policy, preference was to be given in 1976–1977 to production workers for wage raises, in order to make those branches of employment more attractive and to facilitate the vital transfer of employees from services to production. However, service occu-

* The data in this chapter are based on economic background material prepared by A. Ahiezra and S. Zarhi for the Economic Committee of Mapam.

pations such as doctors, engineers, etc., put strong pressure on the government and finally achieved considerable wage raises which quickly spread and included all the services. This development (winter 1976–1977) led to a chain reaction: Now the production workers too asked for an additional raise, and the Histadrut had no choice other than to recommend raising their wages by 4 to 5 percent, in spite of the Finance Minister's and the employers' opposition. When this raise was unilaterally implemented in the Histadrut-owned industries, and after the dockers' strike (March 1977) which paralyzed all the ports and caused much harm to the country's citrus exports—the government and the private employers had to give in: "equality" in salaries has more or less been restored, but nothing had come out of the original plan of giving preference to production over services.

SOURCES

Israel's Balance of Payments—1949–1975
(in $ millions at current prices)

Year	Import of Goods & Services	Export of Goods & Services	Deficit
1949	263.0	43.0	220.0
1954	376.5	135.2	241.3
1959	601.7	286.3	315.4
1964	1,184.0	619.2	564.8
1968	1,834.0	1,128.1	695.9
1971	3,083.0	1,874.0	1,209.0
1972	3,326.0	2,225.0	1,101.0
1973	5,421.0	2,779.0	2,642.0
1974	7,035.0	3,648.0	3,387.0
1975	7,846.0	3,827.0	4,036.0

Source: The Israeli Statistical Monthly, April 1965, May 1969, May 1976.

Real Yearly Growth of GNP in Israel (percent), 1961–1975

1961–1966	8.6
1967–1972	9.0
1972	12.0
1973	5.5
1974	7.0
1975	0.5

Source: Israeli Statistical Monthly

Indicators of Economic Development Before and After the Six-Day War

Indicator	1961–66	1967–72
THE MAGNITUDE OF LOCAL PRODUCTION		
1) Average annual increase in GNP (%)	8.6	9.0
2) Average annual increase in industrial production (%)	11.4	11.9
BALANCE OF PAYMENTS AND FOREIGN DEBT		
3) Annual increase in foreign trade deficit (millions of dollars)	17	105
4) Annual increase in foreign debt (millions of dollars)	112	460
PRICES AND INFLATIONARY PRESSURES		
5) Average annual rise in the consumer price index (%)	6.9	6.1(*10.3)
6) Average annual increase in means of payment (millions of Israeli pounds)	190	500
CAPITAL INVESTMENT		
7) Investment in permanent property as a percentage of GNP (%)	29.6	25.9
8) Average annual increase in the supply of capital within the economy (%)	9.5	**7.6
STANDARD-OF-LIVING AND INCOME		
9) Annual per capita increase in private consumption (%)	4.9	3.9
10) Annual increase per working family in real usable income (%)	3.3	**1.6
11) Average annual rate of completed new apartments per thousand residents	15.0	11.0

*1970–1972   **1967–1971

SOURCE: The above data were gathered from the following sources:
a) The Statistical Yearly of Israel, The Central Statistical Office.
b) The Statistical Monthlies of Israel, The Central Statistical Office.
c) The 1973 National Budget, Research Department of the Bank of Israel and the Treasury Dept.
d) The Bank of Israel Report–1971.

Employment in Israel by economic branch—1975

Branch	(thousands)	Percent
Agriculture	71,0	6.4
Industry	268,6	24.3
Electricity & Water	11,2	1.0
Construction	88,7	8.1
Transport & Communications	80,7	7.3
Commerce, Restaurants & Hotels	135,8	12.3
Public Services	296,7	26.9
Finance & Business Services	75,6	6.9
Personal Services	68,1	6.2
Unknown	6,2	0.6
Total	1.102,6	100,0

Source: Monthly Bulletin of Statistics, Supplement, May 1976

Unemployment 1965–1975
(Daily average of adult unemployed)

Year	unemployed
1965	3,200
1970	1,595
1971	938
1972	744
1973	879
1974	844
1975	1,000

Source: Statistical Abstract of Israel 1976, Central Bureau of Statistics, Jerusalem.

Strikes and Lockouts—1965–1975

Year	Strikes & Lockouts	Strikers & Locked Out	Working Days Lost
1965	288	90,210	207,561
1966	286	85,953	147,846
1967	142	25,058	58,286
1968	100	42,146	71,789
1969	114	44,496	102,162
1970	163	114,941	390,260
1971	169	88,265	178,612
1972	168	87,309	236,058
1973	96	122,348	375,023
1974	71	27,141	51,333
1975	117	114,091	164,509

Source: Statistical Abstract of Israel, 1976.

Average Monthly Wages, 1965–1975, by Economic Branch (in I£)

Year	Whole Economy	Agriculture	Industry	Construction	Commerce	Transport & Communications	Finance & Business Services	Public Services	Personal Services
1965	496	333	471	517	521	640	-	530	341
1972	888	521	863	807	812	1,302	1,069	897	544
1975	2,144	1,523	2,182	1,927	1,919	3,081	2,520	2,044	1,350

Sources: National Insurance and Central Bureau of Statistics, Jerusalem, 1974; Monthly Bulletin of Statistics, 12, December 1976, Jerusalem.

Breakdown of Incomes of Urban Wage-earning Families In Israel by Ten Cohorts
(1971–1975, percentages)

Cohorts	1971	1972	1973	1974	1975
Lowest Cohort	3.0	3.0	3.0	2.6	3.0
Second "	5.1	5.0	4.9	4.7	5.0
Third "	6.2	6.1	6.0	5.8	6.1
Fourth "	7.2	7.1	6.9	6.9	7.2
Fifth "	8.1	8.1	7.9	7.9	8.3
Sixth "	9.3	9.1	9.3	9.3	9.5
Seventh "	10.7	10.6	10.7	10.8	10.9
Eighth "	12.4	12.4	12.7	12.8	12.7
Ninth "	15.2	15.4	15.7	15.6	15.2
Highest "	22.8	23.2	22.8	23.6	22.1
Total	100.0	100.0	100.0	100.0	100.0
Inequality Factor (Lorenz Curve)	0.293	0.298	0.300	0.315	0.289

Sources: "Incomes of wage-earning families 1972–1974," series of special publications, 510, published by the Central Statistical Bureau, Jerusalem, and *Statistical Abstract of Israel,* 1976, No. 27.

HISTADRUT'S ECONOMIC PROPOSALS
(Excerpts)

XII. EQUALITY OF BURDEN-SHARING AND IMPROVEMENT IN TAX ADMINISTRATION

Histadrut believes that it is possible to harness the entire community in a special effort to rehabilitate the economy. Even if this task requires a certain mitigation of the citizenry's expectations for further improvements in the standard of living, it would nevertheless be within the realm of possibility would it be clear beyond doubt that the burdens entailed were shared and apportioned fairly in accordance with the capacity of each segment of society, without exception.

Histadrut is prepared to cooperate with the government in helping apportion the burden equitably among the various sectors of the population, and in fostering the moral ethic to get both direct and indirect taxes fully paid.

A. Implementation of the reform in direct taxation in practice, by all sectors of the population, was the goal of the reform. It intended, among other things, to remove tax distortions and inequities, to broaden the circle of taxpayers and to see that "true" taxes were paid.

A full year has now passed since the reform in direct taxes was instituted, the goal of which was to gather "true" taxes from the entire population, without exception. The fact is however that the reform has been fully implemented only in the case of wage-earners. According to the data conveyed by the tax authorities, only a third of the independent (self-employed) who were required by law to keep bookkeeping records have thus far complied and done so.

Similarly there is a considerable lag in the preparation of tax estimates (appraisals) of the independent and self-employed, whose number is about 200,000. According to the figures of the tax authorities at the end of 1975, final estimates for 1974 had only been forthcoming for about 35,000 (18% of the self-employed); for 1973 for 72,000 (36%), and for 1972 for 110,000 (55%). In the case of about 70,000 self-employed (out of a total of 200,000) there exist no dossiers at all in the income-tax offices.

It is essential that an effective operation be launched to uncover all of the self-employed for the purpose of taxation, to prepare tax records for them, and to have the entire public on the tax rolls.

B. Improvement of the Tax Collection System and the War Against "Black" Capital. A major factor causing increased demand in the economy, and consequently expansion in private consumption, is the influence of "black" capital. The working public has done its share in restraining and modifying its living standards, and Histadrut has, among other things, acted in support of a restrained incomes policy which was expressed in the nature of the new wage agreements and in the new long-term agreement with government on the payment of cost-of-living increments. Nevertheless during this period "black" capital continues to grow and amass profits. Excess profits have not been contained, and the tax authorities admit that many billions have avoided taxation.

This phenomenon, added to the severe tax-burden in our country, is a problem of overriding importance, and its persistence adversely affects the morale and the behavior norms of the population. It is consequentially most essential that the organs of government harness every implement at their disposal to guarantee true collection of direct and indirect taxes and to conduct an unrelenting battle against "black" capital, by:

1. Requiring all who are obliged by law to keep financial records (especially since the introduction of VAT) to do so.
2. The establishment of special courts to try tax evaders, and to set minimum punishment for those found guilty of evasion.
3. To prohibit government, public enterprises of Histadrut undertakings from having commercial relations with any business firm or contractor who does not keep financial records.
4. Making it conditional that tax receipts have to be presented before services of various kinds will be rendered.
5. Imposing a one-time levy on capital, the proceeds of which are to be earmarked for defense and social welfare needs.
6. The uncovering of the sources of "black" capital in the country and abroad.
7. In-depth sampling surveys in the self-employed sector, particularly, to promote "true estimates" and full, accurate tax payments.
8. Establishment of a special unit assisted by the best experts in the field to deal with the most serious manifestations of tax evasion.
9. Shifting the emphasis of the largest part of the tax apparatus and employees from routine activity to active attention to the task of uncovering "black" capital and tax evaders, and to the

realization of "true" tax collections from those who have thus far managed to avoid the net.
10. By the government's utilization of public bodies and institutions to help in the struggle against tax evasion.
11. By affixing in every business enterprise, shop or office which keeps proper records, a display sign reading "We keep records," for the public to see.
12. The publication of a taxpayers' list, and the publication each year of the tax estimate figures and the taxes actually paid, by sub-branch.

C. Closing the Gap Between Tax on Capital and Tax on Work

The existence of this discriminatory differential (to the advantage of capital) is a cause of social injustice and serves to distort the income distribution proportion and pattern as between labor and capital. During the last decade this differential has been considerably widened without justification.

D. Reform of the Capital Market will be insisted upon by Histadrut. The government must bring about a reform in the capital market to abrogate existing and prevent future advantages to capital investment whose interest and c.o.l. linkage increments are tax free.

It is also necessary to institute reforms with regard to the conditions under which government securities are presently sold, and in the manner and criteria of granting of government loans and credits and security guarantees.

It is clear that the c.o.l. linkage conditions should not be impaired or worsened in the case of investments whose purpose it is to safeguard pensions, for social purposes, for education, for housing, and for long-term savings. The government should, though, avoid giving full linkage guarantees to negotiable securities whose principal beneficiaries are the affluent. By having done so capital market investments for real economic development have been blocked.

We cannot accede to the fact that though the maximum a wage earner can expect as compensation for price rises is a 70% c.o.l. increment after a time lag of half a year, compensation for capital invested in securities is 100%, immediate, and tax-free into the bargain.

We are not proposing changing the conditions of government securities issued in the past; however, as stated, we are of the opinion that it is necessary to gradually change the terms of new issues of government securities to capital as follows:

1. New government security issues in the future should be linked at a maximum rate of 70 percent to the c.o.l. index, in accordance with the recommendations of the Ben Shahar Commission.
   There is no reason why security holders should obtain immediate compensatory adjustments for price rises abroad or for price increases which stem from the government's alteration of the value of the currency (devaluation).
2. All newly-issued government guaranteed securities should be issued and registered by name only, and not as bearer bonds. Also, all bearer bonds issued in the past should gradually be exchanged for registered-by-name securities.
3. Holders of negotiable securities should be given the opportunity to convert to long-term (three to five years) saving plans. The guide-

line and principle behind the reform proposals should be to equalize conditions and earnings gained by capital with the compensation labor has been getting.

E. Capital Concessions

It is necessary to establish a commission and to vest it with authority to examine all capital concessions granted to various companies during the last decade, in order to determine, in retrospect, whether there was ample justification in granting extraordinary concessions and easements in real estate tax abatements, for preferred capital.

We are proposing, **inter alia,** that export incentives should not be granted indiscriminately, but only after strict testing in every instance, and through the conduct of a constant audit to ascertain whether the obligations and undertakings of the exporters are being met in fact.

This should be the case with regard to the supply of directed credits, whose availability and granting must be limited to the selected purposes designated, and which should be of proven value on a national-economic priority basis.

From: "Labour in Israel," International Dept. Histadrut, Vol. XXVIII, No. 6, December 1976, T.A.

LIKUD'S ECONOMIC PROGRAM

A Free Economy, and Government Guidance to Assure Its Prosperity

The Likud government will establish a new infrastructure for the national economy, eliminate the faulty structures that prevent economic recovery, promote the better use of the available manpower and capital resources, seek to reduce government involvement in economic activity and promote the establishment of a free economy based on fair reward, efficiency, enterprise and competition, through initiatives in the following fields:–

a) *Halting the Inflation*

It is possible to reduce the increase of prices to reasonable rates, far lower than the inflation rate in the last four years, mainly by means of reducing the deficits of government budgets and the flow of funds to the public sector. Likud will act to reduce nonessential government and public spending and activities and to scale down superfluous administrative machinery, while assuring the orderly conversion of workers to more productive occupations.

b) *Reduction of the Balance-of-Payments Deficit*

The effort to achieve economic independence requires a reduction of the deficit of the current balance of payments to about 40 percent of its present volume within four years. This target will be achieved by a considerable increase of exports and reduction of imports, including defense imports, in real terms. To that end, it will be necessary to adopt an exchange policy that encourages export, makes import more costly, and reflects the true value of the Israel pound.

c) *Taxation*

Likud will take steps to simplify the tax structure and the abolition of double and unnecessary taxes to the point where there will be only two taxes: a progressive Income Tax, and a Value Added Tax at a uniform rate of expenditure.

d) *Labor Relations and Wage Policy*

Likud will promote the stabilization of labor relations, mainly by laying down a policy based on agreements between employees and employers in the different branches and aimed at the establishment of a direct relation between output and wages. Wage linkage between one trade or profession and another will be abolished and a fair reward for know-how, function, specialization, initiative, increase of the real output, effort and responsibility will be assured.

The anarchy in labor relations, which is a result of the Alignment Administration's weakness, makes it essential to introduce compulsory arbitration in *essential services,* so that labor disputes may be settled before they escalate into wildcat strikes with their ruinous effect on the entire economy.

From: Likud—Platform for the Ninth Knesset, Main points, published by Likud Headquarters, Tel Aviv, 1977.

28 • Workers' Hegemony at Stake

The Road to Geneva

In regard to foreign policy, the Israeli public has been split—since the Yom Kippur War, and especially during 1975 and 1976—on a whole series of issues. This controversy had a considerable impact both on the labor movement and on the Rabin government, which was based on the two socialist-Zionist workers' parties and their allies.

The first issue was Israel's struggle in the international arena against its growing isolation, as well as the attitude toward the diverse peace initiatives and repeated demands for reconvening the Geneva Conference. Since the gap between the Israeli and the Arab positions proved to be too wide to bridge, American diplomacy made recurrent efforts to reach at least partial agreements, first between Israel and Egypt, and later between Israel and Syria as well. It is not by chance that the right-wing Likud, which traditionally has taken a hard line against territorial concessions, was strongly opposed to Dr. Kissinger's steps toward negotiations between Israel and Egypt. Likud was in favor of going straight to Geneva, in favor of an all-embracing solution, of "true peace" only. This position was based on the assumption that partial agreements have a real chance of success, and consequently—of withdrawal from territories; while in Geneva the basic Israeli and Arab stands would inevitably be so diametrically opposed to each other, that nothing would come out of it, and the status quo would continue until the day (according to Likud's assumption), when Israel would be able to dictate its own terms for a peace treaty. It is true that the opposition to Dr. Kissinger's moves had not been confined solely to the right wing (Likud, National Religious Party, the hawks within the Labor Party). Among the leftist and "anti-establishment" groups which opposed the Rabin government, there also were strong reservations regarding partial agreement, mainly because they resent a "pax Americana" which excludes the Soviet Union and fear that the Israeli government would content itself with such interim solutions and consider them a substitute for efforts to reach a final and all-around peace agreement at Geneva.

Mapam's position, supported by a large section of the Israel Labor Party, was that the efforts to reach partial agreements should be viewed as positive and realistic steps, as long as they are not considered by the Cabinet substitutes for Geneva, but rather as preparatory steps on the road to Geneva; that it always be kept in mind that no final settlement can be reached without the participation of the Soviet Union; and that there can be no stable and true peace in this region unless the Palestinian problem is solved on the basis of national self-determination.

After the initial failure of Kissinger's mission (March 1975), negotiations were resumed, and in the end an interim agreement between Israel and Egypt was signed—after arousing a fierce controversy in the Israeli public. The Knesset approved the agreement (September 3, 1975) by a majority of 70 to 43, with seven abstentions; three Alignment and two National Religious Party members voted with the Likud; one Independent Liberal abstained (the Labor rebels were Moshe Dayan and two of his close Rafi associates).

The second controversial issue was the illegal establishment of Jewish settlements on the West Bank, carried out against the decision of the Cabinet by the extremist nationalist and orthodox religious Gush Emunim (Bloc of the True). These acts, openly intended to create *faits accomplis* on the West Bank, occurred as early as 1974, but were intensified during 1975, often as an integral part of the political mass demonstrations against the Kissinger mission and the negotiations on the interim agreement. In most cases the Army prevented the illegal settlers from reaching their goals, or removed them by force afterwards. In one case, however, the Defense Minister (Shimon Peres), whose attitude toward settlements in densely populated Arab areas has been ambiguous (favoring their aims on principle, but opposing them on the grounds of contradicting the law), reached a compromise with the settlers, allowing them to stay "temporarily" in a nearby army camp at Kaddum (December 1975). Since then all the efforts to put an end to this "temporary stay" by sending the settlers home or moving them to an area where settlements are legal, and all the Cabinet resolutions to this effect, have been in vain, because the National Religious Party coalition partners, as well as the Defense Minister and his Rafi associates, threatened to create a Cabinet crisis in such an event. This continuous surrender of the Cabinet majority to hawkish blackmail was much resented by the doves within the Cabinet and created tension and a crisis of confidence between Mapam and the Prime Minister. To make the picture complete, we have to mention in this context the provocative behavior of the Gush Emunim inhabitants of Kiryat-Arba (the Jewish Upper Hebron): Their leader, Rabbi Levinger, was not satisfied with a Jewish town overlooking Hebron and wanted to replace the Arab city. He and his zealot associates provoked violence between Jews and Moslems and defied the law and the Army in the riots about changing the status quo at the Cave of the Patriarchs. In this case, however, the Cabinet took firm steps to stop this superfluous and harmful religious conflict, to conduct a thorough investigation of the events in Hebron and Kiryat-Arba and to bring all those guilty of defiling Tora scrolls and Korans to justice.

The third controversial issue was the Palestinian problem. In contrast with the hawks' view that if a Palestinian problem exists at all, it ought to be solved on the East Bank of the Jordan (since the West Bank has to be considered as "part of Israel" and to be kept by her for good . . .), it is accepted by the dovish section of the public in its diverse shades that the Palestinians have a right to national self-determination, parallel to Israeli self-determination, as long as it is based on peaceful coexistence between the states of Israel and Palestine. However, a broader political framework for the Palestinian entity (namely, on *both* banks of the Jordan) would have many distinct advantages for all concerned; whereas the alternative (a small separate Palestinian State on the West Bank and the Gaza Strip) is complicated and dangerous from the point of view of ensuring a stable peace in the Middle East, Israel's security, Palestinian economic development and prospects of solving the refugee problem. Instead of making the political and social struggle for progress and democratization of the regime the focus of national life, it would foster revanchist dreams and irredenta. So far, there is a common denominator among the Independent Liberals, the Labor Party, Mapam and others (in contrast with the leftist groups united in the framework of the Israel Council for Israeli-Palestinian Peace, and with Rakah, who are in favor of a Palestinian State on the West Bank and the Gaza Strip, as well as of negotiations with the P.L.O.) Beyond that point, however, the controversy starts: The Labor Party rejects such a "third state" alternative unequivocally, "under any circumstances whatsoever," while Mapam expresses preference for the one (the broader) solution and points out the disadvantages and risks of the other. In Mapam's opinion, Israel cannot dictate to the Palestinians and Jordanians how to live together, how to shape their mutual relations, whether to live in one joint state or in two separate ones. Instead, Israel should confine herself to insisting on a formal and explicit peace between the sovereign State of Israel and the state (or states) beyond her eastern borders, based on secure and mutually recognized borders, national coexistence and good neighborliness. In other words, Mapam does not advocate the creation of a third, separate Palestinian state, but does not exclude the possibility, either, that under certain circumstances such a solution should be considered as well.

There is a close connection between the different approaches towards the establishment (or the possibility of putting up with the emerging) of a separate Palestinian state, and the problem of finding Palestinian partners for negotiations: if one excludes categorically the alternative of a Palestinian state or the West Bank and the Gaza Strip, then it is not essential at all, and perhaps even embarrassing, to meet moderate Palestinian partners for negotiations. On the other hand, those Israelis who do not rule out entirely the eventual creation of a separate Palestinian state take the stand that, while they cannot negotiate with the P.L.O. as long as the latter adheres to the "National Palestinian Covenant" aimed at the destruction of Israel and performs acts of terror, Israel should express her readiness to negotiate with any Palestinian group or organization willing to recognize Israel on the basis of S.C. Resolution 242 and to abstain from terrorism.[1] There may not be an operative difference between these two stands, in the short run, since virtually all Israelis consider negotiations with the present P.L.O. impossible, while apparently no official "moderate" Palestinian partner is available right now. But in the long run, there no doubt is a significant difference between the two: while the one approach leaves no options open even in the future, the other keeps them open. This difference in approach also leads to different answers to the question of Palestinian representation at the Geneva Conference: while the official stand refuses such separate representation on principle and insists on the Palestinians being represented by the Jordanian delegation, Mapam confines itself to insisting on any eventual Palestinian representation at the Conference being based on the acceptance of S.C. Resolutions 242 and 338—be it by a separate Palestinian delegation or within a united Arab delegation.

Changing Political Scene

During the controversy on the interim agreement with Egypt, some changes in approach became apparent within the Likud camp. Not only did the "liberal" component of the Likud continue its criticism of the intransigent and "old-fashioned" slogans and formulation of "Herut," but differences also emerged in the latter's ranks. As a result, one of the outstanding Herut parliamentarians, one-time member of the High Court of Justice Benyamin Halevy, disassociated himself from Herut and formed a one-man group of his own. Another of the Likud components, the Free Center [four Knesset members (M.K.s)] split over the same issue: the orthodox-hawkish wing (two M.K.s) merged with the ex-Rafi "State List" and the "Greater Israel Movement" into the "La'am" (toward the people) Party, as a component of Likud, while the party leader, Shmuel Tamir, and another M.K. maintained an independent group within the Likud (January 1975).

---

1. The so-called Shemtov-Yariv Formula, since it was suggested to the Cabinet by Minister V. Shemtov of Mapam and Minister A. Yariv of the Labor Party. However, this formula was rejected by the majority of the Cabinet, which considered it to be a commitment to a Palestinian state (in case such a state were to be demanded by moderate Palestinians), while the Labor Party does not accept the idea of such a state, even if suggested by moderate Palestinians, on the basis of national coexistence, mutual recognition and good neighborliness.

Some changes also occurred within the opposition camp on the opposite pole. Maki and the New Left "Blue-Red Movement" that had joined ranks since the elections of 1973 merged finally under the name of "Moked" (Focus—June 1975). In May 1975 the majority of an opposition circle within the Labor Party, the circle for clarification of social and political problems, split away from the Labor Party and, under the leadership of Knesset Member Liova Eliav (one-time Secretary-General of the Labor Party) joined with Shulamit Aloni's Civil Rights Movement in creating a new party, Ya'ad (Goal). However, Ya'ad's anti-establishment platform proved to be insufficient to serve as a common denominator for "wild-gone Liberals" such as Shulamit Aloni's and frustrated socialists such as Liova Eliav, especially since the former Civil Rights Movement was not willing to go further than rather vague and noncomittal slogans in regard to foreign policy. The new party did not last longer than half a year: on December 31 it split finally—Shulamit Alloni and another M.K. reconstituted the Civil Rights Movement, while Liova Eliav with another M.K. from the former C.R.M. formed a new Knesset group, called Independent Socialists. The latter cooperated with Moked and other marginal groups in the framework of the Israel Council for Israeli-Palestinian Peace (founded in February 1976).

In the second half of 1976 more changes occurred, mainly because of the approaching Knesset elections, due at the latest in November 1977. In some sections of the Likud camp ferment spread against the traditional slogans, especially in face of the generally anticipated peace initiatives (and pressures on Israel) by the new Carter administration. In the course of this controversy, Shmuel Tamir's Free Center split away from the Likud (October 1976). Almost at the same time Ariel Sharon left the Likud and founded an independent "national and liberal" movement of his own, Shlomzion (Peace to Zion).

Simultaneously, intensive efforts were initiated to create a strong and united Liberal Center, aimed at drawing a great number of voters both from the unpopular and compromised Alignment and from the sterile and obsolete Likud. In particular these forces hoped to benefit from the spreading unpopularity of the ruling Alignment establishment, both on grounds of its economic austerity policy and a series of financial scandals for which the establishment was being held responsible by the public. On this background a new Democratic List was founded, headed by the one-time Chief-of-Staff of the Hagana, Yigal Yadin, later a famous archaeologist. This group merged with Prof. Amnon Rubinstein's Shinui (Change) movement, which had emerged from one of the protest groups after the Yom Kippur War. The united movement (Democratic Movement for Change—DMC) merged with Shmuel Tamir's Free Center and was joined by one wing of the Black Panthers. It also conducted negotiations with the Independent Liberals, with the Civil Rights Movement and with

Ariel Sharon's Shlomzion—but nothing came of these additional efforts, mainly because of personal rivalries. The common denominator of all those groups was their evasiveness in regard to foreign policy, mainly since they did not want to antagonize any of their new members and followers, hawks and doves alike. They concentrated above all on slogans like "change," "efficient government," "clean hands," etc., with strong emphasis on the need for electoral reform (meaning the abolition of proportional representation by a constituency system), demanding antistrike laws, obligatory arbitration in labor disputes, etc. Most of the above slogans revealed what close political neighbors the Democratic Liberals and the conservative-reactionary Likud were.

In face of the revival of the Center, the Independent Liberals considered leaving the coalition, in order to be unhampered in their election campaign and to be able either to merge with the other liberal groups or to compete with them. When, in addition to the Liberals' threats, the National Religious coalition partners also tried to prove their growing independence, going so far as to abstain during a no-confidence vote[2] (moved by the Tora Front), Prime Minister Rabin reacted quickly by dismissing the N.R. Ministers for violating the law of collective responsibility and announced the resignation of the Cabinet. This step turned it, according to the law, automatically into a caretaker government, to which nonconfidence cannot be voted and from which no Minister can resign. This also meant that the Independent Liberals had missed their chance for leaving the Cabinet before the elections, the date of which had been changed from November to May 17, 1977.

The Workers' Parties at the Crossroads

Since the elections to the 9th Knesset were approaching, Mapam had to make up its mind whether to face the electorate once more in a joint list with the Labor Party (Alignment), or on an independent Mapam list. Yet going it alone necessitated exacting and extensive preparations, and Mapam's 7th National Congress was obliged to take a final decision, based on a realistic and balanced assessment of the achievements as well as of the failures of the partnership with the Labor Party in the framework of the Alignment. In spite of much apprehension in that respect, Mapam proved to be able to keep its independence and unequivocally publicize its own critical views regarding foreign and economic policies; in addition,

---

2. The pretext for this no-confidence motion was the fact that an official reception ceremony, held on Friday afternoon in honor of the long-awaited American F-15 planes, lasted till darkness and led to sacrilege of the Sabbath. Although this motion was a religious-motivated one, it was supported by all the opponents of the coalition, from the Likud on the right to Rakah on the left.

it did find valuable and influential allies in the ranks of the Labor Party, both in the Knesset and in the Histadrut. On the other hand, however, Mapam's hopes of inducing the most influential party in Israeli politics, the Labor Party, to take peace initiatives and effectively defend the interests of the working class, had often been disappointed; and Mapam had to face the bitter truth that the Labor Party has been incapable of overcoming its internal factional split and paralysis in order to make clearcut decisions. At the same time, all these problematics and deliberations were overshadowed by the grave danger that in the forthcoming elections the Likud and its potential liberal and religious allies would put an end to the workers' hegemony in Israel. During the weeks preceding the congress, Mapam conducted negotiations with the Labor Party, presenting it with a "minimum program," the main points of which were:

a. That Israel make public her specific ideas about peace within secure and mutually recognized borders.

b. That the Labor Party abandon for good the fatal "stalling for time," and prove its sincere intentions of keeping up the momentum of negotiations and striving for a reasonable compromise, both on the border and the Palestinian issues.

c. That the estbalishment of Jewish settlements on the West Bank be unequivocally stopped, and those which have been recently illegally established be dismantled.

The results of those negotiations were to be reported to the National Congress, in order to enable it to decide whether to leave the Alignment or to "give it another try." At the Congress, held on June 9–11, 1976 in Tel Aviv, Mapam's Peace Plan, first formulated in August 1967, was modified and complemented on issues such as the Jewish settlements on the West Bank, the Palestinian State and negotiations with moderate Palestinian groups and organizations. As to the future of the Alignment, the Congress adopted an interim resolution almost unanimously: Mapam would make preparations, without delay, to contest the next parliamentary elections independently; at the same time the hope was expressed that the forthcoming National Congress of the Labor Party (due in the winter of 1976–77) would take a clear decision in favor of a dovish policy, particularly regarding Israel's readiness to return the West Bank to Arab-Palestinian sovereignty as part of a peace agreement, and that no more Jewish settlements be established on the West Bank. After the Labor Party's Congress, but not later than in March 1977, a second session of the 7th Congress was to be convened in order to assess the results of the Labor Party's Congress and to conclude finally whether a common election platform with the Labor party was possible.

With the resignation of the Israeli coalition government in December 1976 and the consequent advancement of the parliamentary elections date from November 1977 to May 17, Mapam's timetable was completely disarranged. Since Mapam could not postpone the second session of its Congress any longer, so close to the elections, the session had to be advanced to January 30, i.e., before the Labor Party's Congress on February 22. Thus Mapam faced the unexpected difficulty of taking a final decision on whether to go the elections alone or jointly with the Labor Party, before getting an authorized reply from the latter regarding the conditions for continuing the Alignment. Another complication was the contest for the leadership of the Labor Party and the nomination of the Alignment's candidate for the premiership. Although Mapam, with its organizational independence, could not formally interfere in this contest, it nevertheless made it clear that if the Labor Party nominated Shimon Peres (Rabin's main opponent), it would mean the end of the Alignment. With his hawkish views, Peres could not be trusted to carry out a dovish program, even if it were adopted by the Labor Party's Congress. But this nomination too was to take place after Mapam's Congress. In the last stages of its negotiations with the Labor Party, Mapam made its various demands more concise, in the form of three ultimative conditions for a joint election list:

1. Amendment of their program ("14 Articles") to specify that Israel's declared readiness for territorial compromise applies to the West Bank too.

2. Shimon Peres will not be the Alignment candidate for the premiership.

3. Mapam's demands regarding economic-social problems, and the Arab minority in Israel, be met at least halfway.

The second session of Mapam's Congress, on January 30, unanimously endorsed the above three terms for continuing the Alignment. It was also decided that after the elections Mapam would not join any government of which the right-wing Likud was a component. However, opinions differed on the question of whether to continue the Alignment or to disband it without delay. The majority (527 delegates, 62.8 percent) supported Secretary-General Talmi's resolution stating that after the Labor Party's Congress on February 22, Mapam's Central Committee would assess whether Mapam's terms had been met, and decide accordingly. The minority (313 delegates, 37.2 percent) voted in favor of a motion to the effect that since Mapam's demands have not been met up to now, the National Congress decide to disband the Alignment and go the elections independently.

The duel between Rabin and Peres during January and February 1977 shook the Israel Labor Party to its very foundations. While Shimon Peres could rely from the very beginning upon the support of all his former Rafi associates, Yitshak Rabin could depend upon the former Ahdut Haavoda faction. In addition, the various sections of the kibbutz movement supported Rabin, or—as many preferred to put it—opposed Peres. While Rabin's supporters belonged mainly to the dovish camp with its various shades and degrees of consistency, the Peres camp was made up of hawks and doves alike. Among them could be found former Mapai members who held grievances against Rabin and the party establishment (such as Abba Eban, who had not been included in the Rabin Cabinet), but also many others who gave their support to Peres for so-called "electoral considerations." They believed that in face of the "magic slogans" of Yadin's Democratic Movement for Change (D.M.C.), such as democracy, efficiency, open-mindedness, electoral reform, anti-strike laws, and, above all, change, only a Peres leadership could create a "new and dynamic" image of the Labor Party, immunizing Labor's traditional and potential voters against D.M.C. demagogy. Their opponents in the party accused Peres and his followers of telling the electorate that there was no need to buy the above ideas in the D.M.C. supermarket, since all of them could be found "in their own old shop, now changed and overhauled," without the adventurous risk of disrupting long-accumulated experience, stability and continuity.

The entire kibbutz movement (both the sections affiliated with Mapam or the Labor Party) rejected this "classic" Rafi approach. They (and many others as well) argued that the existence and continuation of workers' hegemony, though seriously threatened, cannot be saved by playing down labor's traditional and unique tenets and values—socialist-Zionism, pioneering spirit, and efforts for peace; by blurring the demarcation line between the labor movement and its rivals, by rapprochement and assimilation with petit-bourgeois liberalism; but only by an audacious return to the sources, to the original labor-Zionist ideology and spirit. The remedy is not in moving toward the center but in fighting the right on a clear-cut leftist and dovish plank.

The 2nd National Congress of the Israel Labor party took place during February 22–25. Yitshak Rabin was chosen as the party leader and candidate for the premiership after a secret ballot of nearly 3,000 delegates, by a narrow margin (1,445 for Rabin; for Peres, 1,404). As for the political platform, the preparatory committee had unanimously recommended the inclusion of the following resolution, partly in order to meet Mapam's ultimative demand: ". . . Israel will continue its political efforts to conclude peace agreements with Egypt, Jordan and Syria, maintaining defensible borders, but being ready for a territorial compromise with each of them, and with Lebanon—with the present boundaries. . . ." At the Congress, however, Moshe Dayan strongly criticized this resolution due to his opposition to evacuating the West Bank. He proposed a resolution that confined itself to expressing readiness for a territorial compromise in general terms only, without specifying where and with whom.

Dayan's motion met with unexpectedly strong support, but in the end it was defeated by a decisive majority. The Congress also rejected, this time by only a narrow majority (659 to 606), another Dayan proposal: to amend the section of the resolution which says that the government should give priority to settlement in the Jerusalem area and the Jordan Valley. Dayan claimed that by specifying that there will be settlement in those regions, the party tacitly was admitting that there will be no settlements elsewhere on the West Bank. On the other hand a resolution by Yitshak Navon, chairman of the Knesset Foreign Affairs and Security Committee, to express readiness to talk to Palestinian groups who will recognize Israel and accept UN Security Council resolutions 242 and 338 (the so-called Yariv-Shemtov Formula) did not win a majority either.[3]

In accordance with the decision taken by Mapam's National Congress (2nd session, January 30, 1977), Mapam's Central Committee convened on February 27 to assess the results of the Labor Party Congress and decide whether they conform to Mapam's ultimative demands. Since both the resolution regarding the West Bank and the choice of the candidate for the premiership complied with Mapam's demands, the Central Committee decided to go to the forthcoming elections jointly with the Labor Party. However, it was stressed that there are still many issues which remain controversial between the two parties, such as the Palestinian problem, the establishment of Jewish settlements in the occupied territories, social and economic policies, etc. Therefore Mapam considered itself free to explicitly express its own view regarding these questions. As on previous occasions, a minority of the Central Committee demanded the disbandment of the Alignment, in spite of the Labor Party's response to Mapam's demands. They emphasized the narrow majority by which Peres' candidacy had been voted down, and the strong support for Dayan's amendments at the Labor Party Congress. This minority resolution was rejected by the Central Committee by 148 to 43, with eleven abstentions (78 percent to 22 percent). After both workers' parties had taken their decisions, all their joint efforts could be devoted to repelling the onslaught of the hawkish and social-reactionary Right, to secure the workers' hegemony, and to win massive support for peace initiatives.

The latest of the crises faced by Israel during the stormy election campaign took place when Prime Minister Rabin resigned as his party's candidate to head the new government as a result of his involvement, together with his wife, in the foreign currency misdemeanor of maintaining an account in an American bank after the return from his term as ambassa-

3. Shortly after the Congress, ex-Rafi'ite M. Ben-Porat left the Labor Party and Alignment Knesset faction, announcing that he was leaving the party in the wake of "dictates by Mapam." Though M. Dayan did not join Ben-Porat, he continued to "sit on the fence": only when he failed to bring his negotiations with Likud to a satisfactory conclusion, he gave his consent to be included in Labor's list of candidates. This ambiguous attitude met with bitter criticism not only by Mapam, but also within his own party.

dor in the United States. In retrospect, he actually gained in moral prestige by his decision to share his wife's blame and to suffer all the consequences—up to resigning the position for which he had fought so hard in the Labor Party Congress. The result was almost inevitable: Security Minister Shimon Peres, who had lost the candidacy by a narrow margin, was now elected to head the Labor Party election list, with Foreign Minister Yigal Allon as his second and Abba Eban, third.

Mapam's Central Committee, which met two days before the closing of the election lists, faced a difficult dilemma. On the one hand, it faced the test of credibility, with many members demanding the fulfillment of the decision taken by the 7th National Congress not to enter an alignment headed by Shimon Peres, known by his hawkish views; on the other hand, others argued that Shimon Peres, nominated in contest with Rabin, was one thing, and Shimon Peres nominated uncontested by the Labor Party was another thing entirely. In addition, there was both the fear that the month remaining before the elections was not sufficient to organize an efficient campaign, and the inclination to accept Peres' pledges that he would remain loyal to the party's political program despite the change in personnel. The sad fact that the rightist forces, headed by the Likud, appeared to be the closest they had ever been to coming to power, and the imperative to do everything possible to prevent such a contingency, eventually swung the balance. The resolution adopted by the Central Committee and which won a majority of 58 percent ratified Mapam's continued participation in a joint election list with the Labor Party, with the proviso that during the course of the first half year of the new government's activities Mapam would evaluate the Labor Party's faithfulness to its pledges and decide on the future of the Alignment on that basis. During this period Mapam would also rediscuss the organization and political partnership of the socialist-Zionist labor movement, since the Alignment in its present form is not satisfactory and will not be able to continue.

Workers' Hegemony Defeated

Although 22 lists participated, the election campaign was mainly a contest among three camps: Ma'arah (Alignment), Likud, and DMC. The last-named particularly tried to draw into its ranks traditional voters of the Labor Party who had become disappointed by their party, but still would not go so far as to support the extreme nationalist and militantly anti-socialist Likud. However, DMC's "positive solutions"—change, true democracy, efficient administration, electoral reform, anti-strike legislation, etc.—were quite vague and certainly did not get to the root of the problems. As for questions of foreign policy, relations between state and religion, etc., DMC was evasive and noncommittal due to the politically heterogeneous composition of this movement, which includes doves and hawks, religious and non-religious alike. At any rate, the militant DMC succeeded in absorbing the traditional moderate groups of the center, as well as in taking some of the wind out of Likud's sails in the sphere of internal policy.

There were no new slogans in Likud's election campaign, but a repetition of the old ones, though on a shriller note: no repartition of Israel by a territorial compromise on the West Bank; application of Israeli law to the occupied territories; free Jewish settlement activity all over the West Bank; electoral reform (abolishment of proportional representation); depolitization (more exactly, "desocialization") of the Histadrut; disbandment of government and Histadrut-owned enterprises, leaving industrial activity exclusively to private initiative; compulsory arbitration and anti-strike legislation (etc.), and, above all, "Begin to power! Begin to the premiership!"

The Alignment was seriously handicapped by a whole series of political, economic and psychological circumstances. Aside from the unpopularity of its economic austerity policy, it failed to present the electorate with a clear-cut alternative policy to those of Likud and DMC. When at last it tried, as a result of strong pressure by Mapam, to correct this shortcoming at the last minute (during the election campaign), it was already too late to erase the impression that had become entrenched in the minds of the public in the course of the last few years, that there was no fundamental and unbridgeable difference between the Alignment and its rivals. One of the main arguments of the Likud and DMC during the campaign was that Labor had been running the country for 29 years and it would be a good thing, for Israel as well as for Labor itself, if the Alignment were to take a four-year holiday and give others a chance. The counter-argument—that such a change in government would inevitably have fatal results not only for the working class and for the further development of the country, but above all for Israel's security and prospects for peace—though realistic and correct in itself, did not sound convincing enough. This was one of the principal reasons for the disastrous loss of votes for the Alignment. In addition, there was the shock caused by the unexpected last-minute change in leadership (Peres instead of Rabin), as well as the desertion of the Labor Party (to the DMC) by members of Knesset and high-ranking directors of Histadrut enterprises. Much harm was done by the ambiguous position of Moshe Dayan, who hesitated until the last moment as to whether to join the Likud or remain in the Labor Party.

4. In the elections of May 17, the Knesset representation of the Independent Liberals was reduced from four seats to one, and of the Movement for Civil Rights from three to one.

This scandalous behavior, bitterly attacked by Mapam and by Dayan's own party colleagues, contributed to blurring the demarcation line between the Alignment and Likud in the eyes of the electorate.

Another fatal handicap was the large number of monetary scandals in which high-ranking officials of the Labor Party had been involved, as well as charges of foreign currency offenses against several of its prominent leaders. The public was inclined to blame these personal failures on the Alignment as a whole, and Likud and DMC campaigners exploited this inclination to the utmost by bluntly stating that "all this is typical of the present rotten system, typical of the Alignment."

On election day, the Labor–Mapam Alignment suffered a landslide defeat (32 seats as compared with 51 in the 1973 elections), Likud and the National Religious Party won several additional seats (Likud, 43 instead of 39; NRP, 12 instead of ten),[5] the new liberal DMC achieved an impressive success in emerging as the third political force in Israel (15 seats). Since the Likud came out as the strongest list, the President of the State asked the Likud leader to form the new government. After hard bargaining, Menahem Begin succeeded in ensuring sufficient parliamentary support for his coalition, consisting of Likud, NRP, Agudat Israel and M. Dayan (June 20, 1977).

Having rejected Begin's offer to join a National Unity Government, the Alignment went into opposition (as far as the Labor party is concerned, for the first time since the foundation of the State of Israel, and even before). This election campaign and its results have put the weaknesses of the workers' hegemony in Israel into focus. The question of how to deal with these weaknesses, how to bring a recovery and renaissance of the Israeli labor movement, is certainly not less important than the question of the new government's composition.

The gradual decline and final defeat of "workers' hegemony" in Israel cannot be fully understood and explained without taking into consideration the deep objective-structural changes in the Israeli working class, with their subjective-political implications. The Israeli labor movement originated from, and has been mainly based upon, workers who had been motivated to immigrate and become workers by socialist-Zionist ideology, and who took for granted the connection between Zionism and socialism, trade union struggle and a progressive political program. However, in the course of realization of the socialist-Zionist ideology, a new working class developed in the urban areas of the country (and to some extent in the moshavim), mainly consisting of new immigrants from the Middle East and North Africa. The latter have no socialist-Zionist background and tradition and do *not* take the connection between Zionism and

---

5. After the elections Shlomzion returned to the ranks of Likud, and Likud's representation increased from 43 to 45 Knesset seats.

Socialism, trade union struggle and a progressive political program for granted. On the contrary, this new working class has up to now been extremely vulnerable to nationalist and social demagoguery, so skillfully practiced by the Israeli Right.

A similar process of alienation has taken place between the founding generation of the Israeli labor movement and many members of the younger generation, who lack the motivation of personal socialist-Zionist revolution which their parents had. In addition, the Labor Party's complacency and emphasized pragmatism, as well as its failure to radiate socialist-Zionist values and to drawing a clear-cut demarcation line between left and right, created a vacuum which was inevitably filled by ideas and values alien to the labor movement. The Oriental Jewish workers and slum-dwellers, as well as the (urban) young generation, were particularly receptive to these ideas. In the past, workers' criticism, dissatisfaction and embitterment over the ruling Labor Party's politics could be mollified on election day, since the working voter ruled out the possibility of voting for a reactionary rightist list. The argument of "absence of options," far too often used and abused by the establishment and for a long time accepted by the voters, gradually eroded. The working people and younger generation finally overcame their former inhibitions and translated their protest against "the establishment" into voting the reactionary Right into office.[6]

The labor movement as a whole will have to adapt itself to these structural changes and ideological-psychological development by plowing deep furrows in this new social reality, endeavoring to bring the Israeli working class and youth back to the socialist-Zionist labor movement by a wide-scale and thorough educational, ideological and trade union offensive. Otherwise all its congresses, discussions, resolutions, splits, and alignments will be hanging in the air, unrooted in social reality.

Already during the Rabin-Peres duel at the end of 1976, one of the characterstistic new phenomena was the active intervention of the kibbutz movement, both the section which forms the backbone of Mapam and the one affiliated with the Labor Party. The kibbutz movement, which was for many years predominantly preoccupied with its own internal consolidation, recently became aware of the imminent danger of an individualistic, neo-capitalist hegemony emerging as a threat to both the development of the country and the prospects of peace, as well as to the

---

6. In the Histadrut elections of June 21, 1977, the process of the Alignment decline continued (56.3 percent as compared with 65.39 percent in 1965, 62.56 percent in 1969 and 58.3 percent in 1973). Nevertheless, the Alignment was this time much more successful than in the parliamentary elections of May 17, 1977, and was able, rather unexpectedly, to keep its overall majority. Obviously, many of those who had voted for Likud or DMC in the Knesset elections were this time mainly influenced by the fear of the Likud Government's reactionary economic policy. Opposite a right-wing bourgeois government they preferred an Alignment-led Histadrut.

future of the labor and kibbutz movements. This awareness induced the kibbutz movement (and induces it even more after the recent electoral disaster), and in particular its young generation and young leaders, to a deep political involvement, both in the struggle against the anti-socialist right and center, and for the return of the labor movement to its sources, to its pioneering spirit and to the radical ideology of original Labor Zionism. Whether the kibbutz movement succeeds in this endeavor, whether it finds sufficient support in the ranks of the urban working class and youth, will be of fateful significance not only for the future of the labor and kibbutz movements, but for the future of Israel and Zionism as well.

A battle lost is never fatal, if the appropriate lessons are learned. Since the Israeli Right has no realistic alternative answers and feasible solutions to Israel's complex problematics in the spheres of foreign, security and economic policy, the Israeli left is confident of winning its forthcoming struggle for the re-establishment of workers' hegemony.

SOURCES

Mapam's Peace Plan

Mapam's Seventh National Congress calls upon the Government of Israel to formulate a program for an inclusive Israeli-Arab peace agreement. This program, which Israel will bring to Geneva or to any other agreed-upon forum, will constitute Israel's suggestions for a solution of the problems in dispute. Such a program would reinforce our position by clarifying our aims to the Arab countries, and would win friendship and support for our struggle for peace and security all over the world. The following premises should be the basis for this program:

A. The peaceful relations between Israel and its neighbors will be founded on recognition of the independence and sovereignty of the State of Israel; the cessation of hostile propaganda and the economic boycott; on economic, scientific and cultural cooperation; and the development of tourism—with the aim of attaining normal relations, including diplomatic relations. The peace program will be implemented within a definite period of time and in predetermined stages.

B. Israel will strive for an inclusive peace agreement, with all of its neighbors. It will therefore be prepared to conduct negotiations, with no preliminary conditions, with all the Arab countries together or with each of them separately.

C. Israel will also be prepared to negotiate the termination of the state of war, as well as interim or partial agreements as a stage towards lasting peace. These negotiations will be conducted by Israel on the basis of its inclusive program.

D. The State of Israel does not seek annexations but rather guarantees for its security. It will come to the negotiations on the basis of Security Council Resolutions 242 and 338, declaring its readiness to evacuate territories it occupied in Sinai, the West Bank and the Golan Heights, and to make far-reaching withdrawals, with necessary border modifications obligated by security needs, to secure recognized and agreed-upon borders. Before peace is achieved, no facts will be established which are not obligated by security needs and which would be obstacles to agreement by political means.

. . . Palestine on both sides of the Jordan river is the mutual homeland of the Jewish people returning to its country and of the Palestinian people living in it. Therefore, in its negotiations with Jordan, Israel will favor a political solution based on the existence of two independent and sovereign states: Israel on the one hand, and an Arab state, Jordanian-Palestinian, on the other. The self-determination of the Palestinian Arab People will find its expression in this neighboring state. Israel will respect the democratic decisions of the Palestinians and the Jordanians in everything concerning self-determination, sovereignty and independence of both these groups, beyond Israel's borders, on condition that the relations with Israel be based on peace agreements and good neighborliness.

Israel will be prepared to negotiate with any Palestinian group which recognizes Israel's right to existence and sovereignty, and rejects and avoids acts of terror or sabotage (recognition on the basis of Security Council Resolution 242). The agreement between Israel and its neighbors to the east will be based on a peace treaty and on economic and cultural cooperation. Combined efforts will be made by both states to mobilize means from international sources for the development of irrigation projects, agriculture, industry and housing. Upon the determination of the border modifications necessary for its security, Israel will withdraw to the agreed-upon borders and the West Bank will be returned and demilitarized according to a timetable determined by the agreement. Armed forces will not cross the Jordan river and the demilitarization will be guaranteed by agreed-upon security arrangements.

. . . Peace agreements between Israel and its neighbors and the consequent termination of hostilities will liberate tremendous human and economic resources capable of advancing the peoples of the region towards economic and political independence. It will free them from the intervention of foreign powers and enable them to achieve a higher standard of living, and work towards the eradication of poverty, disease and illiteracy, the effective utilization of natural resources, large-scale development programs and the use of know-how for the mutual benefit of all the people of the region.

(Excerpts from Resolutions adopted at Mapam's 7th National Congress, Mapam Bulletin No. 36, June 1976, Tel Aviv.)

Labor's Peace Plank

Consistent striving for peace: The central objective of Israel is the attainment of peace with the neighbouring states and the weaving of the fabric of cooperation between the peoples of the region. Israel has been striving for this target ever since it came into being, and the fact that it has not been reached is due to the policy of hostility, war and boycott pursued by the Arab States all these years. Nonetheless, the political efforts to reach permanent peace in defensible borders with Egypt, Jordan and Syria are to be continued with readiness for territorial compromise with each of them, and with Lebanon—with the present boundaries.

Israel will support the convention of the Geneva Conference without delay, composed of the participants as agreed in December 1973. This agreement constitutes the base for the Peace Conference and should not be deviated from. Israel rejects the invitation of representatives of PLO and terrorist organizations.

At the Peace Conference and through all channels of international relations, Israel will strive for peace agreements to be arrived at by negotiation without precondition, without pressures, and without attempts by any party to impose anything.

The peace agreements should ensure:
a) Cessation of all elements of hostililty, blockade, and boycott.
b) Defensible borders enabling Israel to defend itself efficiently against military attack or attempts at blockade, and based upon territorial compromise. Peace borders should replace the cease-fire lines. Demilitarization provisions and political arrangements are to be included in the peace agreements, additional to agreed and recognized defensible borders, and not instead of them. Israel will not return to the borders of June 4, 1967, which constituted an encitement to aggression.
c) United Jerusalem is the capital of Israel. In the peace arrangements, the special religious status of the places holy to Islam and Christianity should be safeguarded, under autonomous administration.
d) The Jewish character of the State of Israel so as to realize its Zionist destination and its tasks in immigration and Ingathering of the Exiles.
e) The beginning of an era of regular relationships between Israel and the neighboring states in the political, economic, social and cultural fields.

The peace agreement with Jordan is to be based upon the existence of two independent states: Israel with its capital in United Jerusalem, and an Arab state to the east of Israel. Israel rejects the establishment of an additional separate Palestinian Arab State to the west of the Jordan River. In the neighbouring Jordanian-Palestinian state, the independent identity of the Palestinian and Jordanian Arabs will be able to find its expression, in peace and good neighbourliness with Israel.

Any peace agreement is to be signed subject to approval by the Government and the Knesset.

> (Excerpts from the political resolutions of the 2nd National Congress of the Israel Labor Party, *The Jerusalem Post*, Feb. 27, 1977)

The Israel Council for Israeli-Palestinian Peace Manifesto

We Affirm
1. That this land is the homeland of its two peoples—the people of Israel and the Palestinian Arab people.
2. That the heart of the conflict between the Jews and the Arabs is the historical confrontation between the two peoples of this land, which is dear to both.

3. That the only path to peace is through co-existence between two sovereign states, each with its distinct national identity: the state of Israel for the Jewish people and a state for the Palestinian Arab people, which will exercise its right to self-determination in the political framework of its choosing.
4. That the establishment of a Palestinian Arab state alongside the state of Israel should be the outcome of negotiations between the government of Israel and a recognized and authoritative representative body of the Palestinian Arab people, without refusing negotiation with the Palestine Liberation Organization, on the basis of mutual recognition.
5. That the border between the state of Israel and the Palestinian Arab state will correspond to the pre-war lines of June 1967, except for changes agreed upon by the parties and after settlement of the problem of Jerusalem.
6. That Jerusalem is the eternal capital of Israel. Being sacred to three religions and inhabited by the two peoples, it deserves a special status. It will remain united under a common municipal roof-organization and will be accessible to people of all nations and faiths. Jerusalem will continue to be the capital of the state of Israel, and the Arab part could become, after the establishment of peace, the capital of the Palestinian Arab state. The Holy Places of all three religions will be administered autonomously by their respective institutions.
7. That the border between Israel and the Palestinian Arab state will be open to the free movement of people and goods throughout the land. Palestinian Arabs will not settle in Israel nor Israelis in the Palestinian Arab state other than by consent of the two governments.
8. That the creation of a Palestinian Arab state will contribute decisively to the solution of the national and humanitarian problem of the refugees. Israel will assist in this solution.
9. That the early stages of Israel-Palestinian co-existence will require mutually-agreed-upon security arrangements. There will be guarantees that foreign military forces will not enter the territory of either of the two states.
10. That the two states will be sovereign in all respects, including matters of immigration and return. The state of Israel will preserve its inalienable link to Zionism and to the Jewish people throughout the world, and the Palestinian Arab state will maintain the link of its people to the Arab world.
11. That the two states will aim to conduct a continuing dialogue in order to forge closer relations between them, to solve common problems in a spirit of cooperation and for the benefit of both nations. The two states shall not engage in any acts to alter the structure of the co-existence between them, except by mutual agreement.
12. That for the benefit of all nations in the area there should be a system of regional co-operation, in which both the state of Israel and the Palestinian Arab state will participate.

(*New Outlook*, Vol. 19, No. 2, February–March 1976. This manifesto appeared as an advertisement in the evening newspapers.)

Likud on Foreign Policy and Security

5. FOREIGN POLICY AND DEFENSE
A. Israeli sovereignty between the Mediterranean and the Jordan; Eretz Yisrael for the Jewish people.
B. Positive initiatives for peace—direct negotiations with the Arab states without preconditions and without foreign directives.
C. The continued strengthening of the I.D.F. with weapons systems and training, together with the reduction and prevention of waste and inflated budgets.
D. Establishing the relationship between Israel and the United States on the basis of cooperation while developing the awareness of the strategic importance of a strong Israel for the United States and the West.
E. An information campaign abroad which will explain the right of the Jewish people to Eretz Yisrael as their homeland—and on the destructive intentions of Israel's enemies; posting of the best professional talents for diplomatic and public duties abroad according to national criteria, not narrow party interests.

(From Likud's Election Platform, May 1977.)

D.M.C. On Foreign Policy and Security

When you vote for the Democratic Movement for Change on May 17 you will be voting for a programme to ensure Israel's security and pave the way for peace by:
  1. Strengthening the country's social and economic structure so that it will be strong enough to withstand foreign pressures during negotiations for a settlement.
  2. Agreeing to the return of some of the territories now under Israeli control in order to achieve peace and to ensure that Israel remains predominantly Jewish and fully democratic.
  3. Insisting that Jerusalem remain Israel's capital and the Jordan River her security border, and that Israel retain control of such territory west of the Jordan as is necessary to hold that border.
  4. Agreeing to only one Arab State between Israel and Jordan's eastern border, with its name, regime and character to be determined by its residents. The Palestinian entity will find its expression in that state.

(From D.M.C.'s Election Platform, May 1977.)

Rakah's Peace Plank

The Front will fight for:
1. JUST AND STABLE PEACE BETWEEN THE STATE OF ISRAEL AND THE ARAB STATES
   Peace will be based on respect for the rights of all peoples and states in our region, including those of Israel and the Arab Palestinian people.

Israel must withdraw from all territories occupied during the Six-Day War. The lines of June 4, 1976, will become recognized and secure borders between the State of Israel and the Arab states.

The Arab Palestinian people's right of self-determination and to establish their own independent state, alongside the sovereign state of Israel, must be recognized.

The Geneva Peace Conference must be convened without further delay, with the participation of all sides involved in the conflict, including the PLO as the agreed and recognized representative of the Arab Palestinian people.

(From the Democratic Front for Peace and Equality's election platform, March 1977.)

POSTSCRIPT

We have attempted in this book to describe and analyze facts, achievements and postures, lines of development and stages of consolidation as parts of the conflicts and pressures so deeply rooted in Palestinian and later Israeli reality, with which the workers' parties have had to contend both in theory and in practice.

During the twenties, reformism was prevalent within the majority of the country's working public, with the pioneering-left, represented by Hashomer Hatsair and its urban allies alone, forming only a small minority. In contrast to the other workers' parties to the right and the left, Hashomer Hatsair wanted to resolve the tension and conflicts between international socialism and Israeli socialism, between "reality" and "program," between constructionism and class struggle, between Jewish patriotism and international fraternity—by means of a synthesis of pioneering Zionism and revolutionary socialism, and by integrating class struggle and construction, concern for security and striving for peace. Such a synthesis, however, with all the implications for various aspects of struggle and creativity, was then still largely considered to be an abstract idea and a deviation.

Today, such ideas have already managed to penetrate deeply into wide circles of the working class and they, or other ideas that are essentially very similar, have become common currency, even within the ranks of the Israel Labor Party. Hashomer Hatsair and Mapam are no longer isolated. They have found important and deeply rooted pioneering-leftist allies, though the relationship with these allies has been woven of both rivalry and cooperation. True, the path of the pioneering-left has been marked by turns and twists, by many deviations and retreats. Its progress has also often been held up and distorted by manifestations of instability and despair, and by defeatist attitudes towards the prospects of its own historic mission, despite the encouraging signs of self-examination and rethinking among the socialist worker and pioneering sections of the reformist majority party.

Nevertheless, when we analyze and sum up the past, then beyond the successes and the failures, the achievements and the defeats, a progressing line of development makes itself evident, both of the labor movement as a whole and of its left-socialist pioneering wing in particular.

The future of Israel's labor movement will depend on, first, its will for renaissance and regeneration, for returning to its revolutionary sources and specific values; second, the ability to integrate the "new working class" of predominantly oriental origin into the modern socialist-Zionist labor movement; and third, the courage to take initiatives and clear-cut decisions on the key issue of peace with Israel's neighbors, based on secure borders and a territorial compromise.

Appendix I. State and Constitution

The President

The President of the State is elected by the Knesset for a period of five years, and may be re-elected for one further term. He has the prerogative of pardon and of commuting sentences. He accepts the accreditation of foreign ambassadors and ministers, appoints Israel's ambassadors and ministers, judges and the State Comptroller, and signs all laws except those concerning the presidential powers.

When a new Government is to be formed, the President consults with representatives of the parties and then calls on a member of the Knesset to undertake the task.

The Legislature: The Knesset

Israel is a parliamentary democracy. Supreme authority rests with the Knesset (Assembly), a unicameral legislative body of 120 members.

The Knesset is elected by universal suffrage under proportional representation for four years, but may, by specific legislation, decide on new elections before the end of its term. Electors choose between national lists of candidates, seats being allocated in proportion to the number of votes obtained by each list.

Knesset consent is required before the installation of a new Cabinet, which must resign on losing its confidence. It approves the annual Budget and keeps Cabinet policy under constant survey by means of questions to Ministers and public debates in the plenary and discussions in the Knesset committees, which hear reports from Ministers and senior officials.

Any member may propose that a subject of public importance shall be debated in the House or submitted to a committee for consideration. A motion of no-confidence in the government may be proposed at any time and takes precedence over all other business.

Debates, which are conducted in Hebrew, are open to the public. The proceedings are translated simultaneously into Arabic for Arab members, who may address the House in that language.

The Cabinet

The Cabinet, headed by the Prime Minister, is collectively responsible to the Knesset. It takes office on receiving a vote of confidence from that body, and continues in office until—after resignation (or death) of the Prime Minister, or upon a vote of no-confidence—a new Cabinet is constituted. Ministers are usually but not necessarily members of the Knesset.

As no party has so far commanded an absolute majority, all Cabinets have been based on coalitions.

Appendix II. Population

A. *Population at end of period 1948–1976*

1948	650,000
1952	1,629,500
1956	1,872,400
1960	2,150,400
1964	2,525,600
1968	2,841,100
1972	3,164,400
1976	3,600,000

B. *Origins of the Jewish population (percentages)*

	1948	1960	1976
Europe & America	54.8	35.0	27.0
Asia & Africa	9.8	27.1	22.1
Born abroad	64.6	62.1	49.1
Born in Israel	35.4	37.9	50.9
Total	100.0	100.0	100.0

C. *Population by type of locality*—December 31, 1976
   (percentages)
Total population—3,600,000, living in 889 localities

Type of Locality	Percent of Total Population	Number of Localities
Urban localities	85.8	104
Towns	69.1	
Other urban localities	16.7	
Rural localities	14.1	785
Large villages	3.3	
Small villages	2.1	
Moshavim	3.7	
Moshavim Shitufiim	0.2	
Kibbutzim	2.8	
Temporary, and Bedouin tribes	1.5	
Institutions, farms	0.5	
Living outside localities	0.1	

	Jews		Non-Jews	
	Localities	Population (percent)	Localities	Population (percent)
Urban	87	90.6	24	59.2
Rural	697	9.2	88	40.8

(Statistical Abstract of Israel, 1976)

Appendix III. Political Parties in the Ninth Knesset (1977)

Israel Labor Party

This social-democratic-type party was founded in 1968 by the union of Mapai, Ahdut Haavoda–Poale Zion, and Rafi. Official organs: *Hapoel Hatsair* (weekly, 1907–1970); *Ot* (weekly, 1971–1974); *Migvan* (monthly, established 1976). Unofficial organs: *Davar* (Histadrut daily, established 1925) and *Molad* (a political and literary magazine, established 1948: at first monthly; later quarterly). In the Eighth Knesset the Labor Party controlled 44 seats, the affiliated Arab lists, 3. In the Ninth Knesset the Labor Party holds 28 seats, the affiliated Arab list, seven. *

United Workers' Party (Mapam)

A Jewish-Arab party, pioneering-Zionist and left-socialist in character, founded 1948 by the union of the Hashomer Hatsair Workers' Party and L'Ahdut Haavoda–Poale Zion. Official organs: *Al Hamishmar* (Hebrew daily, established in 1943); *Al-Mirsad* (Arabic weekly, established in 1954; since 1977, monthly) and *Basha'ar* (bi-monthly ideological journal, founded in 1958). In the Eighth Knesset Mapam held seven seats, in the Ninth, four.*

Likud

Bloc of the right-wing opposition parties, established before the elections of 1973 by Gahal (Herut and Liberals), the Free Center, the State List and the Greater Israel Movement. The Likud held 39 seats in the 8th Knesset, and holds 43 in the 9th. In the 8th Knesset the Free Center split into two factions: the one formed with the State List and the Greater Israel Movement the "La'am" Party (January 1976), within the Likud, while the other one left the Likud (October 1976) and joined the Democratic Movement for Change.

* Since 1969, the Israel Labor Party and Mapam have been united in an Alignment (Ma'arah) and submit a joint list of candidates for elections.

National Religious Party (Mafdal)

Based on the principles of religious Zionism. It was founded in 1956 by the union of Misrahi and its independent labor wing—Hapoel Hamisrahi. Official organ: *Hatsofe* (daily, founded 1938). Ten seats in the Eighth Knesset, 12 in the Ninth.

Agudat Israel

Founded 1911 as an extremely religious non-Zionist party. Official organ: *Hamodia* (daily, founded 1960). In the 1973 elections Agudat Israel constituted, together with its independent labor wing, Poale Agudat Israel, the Religious Tora Front. Agudat Israel held three seats in the Eighth Knesset, and holds four in the Ninth.

Poale Agudat Israel

Founded in 1925 as the independent labor-wing of Agudat Israel. Official organ: *She'arim* (daily, founded 1951). Held two seats in the Eighth Knesset, and holds one in the Ninth.

Independent Liberal Party

Founded in 1965 after a split in the Liberal Party. Official organ: *Tmurot* (monthly, established in 1960). Four seats in the Eighth Knesset, one in the Ninth.

Movement for Civil Rights

Split away from the Labor Party in 1973. In the Eighth Knesset three, and later only two seats; in the Ninth, one.

Democratic Movement for Change

Founded in November 1976 by union of Democratic Movement, Shinui Group, Free Center, and Zionist Panthers. Fifteen seats in the Ninth Knesset.

Shlomzion Movement

Founded by Gen. (res.) Ariel Sharon in November 1976, after leaving Likud. Two seats in the Ninth Knesset. Rejoined Likud after the elections.

Democratic Front for Peace and Equality

Founded 1977 by the Communist Party (Rakah), together with nonpartisan Arab nationalists and one of the various Black Panther groups. Four seats (representing Rakah) in the Eighth Knesset, five in the Ninth. **

Camp for Peace and Equality (Heb. abbr. Sheli)

Founded 1977 as a joint election list by Moked, Independent Socialists and Haolam Hazeh. One seat (representing Moked) in the Eighth Knesset, two in the Ninth. ***

The Press

Although the right-wing Likud has no daily organ of its own, the Israeli bourgoisie has at its disposal the daily *Ha'aretz* (founded in 1915), which pretends to be independent, and two afternoon papers sharing this pretension: *Ma'ariv* (established in 1949) and *Yediot Ahronot* (founded in 1939). Some of the parties also publish papers in other languages than Hebrew— for new immigrants: The *Labor Party* controls dailies in Yiddish, Rumanian, Russian, German, French, Polish, Hungarian and Bulgarian. Mapam publishes a weekly in Rumanian, bi-weeklies in Yiddish, Russian and Bulgarian, and a monthly in Persian. Its International Department publishes a bi-monthly *Mapam Bulletin* in English, and the World Union of Mapam Parties a monthly bulletin in English (for the Diaspora and immigrants)—*Brit Mapam.*

There is also an English daily, *The Jerusalem Post* (independent, established in 1932; before 1948 named *The Palestine Post*). A nonpartisan Middle East monthly, *New Outlook* (English, founded in 1957) states as its purpose "to serve as a medium for the clarification of problems concerning peace and cooperation among all the peoples of the Middle East." Dailies in Arabic include *Al-Anba* (founded in 1968), which supports the government; *Al-Quds* (established in 1968), which is independent, representing Palestinian circles in eastern Jerusalem, who favor a Palestinian-Jordanian federation as well as a negotiated Israeli-Arab agreement; *Al-Sha'ab* (founded in 1972) and *Al-Fajar* (established in 1972) which follow a militant nationalist anti-Israeli and anti-Jordanian line.

** Official organs of Rakah: *Al-Itihad* (Arabic paper, established in 1942, twice a week); *Zu Haderekh* (Hebrew weekly, founded in 1950) and *Al-Darb* (Arabic quarterly, founded 1951).
*** Sheli has at its disposal Moked's bi-weekly *Bamoked* (established in 1975) and the weekly *Haolam Hazeh*.

Appendix IV. Knesset Election Results 1949–1977

Party	First Jan. 25, 1949 Electorate 506,567 Valid Votes Cast 434,684 Percent	Seats	Second July 7, 1951 924,885 687,492 Percent	Seats	Third July 26, 1955 1,057,795 853,219 Percent	Seats	Fourth Nov. 3, 1959 1,218,483 964,337 Percent	Seats	Fifth Aug. 15, 1961 1,274,280 1,006,964 Percent	Seats	Sixth Nov. 2, 1965 1,449,709 1,206,728 Percent	Seats	Seventh Oct. 28, 1969 1,758,658 1,427,981 Percent	Seats	Eighth Dec. 31, 1973 2,037,478 1,566,855 Percent	Seats	Ninth May 17, 1977 2,236,293 1,747,820 Percent	Seats
Labor-Mapam Alignment[1]													46.22	56	39.6	51	24.6	32
Israel Labor Party[2]	35.5	46	37.3	45	32.2	40	38.2	47	34.7	42	44.6	55[6]		49[9]		44		28
Ahdut Ha'avoda					8.2	10	6.0	7	6.5	8								
Mapam	14.7[3]	19	12.5[3]	15	7.3	9	7.2	9	7.6	9	6.6	8	7[10]		7		4	
State List													3.11	4				
Herut	11.5	14	6.6	8	12.6	15	13.6	17	13.7	17	21.3	22[7]	21.67	26				
Liberals	5.2	7	18.9	23	10.2	13	6.1	8							30.2	39[11]	33.4	43
Free Centre													1.20	2				
Independent Liberals	4.1	5	3.2	4	4.4	5	4.6	6	13.6	17	3.8	4	3.21	4	3.6	4	1.2	1
National Religious Party	12.2	16	8.3	10	9.1	11	9.9	12	9.8	12	3.75 8.9	4 11	9.74	12	8.3	10	9.6	12
Agudat Israel			3.7	5	4.7	6	4.7	6	3.7	4	3.3	4	3.22	4	3		3.4	4
Poale Agudat Israel			4.0	5	4.5	6	2.8	3	1.9	2	1.8	2	1.83	2	3.8	2	1.4	1
Communists	3.5	4	4.7	5	4.9	5	3.5	5	4.1	5	3.4	4[8]	2.98	4	4.8	5[12]	4.6	5[13]
Arab lists	3.0	2							3.5	4	3.3	4	3.51	4	3.3	3	1.4	1
Haolam Haze											1.36	1	1.23	2				
Movement for Civil Rights															2.2	3	1.2	1
D.M.C.[4]																	11.6	15
Sheli[5]																	1.6	2
Shlomzion																	1.9	2
Others	10.1	7	3.6	3	1.9	—	2.2	—	0.3	—	1.1	—	1.17	—	2.3	—	2.0	1

1. Joint list Labor Party-Mapam, 7th, 8th and 9th Knesset
2. Until 1968: Mapai
3. In 1949 and 1951 Mapam included Ahdut-Haavoda
4. Democratic Movement for Change
5. Moked, Indep. Socialists, Haolam Haze, Black Panthers
6. Mapai, Ahdut Haavoda and Rafi merged in 1968
7. Herut Liberal Bloc (Gahal, 6th and 7th Knesset)
8. 3 Rakah, 1 Maki
9. Labor Party's share in Alignment seats
10. Mapam's share in Alignment seats
11. In 1973 Gahal, Free Center and State List constituted Likud (8th and 9th Knessets)
12. Four Rakah, one Moked (Maki & allies)
13. Democratic Front for peace and Equality (Rakah & allies)

Appendix V.

National Congresses of the Histadrut

First Congress
December 4–9, 1920; in Haifa; 4,433 members in elections; 87 delegates:
Distribution of seats according to parties
Ahdut Haavoda	38
Hapoel Hatsair	27
"New Immigrant" List (Tseire Zion, Hechalutz, Hashomer Hatsair)	16
M.P.S.	6

Second Congress
January 1923, in Tel Aviv, 6,561 voters, 130 delegates:
Ahdut Haavoda	69
Hapoel Hatsair	36
Gdud Haavodah	6
Hashomer Hatsair	4
"Organizational Group" (Yizhaki-Abramowitch)	4
Haifa Railway Workers	3
"Workers List"	3
Workers Fraction (Communist)	3
United Trade Union (Jerusalem)	2

Third Congress
July 1927, in Tel Aviv, 17,036 voters, 201 delegates:
Ahdut Haavoda	108
Hapoel Hatsair	59
Left Poale Zion	14
Kibbutz List	8
Left Opposition	4
Left Bloc (Communist)	3
Labor Palestine Non-Party List	3

Zionist-Revisionist
Workers List 2

Fourth Congress
First Session: February 1933, Tel Aviv
Second Session: January 1934, Tel Aviv
22,341 voters, 201 delegates:
  Mapai 165
  Left Poale Zion 16
  Hashomer Hatsair 16
  Religious Socialists
    (affiliated with Mapai) 1
  Young General Zionists 1
  Yemenite Workers
    (affiliated—Mapai) 1

Fifth Congress
April 1942, Tel Aviv, 88,198 voters, 424 delegates:
  Mapai (including 100 Siah
    Bet faction delegates) 300
  Hashomer Hatsair and
    Socialist League 83
  Left Poale Zion
    (Erem-Nir) 19
  Poale Zion and
    Marxist Circles
    (Yizhaki-
    Abramowitch) 7
  The Zionist Worker
    (General Zionist) 15

Sixth Congress
First Session: November 1944
Second Session: January-February 1945
Tel Aviv, 106,420 voters, 423 delegates:
  Mapai 226
  Left Front (Hashomer
    Hatsair—65 Left
    Poale Zion—22 87
  Hatnua L'Ahdut
    Haavoda 75
  The Zionist Worker 13
  The New Workers'
    Immigration (Pro-
    gressive Zionists) 13
  The Religious Worker 5
  United Yemenite List 2

National Workers
  (Zionist Revisionists)   1
Communists   1

Seventh Congress
  May 1949, Tel Aviv, 142,833 voters, 501 delegates:
  Mapai   286   (57.06%)
  Mapam   172   (34.43%)
  The Religious Worker   11
  The Zionist Worker   19
  Israeli Communist Party   10
  Hebrew Communist
    Party   3

Eighth Congress
  March 1956, Tel Aviv, 410,451 voters, 801 delegates:
  Mapai   463
  Ahdut Haavoda–Poale
    Zion   117
  Mapam   101
  The Zionist Worker
    (Progressive)   42
  Israeli Communist
    Party   33
  General Zionist
    Workers   30
  The Religious Worker   15

Ninth Congress
  May 1960, Tel Aviv, 480,623 voters, 801 delegates:
  Mapai   444
  Ahdut Haavoda–
    Poale Zion   136
  Mapam   112
  The Zionist Worker   46
  General Zionist Worker   28
  Israeli Communist Party   22

Tenth Congress
  January 1966, Tel Aviv, 669,270 voters, 801 delegates:
  Alignment for Unity of
    Israeli Workers
    (Mapai, Ahdut
    Haavoda-Poale Zion,
    Religious Worker)   408   (50.88%)
  Herut-Liberals   122   (15.20)
  Mapam   116   (14.51)

Rafi	97	(12.13)
Independent Liberals	35	(4.42)
Israeli Communist Party (Maki–Mikunis-Sneh)	13	(1.58)
New Communist List (Rakah–Vilner-Toubi)	10	(1.25)

Eleventh Congress

December 1969, Jerusalem, Tel Aviv, 639,131 voters (65.37%), 1,001 delegates:

Labor Party-Mapam Alignment	622	(62.11%)
Herut Liberals	169	(16.85)
Independent Liberals	57	(5.69)
The State List (Rafi independents, Ben-Gurion)	39	(3.85)
The Religious Worker (Affiliated to Alignment)	31	(3.06)
Free Center (Herut Split)	20	(1.99)
Haolam Hazeh–New Force	13	(1.33)
Maki (Israel Communist Party)	18	(1.79)
Rakah (New Communist List)	22	(2.25)
Ahva (Community List of Iraqi Jews)	5	(0.59)
Left Socialist–Zionist Alliance (Split from Mapam)	5	(0.59)

Twelfth Congress

March 1974, Tel Aviv, 777,733 voters (68.7%), 1,501 delegates:

Labor Party-Mapam Alignment	875	delegates	(58.3%)
Religious Worker (affiliated to Alignment)	64		(4.26)
Alignment & Allies	939		(62.56)
Likud (right-wing front)	341		(22.74)
Independent Liberals	90		(5.97)
Rakah (New Communist List)	36		(2.41)

Moked (Maki & Allies)	26	(1.72)
Meri (Haolam Haze & Allies)	11	(0.75)
Left Alliance (Riftin Group)	4	(0.27)
Black Panthers (Communal List of oriental Jews)	24	(1.63)
Ahva (Communal List of Iraqi Jews)	14	(0.91)
Two Communal Lists of Yemenite Jews	11	(0.75)
List "For Electoral Reform"	5	(0.31)

Thirteenth Congress

October 1977, Tel Aviv, 917,126 voters (69%), 1,501 delegates. One percent barrier:

Labor Party-Mapam Alignment	851	delegates	(56.30%)
(Labor's share—45.3%, Mapam's share—11%)			
Likud	429	"	(28.58)
Democratic Movement for Change	122	"	(8.13)
Democratic Front (Rakah & allies)	46	"	(3.06)
Religious Worker	27	"	(1.80)
Independent Liberals & Civil Rights	19	"	(1.27)
Sheli (Moked, Haolam Haze & allies)	11	"	(1.13)

Appendix VI. Trade Unions, Workers Parties and Youth Movements*

A. Trade Unions

Hahistadrut Haklalit shel Haovdim Haivrim Be'eretz Israel (Histadrut)—
General Federation of Jewish Workers in Israel. Founded in 1920, it was preceded by regional organizations of agricultural workers (Judea: 1911, Galilee: 1915), United Committee of Workers of Palestine (1914), Organization of Agricultural Workers of Palestine (1919). Since 1959 the Histadrut has been open to Arab workers. By the decision of the 10th Congress (January 1966) its name was changed to General Federation of Workers in Israel.
Brit Poale Eretz Israel—Union of Palestinian Workers (1927–1959). According to the decision of the Histadrut's 3rd Congress, the Brit was to be a sort of overall organization joining a Jewish workers' federation and an Arab workers' federation. The Arab federation never came into being, most of the Arab workers joining the nationalistic Palestinian Union of Arab Workers, under the influence of the Mufti of Jerusalem. Because of this, the Union of Palestinian Workers (Brit), remained an Arab organization under Histadrut patronage.
Congress of Arab Workers (1945–1959)
A trade union organization under communist influence. It was preceded by the Union of Arab Trade Unions (established in Haifa in 1942). After the creation of the State of Israel, the Congress represented the majority of the organized Arab workers. It disappeared in 1959–1960 when Arab workers were accepted into the Histadrut.

B. Workers Parties (including election lists and political groupings).

Ahdut Haavoda—Unity of Labor (1919–1930).
Its complete name was Socialist-Zionist Union of Jewish Workers of Palestine—Ahdut Haavoda. It was born of union of Poale Zion and the non-partyites at the time of the Second Aliya.
Agriculture and Development. Arab list affiliated with Mapai in 2nd, 3rd, 4th elections.
Arab-Israeli Labor Party (1958–1960). Arab party linked federatively with Ahdut Haavoda–Poale Zion Party.
Borochov Opposition. Left Poale Zion formation within Histadrut and trade unions.
Committee for Unity (1926–1928). Palestinian branch of international

* For the period, preceding the establishment of the State of Israel, when the name Eretz Israel is used as part of a name of a party, it is translated as Palestine.

movement for restoration of trade union unity; participated in by Palestinian Communist party, Left Poale Zion and independents.
Cooperation and Fraternity. Arab list affiliated with Mapai in 4th, 5th, 6th elections.
Democratic Front for Peace and Equality (1977–). Joint election list of Rakah and allied groups to the Ninth Knesset.
Democratic List of Israeli Arabs. Arab list affiliated with Mapai in 1st, 2nd, 3rd elections.
Hakibbutz Ha'artsi Hashomer Hatsair (founded in 1927). National Federation of Kibbutzim of Hashomer Hatsair (Young Guard). Up to formation of Hashomer Hatsair Workers Party also served as the political instrument of Hashomer Hatsair kibbutzim.
Haliga Hasotzialistit (Socialist League) (1936–1946). Workers organization not belonging to Kibbutz Artsi Hashomer Hatsair federation, but identifying itself with it ideologically and politically.
Hamaarach L'ahdut Poale Israel (1965–1968). Front for the Unity of the Workers of Israel. United front of Mapai & Ahdut Haavoda-Poale-Zion Party in the 10th Histadrut Congress and 6th general elections.
Hamaarach shel Mifleget Haavoda ve-Mapam (Founded in 1969). United front of Israel Labor Party and Mapam.
Hamiflaga L'ahdut Haavoda-Poale Zion (1940–1948). Unity of Labor Poale Zion Party. The unification of the Movement for the Unity of Labor and the Poale Zion Palestinian Workers Party.
Hapoel Hatsair (1905–1930). The Young Worker. Non-Socialist Zionist workers' party, fused in 1930 with Ahdut Haavoda to form Mapai.
Hatnua L'ahdut Haavoda (1944–1946). Movement for the Unity of Labor. Left opposition of Mapai (Siah Bet) after schism, as independent organization.
Hazit Hasmol (1944–1945). Election alliance of Hashomer Hatsair, Socialist League and Left Poale Zion toward the 6th Histadrut Congress.
Hashomer Hatsair Workers Party (1946–1948). The joint political framework for Kibbutz Ha'artsi and Socialist League.
Hebrew Communist Party (1945–1949). Previously called Communist Educational Association, Communist Association of Palestine. Split with official Communist Party over problems of Jewish settlement in Palestine. Most of its members joined Mapam.
Independent Socialists, parliamentary group founded 1976 after split of Shulamit Alloni's and Liova Eliav's joint anti-establishment party Ya'ad (goal); joined 1977 Sheli.
Israeli Camp for Peace and Equality (abbr. Sheli), joint election list of Moked, Independent Socialists, Haolam Haze and one of the Black Panther groups. Established 1977.
Israel Communist Party (Maki), founded in 1919. Names before the establishment of Israel: Socialist Workers' Party (M.P.S.), Jewish Communist Party (I.C.P.), Palestinian Communist Party (P.C.P.). Split 1965 into Maki and Rakah. Maki merged 1975 with Blue-Red Movement, founding Moked (Focus).

Israeli Workers List (RAFI) (1965–1968). Minority opposition in Mapai, after formation as an independent party headed by Ben-Gurion, Moshe Dayan and Shimon Peres.

The Kibbutz List, Union of the majority of Hashomer Hatsair kibbutzim, Gdud Haavoda and other groups, towards the 3rd Congress of the Histadrut (1926–1927).

League to Fight Against Racism and Anti-Semitism (1934–1937). Founded by initiative of Left Poale Zion as Palestinian branch of International Anti-Fascist Committee, with headquarters in Paris; composed of Left Poale Zion, communists and independents (known as Anti-Fa).

League for National Liberation (1945–1948). Arab nationalist trend that split away from the official Communist Party and rejoined it after the creation of the State of Israel.

Left Opposition (1926–1927). Union of Left Gdud Haavoda and some members of Bet-Alfa, Hefziba, etc., in elections to 3rd Histadrut Congress.

Marxist Poale Zion (1923–1924). Vesher Erem group, affiliated with World Union of Left Poale Zion until its union with "Social Democratic Poale Zion" headed by Abramovitch and Yizhaki.

Matzpen ("Socialist Organization of Israeli") founded in 1962. Group of pro-Chinese, anti-Zionist communists which split from Maki in 1962.

Mifleget Ahdut Haavoda–Poale Zion (1954–1968). L'Ahdut Haavoda and Erem Left Poale Zionist factions, previously within Mapam, after splitting away and organizing independent party.

Mifleget Haavoda Ha'israelit (Israel Labor Party) founded in 1968 by union of Mapai, Ahdut Haavoda–Poale Zion and Rafi, in January 1968.

Mifleget Hapoalim Hameuchedet (United Workers Party–Mapam) founded in 1948. Union of Hashomer Hatsair Workers' Party and Ahdut Haavoda–Poale Zion.

Mifleget Poale Eretz Israel. Palestine Workers Party (Mapai), founded by union of Ahdut Haavoda and Hapoel Hatsair in January 1930.

Moked (Focus), founded 1975 by union of Maki and New Left Blue-Red Group.

The New Communist List (1965–). Party of neo-Stalinite Arab Communists headed by Meir Vilner and Toufig Toubi, after split from Maki. Abbreviated as Rakah.

Nonparty. An ideological trend without an organization, born during the second Aliya. Refused to join the various parties and demanded the organizational and political unification of Jewish workers in Palestine.

Organizational Committee of Trade Unions (1922–1923). Opposition group, mainly from leaders of rank and file of the building workers, under influence of Left Poale Zion. Called Organizational Committee or Organizational Group.

Party of the Socialist Left in Israel (1953–1954). Leftist group headed by Dr. Moshe Sneh after his expulsion from Mapam; joined Maki in 1954.

The List for Peace (Founded in 1965). Arab list affiliated with Rafi, in election to Sixth Knesset.

Poale Zion (Workers of Zion) (1905–1919). Marxist Socialist-Zionist Party of 2nd Aliya period. Complete name: Jewish Social Democratic Workers Party of Palestine–Poale Zion.
Poale Zion Smol (Left Poale Zion) 1923–1946. Complete name: Palestine Workers Party—Poale Zion. Preceded by: Initiating Committee for Social-Democratic Poale Zion; Propaganda Committee for Jewish Social Democrats (Poale Zion) in Palestine, Marxist Poale Zion in Palestine. United in 1946 in "Movement for Unity of Labor." After splitting from Mapam in 1954, majority remained in Mapam, while a minority (Erem Group) helped found the Ahdut Haavoda-Poale Zion Party.
Progress and Development. Arab list affiliated with Mapai in 4th, 5th, 6th elections.
Progress and Labor. Arab list affiliated with Mapai in 2nd, 3rd, 4th elections.
The Religious Workers (founded in 1934). Religious formation within Histadrut, close to Mapai; was preceded by "Religious Socialists" list in elections to 4th Histadrut Congress.
The Third Force (founded in 1952). Anti-Zionist Trotskyite group.
Tnuat Min Hayesod (founded in 1964). "From the Basis" Movement after split from Mapai, under the leadership of Pinhas Lavon, Prof. Rottenstreich and Y. Kesseh.
Union of Arab Students and Intellectuals in Palestine (1945–1948) Leftist organization under Communist Party influence.
Union of Independent Socialist Zionist Left (founded in 1969). Pro-Soviet faction that split from Mapam because of its opposition to the united front between Mapam and Labor Party.
Union of Internationalist Socialists of Palestine (1934–1943) Leftist opposition Socialist List, after its expulsion from Mapai in 1932.
Workers Fraction. A group representing the Palestinian Communist Party within the Histadrut and within the trade unions.
Workers Party of Palestine (Poale Zion) and Marxist circles. (1935–1942). Yizhaki-Abramovitch wing of Left Poale Zion reunited with Erem-Nir-Zerubavel group in Palestine Workers' Party—Poale Zion.

C. Youth Movements Linked to the Labor Movement

Baharut Solzialistit Ivrit (Jewish Socialist Youth) 1926–1942. Younger members of L'ahdut Haavoda, and of Mapai after unification in 1930.
Gordonia Pioneer Scout Movement (1937–1945). Pioneering youth movement affiliated with Hever Hakvutzot (predecessor of Ihud Hakvutzot V'hakibbutzim) and with Mapai. In 1945 joined the Tnua Hameuhedet (United Movement).
Hahistadrut Haklalit shel Hanoar Haoved (General Federation of Working Youth (1924–1959). In principle, affiliated to the Histadrut generally, but actually led by Ahdut Haavoda and Hapoel Hatsair and later by Mapai. After the 1944 split, run by agreement with Ahdut Haavoda though always predominantly Mapai-controlled.

Hamahanot Ha-olim (The Ascending Camps.) Founded in 1930. Socialist Zionist pioneer youth organization formed by the fusion of the Circle of Student Youth, the Jerusalem Scout Brigade and the Scout Communities of Haifa, Hadera, Petah Tikva and Rehovot. Originally affiliated with the Kibbutz Meuchad and Mapai, after the 1944 split it was affiliated with L'ahdut Haavoda-Poale Zion party. Since 1958, after union with Dror (Freedom) movement abroad, official name became "Dror-Mahanot Ha-olim."

Hatnua Hameuhedet (The Unified Movement) (1945–1959). Socialist Zionist pioneer youth movement, formed by the union of Gordonia and a pro-Mapai section of Hamahanot Ha-olim. Since 1954 when it united with Habonim abroad, the name has been Habonim-Hatnua Hameuhedet. It was affiliated with the Mapai-oriented Ihud Hakvutzot Vehakibbutzim. In 1959 it fused with the Histadrut Haklalit shel Hanoar Haoved.

Histadrut Hanoar Haoved V'hanoar Halomed (Organization of working and student youth) Founded in 1959. Formed by the union of the General Federation of Working Youth and Habonim-Hatnua Hameuhedit. Officially affiliated with the Histadrut as such, it was actually directed by Mapai and Ahdut Haavoda–Poale Zion working by agreement, though Mapai was always dominant. Now exclusively under influence of the Labor Party.

Histadrut Hashomer Hatsair Be'eretz Israel (Organization of Hashomer Hatsair in Palestine [Israel]) founded in 1930. Socialist Zionist Pioneer youth movement affiliated with Kibbutz Artsi-Hashomer Hatsair and politically with Mapam.

Jewish Scout Organization in Palestine (founded in 1930). Educational movement without direct links with the labor movement but actually under Mapai influence.

The Mapai Youth Group (1942–1957). Reorganized 1965–1968; new Youth Group of Israel Labor Party (founded in 1968).

Mapam Youth Section (founded in 1948).

Marxist Circles in Palestine (1932–1935). Young people's organization linked ideologically to Left Poale Zion (Yitzhaki-Abramovitch trend) without any official links to that party. United with Yitzhaki-Abramovich trend in 1935 and official name became: "Palestine Workers' Party Poale Zion and the Marxist Circles."

The Marxist Youth (1935–1942). Young Generation of Palestine Workers Party (Poale Zion) and of the Marxist Circles.

The Marxist Youth in Memory of Borochov (1942–1946). Organization of the Younger Generation of Left Poale Zion from the unification of the separate wings up to the union of Left Poale Zion with Hatnua L'ahdut Haavoda in 1946.

Organization of Palestinian Working Youth in Memory of Borochov (1924–1928). Young Generation of Left Poale Zion, after 1928 its name became Borochovist Youth.

Pioneer Arab Youth (founded in 1954). Fraternal Arab movement of Hashomer Hatsair organization.

Tsofim Halutzim (Pioneer Scouts) 1950–1955. Movement of Socialist-Zionist pioneer youth which split in 1950 from the Jewish Scout Organization. Was affiliated with Kibbutz Hameuchad and united in 1954 with Hamahanot Ha-olim.

Union of Israeli Communist Youth (founded in 1948). Known in short as "Banki." Young Generation of Communist Party in Israel. Before Israeli independence, called Union of Palestinian Communist Youth. After 1965 split, there were two Unions of Communist Youth—one affiliated with Maki and the other with Rakah.

Young Generation of Ahdut Haavoda-Poale Zion Party (1954–1968).

Youth Group of Rafi (1965–1968).

Appendix VII. National Congresses of the Labor Parties

1. Hapoel Hatsair
    1st meeting—Petah Tikva, 1905
    21st Congress (last)—Tel Aviv, 1930
2. Poale Zion
    1st meeting—Jaffa, 1905
    13th Congress (last)—Jaffa, 1919
3. Ahdut Haavoda
    Constitute Assembly—Petah Tikva, 1919
    6th Congress (last)—Tel Aviv, 1930
4. Mapai
    Unification Congress
    (Ahdut Haavoda & Hapoel Hatsair)—Tel Aviv, Jan. 1930
    2nd Congress—Tel Aviv, 1932
    3rd Congress—Tel Aviv, 1935
    4th Congress—Tel Aviv, 1938
    5th Congress (I session)
      Tel Aviv 1941
      (II session) Tel Aviv 1942, April
      (III session) 1942, October (Kfar Vitkin)
    6th Congress—Tel Aviv 1946
    7th Congress—Tel Aviv 1950
    8th Congress (I session) Tel
      Aviv 1956
      (II session) Tel Aviv 1958
    9th Congress (I session)
      Tel Aviv 1959
      (II session) Tel Aviv 1960
      (III session) Tel Aviv 1963
    10th Congress—Tel Aviv 1965
    Unificatiion Convention (Mapai &
    Ahdut Haavoda–Poale Zion & Rafi)
    Jerusalem, January 1968
5. Ahdut Haavoda–Poale Zion
    1st Congress Tel Aviv, 1958
    2nd Congress (I session)
    Haifa, 1961
    (II session) T.A., 1962 (partly in Shfaim)
    Unification Convention with Mapai
      and Rafi–Jerusalem, 1968

6. Rafi
   Constituent Assembly—
   Tel Aviv, 1965
   1st Congress —Tel Aviv 1966
   2nd Congress —Tel Aviv 1967
   Unification Convention,
   Jerusalem 1968

7. Israel Labor Party
   Constituent Congress
   (Unification Congress)—
   Jerusalem, January 1968
   Nominated Congress—
   Tel Aviv, 1969
   1st elected Congress—
   Jerusalem, Tel Aviv 1971
   2nd elected Congress—
   Jerusalem, Tel Aviv 1977

8. Communist Party
   1st Congress (M.P.S.)—
   Tel Aviv 1919
   14th Congress (last before
   split) Tel Aviv 1961
   15th Congress (Maki,
   Rakah, separately) Tel
   Aviv 1965
   16th congress (Maki,
   Rakah, separately) Tel
   Aviv 1969
   17th Congress (Maki,
   Rakah, separately) Tel
   Aviv 1972
   18th Congress (Rakah)—
   Haifa 1976

9. Hashomer Hatsair
   (Until the formation of the Hashomer Hatsair Workers' Party, the Kibbutz Artzi National Federation of Hashomer Hatsair Kibbutzim also served as a tool for political acitivity).
   Constituent Assembly
   (Kibbutz Artzi)—Haifa 1927, April
   2nd General Meeting
   (Kibbutz Artzi)— 1929
   3rd General Meeting
   (Kibbutz Artzi)— 1930
   4th General Meeting
   (Kibbutz Artzi)— 1933
   5th General Meeting
   (Kibbutz Artzi)— 1935

6th General Meeting
   (Kibbutz Artzi)—   1942
Constituent Assembly
   (Hashomer Hatsair
   Workers' Party)—Haifa   1946, February
2nd Congress (Hashomer
   Hatsair Workers' Party)
   —Tel Aviv,   1948, January

10. Left Poale Zion
(This party has gone through successive splits: it was unified from 1924–1928; 1931–1934; 1943–1946; and divided in 1928–1931; 1934–1943)
   1st Congress—Tel Aviv   1924
   10th Congress (last)— Tel
      Aviv,   1946

11. Hatnua l'Ahdut Haavoda
   Constituent Assembly—Tel
      Aviv,   1944, May
   Congress of Unification
      with Left Poale Zion—
      Tel Aviv,   1946, April

12. Mapam
   Unification Congress
      (Hashomer Hatsair Workers'
      Party & L'Ahdut Haavoda-
      Poale Zion)—Tel Aviv,   1948, January
   2nd Congress—Haifa,   1951
   3rd Congress—Haifa,   1958
   4th Congress—Tel Aviv,   1963
   5th Congress (I session)—
      Tel Aviv,   1968, March
      (II session)—Tel Aviv,   1968, October
   6th Congress—Tel Aviv,   1972
   7th Congress (I session)—
      Tel Aviv,   1976, June
      (II session)—Holon,   1977, January

13. Moked
   Unification Assembly (Maki
      & "Blue-Red")—Tel Aviv,   1975, July
   1st Congress (I session)—
      Tel Aviv,   1976, June
      (II session)—Tel Aviv,   1976, July
      (III session)—Tel Aviv,   1977, March

Evolution of Workers' Parties

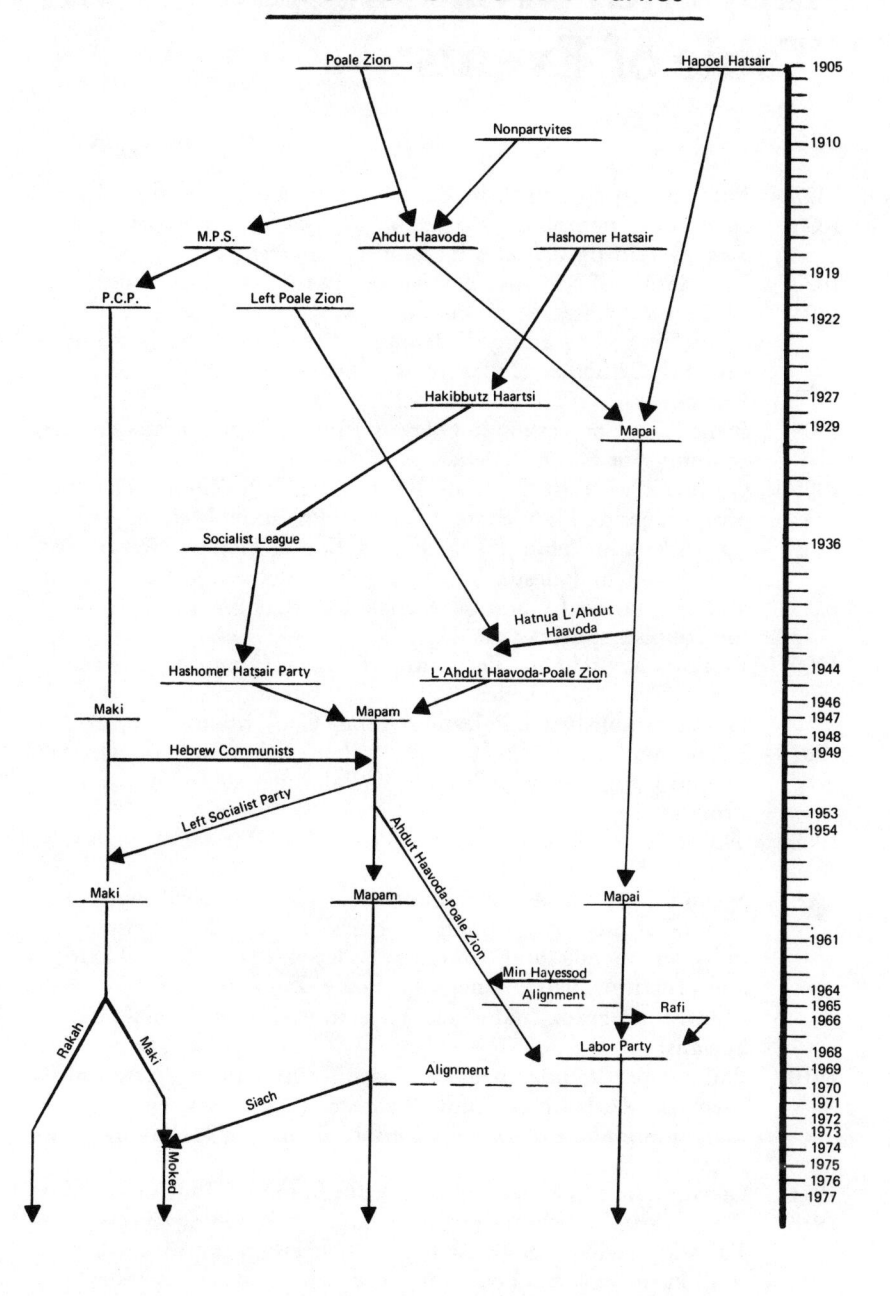

Appendix IX. Chronological Table of Events

1897   First Zionist Congress, in Basle; foundation of Bund in Vilna.

1898   N. Syrkin's pamphlet, *The Jewish Question and the Socialist Jewish State*; Syrkin participates in Zionist Congress.

1899   Foundation of Socialist Zionist societies in East and West.

1903   "Uganda debate" at Sixth Zionist Congress; Poale Zion Council in Vilna; beginning of debate between Sjemists, Territorialists and Orthodox (Palestinians); beginnings of Zeire Zion in Russia.

1904   Poale Zion Convention in Odessa; schism of Territorialists (S.S.); beginning of Second Aliya.

1905   Outbreak of First Russian Revolution; 7th Zionist Congress rejects Uganda Plan; Second Aliya to Palestine; Meeting of Jewish workers in Petah Tikva; Foundation of Hapoel Hatsair and Poale Zion in Palestine; Borochov's pamphlet "Class Struggle and the National Question"; Poale Zion Congress in Berdichev; the Sjemists split away.

1906   B. Borochov's "Our Platform"; Poltava Congress of Russian Poale Zionist adopts clear Palestinian definition; Hapoel Hatsair journal established in Palestine; Ramle Convention.

1907   Foundation of World Union of Poale Zion in The Hague; Second Congress of Poale Zion in Palestine; adoption of Ramle Program.

1908   Third Congress of Palestinian Poale Zion; formation of Hashomer.

1909   Second Congress of Poale Zion World Union in Krakow; formation of Kapai (Palestinian Workers' Fund); Negotiations on unity in Vienna and America between Poale Zion, Sjemists and Territorialists; American Poale Zion adopts new non-Marxist program; name changed from Social Democratic to Socialist.

1910   Failure of Vienna negotiations; in America, Territorialists (Symkis, Zuckerman) and Sjemists (Zhitlovski) join Poale Zion; foundation of Dagania; establishment of Ha'ahdut (journal).

1911   Convention of Galilee workers; convention of Judean workers.

1913   Third World Congress of Poale Zion greets kibbutz projects in Palestine; debate on Russian party's decision not to participate in Zionist Congress; Poale Zion and Zeirei Zion delegates appear together at Zionist Congress; joint committee for Galilean and Judean workers; beginnings of Histadrut Hapoalim Hahaklaim

(United Committee of Palestinian Workers), beginnings of Hashomer Hatsair in Galicia; beginnings of Dror in the Ukraine.
1914 Outbreak of World War I.
1915 Expulsion to Egypt; debate over volunteering for British Army; Hechalutz formed in America by Ben-Zvi and Ben-Gurion.
1916 Palestinian Poale Zion accepted into Socialist International's Bureau; beginnings of enlistment; establishment of Kfar Giladi, Federation of Samarian Workers formed.
1917 Outbreak of Russian Revolution; Hechalutz established in Russia by Y. Trumpeldor; Russian Territorialists and Sjemists unite; Kiev Congress of Russian Poale Zion; October Revolution; Balfour Declaration; Borochov dies.
1918 British Army enters Palestine; enlistments in America and Palestine; beginnings of movement for unity among the Jewish battalions.
1919 Third Aliya; members of Russian Hechalutz and Zeire Zion, first Hashomer Hatsair members come to Palestine; Congress of Agricultural Federation (Unification Congress) in Petah Tikva; the debate over establishing Ahdut-Haavoda; Hapoel Hatsair refuses and Ahdut Haavoda formed by fusion of Poale Zion and nonpartyites; Council of World Union of Poale Zion in Stockholm; beginnings of debate over Zionist Congress and recognition of Ahdut Haavoda; formation of M.P.S.–Poale Zion in Palestine by opponents of unification.
1920 Fifth World Congress of Poale-Zion in Vienna; debate over Zionist Congress and joining Comintern; World Union splits into right and left unions; split among Russian leftist Poale Zionists into "Social Democrats" and "Communists"; Third Congress of Russian Zeire Zion in Kharkov decides to establish independent Socialist-Zionist party (Z.S.); Union of Hapoel Hatsair and (non-Socialist) Zeire Zion in Hitachdut, in Prague; organization of Union of Zeire Zion (Z.S.) in Warsaw; Trumpeldor's appeal to Palestinian workers against party strife and for federative union; defense of Tel Hai; Trumpeldor's death; meeting of new immigrants on Mount Carmel: Russian Hechalutz, Zeire Zion and Hashomer Hatsair; Gdud Haavoda (Labor Battalion) formed; formation of General Federation of Jewish Workers' (Histadrut) in Haifa; members of Z.S. join Ahdut Haavoda.
1921 Negotiations between Poale Zion Left Union and Comintern on former's adhesion and on recognition of Zionism; growing liquidationist trends within sections of the Left Union (Kampferbund) and its Palestinian branch (I.C.P. as section of P.C.P.); formation of World Hechalutz Organization; Jaffa events; murder of Y. H. Brenner and Z. Shatz; Gdud Haavoda settles in Ein Harod and Tel Yosef; first moshav ovdim: Kfar Yehizkel; Moshav Nahalal established; members of Hashomer Hatsair in Betania Ilit and Nahalal-Gedra road.

1922 Failure of negotiations between Left Poale Zionists and Comintern; growing liquidationist trends in Palestine and abroad; expulsion of (Palestinian-centered) Berlin Organizing Committee from leftist World Union; formation of the Organization Group (Yitzhaki-Abramovitch) in Palestine; Hashomer Hatsair settlement in Bet Alfa.

1923 Liquidationists in Poale Zion join Yevsektzia abroad and establish P.C.P. in Palestine Second Congress of Histadrut; formation of Marxist Poale-Zionists in Palestine; Right Poale Zion (with 2½ International) join Socintern; split in Gdud Haavoda: Ein Harod and Tel Yosef.

1924 Members of Hashomer Hatsair meet in Bet Alfa; founding convention of World Hashomer Hatsair Organization in Danzig; fusion of Left Union of Poale Zion with Berlin Organizing Committee to join Committee for Labor Palestine (together with Right Poale Zion, Z.S., Hitachdut and Hashomer Hatsair; the two Left Poale Zion groups in Palestine merge; beginning of Fourth Aliya.

1925 Establishment of daily "Davar," Hanoar Haoved, Hapoel and Ohel; Right Poale Zion unites with Z.S.; moshav ovdim movement established.

1926 Economic crisis and unemployment; liquidationist trends on margins of workers' camp; split in Gdud Haavoda; the Left Gdud; Left Opposition; Unity Group; the Kibbutz List (Hashomer Hatsair, Gdud Haavoda, etc.); elections to Third Congress of Histadrut.

1927 Third Congress of Histadrut; organization of Kibbutz Ha'artsi Hashomer Hatsair, in Haifa; establishment of Kibbutz Hameuchad, in Petah Tikva; Elkind and his comrades return to Russia; Second World Convention of Hashomer Hatsair, in Danzig; orange-picking disturbances in Petah Tikva.

1928 Left Poale Zion closed down in Soviet Union; parties in Palestine renew debate over unification; split in Left Poale Zion; beginning of Fifth Aliya.

1929 Fifth Aliya; Young Hashomer Hatsair kibbutzim go to colonies (moshavot); Unity Agreement between Ahdut Haavoda and Hapoel Hatsair, and referendum on this question; riots; remnants of Gdud Haavoda (Kfar Giladi, Ramat Rachel, Tel Yosef) join Kibbutz Hameuchad.

1930 Ahdut Haavoda and Hapoel Hatsair unite: formation of Mapai (in Tel Aviv); Poale Zion-Z.S. unites with Hitachdut abroad; third World Convention of Hashomer Hatsair, in Vrutky; schism of Russo-Latvians to form Netzah; Kibbutz Ha'artsi Council in Mishmar Haemek; formulation of minimum program for unity.

1931 Unemployment in colonies, Palestinian Left Poale Zion groups merge.

1932 Renewed immigration; beginnings of economic upsurge.

Chronological Table of Events · 361

1933	Hitler comes to power in Germany; increased immigration; fourth congress of Histadrut; Arlozoroff assassinated.
1934	Anti-fascist ferment among Palestinian Jewish workers; Ben-Gurion–Jabotinsky agreement; Gordonia unites with Hever Hakvutzot; split in Left Poale Zion.
1935	Histadrut referendum on Ben-Gurion-Jabotinsky agreement; united front of Hashomer Hatsair, Hakibbutz Hameuchad and Left Poale Zion; Vesher wing of left Poale Zion leaves to join Mapai; Kibbutz Ha'artsi Council in Hadera: debate over organizing Hashomer Hatsair voters in cities and colonies; fourth World Convention of Hashomer Hatsair in Poprad.
1936	Immigration reaches a peak; beginning of riots; settlement renewed; "wall and tower" settlements; formation of "Socialist League."
1937	Peel Committee publishes report on partition; changes in Poale Zion.
1938	Debate over partition; White Paper published; opposition formed in Mapai's urban branches; appearance of Siah Bet on national level.
1939	1st Zionist Congress–Partition Congress; left Poale Zion participates in Congress; beginning of World War II.
1940	Expanding enlistments and construction for army camps; radicalization within working class; opposition within Mapai (Siah Bet); law bans land sales; debate over "gdudism" vs. "defending the country"; workers debate over Soviet Union and implication of Molotov-Ribbentrop Agreement; ferment within P.C.P.
1941	Formation of Palmach; Nazi invasion of U.S.S.R.; elections to fifth convention of Histadrut; Hashomer Hatsair wins 20 percent (17,000 votes).
1942	Fifth Histadrut Congress: debate over leftist parties' participation in administrative organs and over attitude toward Red Army; Kibbutz Ha'artsi Council in Mishmar Ha'emek decides to prepare the ground for an independent party of Hashomer Hatsair; dispute within Tel Aviv Workers Council; Mapai Convention in Kfar Vitkin; union of Left Poale Zion groups.
1943	Intensified friction within Mapai; daily *Mishmar* established.
1944	Split in Mapai; formation of Tnua L'ahdut Haavoda; death of Berl Katznelson; beginnings of negotiations on left unity and formation of Left Front (Hashomer Hatsair and Poale Zion); elections to Sixth Congress of Histadrut; formation of Arab League for National Liberation; first session of Histadrut's Sixth Congress.

1945 End of World War II; disintegration of Left Front; second session of Histadrut's Sixth Congress; negotiations on left unity; Labour Party in England; formation of Hebrew Communist Party.

1946 Illegal immigration and struggle against British administration; debate over forms of struggle; failure of negotiations on left unity; Left Poale Zion unites with Hatnua L'ahdut Haavoda; Anglo-American Committee of Investigation presents report; elections to 22nd Zionist Congress; equal status for Hashomer Hatsair and L'ahdut Haavoda–Poale Zion.

1947 First Palestinian debate in U.N.; Gromyko's speech; report by U.N. Enquiry Commission; partition; Hashomer Hatsair and Ahdut Haavoda–Poale Zion appear together and present joint resolution; discussion in U.N. and campaign to win two-thirds; Zarapkin's address; U.N. decides to establish State of Israel; renewed negotiations on left unity; outbreak of riots.

1948 Formation of United Workers' Party (Mapam) in Tel Aviv; declaration of the State of Israel and formation of provisional government; outbreak of War of Independence; Communist factions unite in Israel Communist Party (Maki); Palmach staff disbanded; elections to constitutional Assembly.

1949 Mapam Council decides not to join coalition government; Hebrew Communists expelled from Maki and many join Mapam; Maki returns to militantly anti-Zionist line.

1950 Intensified internal debate within Mapam; growing differences with Mapai minority within Kibbutz Hameuchad.

1951 Mapam's Second Convention in Haifa ratifies program; Kibbutz Hameuchad splits; formation of Ihud Hakvutzot Vehakibbutzim; elections to Second Knesset; failure of negotiations on Mapam participation in new government.

1952 Growing internal divisions within Mapam; leftist ferment within unity front; Oren's arrest and the Prague trials; rejection of leftist criticism of Mapam's vigorous reaction to Prague trials.

1953 Sneh and his group expelled from Mapam; formation of the party of the Socialist Left; debate with ultra-leftists within Kibbutz Ha'artsi; trial of Jewish physicians in Moscow; Arab workers accepted into Histadrut trade unions; Ben-Gurion leaves for Sde Boker; Moshe Sharett becomes Prime Minister and Foreign Minister; Pinhas Lavon becomes Minister of Defense.

1954 M. Yaari publishes thesis on "Ingathering of the Exiles in the Mirror of our Days"; Kibbutz Ha'artsi Council in Givat Haviva; summing-up debate with ultra-leftists; Ahdut Haavoda and Erem group leave Mapam to form the Ahdut Haavoda–Poale Zion Party; Mapam Council in Haifa ratifies organizational statutes and accepts Arabs into membership; formation of Pioneering Arab Youth; the security scandal; Party of Socialist Left unites with Maki.

CHRONOLOGICAL TABLE OF EVENTS · 363

1955 Lavon removed and replaced by Ben-Gurion as Defense Minister; elections to Third Knesset; Mapam and Ahdut Haavoda join the new government.
1956 Twentieth Congress of C.P.S.U.; Hungarian revolt; the "Polish October"; Sinai Campaign.
1957 Retreat from Sinai and Gaza Strip; Israel adheres to Eisenhower Doctrine; Mapam ranks debate Sinai Campaign; revelations of 20th C.P.S.U. Congress and Hungarian events; *Facing of our Generation* by Meir Yaari is published.
1958 Mapam's Fourth Convention, establishment of theoretical and political journal *Ba-Shaar*.
1959 Knesset campaign to abolish military administration; arms deal with West Germany; government resigns; elections to Fourth Knesset.
1960 Renewed government coalition including Mapam and Ahdut Haavoda; Arab workers accepted into Histadrut; "Lavon Affair" and growing dissension within Mapai.
1961 Government resigns; Lavon removed from post as Histadrut Secretary; formation of government coalition including Ahdut Haavoda, with Mapam in opposition; beginnings of crystallized ideological opposition within Mapai.
1962 New Economic Policy; five-party proposal to abolish military government rejected in Knesset by 59 to 55; Ben-Aharon resigns from government; Ahdut Haavoda–Poale Zion Convention; Lavon Group publishes bi-weekly *Min Hayesod*.
1963 Ben-Aharon proposes federative union of workers' parties; M. Yaari publishes *From Vision to Reality*; military government saved by one vote; affair of German scientists in Egypt, Ben-Gurion restrains campaign; Mapam's Fourth Convention; negotiations on a new alignment of the labor movement; Mapam suggests pioneering-left unity to Ahdut Haavoda; campaign against visit by F. Y. Strauss to Israel; Ben-Gurion's government resigns and Eshkol government formed; Mapam wins success in Beersheba; growing factional strife within Mapai; Mapai Convention; modification of military government; Ahdut Haavoda–Poale Zion Council calls for general federative unity (new Alignment); third session of Mapai Convention.
1964 Negotiations on Mapam adherence to government coalition; Mapam Council decides against; Min Hayesod group threatens secession from Mapai; Min Hayesod organizes Hulda meeting; Eshkol's reconciliation letter to Hulda; Ben-Gurion and Mapai Younger Men against Eshkol's letter; "abrogation of (Lavon's) removal" held up by Eshkol; negotiations on a dual alignment between Mapai and Ahdut Haavoda–Poale Zion; both parties debate dual alignment; Min Hayesod leaves Mapai and forms Min Hayesod Movement; Ben-Gurion renews the Affair;

Mapai Central Committee ratifies Alignment; Eshkol government resigns because of renewal of Affair; Mapai Central Committee supports Eshkol and rejects Ben-Gurion's demands to reopen Affair; coalition government under Eshkol re-established with same party and personal composition.

1965 Mapai's Tenth Convention; Eshkol's majority a majority of 60 percent as compared with Ben-Gurion for the Alignment and against reopening the Affair; the Ahdut Haavoda–Poale Zion Council votes for Alignment with Mapai; public debate over diplomatic relations with Germany; debate renewed over "preventive war" in view of Arab decisions concerning diversion of Jordan's sources; Bourguiba, President of Tunisia, in favor of peace negotiations between Arab countries and Israel; growing factional dissension within Maki—15th Convention approaches; Alignment between Mapai and Ahdut Haavoda–Poale Zion formed; split in Liberal Party over establishing parliamentary bloc with Herut (Gahal); opponents of the bloc form Independent Liberal Party; intensified struggle between partisans of Eshkol and Ben-Gurion over choice of head of candidates for Knesset elections and role of Prime Minister afterwards; split in Mapai; minority, headed by Ben-Gurion, forms Israeli Workers List (Rafi), establishes itself as separate party in Knesset, and its members are expelled from Mapai; sabotage activities by Al-Fatah Palestinian terrorist organization in Jewish communities; retaliatory raids by Zahal in Jordan; debate over this between Mapam and government; Herut members of Histadrut join with liberal Labor Movement faction in Blue-White faction in preparation for Histadrut elections; split in Maki—each of the two factions holding its own 15th Convention and claiming the name of Maki; elections to 10th Congress of Histadrut; elections to Sixth Knesset and municipalities; negotiations on formation of new government.

1966 Tenth Congress of Histadrut; Mapam representative, Abdul Aziz Z'ubi, Mayor of Nazareth; new government, headed by Levi Eshkol, composed of Alignment, Mapam, National Religious Party, Independent Liberals, and Poale Agudat Israel; policies of economic slowdown; growing unemployment; Mapam suggests alternative economic program; crisis in Herut; infiltrations, mines and sabotage activities by Al-Fatah, from Jordan and Syria, and Zahal reprisals (Sam'u, etc.); abolition of military administration apparatus in Arab-populated frontier areas.

1967 Demonstrations against firings and unemployment; Mapam demands "slowing down the slowdown," and enactment of unemployment insurance legislation; intensified infiltrations from Syria and Jordan, increased Syrian activity to divert Jordan sources and prevent water flowing to Israel; J.-P. Sartre and

Simone de Beauvoir visit Egypt and Israel; intellectuals throughout world come out for peace and against dangers of Israel's annihilation; growing tension between Israel and Egypt; U.N. Forces evacuated by Nasser's demand; Tiran Straits closed, Egyptian-Jordinian military alliance, Egyptian forces flow to Sinai Peninsula; Moshe Dayan co-opted to government as Defense Minister, Menahem Begin (Herut) and Yosef Sapir (Liberals) join as Ministers without Portfolio; Six-Day War ends with Israeli victory; Knesset decides to unify Jerusalem and integrate it into Israel; U.S.S.R., Hungary, Bulgaria, Czechoslovakia and Yugoslavia sever diplomatic ties, with Israel, Rumania and Cuba not following suit; U.N. Assembly rejects Yugoslavia's demand for unconditional Israel retreat; Security Council adopts British resolution to establish stable peace by combining Israeli evacuation from Arab territories with cessation of belligerency, the determination of secure and recognized borders, freedom of shipping and a solution for the refugee problem; Arab Summit Conference in Khartoum—for a political settlement but without negotiations, without recognition and without peace; Mapam publishes peace plan, including return of West Bank to Jordan in the event of peace, and the perspective of confederation between Israel and Jordan; formation of Movement for Greater Israel (against returning territories), and of Movement for Peace and Security by university people; policies of "open bridges" over the Jordan; increased Al-Fatah activities; unity negotiations between Mapai, Ahdut Haavoda–Poale Zion, and Rafi; Mapam suggests to Mapai and Ahdut Haavoda–Poale Zion forming union without Rafi; Rafi supporters within Mapai cause its rejection; the "Czechoslovakian Spring."

1968 Formation of Israel Labor Party by union of Mapai, Ahdut Haavoda–Poale Zion and Rafi (Ben-Gurion does not join); Mapam debates entering into negotiations with the Labor Party for the establishment of an Alignment; Mapam's Fifth Convention (first session in March) authorizes negotiations; second session, in October, votes to establish Alignment with Labor despite Rafi oppositions; El Al plane hijacked by Al-Fatah and taken to Algeria; plane released after extended negotiations and after release of Arab terrorists imprisoned in Israel; growing terrorism against Israeli civilian population; Zahal operation against Al-Fatah base in Karame in Jordan; Labor Party, government and public debate future of occupied territories—whether or not to return them as part of peace treaty, and where the "secure and recognized borders" are to be; Abba Eban presents nine-point program; El Al plane attacked in Athens; Zahal reprisal against Beirut Airport; Maki conducts 16th Convention; student revolt in France;

Warsaw Pact countries invade Czechoslovakia. Nixon elected president of the United States.

1969 French embargo on arms sales to Israel; government crisis in Lebanon over terrorist activities; show trials of "spies" (mostly Jews) and public hanging in Bagdad; El Al plane attacked in Zurich; Israeli air force bombs terrorist bases in Syria as reprisal; King Hussein presents "six-clause program"; four-power meetings on Middle East crisis; escalation along the Suez Canal; Zahal reprisal forays into Egyptian territory; Labor–Mapam Alignment established; Rakah holds 16th Convention; Levi Eshkol dies; Golda Meir chosen as Israel's fourth Prime Minister; Labor Party and government debate economic integration of occupied territories with Israel, integration rejected as disguised annexation; deteriorating relations within the Labor Party, some former Rafi'ites threatening to secede; small extremist group of opponents of Alignment leaves Mapam; elections to 11th Congress of Histadrut; elections to 7th Knesset.

1970 Golda Meir forms new Cabinet with increased Gahal representation; Mapam participates with two Ministers without Portfolio, not joining the Labor Party–Gahal programmatic coalition; the "Who Is a Jew" crisis; "Goldmann Affair"; Hebron Controversy; G. Meir reaffirms acceptance of S.C. resolution of November 1967, as well as readiness to conduct peace talks according to the Rhodes Formula; the Labor Party and Gahal are drawing apart; Mapam reverses its decision of not joining the coalition—accepts Ministry of Health and Ministry of Absorption of New Immigrants; American Peace Initiative ("Rogers' Plan"), with Israel, Egypt and Jordan responding; Gahal ministers resign from government; agreement on cease-fire and "Military Stand-Still" along Suez Canal; the violation of the "Stand-Still" by the Egyptians and Russians postpones the starting of Jarring peace talks; wave of Palestinian air piracy; civil war in Jordan; President Nasser's death; Anwar Sadat Egypt's new President.

1971 Jarring's proposals for frontier settlement between Israel and Egypt; Rogers' proposals for partial agreement with a view to opening of Suez Canal; Brezhnev "Doctrine" of Soviet responsibility for stability of East European regimes; clashes between Army and Palestinian organizations in Jordan; Syrian military intervention in Jordan; war between India and Pakistan; Bangladesh an independent state; show trials against Jews in U.S.S.R.; world conference to help Soviet Jewry (Brussels); political purges in Egypt; Black Panthers demonstrate in Jerusalem and elsewhere in Israel; death of Yitshak Tabenkin and Eliezer Hacohen; devaluation of Israeli pound; resolution on principle for creating federation among Egypt, Libya and Syria;

People's Republic of China admitted to U.N. instead of Taiwan; delegation of African presidents visits Israel and Arab states; Mapam Council sums up debate on problems of contemporary socialism.

1972 Student riots in Egypt; King Hussein's plan for federation between East and West banks of Jordan; death of Dr. Moshe Sneh; rupture between Uganda and Israel; municipal elections in occupied territories; Israel's P.M. visits Rumania; Soviet advisers and experts leave Egypt; resolution on merger between Egypt and Libya in 1973; Nixon visits Peking and Moscow; ransom payment imposed on university graduates wishing to leave U.S.S.R.; coalition crisis in Israel over civil marriage; skyjacking and terror activities of Black September abroad; Israeli Olympiad participants murdered in Munich; Japanese terrorists' assault on civilians at Lod airport; Zahal and Israeli air force raid terrorist bases in Lebanon and Syria; peace agreement in Vietnam; Nixon re-elected president of United States; Mapam's Party Congress confirms with big majority continued participation in alignment with Israel Labor Party. Meir Talmi succeeds Meir Yaari as Mapam Secretary-General.

1973 Ephraim Katsir elected President of Israel; many African countries sever diplomatic ties with Israeli; struggle between doves and hawks within Israel Labor Party leadership intensifies; right-wing parties join in National Liberal Union (Likud); factional struggle within Israel Communist Party (Maki)—opposition group, led by Ester Vilenska, expelled; Maki joins Blue-Red Movement in Moked (Focus) election list; Haolam Hazeh joins Siah (New Israeli Left) and Vilenska group in Meri (Israel Radical Camp) election list; interfactional compromise within Labor Party leadership (Galilee Document); polling for Histadrut Convention; the Ben-Aharon Affair; suprise invasion of Syrian and Egyptian armies (Yom Kippur War); Arab oil boycott, Security Council resolutions on cease-fire (Resolutions No. 338 and 339); "Six Points" agreement between Israel and Egypt and talks at Kilometer 101 on implementation of cease-fire; Ben Gurion dies; judicial committee appointed to investigate the military shortcomings of October 6, 1973; dovish election platform adopted by Israel Labor Party (14 principles) after heavy pressure for ousting Moshe Dayan from Labor Party leadership and Cabinet; Peace Conference opens at Geneva—Israel, Egypt and Jordan participating; polling for Eighth Knesset.

1974 Energy crisis in Europe and America; disengagement agreement between Israel and Egypt; Syrian "war of attrition" against Israel on the Golan Heights; death of Deputy Minister of Health Abdul Aziz Zu'abi; coalition government in Israel with Golda Meir as Prime Minister; 12th Histadrut Congress; protest movements; widespread demand for Moshe Dayan to resign from government—crisis and threatened split within the Labor Party; Golda Meir's government resigns; Yitshak Rabin elected Labor Party's candidate to form the new Cabinet; terrorist attacks from Lebanese bases on women and children in Galilee—Israel retaliates against bases in Lebanon; intensified efforts by U.S. Secretary of State Henry Kissinger to negotiate disengagement agreement between Syria and Israel—the agreement is signed in Geneva; Rabin government constituted, based on Alignment, Independent Liberals and Civil Rights Movement (later National Religious Party joins, Civil Rights Movement walks out); armed conflict between Turkey and Greece over Cyprus; fall of fascist junta in Greece; illegal Gush Emunim settlement at Sebastya near Nablus—removed by the Army; Gerald Ford succeeds Nixon as U.S. president; Arab Summit at Rabat declares P.L.O. only representative of Palestinians; P.L.O. admitted as observers to U.N.; Israel expelled from UNESCO.

1975 King Faisal assassinated—Khaled crowned King of Saudi Arabia; death of Chou En-lai; end of American intervention in Vietnam; European Security Conference at Helsinki; civil war in Lebanon and Syrian military intervention; Kissinger missions to the Middle East to bring about interim agreement between Israel and Egypt; mass demonstrations in Israel for and against the agreement with Egypt; endorsement of the agreement by the Knesset and signature at Geneva; opening of the Suez Canal; rift between Egypt and Syria because of Egyptian-Israeli Interim Agreement; rapproachement between Jordan and Syria; U.N. Assembly condemns Zionism as "a form of racism"; municipal elections in West Bank villages; illegal Gush Emunim settlement at Sebastya—removed by the Army, but settlers allowed to stay temporarily at nearby army camp (Kaddum); municipal elections in Nazaret—Communist mayor elected.

1976 Mounting unrest and clashes on the West Bank; unrest among Arab villagers in Galilee following land requisitions for development projects—clashes with the police; municipal elections in West Bank towns and large villages—the majority of the victors nationalists and leftists; E. Sarkis President of Lebanon; "good fence" on Israel-Lebanon border; Riyadh meeting and Cairo summit to end civil war in Lebanon and bridge Syrian-Egyptian rift; death of Mao Tse-tung and succession by Hua Kuo-feng; Israeli commando rescues Air France passengers kidnapped by Palestinian terrorists and brought to Entebbe in Uganda; presidential elections in the United States—J. Carter elected; Gush Emunim leader Rabbi Levinger of Kiryat Arba provokes clashes between Jews and Muslims in Hebron about status of Cave of the Patriarchs; Mapam's 7th National Congress discusses peace initiatives and future of the Alignment; negotiations between Mapam and Labor Party on common platform in forthcoming elections; National Religious ministers expelled from government coalition for abstaining during no-confidence vote in the Knesset; Rabin Cabinet resigns and new elections announced for May 1977; Rabin heads caretaker Cabinet till elections.

1977 (Jan.–June) Violent demonstrations in Egypt against higher food prices; tension on the northern border following entrance of Syrian troops into South Lebanon; Rabin meets Ivory Coast President Houphouet at Geneva; U.N. Secretary K. Waldheim and U.S. Secretary of State C. Vance visit the Middle East; Congress of Israel Labor Party chooses Y. Rabin as party leader and candidate for premiership; Mapam decides to continue Alignment with Labor Party; U.S. President J. Carter meets Prime Minister Y. Rabin, Presidents A. Sadat and H. Assad, and King Hussein; Palestine National Council meets in Cairo; continuous clashes between Christians and P.L.O. in south Lebanon; serious labor unrest in Israel; Y. Rabin steps down as head of the Alignment's list of Knesset candidates and is replaced by S. Peres; elections to the Ninth Knesset: heavy losses for Alignment, success for DMC; Likud emerges as strongest party, Likud leader M. Begin; Prime Minister M. Dayan deserts Labor Party and accepts post of Foreign Minister in Begin's Cabinet; Alignment in opposition; Histadrut elections; Alignment keeps its overall majority.

Appendix X: Suggested References

Jewish Problem: Zionism
Arnoni, M. S. *Zionism as a Movement of National Liberation*, Tel Aviv, 1969.
Ben-Gurion, David. *The Jews in Their Land*, London, 1966.
Buber, Martin. *Israel and Palestine: The History of an Idea*, London, New York, 1952.
Cohen, Israel. *A Short History of Zionism*, London, 1951.
Herzl, Theodor. *The Jewish State: An Attempt at a Modern Solution of the Jewish Question*, New York, 1970.
Hertzberg, Arthur (ed.). *The Zionist Idea*—A Historical Analysis and Reader, New York, 1969.
Laqueur, Walter. *A History of Zionism*, New York, 1972.
Leon, Avraham. *The Jewish Question—A Marxist Interpretation*, New York, 1970.
Parkes, J. *A History of the Jewish People*, London, 1962.
Tsur, J. *Zionism—National Liberation Movement*, Jerusalem, 1968.
———. *Zionism in Question*, London, 1969.
Periodicals: Jewish Chronicle, Jewish Quarterly, Jewish Observer (L.) *Commentary, Midstream, The American Zionist, Jewish Frontier, Youth and Nation, Israel Horizons* (New York)

The State of Israel—Facts and Problems
Absorption of Immigrants ("Israel Today" Pamphlets), Jerusalem, 1965.
Arian, Alan (ed.). I. *The Elections in Israel—1969;* II. *The Elections in Israel—1973*, Edison, N.J., 1975.
Aumann, Moshe. *Land Ownership in Palestine, 1880–1948*, Jerusalem, 1976.
Avineri, Shlomo. *Israel in the Post-Ben-Gurion Era; the Nemesis of Messianism* (reprint of *Midstream*, New York, September, 1965).
Bauer, Yehuda. "From Cooperation to Resistance: The Haganah 1938–1946," *Middle Eastern Studies* Vol. II, No. 3, August 1966.
Begin, Menahem. *The Revolt, Story of the Irgun*, New York, 1957.
Ben-Gurion, David. *Years of Challenge*, London, 1964.
Ben-Gurion Looks Back, London, 1965.
Bentwich, Norman. *Israel Resurgent*, London, 1960.
Brenner, Y. S. "The Stern Gang 1940–1946," *Middle Eastern Studies*, Vol. II, No. 1, October 1965.
Crossman, R. H. S. *Palestine Mission*, London, 1947.
Curtis, Michael, and Gitelson, Susan Aurelia (eds.). *Israel in the Third World*, New Brunswick, N.J., 1976.
———, and Chertoff, Mordecai (eds.). *Israel: Social Structure in Change*, New Brunswick, N.J., 1973.
Dayan, Moshe. *Diary of the Sinai Campaign*, London, 1965.
Eban, Abba. *Voice of Israel*, New York, 1957.
Eisenstadt, S. N. *Israeli Society*, New York, 1967.

Elon, Amos. *The Israelis: Founders and Sons*, London, 1971.
Elston, D. R. *The Making of a Nation*, London, 1963.
Etzioni-Halevy, Eva. *Political Culture in Israel, Cleavage and Integration Among Israeli Jews*, New York, 1971.
Eytan, Walter. *The First Ten Years: A Diplomatic History of Israel*, New York, 1968.
Facts About Israel (Ministry for Foreign Affairs), Jerusalem
Fein, Leonard. *Politics in Israel*, Boston, 1967.
Goldberg, Y. *Haganah or Terror?* New York, 1938.
Great Britain and Palestine, 1916-1945, London, 1946.
Greenberg, H. I. and Nadler, S. *Poverty in Israel: Economic Realities and the Promise of Social Justice*, New York, 1977.
Henriques, R. *One Hundred Hours to Suez*, London, 1957.
Horowitz, David. *The Economics of Israel*, London, 1967.
Hurewitz, J. C. *Diplomacy in the Near and Middle East: A Documentation Record, 1914-1956*, Princeton, N.J., 1958.
Hurewitz, J. C. *The Struggle for Palestine*, New York, 1950.
Hyamson, A. M. *Palestine and the Mandate*, London, 1938.
Kish, E. H. *Palestine Diary*, London, 1938.
Kreinin, M. E. *Israel and Africa: A Study in Technical Cooperation*, New York, 1964.
Kurland, S. *Biluim, Pioneers of Zionist Colonization*, New York, 1943.
Laqueur, Walter. *Communism and Nationalism in the Middle East*, New York, 1956.
Lorch, N. *The Edge of the Sword: Israel's War of Independence, 1947-1949*, London, 1961.
Macdonald, J. M. *My Mission to Israel*, New York, 1951.
Matras, Judah. *Social Change in Israel*, Chicago, 1965.

Nahumi, Mordechai. "Ten Years After Suez," *New Outlook*, Vol. IX, No. 9, Dec. 1966.

Parkes, J. *A History of Palestine from 135 A.D. to Modern Times*, London, 1949.

Sharet, Moshe. *Rise of Israel*, Tel Aviv, 1963.
Statistical Abstracts of Palestine, Jerusalem.
Statistical Abstracts of Israel, Jerusalem.
Sykes, Christopher. *Crossroads to Israel, 1917-1948*, New York, 1965.
Talmon, J. L. *Israel Amongst the Nations*, London, 1970.
Thomas, Hugh. *The Suez Affair*, New York, 1969; London, 1970.

Periodicals: Zionist weeklies, monthlies and yearbooks in Great Britain, United States, Canada, Australia and South Africa; government yearbooks (Jerusalem), *Israel Yearbook* (Tel Aviv), *Jerusalem Post Economic Annual* (Jerusalem).

Jewish Labor Movement in the Diaspora; Labor Zionism
A Great Collection. The Archives of the Jewish Labor Movement, New York, 1945.
Abramovitch, Z. "The Poale Zion Movement in Russia; Its History and Development," Essays in memory of Dr. Noah Barou (Infield, H. F., ed.), London, 1962.
Borochov, B. *Nationalism and the Class Struggle: A Marxian Approach to the Jewish Problem*, New York, 1937.
Borochov, B. *Selected Essays in Socialist Zionism*, London, 1948.
Epstein, M. *Jewish Labor in the U.S.A.*, New York, 1947.
Gal, Allon. *Socialist-Zionist Theory and Issues in Contemporary Jewish Nationalism*, Cambridge, Mass., 1973.
Hertz, J. S. *The Jewish Labor Bund: A Pictoral History, 1897-1957*, New York, 1957.
Jewish Labor Bund, 1897-1957, New York, 1958.
Johnpoll, B. K. *The Politics of Futility: The General Jewish Workers' Bund of Poland, 1917-1943*, New York, 1967.
Levenberg, S. *The Jews and Palestine: A study in Labor Zionism*, London, 1945.
Locker, B. *What Is Poale-Zionism?*, London, 1937.
Syrkin, N. *Essays on Socialist Zionism*, New York, 1937.
The History of Labor Zionist Organization in America–Poalei Zion, New York, (n.d.)
Tscherikover, E. *The Early Jewish Labor Movement in the United States*, New York, 1967.
Yaari, Meir. *Ingathering of the Exiles*, Tel Aviv, 1954.
Yaffe, R. (ed.). *Borochov for Our Day* (the Socialist-Zionist View of the Jewish People), New York, 1958.
See also: *Encyclopaedia Judaica*, Jerusalem & New York, 1971.
Periodicals: Jewish Vanguard; Labour Israel (London), *Jewish Frontier; Israel Horizons* (New York).
Jewish Labor Movement in Israel
Derekh, Shlomo. *Israeli Socialism*, Tel Aviv, 1970 (Attitudes–World Labor Zionist Movement).
Documents and Essays on Jewish Labor Policy in Palestine, Tel Aviv, 1930.
Forging the Link—A Handbook of Hashomer Hatzair, London, 1952.
Gordon, A. D. *(Gleanings)*, New York, 1947.
Gordon, A. D. *Selected Essays*, New York, 1947.
Gotthelf, Yehuda (ed.). *Israel Towards a New Society* (articles and essays), Tel Aviv, 1969.
"Hechalutz—Builders and Fighters," *Hechalutz Yearbooks*, New York.
Katznelson, Berl. *Reaction v. Progress in Palestine*, London, 1937.
———. *Revolutionary Constructivism: Essays on the Jewish Labor Movement in Palestine*, New York, 1937.
———. *The Next Stage in Palestine*, London, 1938.
Mapam—Portrait of a Party, Tel Aviv, 1969.
Medding, Peter. *Mapai in Israel, Political Organization and Government in a New Society*, Cambridge, 1972.

Nahas, Dunia Habib. *The Israeli Communist Party*, New York, 1976.
Preuss, Walter. *The Labor Movement in Israel*, 3rd ed., Jerusalem, 1965.
Right and Left in Israel, London, 1949.
The Alignment: For and Against, Tel Aviv, 1973 (Mapam).
The Israeli Road to Socialism, Tel Aviv, 1971 (Mapam).
The Jewish Labor Movement in Palestine—Its Aims and Achievements (Report to the Labor and Socialist International Congress in Brussels), Berlin, 1928.
The United Workers' Party—Mapam, Tel Aviv, 1966.
What Is Hechalutz?, New York, 1937.
With Strength and Courage 1913–1963, 50 Years of Hashomer Haitsair, New York, 1963.
Yaari, Meir. *Ingathering of the Exiles*, Tel Aviv, 1963.
Yaari, Meir. *Facing Our Generation*, Tel Aviv, 1958.
———. *From Vision to Reality*, Tel Aviv, 1969.
———. *Israel 1968: On the Road to Socialism*, Tel Aviv, 1968.
Zweig, F. *The Israeli Worker*, New York, 1960.
See also: *Encyclopaedia Judaica*, Jerusalem and New York, 1971.
Periodicals: Labour Israel; Jewish Vanguard (London); *Israel Horizons, Youth and Nation; Jewish Frontier; Hechalutz Yearbooks* (New York); *Bulletin* (Israel Labour Party, Tel Aviv); *Israel at Peace* (Organ of Maki, Tel Aviv); *International Bulletin* (Rakah, Tel Aviv); *Mapam Bulletin* (Tel Aviv); *Work; Labour in Israel* (Histadrut, Tel Aviv); Publications of the Zionist-Socialist Youth Organizations and Kibbutzfederations (Tel Aviv)

Biographies:
Aaronovitch, J., and Dayan, S. *A. D. Gordon; Two Biographical Sketches*, New York, 1930
Ben-Zvi, R. (Yanait). *Coming Home*, Tel Aviv, 1963.
Cohen, I. *Haim Arlosoroff*, Tel Aviv, 1957.
Edelman, M. *Ben-Gurion, A Political Biography*, London, 1964.
Halevy, M. *A. D. Gordon and his Philosophy*, New York, 1947.
Infield, H. F. (ed.) *Essays in Memory of Dr. Noah Barou*, London, 1962.
Katznelson, B. *My Way to Palestine*, London, 1946.
Kohn, M. "Moshe Sharett, Servant of his People," *Israel Youth Horizon*, Vol. VII, No. 4, 1965.
Lipovetzki, P. *Joseph Trumpeldor, Life and Works*, Jerusalem, 1953.
Meir, Golda. *My Life*, Jerusalem, New York, 1976.
Syrkin, M. *Golda Meir, the Woman with a Cause*, New York, 1963.
Syrkin, M. *Nachman Syrkin, Socialist Zionist: A biographical Memoir and Selected Essays*, New York, 1961.
See also: *Encyclopaedia Judaica*, Jerusalem and New York, 1971.

Histadrut
Becker, A. *Histadrut—Program, Problems, Perspectives*, Tel Aviv, 1966.
Daniel, A. *Labor Enterprises in Israel*, 2 volumes, Edison, N.J., 1975.
Histadrut—The General Federation of Labor in Israel, Tel Aviv, 1969.

Kurland, S. *Cooperative Palestine: The Story of Histadrut*, New York, 1947.
Malkosh, N. *Cooperation in Israel*, Tel Aviv, 1966.
Malkosh, N. *Histadrut in Israel, Its Aims and Achievements*, Tel Aviv, 1961.
Muenzner, G. *Labor Enterprise in Palestine: A Handbook of Histadrut Economic Institutions*, New York, 1947.
Onn, Z. *Hevrat Ovdim: Israel's Labor Economy*, Tel Aviv, 1964.
Revutsky, A. *The Histadrut, a Labor Commonwealth in the Making*, New York, 1938.
Shachar, B. *Culture and Education in the Histadrut*, Tel Aviv, 1968.
Periodicals: Work; Labour in Israel (Tel Aviv)

Kibbutz, Moshav, Rural Cooperation
Baldwin, Elaine. *The Making of a Moshav: Differentiation and Cooperation in a Veteran Israeli Moshav*, Manchester, 1975.
Baratz, J. *Village by the Jordan*, London, 1954.
Ben-Shalom, A. *Deep Furrows:* Pioneer Life in the Collectives in Palestine, New York, 1937.
Bentwich, N. (ed.) *A New Way of Life: The Collective Settlements of Israel*, London, 1949.
Darin-Drabkin, H. *The Other Society*, London, 1962.
Dayan, S. *Man and the Soil: The Story of the First Fourt Decades of Nahalal*, Tel Aviv, 1962.
Goldy, R. *Kibbutz Socialism* (Friends of the Histadrut), Tel Aviv, 1973.
Hacohen, E. *The Economic Basis of the Kibbutz*, Tel Aviv, 1962.
Kibbutz Bibliography, compiled by Shimon Shur, Tel Aviv, 1972.
Labes, E. *Handbook of the Moshav*, Jerusalem, 1959.
Leon, D. *The Kibbutz: A Portrait from Within*, London, 1969.
Leviatan, U. "Industry and Kibbutz Values," *New Outlook*, Vol. 19, No. 4, June 1976.
Merhav, P. "A New Profile for the Kibbutz," *New Outlook*, Vol. 18, No. 1, January 1975.
Messinger, Y. (ed.). *Kvutzah, Moshav, Kibbutz; Principles of Cooperative Settlements in Palestine*, New York, 1952.
Orni, E. *Forms of Settlements*, Jerusalem, 1960.
Pearlman, M., Yisraeli, A., Wurm, S. *Essays on the Collective Settlement—the Kvutza*, Tel Aviv, 1946.
Shatil, J. *The Economy of the Kibbutz Form*, Tel Aviv, 1956 (mimeo).
The Kibbutz (Israel Today Pamphlets), Jerusalem, 1965.
The Moshav (Israel Today Pamphlets), Jerusalem, 1966.
"The Place of the Kibbutz in Present-Day Israel Society: A Jewish Quarterly Symposium," *Jewish Quarterly* No. 11 (2), London, 1963.
Periodicals: Israel Horizons; Youth and Nation (New York); *Work; Labour in Israel; Shdemot*, Publications of the Socialist-Zionist Youth Movements and of the Kibbutz federations (Tel Aviv).

Jewish-Arab Problems till 1948
Abramovitch, Z. *Wither Palestine?* London, 1936.
Al Kilai, Abd-el Wahab. *The Palestinian Struggle against British and Zionist Aggression, 1917–1939*, Beirut, 1967.
Antonius, G. *The Arab Awakening,* London, 1938; reprinted 1945.
Arlosoroff, C. *Jews, Arabs and Great Britain,* New York, 1930.
Bauer, Y. "The Arab Revolt of 1936," *New Outlook,* Vol. IX, No. 6 & 7, July-Aug. and September 1966.
Ben-Gurion, D. *My Talks with Arab Leaders*, Jerusalem, 1972.
Canaan, T. *The Palestine Arab Cause,* Jerusalem, 1936.
Cohen, A. *Israel and the Arab World,* New York, 1970.
———. *Israel and Jewish-Arab Peace: Governmental and Nongovernmental Approaches;* reprint of *The Elusive Peace in the Middle East*, Malcolm H. Kerr, (ed.), New York, 1975.
———. "An Idea Cannot be Murdered," *New Outlook,* Vol. 19, No. 8, December 1976.
Goitein, S. D. *Jews and Arabs,* New York, 1955.
Haim, G. S. (ed.). *Arab Nationalism: An Anthology,* Los Angeles, 1962.
Hashomer Hatsair Workers' Party. *The Road to Bi-National Independence of Palestine* (memorandum), Tel Aviv, 1946.
Hashomer Hatsair Workers' Party. *The Case for a Bi-National Palestine,* Tel Aviv, 1946.
Hattis, S. L. *The Bi-National Idea in Palestine During Mandatory Times, 1917–1948,* Haifa, 1970.
Hitti, O. H. *History of the Arabs,* London–New York, 1953.
Kanaan, H. "The Arabs in Mandated Palestine," *New Outlook,* Vol. V, No. 6, July–August 1962.
L'ahdut Ha'avoda–Poale Zion. *Statement of Policy on the Palestine Question*, Tel Aviv, 1947.
Mansur, G. *The Arab Worker under the Palestine Mandate,* Jerusalem, 1937.
Marlowe, J. *Rebellion in Palestine,* London, 1946.
Memmi, A. *Jews and Arabs,* Chicago, 1975.
Middle East Information Series XXIV, *Palestine and Palestinism,* Part 1, New York, 1973.
Nuseibeh, Hazem Zaki. *The Idea of Arab Nationalism,* New York, 1959.
Nutting, A. *The Tragedy of Palestine from Balfour Declaration to Today,* London, 1967.
Orenstein, M. *Jews, Arabs and British in Palestine: A Left Socialist View,* London, 1936.
Orenstein, M. *Palestine: A Plea for Arab-Jewish Unity,* London, 1939.
The Jewish Plan for Palestine. Memorandum and Statements presented by the Jewish Agency for Palestine to the United Nations Special Committee on Palestine, Jerusalem, 1947.
Towards Union in Palestine. Essays on Zionism and Jewish-Arab Unity; edited by Martin Buber, J. L. Magnes, Ernst Simon, Jerusalem, 1947.

Israelis, Arabs, Palestinian—Between War, Terror and Peace
Abdul Kader, A. R. "The Real Enemy of the Arab People," *The Jerusalem Post*, August 1, 1969.
Abu-Lughod, Ibrahim (ed.). *The Transformation of Palestine*, Evanston, Ill., Northwestern University Press, 1971.
Arab-Israel Parley. *Israel Magazine*, Vol. 1, No. 8, Tel Aviv, 1968.
Arnoni, M. *Rights and Wrongs in the Arab-Israeli Conflict*, New York, 1968.
Avineri, S. (ed.). *Israel and the Palestinians: Reflections on the Clash of two National Movements*, New York, 1971.
Avneri, U. *Israel Without Zionists: A Plan for Peace in the Middle East*, New York, 1968.
Benvenisti, Meron. *Jerusalem: The Torn City*, Minneapolis, 1977.
Buber Memorial Seminar on Jewish-Arab Understanding, *New Outlook*, Vol. IX, Nos. 8 & 9, 1966.
Chaliand, G. *The Palestinian Resistance*, London, 1972.
Cohen, A. *Israel and the Arab World*, New York, 1970.
⸺⸺⸺. *Israel and Jewish-Arab Peace*, New York, 1975 (reprint from *The Elusive Peace in the Middle East*.
Curtis, M., Neyer, J., Waxman, C. and Pollack, A. (eds.) *The Palestinians—People, History, Politics*, New Brunswick, N.J., 1975.
Deutscher, I. "On the Arab-Israel War," *New Left Review*, London, 1967.
Dobson, C. *Black September—Its Short Violent History*, New York, 1975.
Flapan, S. *The Arab-Israeli War of June 1967* (reply to Isaac Deutscher), Tel Aviv, 1968).
Flapan, S. "Terrorism versus Peace" (reply to Majdalani), *New Outlook*, Vol. XII, No. 2, February 1969.
Four Solutions to the Palestinian Problem (Assoc. for Peace) Tel Aviv, 1969.
Gabbay, R. *A Political History of the Arab-Jewish Conflict*, Geneva, 1969.
Hadawi, S. (ed.). *United Nations Resolutions on Palestine, 1947-1966*, Beirut, 1967.
Harkabi, Y. *Fatah's Doctrine*, Jerusalem, 1968.
Harkabi, Y. *Arab Attitudes to Israel*, Jerusalem, 1972.
Harkabi, Y. *Palestinians and Israel*, Jerusalem, 1974.
Hazan, Y. *The Core of the Problem: Analysis of the Arab-Jewish Conflict*, Jerusalem, 1976.
Hazan, Y. *Peace and the Future of Jerusalem*, Tel Aviv, 1976.
Ismael, Tareq Y. *The Arab Left*, New York, 1976.
Kadi, Leila (ed.). *Basic Political Documents of the Armed Palestinian Resistance Movement*, Beirut, 1969.
Kaplan, D. *Arab Refugees*, Jerusalem, 1959.
Kazzina, Walid. *Revolutionary Transformation of the Arab World: Habash and His Comrades from Nationalism to Marxism*, New York, 1975.
Kerr, M. H. (ed.) *The Elusive Peace in the Middle East*, New York, 1975.
Khouri, F. J. *The Arab-Israeli Dilemma*, New York, 1976.
Laqueur, W. *The Israeli-Arab Reader: A Documentary History of the Middle East Conflict*, New York, 1970.

Majdalany, J. "Anti-Racialism, Zionism and the Arabs," *New Outlook*, Vol. XII, No. 8, 1969.
Mapam's Peace Plan. "Resolution of the 7th National Congress," *Mapam Bulletin*, No. 36, Tel Aviv, June 1976.
Moore, J. N. (ed.) *The Arab-Israeli Conflict* (3 volumes), Princeton, N.J., 1974.
Nahumi, M. *Rise and Decline of Arab Guerrilla and Terror*, Tel Aviv, 1973.
New Outlook's Editors Debate Peace and Territories. Symposium, Vol. XI, No. 3, March-April 1968.
New Paths to Peace between Israel and the Arabs. Symposium, *New Outlook* Vol. VI, No. 2, 3, 4, Tel Aviv, 1963.
Peace Proposals for a Middle East Settlement. *Middle East Review*, Vol. IX, No. 4, Summer 1977.
Peretz, D. *A Palestinian Entity?* Washington, D.C., 1970.
Rodinson, M. *Israel and the Arabs*, London, 1968.
Safran, N. *From War to War: The Arab-Israeli Confrontation, 1948-1967*, New York, 1969.
Sid-Ahmed, Mohamed. *After the Guns Have Gone Silent*, New York, 1976.
The Arab-Israeli Conflict, Special Issue of Bulletin for Peace Proposals, Oslo.
The Hashemite Kingdom of Jordan and the West Bank. A Handbook, Anne Sinai and Allen Pollack (eds.), New York, 1977.
The Israel Council for Israeli-Palestinian Peace. Manifesto, *New Outlook*, Vol. 19, No. 2, February-March, 1976.
The Other Israel. The Israeli Socialist Organization (Matspen), Tel Aviv. 1968.
The Palestinian National Covenant, July 1968. Articles of the Covenent. New York University Journal of International Law and Politics, Vol. 3 (1), Spring, 1970.
To Make War or to Make Peace. Symposium on the Middle East. Special Issue of *New Outlook*, Tel Aviv, April 1969.
Weigert, G. *What the Palestinians Say*, Jerusalem, 1974.
"When the Guns Fall Silent," *New Outlook* 20th Anniversary Sumposium, special issue, Tel Aviv, 1977.
Yatziv, G. "With Folded Banners" (review of Uri Avneri's "Israel Without Zionists," *New Outlook*, Vol. XII, No. 8, Oct. 1969.
Periodicals: ARR—Arab Research and Record; Free Palestine; Jewish Observer and Middle East Review; Jewish Quarterly; The New Middle East; The Arab (Arab League), *New Statesman; The Observer; The Times Weekly Supplement* (London); *Israel Horizons; Middle Eastern Studies; Time; Newsweek* (New York); *Middle East Information Series; Middle East Review* (New Brunswick, N.J.); *Le Monde Diplomatique* (Paris); *New Outlook* (Tel Aviv); *Middle East Record* (Jerusalem); *The Middle Eastern Newsletter* (Beirut).

Israel's Arabs
El-Asmar, F. *To Be an Arab in Israel*, London, 1975.

Harari, Y. *The Arabs in Israel: Statistics and Facts*, Givat-Haviva, 1970.
Israel's Arabs after October 1973. Symposium, *New Outlook*, Vol. 18, No. 7, 1975.
Jirys, S. *The Arabs in Israel*, New York, 1976.
"Koenig Document." Mapam Bulletin No. 37, Tel Aviv, December 1976.
Landau, J. M. *The Arabs in Israel*, London, 1970.
Mansur, A. *Waiting for the Dawn*, London, 1975.
Rosen, H. M. *The Arabs and Jews in Israel: The Reality, the Dilemma, the Promise*, New York, 1970.
Schwartz, W. *The Arabs in Israel*, London, 1959.
The Arabs of Israel. Resolution adopted at the 7th National Congress of Mapam, Mapam Bulletin No. 36, Tel Aviv, June 1976.
The Histadrut's Arab Members, Tel Aviv, 1969.
"The Struggle for Equality: Israel's Arab Citizens," *New Outlook*, Vol. 18, No. 7, October-November 1975.
Watad, M. "Israeli Arabs," *New Outlook*, Vol. 15, No. 9, November-December 1972.
Weigert, G. *Israel's Minorities at a Turning Point*, Jerusalem, 1976.
Zaid, K. "Israel's Arabs after Twenty-Five Years," *New Outlook*, Vol. 16, No. 6, July-August 1973.
Zu'bi, A. A. "The Arab Minority in Israel," *New Outlook*, Vol. 17, No. 5, June 1974.
Periodicals: New Outlook (Tel Aviv); *Israel Horizons* (New York)

Great Powers, Oil etc.
Anthony, J. D. (ed.). *The Middle East: Oil, Politics and Development*, Washington, D.C.
Freedman, R. O. *Soviet Policy Towards the Middle East Since 1970*, New York, 1975.
Hurewitz, J. C. (ed.). *The Soviet-American Rivalry in the Middle East*, New York, 1969.
Kleiman, A. S. *Soviet Russia and the Middle East*, New York, 1970.
Majus, Y. *Détente* (Middle East Peace Institute), Tel Aviv, 1976.
Merlin, S. (ed.) *The Big Powers and the Present Crisis in the Middle East. A Colloquium*. New Jersey, 1968.
Stevens, G. G. (ed). *The United States and the Middle East*, New York, 1962.
Stevens, R. *Oil Billions—Exemplary Investment: The Arabs' New Frontier*. London, 1973.
The U.S.S.R. and the Middle East: Problems of Peace and Security (documents and other material), Moscow, 1972.
"United States-Soviet Détente and the Middle East," *Middle East Review* 8, New Brunswick, N.J., Spring-Summer, 1976.
"United States Foreign Policy and the Middle East," *Middle East Review*, 9, New Brunswick, N.J., Spring, 1977.

Index

Abramovitz, Zev, 57n., 64, 68, 137n., 350, 351
Afikim, 169
Affair, the, 204, 205, 207, 220, 235ff. *See also* Lavon Affair.
Afula, 184
Agranat Inquiry Commission, 290
Agricultural Workers Congress, 1919, 36
Agricultural Workers Union, 194
Agudat Israel, 70, 325, 340
   in Knesset elections, 342
Ahdut (Unity), 35n., 40
Ahdut Haavoda (Unity of Labor), 23, 36ff., 46ff., 82-84, 86, 93, 98, 102-104, 108n., 109-110, 114, 117-118, 139-140, 156, 168ff., 177, 178, 187, 191, 195, 209, 211ff., 218n., 219, 220ff., 228, 231-233, 265ff., 270, 277, 291, 320, 339
   Council of, 232
   in Knesset elections, 342
   leaders of, 45n.
   makeup of, 46
   Mapam, differences with, 213
   Ministers, 142
   Notebooks, 40
   Tel Aviv branch, 53
Ahdut, Haavoda-Poale Zion (Unity of Labor-Workers of Zion), 139, 157, 178, 183-185, 186n., 205, 207-208, 213, 218, 222, 224ff., 236-237, 239, 242, 243, 245, 247, 257, 268, 273, 282
   Council, 232, 235
   Party, 93, 111, 136, 137n., 222ff., 233
Ahiezra, A., 303n.
Al-Anba, 341
Alder, Max, 93
Al-Fajr (The Dawn), 216, 341
Al Fatah, 141n., 148n., 184n., 255

Al Hamishmar, 131, 136n., 140, 144, 189ff., 212, 218, 220, 227, 231, 233, 241, 245, 249, 261, 262, 275, 279, 339
al-Husseini, Fawzi, 92n., 100
Alignment, the, 76, 191-193, 207, 216, 222, 228, 231ff., 265, 266, 272n., 274ff., 288, 289, 291, 292, 314, 317, 318, 320, 323-325, 326n.
   Ahdut Haavoda-Poale Zion and, 232
   decline, 276-280
   Histadrut and, 243
   Knesset faction, 322n.
   Labor Party, 318
   Mapai and, 228, 237
   new, 226, 228
   organizational structure, 284
   Political Committee, 275, 278, 279
   Program for the Histadrut, 193
   Statement of, 234
Alignment-affiliated Arab lists, 289
Alignment-Ahdut Haavoda-Poale Zion, 228
Alignment for the Unity of the Workers of Eretz Israel, 233, 234
Alignment for the Unity of the Workers of Israel, 237
Alignment-Israel Labor Party-United Workers Party, 283, 284
Al-Itihad, 341n.
Aliya (Immigration)
   dates of, 31n.
   defined, 31n., 66
   Second, 31-34, 38ff., 47, 49, 52, 54, 58, 61, 96, 98, 113, 167, 168, 213
   main sources of, 32
   reasons for, 31
   Third, 37, 38, 40, 44, 48, 52, 55, 62, 81, 82, 90, 113, 156, 157, 167ff., 213, 270

components of, 37
utopianism of, 40
Fourth, 48, 49, 52, 55, 65, 70, 83n., 156, 169, 170, 176
  discussion of, 48n.
Fifth, 53, 70n., 86, 172
Allende, Salvatore, 148n.
Alliance of Socialist-Zionist Workers-Zeire Zion, 23
Allon, Yigal, 118n., 195, 216, 217, 229, 245, 273
  Foreign Minister, 323
  General, 118n.
  Labor Minister, 250
Al-Mirsad (*The Guard*), 149n., 216, 339
Almogi, Yosef, 236n., 237, 239, 273
Aloni, Shulamit, 289, 292, 293, 317
Al-Quds, 341
Al-Sha'ab, 341
American Zionists, 96n.
A New View (*Mabat Hadash*), 239n.
Anglo-French Suez War, 141
Anilevitz, Mordehai, 95n.
Anti-Fa (League to Fight Fascism and Anti-Semitism), 70
Arabization, 70
Arab Labor Party, 215
Arab League for National Liberation, 71, 74
Arab Lists, 186, 218, 278
  in Knesset elections, 342
Arab Pioneering Youth Organization, 178, 217
Arabs
  Communist, 72
  homeland, 256
  Israeli, 198
    civil equality of, 199
    development and industrialization of, 198
    education of, 199
    minority, 195, 197, 216, 320
    youth, 199
Arab Third World, 252
Arbeiter Ring (Workers Circle), 14, 17
Arlosorov, Chaim, 23, 45, 53

Armed Jewish Brigade, 95
Army Workers Union, 194
Aronovitz, Yosef, 45n.
Ascending Camps (Hamahanot Haolim), 176
Asefat Hahamin (*Council of Scholars*), 13
Avihail, 238
Avneri, Uri, 76, 252n., 281
Avuka (Torch) Group, 51, 53
Ba'ayot, 100
Bader, Menahem, 45n.
Bahrut Sotsialistit Ivrit (Jewish Socialist Youth), 49
  described, 49n.
Balfour Declaration, 57, 59, 78, 256
"Bamoked," 341n.
Barali, Yitzhak, 23
Baratz, Yosef, 45n.
Barrou, N., 57n.
Bar-Yehuda, Y. Galili, O. Livshitz Resolution, 122
Bar-Yehuda, Yisrael (Idelson), 23, 45n., 139n., 143, 229
Barzilai, Yisrael, 139n., 218, 245, 278, 279
Basha'ar (*At the Gate*), 149n., 195, 339
Bauer, Otto, 93
Becker, Aharon, 204
Beersheba, 188
Begin, Menahem, 92n., 140, 243n., 244, 250, 325
Beilinson, Moshe, 45n.
Ben-Aharon, Yitzhak, 138, 218, 222-224, 229, 252n., 277n.
Ben-Gurion, David, 35-36, 45n., 53-54, 73, 102, 114, 118-119, 128, 139, 181ff., 189, 200ff., 211, 217ff., 225, 229ff., 243n., 245ff., 266-268, 274ff., 350
  Ahdut Haavoda leader, 46-47, 49
  Jabotinsky agreement, 103n., 104
  Lavon Affair, 200
  State List, 277
  State Party, 276
Ben-Gurion-Peres German policy, 204
Ben-Moshe, Naftali, 194

Ben-Porat, M., 322n.
Bentov, Mordehai, 118, 139n., 218, 245
Ben-Zvi, Yitzhak, 35, 36, 45n., 54, 56, 114, 335n.
Bergelson, D., 31
Bergmann, Hugo, 43
Bet Alfa, 83n., 84
Betaniya Ilit, 167
"Betar," 92n.
Biltmore Program, 96, 98, 100
 described, 96n.
Biltmore Resolution, 99
Bilu'im, 31n.
Biria, 106
"bi-state solution," 255
Black Panthers, 77, 282, 289, 317
 described, 297-298
Bloch-Blumenfeld, David, 45n.
Bloc of the Truth (Gush Emunim), 314
Blocs, the, 203, 204
Blue-Red Movement (Siah New-Leftists), 76, 77n., 281
Blue-White faction of Histadrut, 242n.
Borochov, Ber, 17-19, 25-27, 30, 33, 43, 58ff., 66, 68, 85n., 133ff, 147n.
Borochovism, 45, 54, 60, 62, 66, 72, 85
Borochovist Platform, 34
Borochovist Poale Zion, 68
Brenner, Y.H., 31
Breslavsky, M., 106
"Briha," 95
British Army, 94
British Mandate, 70, 101, 111
British Mandatory Power, 95
Brit Mapam, 194, 341
Brit Poale Eretz Israel (Union of Palestinian Workers)
 background and nature, outlined, 348
Brit Shalom (Peace Alliance), 92n.
Buber, Martin, 92n.
"Buffs," the, 94
Bund, the (General League of Jewish Workers), 14-15, 18-19, 24
 liquidation in Soviet Russia, 17
 national program of, 15-16, 20
 purpose of, 14
Busel, Yosef, 45n.

"Cabinet of National Unity," 250
Cahan, Abe, 14
Camp for Peace and Equality. *See* Sheli.
Canadian New Democratic Party (N.D.P.)
 and Mapam, 148
Carmel, Moshe, 139n., 245
Castro, Fidel, 258, 259
Center for Progressive Culture, 92
Chaluziut. *See* Pioneering.
Change (Shinui), 317
Circle (*Hugim*), 176
Civil Rights Movement, 291, 317, 324n.
Cohen, Aharon, 100
Cohen, Shmuel, 192
Cold War, 117, 127
Colonialism, 79, 141, 259
 anti-colonialism, 184, 252, 255-256
Coltun, Zvi, 53
Comintern, 62-64, 93, 125-127, 130
Committees of Intellectuals for a Negotiated Peace in the Middle East, 148
Committee of Seven. *See* Lavon Affair.
Communist Faction, 83
Communist International, 16, 57
Communist Party. *See also* Maki.
 Cuba, 148
 Hebrew, 71, 72
 Israeli, 70, 73n., 75
 Italy, 148
 Jewish, 63, 64
  in Russia, 63
 Palestinian, 41, 48, 70, 71
 Rumania, 148
 Soviet,
  Jewish Dept. of, 16
 Sweden, 148
 Yugoslavia, 148
Compass (Matspen), 251
Congress in Vienna, 1920, 57
Congress of Arab Workers, 186
 background and nature, outlined, 348

Constituent Assembly, 1949, 118
Constructive socialism, 103
Constructive Zionism, 92n.
Constructivism, 40, 52, 119
"Continuers of Rafi," 274, 276
Cooperative movement, 152-153
Cooperative villages in Israel
  types of, 160
Council of Ahdut Haavoda, 232
Council of Scholars (Asefat Hahamin), 13
Council of the Kibbutz Ha'artzi, 136
Council of the World Union, 57
Crossman, R., 190
Cuban Legation in Israel, 148n.

Davar, 99, 109, 143, 189ff., 201-202, 206, 221, 232, 253n., 255n., 278, 339
Dawn, The. *See* Al-Fajr.
Dayan, Moshe, 185, 188, 200ff., 217, 230, 239, 243n., 250-251, 265, 273-274, 278, 281, 287-288, 314, 321ff., 350
  General, 290
  Minister of Security, 287
Dead Sea, 195
de Beauvoir, Simone, 257, 261
Democratic Front for Development of Nazareth, 77
Democratic Front for Peace and Equality, 77, 341
  in Knesset elections, 342n.
Democratic Liberals, 318
Democratic Movement for Change (D.M.C.), 289n., 317, 321, 323ff., 331, 339, 340
  in Knesset elections, 342
Diaspora, 7ff., 64-66, 72, 75, 82ff., 98, 113, 130-131, 140, 170-171, 176, 182, 189, 260, 271
Die Zunkunft (The Future), 14
Divrei Haknesset, 198, 216, 217
D.M.C. *See* Democratic Movement for Change.
Doves, the, 279, 280, 285-288. *See also* Hawks; Hawks and Doves.

"Dror," 55, 56n., 175
Dror Socialist-Zionist Federation, 23n.

Eastern Alliance of Zeire Zion, 23
Eastern European Poale Zionists, 57
Eban, Abba, 265, 273-275, 321-323
  Foreign Minister, 265, 273, 278, 288
Economic Development
  Indicators before and after the Six-Day War *(chart)*, 305-307
Economic Slowdown, 1966, 294
Economic Stability
  approaches to, 302, 303
Ein Harod, 168, 169
Einigkeit, 127n.
Eisenhower Doctrine, 184
Eisenstadt, S., 18
El Ard, 72, 75
El Arish-Abu Aglielah-Quseima, 143
Eliav, Liova, 317
Elkind, Menahem, 48, 169
Emek group (Havurat Haemek), 169
Emes (Truth), 24n., 127n.
Emet group, 71
Enfurt Program, 88
Erem, Moshe, 57n., 63, 120n., 229
Erem Group, 120-121, 124-125, 129, 136
Eretz Israel, 56, 79, 100, 331
"Eretz Israelian," 71
Eretz Israel (Palestine) Workers Fund. *See* Kapai.
Eretz Israel Workers Party (Mapai), 56, 233
Eshkol, Levi, 45n., 73, 186, 196, 204ff., 211, 225-226, 229-230, 235ff., 243ff., 249-251, 265, 273, 294
  Prime Minister, 196, 211, 265
Eshkol-Galili agreement, 229
Etatism (cult of the state), 182, 200, 240
"Etzel," 92n., 105n.
Extraordinary Zionist Conference, 99
Faction "B" (Siah Bet), 105n.
Faction "C" (Siah Gimel), 107
Falastin Jedida (New Palestine Society), 92n., 100

INDEX • 383

Fardis, 78
Fedayeen, 141-142, 145
Federation of Agricultural Laborers, 154
Fighters for Israel's Freedom. *See* Lehi.
"Focus (Moked), 281, 288, 317
Food Workers Union, 194
Forvartz (Forward), 14
Four Party Club, 219
Free Center, the, 276, 280, 316, 317, 339-340
  in Knesset elections, 342
Freedom Movement (Thuat Herut), 92n.
Free Youth Movement, 81
Freheit, 49
French Socialist Party, 148
From the Roots (Min Hayesod), 204
Front, the, 124, 125, 129-130, 138
Front for the Unity of the Party, 120, 123

Gahal, 242-244, 250, 253n., 269, 276ff., 297, 339
Gahal bloc, 250
Galili, Yisrael, 118, 138, 140, 217, 229, 245, 287
Galili-Eshkol agreement, 235
Galili paper, 281, 288
Gaza Strip, 142-145
Gdud, 39, 46-48, 84, 86, 94, 168ff.
  split of, 1926, 169
Gdud Avoda. *See* Gdud Haavoda.
Gdud Haavoda, 41, 54, 65, 70, 82-83, 98, 167-168, 170
  aims and principles of, 167
  Joseph Trumpeldor Labor Battalion, 167
  Left, 70n.
Gdud Shomriya, 167
Gelfat, Yitzhak, 45n.
General Commune of the Workers of Palestine, 168
General Cooperative Association of Labor in Israel. *See* Hevrat Ovdim.

General Federation of (Jewish) Workers in Israel. *See* Histadrut.
General Federation of Working Youth. *See* Hanoar Haoved.
General League of Jewish Workers (The Bund), 14, 15
General Zionist Organization, 22, 57, 139, 183, 190, 234. *See also* Zionism.
Geneva Peace Conference, 288, 313, 316, 329, 332
Germany, Nazi, 93, 94
Gileadi, Yisrael, 35n., 47
Givat Brenner Council, 1951, 172
Givat Brenner Council, 1955, 173
Gnessin, A.N., 31
Golan Heights, 286, 298, 327
Gold, Lea, 92
Golomb, Eliyahu, 45n.
Gordon, Aharon David, 44-45, 81, 172, 204, 247
Gordonia Youth Movement, 44, 172, 175n., 177, 205
Goren, Rabbi, 262
Government Employees Union, 194
Government of National Unity, 250, 278, 280
Grabsky's Aliya, 48n.
Greater Israel Movement. *See* Land of Israel Movement.
Great Powers, 250, 253-254, 260
Greenberg, Chaim, 23
Gromyko, A., 112, 145
Gromyko Declaration, 117, 118, 126
Guard, The. *See* Al-Mirsad.
Guevara, Che, 259
Gulf of Eilat, 142-144
Gush Emunim (Bloc of the Truth), 314
Ha'aretz, 188, 201, 341
Habibi, Emile, 74
Habonim, 169, 175n.
Hadera, 176
Ha-Emet (The Truth), 13
Haganah (self-defense force), 47, 92n., 94, 105, 118, 283, 317
Hahoresh, 33
Haifa, 106, 176, 277, 286

Haifa bloc, 203, 237, 238
Haifa Congress, 137, 138, 148
Haifa Party Congress, 218n.
Haifa Program, 120, 128, 146, 147
Hakibbutz Ha'artzi, 94n., 99n. *See also* Kibbutz Ha'artzi.
Hakibbutz Hameuchad,172,175n.,177
Halevy, Justice Benyamin, 316
Hamahanot Haolim (Ascending Camps), 176-178
Hamodia, 340
Hanoar Haoved (General Federation of Working Youth), 49, 177, 178
Haolam Hazeh, 76, 77, 276, 281, 289, 341
  in Knesset elections, 342
  List, 1965, 252n.
Haolam Hazeh-Koah Hadash, 277
Haolam Hazeh-New Force, 243n.
Hapoel Hamisrahi, 340
Hapoel Hatsair (The Young Worker), 23, 33-35, 36ff., 81-83, 86, 102, 173, 177-178, 204-205, 339
  leading personalities, 45n.
  Second Aliya,
  special characteristics, 42
Hashomite rule, 261
Hashomer, 33, 46-48
  defined, 33n.
Hashomer Hatsair, 37, 53, 55, 62, 71, 81ff., 101, 104-106, 108ff., 113, 117, 119-120, 122, 124ff., 136-138, 156, 167, 169-170, 176-178, 213, 216, 255, 270, 332, 339
  Central Committee of, 101
  Convention, 177
  Council, 101
  development, growth, cohesion of, 9t
  origins of, 81
  Socialist league, 66
Hashomer Hatsair Kibbutzim, 70, 170, 173, 176
Hashomer Hatsair Workers Party, 92, 99-100, 111-112, 120n.
  formation of, 91
Haskala movement, 32n.

Hatechiya (The Renaissance), 21
Hatnua Le'Ahdut Haavoda (Movement for Labor Unity), 91, 94n., 97, 105, 108, 112, 177
  defined, 91n.
Hatsofe, 340
Havaad Haleumi (National Council), 94n.
Havurat Haemek (the Emek group), 169
Hawks, the, 280, 285ff., 313, 321. *See also* Doves; Hawks and Doves.
  argument of, 280
Hawks and the Doves, the, 280ff., 321, 324. *See also* Hawks; Doves.
  essence of conflict between, 286-287
Hazan, Yaakov, 114, 120, 124, 140, 189, 198, 220
  Mapam leader, 262
Hebrew Communist Party, 71-72
Hebrew Communists, 72, 120, 137
Hebrew Socialist Party, 13
Hebron, 314
Hechalutz, 37, 39, 49, 58, 81, 118, 169
  Russian, 55, 56n., 167
Hechalutz Hatsair, 49, 169
Hechalutz Hatsair-Freheit, 175n.
Hefziba, 83n.
Herut, 139-140, 186n., 229, 234, 242, 244, 250, 297, 316, 339
  in Knesset elections, 342
Herut-Liberal Party bloc. *See* Gahal.
Herzl, Theodor, 20, 41
Hess, Moses, 20
Hever Hakvutzot, 172, 175n., 177
Hevrat Haovdim (Workers Economy), 271
Hevrat Ovdim (General Cooperative Association of Labor in Israel *or* Workers Society), 39, 156, 163, 283
  defined, 39n.
  described, 152
Hibat Zion, 32n.
Histadrut (General Federation of Workers in Israel), 34, 37-38, 44ff., 82-84, 92n., 95, 102, 104, 108n.,

109, 117-118, 120n., 121, 136, 138, 153ff., 164, 167, 169, 173-176, 180-181, 186-187, 190ff., 198, 200-202, 205ff., 216, 221, 223-224, 226ff., 239, 243n., 246-247, 257, 265, 269-271, 276-277, 280ff., 289, 294, 297-298, 303-304, 319, 324, 326n.
  Alignment and, 243
  background and nature, outlined, 348
  Blue-White faction, 242n.
  composition (*chart*), 157-159
  Congresses,
    First, 343
    Second, 47
    Third, 83
    Fourth, 89
    Fifth, 90, 105, 107
    Sixth, 90-91, 108, 110
  Congress and Council, 108
  constructive activity, 152
  Convention, 242, 245
  economic proposals, 308ff.
  Executive Committee (Vaad Hapoel), 48, 108
  Mapam Resolutions on, 163ff.
  National Congresses 1920-1977 participating parties and seat distribution (*tables*), 343-347
Hitachdut (Zeire Zion World Union), 44
Hitachdut World Labor Party, 23n.
Hitler, 70, 208
Holocaust, 79, 95
Hotam, 241
Houshi, Abba, 203n.
Hugim (Circles), 176-177
Hulda meeting, 205, 206, 211
Idelson. *See* Bar-Yehuda.
Ihud, 92n., 97, 99, 100, 172-173
Ihud Hakvutzot Vehakibbutzim (Union of Kvutzot and Kibbutzim), 172, 177-178, 200, 204-206, 235, 238, 246
Immigration. *See* Aliya.

Imperialism, 79-80, 132
  anti-imperialism, 78ff.
Independent Left-Socialist Groups, 148
Independent Left Socialist-Zionist Alliance, 272
Independent Liberal Party, 243-244, 255, 276, 278, 282, 288ff., 314ff., 324n.
  in Knesset elections, 342
Independent Socialists, 77, 317, 341
Ingathering of the Exiles, 146, 147, 182, 220, 270, 271, 329
"Ingathering of the Exiles in the Mirror of Our Times," (Yaavi), 133-135
International Bureau, 93
International Federation of Women and Democratic Youth, 148
Irgun Zvai Leumi (National Military Organization), 92n.
Isolation
  Israeli struggle against, 313-314
Israel, 71, 98, 112, 117, 128, 130-132, 140-141, 144, 147, 178, 189, 195, 197, 240, 253ff., 270, 279, 282-283, 325, 327, 329, 332
  Arab minority, 142, 198
  Balance of Payments (*chart*), 304
  border, 250
  bourgeoisie, 174
  Cabinet, 291
  described, 336
  defense
    forces, 94n., 143, 185, 217, 250, 256, 275, 283
    policy of "activism," 185
  Economy 1972-1976, 299-302
  ethnic discrimination in, 296-299
  family income, 1971-1975 (*table*), 308
  Foreign Ministry, 184
  foreign policy
    Paris-Bonn-Jerusalem axis, 184
    "preventive war," 185, 216
    three controversial issues in, 313-316
  Government, 196, 199, 222, 233, 286, 335-336

High Command, 286
Land Authority, 199
population
  changes 1948-1976 (*table*), 337
  current, by types of locality (*table*), 337-338
  origins of (*table*), 337
reformism, 181
social problems of, 296-299
strikes in, 298
Israel Communist Opposition (Vilenska group), 76
Israeli Communist Party. *See* Maki.
Israel Council for Israeli-Palestinian Peace, 1976, 315, 317, 329
  Manifesto, 329-330
Israel-Cuba Friendship League, 148n.
Israeli-Arab disputes (conflicts, 72, 74, 100, 184. *See also* Fedayeen; Israel, defense, foreign policy; P.L.O.; Sinai Campaign; Six-Day War; United Nations; War of Liberation; Yom Kippur War.
Israeli Left, 103, 254, 255, 259
  history 1897-1977 (*chronological table of events*), 358-369
Israeli New Left (Siach), 272n.
Israeli Radical Camp. *See* Meri.
Israeli Socialist Organization. *See* Matspen.
Israeli Workers List. *See* Rafi.
Israeli Workers Party. *See* Mapai.
Israel Labor Movement, 184, 187, 205ff., 222, 257, 267, 282, 326, 333. *See also* Histadrut; Israel Labor Party; Kibbutz Movement.
Israel Labor Party (Mifleget Haavoda Hayisraelit), 76, 77, 214, 252n., 257, 269-271, 277n., 280ff., 313, 320, 332, 339, 341. *See also* Labor Party.
  Central Committee
  "Young Guard," 255n.
  Charter, 282
  formation of, 267-268
  in Knesset elections, 342
  Peace Plank, 328-329
  Second National Congress, 321

Israel Peace Council, 257
Italian Socialist Party (P.S.I.). *See* Mapam, ties with foreign parties.
Ivanov, K., 136

Jabotinsky, Vladimir, 92n.
Jankelevitch, V., 261
Jerusalem, 251, 254, 262, 329, 330
Jerusalem Post, The, 253n., 255n., 276, 329, 341
Jerusalem Program, the, 96n.
Jerusalem Scout Legion, 176
Jewish Agency, 94, 107, 200
Jewish Anti-Fascist Committee, 127
Jewish-Arab Association for Peace and Equality, 1956, 186
Jewish-Arab Association for Peace and Tranquility, 1956, 216
Jewish Commonwealth, 96n., 99
Jewish Communist Party (Poale Zion), 63, 64
Jewish Community (Yishuv), 106
Jewish Free Press, 13
Jewish Legion, 34n., 35
Jewish National Fund, 59
Jewish National Home, 101, 105n.
Jewish National Parliaments
  functions of, 24
Jewish National Workers Alliance (*Verband*), 25
Jewish Question and the Socialist Jewish State, The, (Syrkin), 20, 28
Jewish Section of the Palestinian Communist Party, 64
Jewish Section of the Soviet Communist Party. *See* Yevsektzia.
Jewish Socialist Democratic Party, 17, 32, 63
Jewish Socialist Society (U.S.A.), 17
Jewish Socialist Workers Party, 63, 64
Jewish Socialist Youth (Bahrut Sotsialistit Ivrit), 49
Jewish State (Herzl), 20, 41
Jewish Workers in Palestine, 152
Jordan, 184n., 195, 269, 329
Jordanian-Palestinian state, 329

Jordan River, 217, 328
  East Bank of, 315
  West Bank of, 289, 315, 329
Jordan Valley, 322
Joseph, Dov, 236n.
Joseph Trumpeldor Labor Battalion (Gdud Ha'avoda), 41n., 47, 167, 169
Kaddum, 314
Kahane, J.P., 261
Kalkilya, 217
Kapai (Eretz Israel Workers Fund), 33, 59
Kaplan, Eliezer, 23, 45n.
Kaplansky, Shlomo, 25, 45n., 51, 57n., 61-62
Katsir, Ephraim, 335n.
Katznelson, Berl, 33, 36ff., 45, 50n., 53, 54, 88, 102, 105, 114, 177
  Ahdut Haavoda leader, 47, 49
Kesseh, Y., 351
Kfar Gileadi, 169
Kfar Vitkin, 108, 204, 238
Kfar Yeheskel, 167
Kibbutz Artzi, 84, 86, 248, 268, 272. *See also* Hakibbutz Ha'artzi.
Kibbutz Bet Alfa, 82
Kibbutz Ein Harod, 169
Kibbutz Ha'artsi, 87, 89ff., 94n., 98, 99n., 137, 146, 170ff., 175n.
  Conference at Mishmar Hemek, 1942, 90
  Council, 136
  Council at Givat Haviva, 1954, 133
  Council in Hadera, 1935, 89
  ideological assumptions, 85, 170-172
Kibbutz Ha'artzi Hashomer Hatsair, 84, 91, 170
Kibbutz Hameuchad (United Kibbutz), 53-55, 60, 84, 94, 104-105, 108, 110, 118n., 123, 137, 169ff., 178, 187, 230
  Council in Alonim, 195
Kibbutz List, 83-86, 169
Kibbutz Meuhad (United Kibbutz Federation), 39

Kibbutz Mishmar Haemek, 280n.
Kibbutz Movement, 86, 321, 326-327
  specific discussion of, 154-156
  stages of development, 167ff.
Kibbutz Sde-Boker, 202
Kinneret, 167
Kiryat-Arba, 314
Kissinger, Henry, 285, 313, 314
Knesset (Assembly), 74-76, 119, 124, 136, 140ff., 183, 185, 190, 196ff., 207, 215ff., 231-232, 235ff., 243ff., 249, 268, 272n., 274ff., 284-285, 289, 292, 298, 314, 316ff., 324, 325n., 329
  Arab members, 186n.
  constitutional powers, 335-336
  debates in Hebrew, 335
  described, 335
  Eighth, 288
  election results and party alignments 1949-1977 (*table*), 342
  Fifth, 218, 220, 222, 228, 243
  First, 71
  Foreign Affairs and Security Committee, 219, 322
  Fourth, 220
  Ninth, 318
  political parties in, 339-341
  Seventh, 277
  Sixth, 228, 232, 238, 239n.
  elections, 1965, 242-243
Kol Ha'am (*Voice of the People*), 74
Kol Ha'am group, 71
Komverband (Communist Union), 24n.
Kultur Kampf, 184
Kupat-Holim, 182
Kvutsa (*Commune*), 37n.

"La'am" Party, 316, 339
Laborists (Socialists of the Future), 22
Labor-Mapam Alignment, 76, 77, 291, 325, 339n.
  in Knesset elections, 342
Labor Movement. *See* Israel Labor Movement.

Labor Parties
  National Congresses 1905-1977
    (*table*), 254-356
Labor Party, 174-175, 181, 184, 194,
    252ff., 268n., 271, 274ff., 284, 286,
    289ff., 302, 313, 315ff., 340. *See also*
    Israel Labor Party.
  Central Committee, 287, 288
  Congress, 319ff.
  General Committee, 287
  present day, 156, 157
  Rafi wing, 292
Labor Zionist Parties, 63
Labour Party (Australia). *See* Mapam
    ties with foreign parties.
Labour Party (Great Britain). *See*
    Mapam, ties with foreign parties.
L'Ahdut Haavoda, 112, 117ff., 128-130,
    136-138, 143. *See also* Ahdut
    Haavoda.
L'Ahdut Haavoda-Poale Zion, 108n.,
    111-114, 129, 143, 339. *See also*
    Ahdut Haavoda-Poale Zion.
Lamerhav, 136, 138, 143, 195, 208, 224,
    232, 234
"Land of Israel Movement," 252, 316,
    339
Latsky, Zev, 24
Lavon, Pinhas, 187, 189, 202, 204-206,
    208-209, 211, 218, 222n., 229, 235,
    351. *See also* Lavon Affair.
Lavon Affair, 188, 219
  Committee of Seven, 202, 235
  described, 202-203
Lavon-Ben-Gurion Affair, 219. *See also*
    Lavon Affair.
Lavon group, 209, 211, 218n.
League for Friendship Ties, 62
League for Jewish-Arab
    Rapprochement, 92
League of Kibbutz Movements, 173
League of Nations, 93
League to Fight Fascism and Anti-
    Semitism. *See* "Anti-Fa."
Left Alliance, 76, 80
Left forum, composition of, 281

Left Gdud Haavoda, 70n.
Left Labor Unity, 76
Left Opposition, 65, 83-84
Left Party. *See* Socialist Left Party.
Left Poale Zion, 62, 64, 70, 83, 85n., 87,
    90, 91, 97, 104, 108, 110, 112, 117,
    120, 137
  foundation of, in Palestine, 62
  Party, 1924, 64ff.
  Russia, 63
Left Poale Zionists, 59, 65, 66, 129, 130,
    170. *See also* Left Poale Zion.
Left Section. *See* Mapam.
Left Union, 62
  outstanding personalities of, 57n.
  trends of, 63
Left-Wing Gdud, 169
Left World Union, 63, 64
Legion of Jerusalem Scouts, 176-177
Lehi (Fighters for Israel's Freedom),
    92n., 105n.
Lestchinsky, Yaakov, 24
Levinger, Rabbi, 314
Levinson, Avraham, 23
Levite, L., 137n.
Liberal Center, 317
Liberal Party (Liberals), 186n., 218,
    242, 250, 339-340. *See also* Likud.
  in Knesset elections, 342
Liberman, Aharon Shmuel, 13
Liberty Workers and Slum Dwellers
    List, 289n.
Likud (National Liberal Union), 77,
    175, 280-281, 285-286, 288ff., 311ff.,
    323ff., 331
  described, 339
  economic program, 311-312
  in Knesset elections, 342n.
Litvakov, Moshe, 24
Lufban, Yitzhak, 45n.
Lwoff, MM A., 261

Ma'arah (Alignment), 323
Ma'ariv, 107, 341
Mabat Hadash (*A New View*), 239n.
Madaule, J., 261

Mafdal (National Religious Party), 219, 243-244, 250, 252-253, 277-278, 288ff., 313-314, 318, 325, 340.
  in Knesset elections, 342
Magnes, Judah L., 92n.
Maki (Israeli Communist Party), 72ff., 80, 108n., 132, 135-136, 138, 186n., 251, 257, 280-281, 288, 317. *See also* Rakah.
  beginnings of, 70ff.
  Central Committee, 76
Malta Labor Party. *See* Mapam, ties with foreign parties.
Mandate (British), in Palestine, 70-71, 95, 98ff., 256
Mapai (Israeli Workers Party), 46, 55, 62, 65-66, 71, 84, 86ff., 95, 97-98, 102ff., 113ff., 120, 124-125, 129, 137-139, 153ff., 170-172, 181ff., 190-191, 200ff., 213ff., 224ff., 236ff., 242ff., 250, 257, 265ff., 270, 273, 277, 282, 291, 295, 321, 339
  Central Committee, 102, 108, 202, 206, 207, 230-231, 235ff.
  central problems of, 1965, 246-247
  Congress, 1942, 108
  dissidents, characteristics of, 239
  economic change plans, 294
  in Knesset elections, 342n.
  Ministry of Defense and, 200
  Rafi-oriented wing, 266, 267
  Secretariat, 207, 238
  splits in, 102, 172, 177-178
  Tel Aviv Council, 105n.
  unity struggle, 187
  veteran leadership, 203-204
  young men of, 200, 203
Mapam (United Workers Party), 72n., 73n., 76, 80, 99, 102, 108n., 114, 117ff., 128ff., 136-138, 141ff., 156-157, 164, 175, 178, 183-186, 191, 193-196, 198, 204, 208, 214-216, 218ff., 240, 242ff., 253, 255, 257, 258, 261ff., 274ff., 284, 286-288, 290ff., 300, 303, 313-316, 318ff., 332

Ahdut Haavoda and, differences between, 213
beginning of, 111-112
Central Committee, 143-144, 267-268, 275, 279, 320, 323
Congresses
  Second, 120, 122, 146
  Third, 146
  Fourth, 224, 225
  Fifth, 166, 268, 271
  Sixth, 280n.
  Seventh, 198, 318, 320-323, 327-328
Council, 273
Council, 1954, 137
described, 339
differences within, 119, 136
economic change plans, 294
Economic Committee, 303n.
Histadrut and, present-day relations between, 194
important aspects of, 113
in Knesset elections, 342
Jewish, 117
key problems of, 1965, 247-248
Left Section, 132
Ministers, 118
Palestine problem, views, 315
Peace Plan, 195-196, 327-328
Pioneering Left appellation, 154n.
policy for 1970-1971, 193
Political Committee, 138, 263
  on West Bank problems, 261
Resolutions on the Histadrut, 163ff.
Soviet policies criticized by, 263-264
ties with foreign parties, 148
Mapam Bulletin, 149n., 341
"Mapam on the Trade Union Struggle," (Ben-Moshe), 194
Marshak, Benny, 229
Marxist Poale Zionism, 62, 68
M.A.S. (Movement for Socialism), Venezuela. *See* Mapam, ties with foreign parties.
Mass Movement of the Colombian People. *See* Mapam, ties with foreign parties.

Matspen (Compass), Israeli Socialist Organization, 251-252
Mayer, D., 261
Meir, Golda, 45n., 204n, 237, 265, 273, 278-279, 289, 292
  resignation, alternatives after, 290
Meirson, 63
Mereminsky. *See* Merom, Yisrael.
Merhavia, H., 29
Merhavia, 209
Meri (Israeli Radical Camp), 76, 281, 289
Merom, Yisrael, 23
Meshel, Yeruham, 193, 194
Migvan, 339
Mikunis, Shmuel, 71, 73, 77n.
Mikunis-Sneh-Vilenska group, 74, 75
Mikve-Israel, 176
Min Hayesod (From the Roots), 173, 188-189, 204-205, 209
Min Hayesod Anthology, 207
Min Hayesod group, 154, 200n., 203-205, 207, 210-212, 228ff., 240
  discussion of, 204
Ministers Committee (Committee of Seven). *See* Lavon Affair.
Mishmar, 100
Misrahi, 340
Mitterand Group, 148n.
Moked (Focus), 75n., 76, 77, 281, 288, 289n., 317, 341
Molad, 339
Mollett, Guy, 208
Moshav Movement, 235, 238
Moshavot (Jewish colonies), 96
Moshav Ovdim, 269
  definition, 155n.
Moshav Shitufi, 155n.
Movement for an Undivided Israel. *See* Land of Israel Movement.
Movement for Citizen's Rights, 289
Movement for Civil Rights, 340
  in Knesset elections, 342
Movement for the Unity of Labor, 105n., 108

M.P.S. Poale Zion. *See* Socialist Workers Party.
Mufti of Jerusalem, Arab nationalist leader
  Fascist and Nazi tendencies of, 71

Nahalal, 167
Nahariya Conference, 1946, 91
Namir, Mordehai, 204
Narodisn (Populism), 13, 32
Nasser, Abdul, 72, 73, 141ff., 258, 261
National Congress of the Labor Parties 1905-1977 (*table*), 354-356
National Council. *See* Havaad Haleumi.
National Funds, 65, 87
National Insurance Bureau, 199
National Kibbutz Federations (*chart*), 179
National Labor Federation, 92n., 104
National Liberal Union. *See* Likud.
National Military Organization. *See* Irgun Zvai Leumi; Israel, defense.
National Palestinian Covenant, 316
National Religious Party. *See* Mafdal.
National Union Government, 287
National Unity Government, 292, 325
Navon, Yitshak, 322
Negev, 142
Netzer, Shraga, 203n.
New Alignment in the Labor Movement, 224, 226, 228
New Communist List. *See* Rakah.
New Democratic List, 317
New Force-Haolem Hazeh, 243
"New Immigrants, The," 81
New Israeli Left. *See* Siah.
New Left "Blue-Red Movement," 317
New Outlook, 216, 330, 341
New Path, the (Via Nova), 48, 169
New Zionist Organization, 92n.
Nir, Nahum, 57n., 63, 120n.
Nuris Block, 168

October Revolution, Russia, 57, 62, 66, 81, 112, 118, 125, 258, 263, 358
October War. *See* Yom Kippur War.
Oren, Mordehai, 130, 131
"organic kibbutz," 86, 170
Organization of Working and Student Youth in Israel, 177, 178
Oriental Jewish workers and slum dwellers, 326
Ot, 339
Our Platform (Borochov), 17, 25, 60
Our Socialism (Bergman), 43

Pacifist Socialist Party (PSP), Holland. *See* Mapam, ties with foreign parties
Palestine (Eretz Israel), 32, 62, 64, 85, 94, 98, 101, 112-113, 174, 176, 195
Palestine Liberation Organization. *See* P.L.O.
"Palestine Post, the," (*The Jerusalem Post*), 341
Palestine Workers Fund. *See* Kapai.
Palestine Workers League, 186
Palestine Workers Party (Mapai), 115
Palestinian Communist Party (P.C.P./Workers Fraction), 48, 64, 103n., 169
  beginnings, 70ff.
  name change, 71
Palestinian Labor Movement, the, 106
Palestinian problem, the, 254ff., 269, 315-316, 329-330
Palestinian Social-Democratic Party, 103
Palmach (Israel Defense Army), 94-95, 105, 118, 187
  described, 94n.
Parties, political. *See also* Agudat Israel; Ahdut Haavoda; Alignment, the; Arab Lists; Democratic Front for Peace and Equality; Democratic Movement for Change; Free Center; Gahal; Greater Israel Movement (Land of Israel Movement); Haolam Hazeh; Hapoel Hamisrahı; Hapoel Hatsair; Hashomer Hatsair Workers Party; Herut; Independent Liberal Party; Independent Socialists; Israel Labor Party; La'am Party; Labor Party; Labor-Mapam Alignment; L'Ahdut Haavoda-Poale Zion; Liberal Party; Likud; Mafdal (National Religious Party); Maki; Mapai; Mapam; Meri; Misrahi; Moked; Movement for Civil Rights; Poale Agudat Israel; Poale Zion; Rafi; Rakah; Religious Torah Front; Sheli; Shinui Group; Shlomzion Movement; State List; Workers Fraction (P.C.P.); Zionist Panthers.
Knesset
  election results and party alignments 1949-1977 (*table*), 342
  National Congresses of the Histadrut, seats held (*tables*), 343-347
  Ninth Knesset, 339-341
Party of the Left Poale Zion, 70
Party of the Workers of Eretz-Israel, 109
P.C.P. *See* Palestinian Communist Party.
Peace to Zion. *See* Shlomzion.
Peace List, 272n.
Peel Report, partition plan, 96-98, 104
Peled, Nathan, 279
People and Homeland (Merhavia), 29
Peoples Socialist Party (SF), Denmark. *See* Mapam, ties with foreign parties.
Peres, Shimon, 185, 200ff., 225, 237, 239, 273-274, 320-324, 350
  Defense Minister, 314
  Information Minister, 291
  Security Minister, 323
Peri, Eliezer, 272

392 • INDEX

Petach-Tikva, 32, 176
Picasso, Pablo, 261
Pioneering (Chaluziut), 88, 95, 215, 220
Pioneering, Left, identified, 154n.
Pioneering Scouts, 178
Pioneering Zionism, 70, 84
P.L.O. (Palestine Liberation Organization), 315, 316, 329, 332
Poale Agudat Israel, 219, 244, 340
  in Knesset elections, 342
Poale Zion (The Workers of Zion), 20, 32ff., 56, 57ff., 63-64, 68, 70, 110, 112, 117
  American, 25, 34-35
  Borochov and, 33, 68
  Czarist Russian, 34
  European, 25, 34
  Left, 59, 62ff., 70, 83, 85n., 87, 90-91, 97, 104, 108, 110-112, 117, 120, 130, 137, 170
  Palestinian
    accomplishments of, 33-35
  Right, 50, 55, 102
  Societies, 23
  split of, 57
  Zionism, view of, 22
Poale Zion Jewish Social-Democratic Party, 25
Poale Zion Palestine Workers Party, 64
Poale Zion S.D., 64
Poale Zion-Z.S., 23n.
Political parties. (*See* Parties, political.)
Political Radical Party (P.P.R.), Holland. *See* Mapam, ties with foreign parties.
Popular Front, 93
Popular Socialism of the Jews, The (Arlozorov), 45
Popular Zionist Hapoel Hatsair Faction, 23
Popular Zionist Zeire-Zion Faction, 22-23
Populism (Narodism), 13, 22
Portuguese Socialist Party. *See* Mapam, ties with foreign parties.
Prague trials, 72, 130-131, 145

President, of Israel. *See also* Israel.
  constitutional powers and duties, 335
Press
  contemporary Israeli, described, 341
Prime Minister, of Israel. *See also* Israel.
  Cabinet, Knesset and, 336
Proletarian Fraction (CPP), 64
P.S.I. (Italian Socialist Party). *See* Mapam, ties with foreign parties.
P.S.U. (United Socialist Party), France. *See* Mapam, ties with foreign parties.

Rabin, Yitshak, 292, 320-324
  Cabinet of, 321
  Chief of Staff, 251
  government of, 313
  Labor Minister, 291
  Prime Minister, 291, 318, 322
Rabinowitz, Y., 229
Rafi, 73, 108n., 154n., 173, 185, 239-240, 242ff., 250, 265ff., 272ff., 290-292, 314, 320-321, 339
Rafi List, the, 239n.
Raik Haviva, 95n.
Rakah (New Communist List), 74ff., 216n., 251-252, 288, 289n., 315, 318, 331, 341. *See also* Maki.
  Democratic Front, 77
  in Knesset elections, 342
  Peace Plank, 331-332
Ramat David Council, 1934, 172
Ramat Hakovesh, 184
Ramat Rachel, 169
Ramle Platform, 1906, 34
Ratner, Mark, 24
Rechev, Shlomo, 78
Red Army, 105, 145
Reformism, 180ff., 332
Rehav, S., 190
Rehovot, 176
Reiner, A., 241
Religious Kibbutz, the, 224
Religious Torah Front, 340
Religious Workers, the, 276, 282
Remez, Aharon, 202, 210
Remez, David, 33, 36, 45n., 114

Revutsky, A., 57n., 63, 64
Rhodes formula, 279
Ribbentrop-Molotov agreement, 94
Riftin, Yaakov, 106, 272
Riftin Group. *See* Left Alliance.
Rightist Bloc, 234, 241
Rightist Gdud, 169
Rightist Union, outstanding personalities of, 57n.
Right Poale Zion. *See* Poale Zion, Right.
Rogers Plan, 280
Rome and Jerusalem (Hess), 20
Rotenstreich, Nathan, 188, 202, 204, 351
Roy, C., 261
Rubashov (Shazer, S.Z.), 57n.
Rubinstein, Ammon, 317
Russian Hechalutz, 167. *See also* Hechalutz.
Russian Poale Zion Congress, Kiev, 1917, 86n.
Russian Revolution, 1917, 38, 57, 359

Sadeh, General Yitzhak, 120
S.A.P. *See* Socialist German Workers Party.
Sapir, Pinhas, 204n., 245, 274, 275, 291
  Finance Minister, 191, 265, 290
  Labor Party General Secretary, 273
Sapir, Yosef, 250
Sartre, Jean-Paul, 257, 261
Schwartz, L., 261
Scouting Organization, 176, 178
Second International, 87, 93
Second Israel, the, 248
Second World War. *See* World War II.
Security Council. *See* United Nations.
Security Scandal, 202. *See also* Lavon Affair.
S.E.R.P. (Socialist Jewish Workers Party). *See* Sjemists.
Sharrett, Moshe, 45n., 177, 182, 202, 204n., 237, 362
Sharon, Ariel, 317, 318, 340
Shazer, S.Z. (Rubashov), 57n.
Shazar, Zalman, 335n.

She'arim, 340
Shekel, 58
Sheli (Camp for Peace and Equality), 75n., 77, 341
  in Knesset elections, 342
Shem-Tov, Victor, 278, 279, 316n.
Shemtov-Yariv formula, 316
Shinui (Change), 317, 340
Shlomzion (Peace to Zion) movement, 317, 318, 325, 340
  in Knesset elections, 342
Shlonsky, Abraham, 92
Shohat, Eliezer, 45n.
Shohat, Yisrael, 45n.
  and Manya Shohat, 47
Shomer Community, 81ff.
"Shomrim," 82
Siah (New Israeli Left), 76, 80
Siah Bet (Faction B), 90, 97, 105, 107-109, 120, 129, 172, 187, 200, 213, 214
Siah Bet Mapai, 108
Siach (Israeli New Left), 272n.
Siah Gimel (Faction C), 107
Sifriat Hapoalim. *See* Workers Book Guild.
Silberfarb, Moshe, 24
Simon, Ernst, 92n.
Sinai Campaign (Sinai War) 1956, 139ff., 201, 251, 327, 363. *See also* Anglo-French Suez War.
Sinai War. *See* Sinai Campaign.
Six-Day War (June 1967), 75, 250ff., 265, 267, 270, 291, 298, 305, 332, 365
Sjemists (Socialist Jewish Workers Party/S.E.R.P.), 24-25, 32-34
  Renaissance Group, 33
Slansky Trials, 130
Sneh, Moshe, 73, 75n., 76, 80, 120, 123, 129, 131ff., 281, 350
  Party of the Left program, 133
Sneh group, 137
Social Democratic Party, Germany. *See* Mapam, ties with foreign parties.
Social-Democratic Party, Palestinian, 103

Social Democratic Party, Sweden. *See* Mapam, ties with foreign parties.
Social-Democratic Poale Zionists, 59
Socialist Democratic Party, Jewish, 63
Socialist German Workers Party (S.A.P.), 102
Socialist International, 46, 103, 187, 257
Socialist Jewish State, idea of, 41, 99
Socialist Jewish Workers Party (S.E.R.P.). *See* Sjemists.
Socialist League in Palestine, 90-92
  summary of, 91
Socialist Left Party in Israel, 132
Socialist Notes, 102, 104, 108n.
Socialist Party, Austria. *See* Mapam, ties with foreign parties.
Socialist Party, Chile. *See* Mapam, ties with foreign parties.
Socialist Party, India. *See* Mapam, ties with foreign parties.
Socialist Party, Japan. *See* Mapam, ties with foreign parties.
Socialist Peoples Party, Spain. *See* Mapam, ties with foreign parties.
Socialists of the Future (Laborists), 22
Socialist Workers Party, 63
Socialist Workers Party, Spain. *See* Mapam, ties with foreign parties.
Socialist Workers Party Poale Zion (M.P.S.), 70
Socialist-Zionism, 22, 54, 84, 180, 210, 282, 321
  ideology, 325
  labor movement, 323, 326, 333
Socialist-Zionist Party, 75
Socialist Zionist Workers Front, 230
Socialist-Zionist Workers Party (S.S.), 23
Solel Boneh (Paver-Builder), 152-153
  described, 152n.
Soviet Union (U.S.S.R.), 105, 117-118, 125-126, 128, 130, 145-146, 169, 184, 204, 225, 257-258, 297, 313
  Jewish minority, 149-150

Mapam's attitude toward, 263-264, 272n.
Sprinzak, Yosef, 45n.
S.S. (Socialist-Zionist Workers Party), 23
Stalin, 79, 134, 135, 145n.
State List, 280, 316, 339
  in Knesset elections, 342
State of Israel. *See* Israel.
Stolypin, 31
Student Youth Circle in Tel Aviv, 176
Stychic process, 85-86
Suez Canal, 144, 251, 254
Suez War. *See* Anglo-French Suez War; Sinai Campaign.
Surkis, M., 236
Syrkin, Hahman, 20, 24, 25, 28-29, 45, 157
  socialist-Zionist theoretician, 40-41

Tabenkin, Yitzhak, 33, 36, 38, 45n., 54, 56, 105, 114, 122, 229, 232
Talmi, Meir, 280n., 320
Tamir, Shmuel, 316, 317
Teitlebaum, Raoul, 80
Tel Aviv bloc, 237
  Haifa bloc and, 203, 207
Tel Aviv Siah Bet, 108
Tel Aviv Workers Council, 108
Tel Hai, 37
Tel Yosef-Ein Harod, 48, 168
territorialism, 25, 32, 34
The Future (Die Zunkunft), 14
This Is the Way (Zu Haderekh), 74
Tiran, Straits of, 142-143, 250, 251
"Tmurot," 340
Tnua L'Ahdut Haavoda, 62, 97, 109ff., 214
Tnuat Herut (Freedom Movement), 92n.
Torah Front, 288, 318
Toubi, Toufik, 71, 74, 350
Trade Union Department, 191
Trade Union International, 126

Trade Unions
  background of major, outlined, 346
Tri-Continent Movement, 258
Trumpeldor, Yosef (Joseph), 37, 43n., 81. *See also* Joseph Trumpeldor Labor Battalion.
Tsahal (Israeli Defense Forces), 250. *See also* Israel, defense; Six-Day War.
Tubin, Pinhas, 75n.
Tzur, Zev, 229

Uganda Plan, 23, 31
Ulbricht, Walter, 73
Ultra-Leftists, 124ff., 130, 133ff., 272
Union of International Socialists in Palestine, 102, 103
Union of Kvutzot and Kibbutzim. *See* Ihud.
"Union of the Left," 93
United Jerusalem, 329
United Jewish Trade Union, 14
United Kibbutz. *See* Kibbutz Hameuchad.
United Movement, 176-178
United Nations, 100, 101, 233, 259
  Charter, 233, 259
  General Assembly, 98, 275
  Security Council, 256, 259-260, 273, 279, 285, 316, 322, 327
  Resolution No. 242, Nov. 22, 1967, (*text*), 259-260
  Resolution, Nov. 1947, 71
United Socialist Party (P.S.U.), France. *See* Mapam, ties with foreign parties.
United Workers Front, 265, 269, 272n.
United Workers Party, 93, 99, 111-112, 121-122, 137n., 138, 147, 208, 283. *See also* Mapam.
Unity Front, 120n., 122, 124, 129-131, 136
Unity of Labor. *See* Ahdut Haavoda.
Unity of Labor-Workers of Zion. *See* Ahdut Haavoda-Poale Zion.
U.S.S.R. *See* Soviet Union.

Vaad Haleumi, 46
Vaad Hapoel (Histadrut Executive Committee), 108.
  See also Histadrut.
Vaad Leumi (Havaad Haleumi), 94
Vescher, Hashin Y., 57n.
Via Nova. *See* New Path.
Victory League to Aid the U.S.S.R. at War ("V League"), 105
Vidal-Naguet, P., 261
Vilenska, Esther, 71, 73, 76, 281, 367
Vilna Circle, 13
Vilner, Meir, 350
Vision and Path (Ben-Gurion), 189
Vitkin, Yosef, 45n.
Voice of the People. See *Kol Ha'am*.
Vozrozhdenia (The Renaissance), 24, 32

War of Independence (1948). *See* War of Liberation.
War of June 1967. *See* Six-Day War.
War of Liberation (War of Independence) 1948, 113, 117-118, 142, 145, 201, 251, 263, 362
Warsaw Ghetto Revolt, 95n.
Weitzmann, Haim, 92n., 335n.
West Bank (of Jordan River), 217, 255, 261, 278, 289, 292, 314-315, 319, 321ff. *See also* Jordan River.
  Jewish settlements on, 314
  Palestinian state on, 315
"White Paper," 71, 95, 105n., 106, 361
"wild-gone Liberals," 317
Wilner, Meir, 71, 73
Wilner-Toubi faction, 74
Winchevsky, Morris, 13-14
Workers Book Guild (Sifriat Hapoalim), 92
Workers Circle (Arbeiter Ring), 14
Workers Commonwealth in the State of Israel, 282
Workers Council, 163, 164
Workers Economy (Hevrat Haodim), 271
  weaknesses of, 153

Workers Fraction. *See* Palestinian Communist Party.
Workers Movement, Israeli, 270
Workers of Israel List. *See* Rafi.
Workers of Zion. *See* Poale Zion.
Workers Parties
  background, nature, and political groupings, outlined, 348-351
Workers Society. *See* Hevrat Ovdim.
"Workers Stream," described, 181
Working Youth, 178
World Jewish Congress, 132
World Union, 23n., 61ff.
World Union of Mapam, 166
World Union of Mapam Parties, 341
World Union of Poale Zion, 34, 49, 50, 54, 57n.
  formation of, 25
World War II, 94, 104-106, 117, 127, 263-264, 361
World Zionist Congress, 67
World Zionist movement, 182
World Zionist Organization, 20, 58n., 87, 92n., 96n., 130-132
  first president, 20n.

Ya'ad (Goal), 317
Yaari, Meir, 89, 120, 124, 127, 133, 135ff., 141, 145, 196, 208-209, 221, 241, 249, 280n.
Yadin, Yigal, 317, 321
Yaffe, Eliezer, 45n.
Yariv, A., 316n.
Yariv-Shemtov formula, 322
Yavnieli, Shmuel, 33, 36, 45n., 114
Yediot Ahronot, 341
Yevsektzia (Jewish Section of Soviet Communist Party), 16, 24n., 62, 64, 127n.
Yishuv (Jewish Community), 106, 109, 188, 190
Yitshaki, Yitshak, 64, 120, 124, 350-351
Yom Kippur War (October War, 1973), 258, 288, 298-299, 313, 317
Yotbat (Tiran), 142

"Younger Men," (of Mapai), 203ff, 219-220, 229-230, 235ff.
"Younger young circle," 200n.
"Young Guard," Central Committee of the Israel Labor Party, 255n.
Young Guardian, The, 81ff. *See also* Hashomer Hatsair.
Youth Movements
  identified and Labor Movement links outlined, 351-353
Youth of Zion. *See* Zeire Zion.

Zahal (Tsahal), 118n., 285
Zahri, S., 303n.
Zalman, Aranne, 204n.
Zayad, Toufik, 77
Zeire Zion (Youth of Zion), 20, 37
  goals of, 32
  differences with Poale Zion, 22
  leaders, 23
  Zionism, views of, 22
Zeire Zion World Union (Hitachdut), 44
Zerubabel, Yaakov, 35n., 57n., 63, 120n.
Zhitlowsky, Chaim, 20, 24, 25
Zionism, 42, 60-62, 66, 83ff., 101, 129ff., 153, 169, 171, 181-182, 189, 227, 233, 252n., 254, 258, 262, 325, 327, 330, 332
  anti-Zionism, 75, 117, 127, 130, 169
  constructive, 92n.
  declarative, 21
  First Congress, 20n.
  General, 21
  Israeli Left and outline, history (*table*), 358-369
  Labor, 20ff.
  political, 92n.
  practical, 21
  proletarian, 22
  Socialism and, 22, 52, 84, 98
  Workers', 21
Zionist Action Committee, 96n.
Zionist Congresses, 50, 58-59, 65ff., 87, 189

Zionist Executive, 46, 92n.
Zionist Labor Party Zeire
  Zion-Hitachdut, 23
Zionist Movement, 106, 200, 220, 227, 271
Zionist Organization, 58, 68, 69, 80, 131
Zionist Panthers, 289n., 340
Zionists, American, 96n.
Zionists, General. *See* General Zionist Organization.
Zionist-Socialist labor movement, 175
Zionist Socialist Party (Z.S.), 55, 56n., 81
  identified, 22
Zionist-Socialist workers parties, consolidation of, 270
Zionist-Socialist World Union, 51
Zionists-Revisionists, described, 92n.
Zionist Youth, 102
Zisling, Aharon, 45n., 118
Z.S. *See* Zionist Socialist Party.
Z'ubi, Aboul Aziz, 215-216
Zu Haderekh (This Is the Way), 74, 136, 341n.
Zukerman, Baruch, 25
Zundelevicz, Aharon, 13